THE COMPLETE IDIOT'S GUIDE® TO

Feng Shui

Third Edition

by Elizabeth Moran, Master Joseph Yu, and Master Val Biktashev

ALPHA

A member of Penguin Group (USA) Inc.

ALPHA BOOKS

Published by the Penguin Group

Penguin Group (USA) Inc., 375 Hudson Street, New York, New York 10014, USA

Penguin Group (Canada), 90 Eglinton Avenue East, Suite 700, Toronto, Ontario M4P 2Y3, Canada (a division of Pearson Penguin Canada Inc.)

Penguin Books Ltd., 80 Strand, London WC2R 0RL, England

Penguin Ireland, 25 St. Stephen's Green, Dublin 2, Ireland (a division of Penguin Books Ltd.)

Penguin Group (Australia), 250 Camberwell Road, Camberwell, Victoria 3124, Australia (a division of Pearson Australia Group Pty. Ltd.)

Penguin Books India Pvt. Ltd., 11 Community Centre, Panchsheel Park, New Delhi—110 017, India

Penguin Group (NZ), 67 Apollo Drive, Rosedale, North Shore, Auckland 1311, New Zealand (a division of Pearson New Zealand Ltd.)

Penguin Books (South Africa) (Pty.) Ltd., 24 Sturdee Avenue, Rosebank, Johannesburg 2196, South Africa

Penguin Books Ltd., Registered Offices: 80 Strand, London WC2R 0RL, England

International Standard Book Number: 978-1-59257-344-8
Library of Congress Catalog Card Number: 2004116015

12 11 10   9 8 7

Interpretation of the printing code: The rightmost number of the first series of numbers is the year of the book's printing; the rightmost number of the second series of numbers is the number of the book's printing. For example, a printing code of 05-1 shows that the first printing occurred in 2005.

Printed in the United States of America

Note: This publication contains the opinions and ideas of its authors. It is intended to provide helpful and informative material on the subject matter covered. It is sold with the understanding that the authors and publisher are not engaged in rendering professional services in the book. If the reader requires personal assistance or advice, a competent professional should be consulted.

The authors and publisher specifically disclaim any responsibility for any liability, loss, or risk, personal or otherwise, which is incurred as a consequence, directly or indirectly, of the use and application of any of the contents of this book.

Most Alpha books are available at special quantity discounts for bulk purchases for sales promotions, premiums, fundraising, or educational use. Special books, or book excerpts, can also be created to fit specific needs.

For details, write: Special Markets, Alpha Books, 375 Hudson Street, New York, NY 10014.

Publisher: *Marie Butler-Knight*
Product Manager: *Phil Kitchel*
Senior Managing Editor: *Jennifer Bowles*
Senior Acquisitions Editor: *Mike Sanders*
Development Editor: *Lynn Northrup*
Production Editor: *Janette Lynn*

Copy Editor: *Kelly D. Henthorne*
Illustrator: *Tim Neil*
Cartoonist: *Richard King*
Cover/Book Designer: *Trina Wurst*
Indexer: *Brad Herriman*
Layout: *Becky Harmon*
Proofreading: *Donna Martin*

Contents at a Glance

Contents

Foreword

Much has been written about feng shui in English: At the time of this writing there are more than 600 separate titles in English and many thousands of websites on the subject. Yet 25 years ago the subject was virtually unheard of in the United States and very difficult to discover among Western-educated Chinese. Before that there were only books written by missionaries and colonial administrators living in the nineteenth century. Western interest was probably sparked by my first book, *The Living Earth Manual of Feng Shui*, which was written in 1976 when most material on feng shui was still available only in Chinese. Feng shui did not, however, become "dinner party conversation" until the late 1980s, and Lillian Too did much to popularize it in the 1990s.

However, when interest in feng shui did finally gather speed, because of the lack of source material, many well-meaning teachers and writers seemed to forget that it is a really precise and exacting subject and extended it in ways not originally part of its traditional Chinese roots. Now, although any science can be extended by new research and testing, this must be done with a full knowledge of all that has gone before. It is sometimes forgotten that feng shui is *not* a branch of interior decorating, but a practical science in its own right.

To put not too fine a point on it, a lot of later-day Western feng shui has been simplified beyond the point where it works or has been invented or *intuited*. Often intuition has provided a key or a direction in which to look, but it is never sufficient in itself to declare "it must be so" because I feel it to be so.

It, therefore, came as a delight and a breath of fresh air when I laid my hands on *The Complete Idiot's Guide to Feng Shui*. It was even more of a surprise to find that what at first glance (from its cover) was just another popularization of the subject, was in fact a very detailed text going a lot further than many of the apparently more ponderous texts, but starting with the real basics.

Elizabeth Moran and Masters Joseph Yu and Val Biktashev have among them produced an excellent and detailed book, explaining precisely the detailed calculations undertaken to this day by professional Chinese feng shui practitioners. As complex as these calculations are, the authors have presented them in a way that is easy to grasp. Even if you fail to absorb all the detail, many excellent tables make it easy to read the type of house, the Four Pillar horoscope of its owner, and the subtle interaction between these two, which modifies the luck, health, wealth, and happiness of its occupants.

Even now people question the effectiveness of such feng shui "luck manipulation." Let me assure you that, properly done, it is every bit as effective as the curative properties of acupuncture, and if wrongly applied, every bit as devastating as a karate blow.

Feng shui, acupuncture, and karate are the products of thousands of years of refinement by one of the most practical races on earth. Their recent arrival in the West does not diminish their effectiveness. The fact that these three traditional Chinese sciences have only recently made their presence felt in the West is a tribute to the canniness of the Chinese, who kept the knowledge of gunpowder (among other things) from the West for hundreds of years.

To transplant from one culture to another a science that is based on a completely different worldview is a very difficult thing to do. To counter some of the myths that have sprung up around modern feng shui is even more so, but to do this in bite-sized chunks and with considerable humor is truly a *tour de force*. Tying in Isaac Newton, Albert Einstein, and David Bohm sets feng shui in the context of science, and using the latest scholarly approaches to Chinese civilization and science keeps the material up-to-date.

Feng shui is such a huge subject that, as with any book on the subject, the main problem is what to leave out. The authors have handled this dilemma by touching briefly upon the fundamentals of feng shui and one of its most sophisticated and popular methods—Flying Star and its interrelation with that branch of Chinese astrology that deals with your personal Four Pillars of Destiny. Both of these aspects make up a large portion of the feng shui currently practiced in Hong Kong today.

I heartily recommend this book.

—Stephen Skinner

Stephen Skinner, originally an academic and lecturer in geography, first came across feng shui in the 1970s in Hong Kong and Singapore, where he observed the work of feng shui practitioners firsthand. As a result of what he saw, he wrote the first English book on the subject in the twentieth century, *The Living Earth Manual of Feng Shui*, in 1976. He is the founder of *Feng Shui for Modern Living* magazine, the world's largest-selling feng shui magazine, which even publishes a regular monthly edition in Chinese. Therefore, Stephen is uniquely placed to comment on the rise of feng shui in the West. He is the author of many books on feng shui, including the *KISS Guide to Feng Shui* and *Flying Star Feng Shui*.

Introduction

So, you want to try feng shui? You've heard it discussed at parties; you've read about it in magazines; and now you're willing to give it a try. Why not? But what is feng shui, exactly? Something to do with moving furniture around and hanging mirrors? Something to do with the flow of qi? (Don't worry, we'll tell you all about qi in Chapter 4.) How do you even pronounce feng shui, anyway? (We'll tell you that, too.)

Well, all of your questions about this ancient Chinese tradition will be answered in a way that you, the Western reader, can understand. No boring treatise—just the need-to-know basics presented in a fun, interesting, and enlightening manner.

Okay, but what *is* feng shui? Feng shui is the art and science of living in harmony with your living space. Specifically, feng shui seeks to harness nature's positive forces and correct the negative ones with the intention of promoting better health, wealth, and relationships. You see, beginning 6,000 years ago, the Chinese monitored the cyclic movement of nature and recorded how its changes affected us. This may sound goofy, but science is coming to agree with the ancient Chinese notion that we're all bundles of one interconnected energy.

Out of the ancients' reverence for nature, three fundamental principles developed: yin and yang, the five phases, and the eight trigrams. Shared by other Chinese traditions such as acupuncture, acupressure, and herbs, these principles form the basis of Flying Star feng shui, which you'll learn about in Parts 4 and 5. This system will help you find a house compatible with your qi. You'll discover how external and internal factors influence your health and livelihood. You'll learn the most auspicious positions to place your bed and desk.

But, hey, we also offer a short study of Chinese astrology. Besides helping you to identify your animal sign, we'll show you how to calculate your life chart using a method called The Four Pillars of Destiny. You'll learn how to forecast your destiny and determine your life's purpose. You'll learn your favorable colors, careers, and environments—and how certain time periods impact your destiny positively or negatively.

Feng shui will not only help you to improve many aspects of your life, but it will also help *you* to understand *you!* By making simple adjustments, you'll gain harmony in your home and workplace. With harmony comes the likelihood of better health, wealth, and relationships.

How to Use This Book

The Complete Idiot's Guide to Feng Shui, Third Edition, is divided into six parts, each advancing you further along the feng shui path:

Part 1, "Let's Get into Feng Shui," eases you into the concept of feng shui. We explain what feng shui is and what it isn't. We explain why this ancient Eastern tradition is relevant to modern Westerners.

Part 2, "The Fundamental Principles of Feng Shui," teaches you all about the basic principles of feng shui. You will learn how these age-old concepts apply to the here and now—and you!

Part 3, "Understanding Your Environment," helps you recognize, avoid, and alter external and internal factors that may influence your well-being.

Part 4, "Feng Shui Mechanics," introduces you to a method of classical feng shui called "Flying Star."

Part 5, "Practical Application," gives you practical experience evaluating and remedying an apartment, a split-level home, and a business.

Part 6, "Fate or Free Will: What's Your Destiny?" teaches you about the Chinese Zodiac and a system of astrology called The Four Pillars of Destiny.

We've also included six handy appendixes designed to complement your expanding knowledge of feng shui.

Feng Shui Features

In addition to all the information you'll find in the parts, you'll find five types of boxes throughout the text. These boxes will explain unfamiliar terms, further explore certain topics, give you helpful information or interesting quotes about feng shui, or alert you to any pitfalls.

Feng Alert

In these boxes, you'll find cautions that will keep you on the right path.

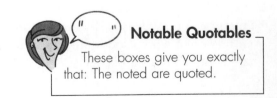

Notable Quotables

These boxes give you exactly that: The noted are quoted.

Master Class _____

These boxes offer tips to make the most of your feng shui journey, as well as quick and interesting facts about feng shui.

Wise Words _____

These boxes define new words so that you can speak the lingo.

Feng Facts

In these boxes, you'll find interesting tidbits and helpful information that are related to feng shui principles.

Acknowledgments

Compiling material on a subject as esoteric as feng shui is not easy. We sincerely wish to thank our students, clients, and friends for urging us to present a deeper level of understanding of classical feng shui. Also, we wish to acknowledge …

Andree Abecassis: Our agent, advisor, mediator, cheerleader, and friend. We appreciate your professionalism more than you can ever know. Mike Sanders: Thanks for allowing us to compile new information for this third edition. Lynn Northrup, Jan Lynn, and Kelly Henthorne: Thanks for your attention to detail. Tim Neil: The most fabulous art slave in the world! Thanks. Scott Ransom: Thanks for the best sitting/facing explanation around! Pauline and Ralph Warren: Thanks for allowing us to use your floor plan!

Val Biktashev would personally like to thank Viktoriy Yudkin, a very wise and kind friend, who unwaveringly supports and encourages him. In large part, Val owes his success to him.

The authors would like to thank the following for permission to use their original work:

Chapter 1:

Photograph of Silva Explorer Model 203 used with permission of Johnson Outdoors Inc.

Chapter 2:

Quotation from *The World Order of Bahá'u'lláh* by Shoghi Effendi used with permission of the publisher, the Bahá'í Publishing Trust, Wilmette, IL. © 1938, 1955, 1974, and 1991 by the National Spiritual Assembly of the Bahá'ís of the United States.

Definitions of the terms conscious and subconscious mind, the critical area of the mind, knowns and unknowns are used with permission of the Hypnosis Motivation Institute.

Quotation by Albert Einstein taken from *The Quotable Einstein*, collected and edited by Alice Calaprice, is used with permission of Princeton University Press © 1996.

Information about Fibonacci numbers is taken from *Fascinating Fibonacci: Mystery and Magic in Numbers*, by Trudi Hammel Garland © Dale Seymour Publications, an imprint of Pearson Learning, a division of Pearson Education, Inc. Used with permission.

The idea of "McFeng shui" is used with permission of Cate Bramble.

The nine aspirations for a New World Vision for the Millennium are identified with the Bahá'í Faith. For more information, go to www.bahai.org/.

Chapter 3:

Quotation from *Tao Te Ching* (St. John's University Press, 1961) by Lao Tzu, translated by John C. H. Wu. Reprinted by arrangement with Shambhala Publications, Inc., Boston, www.shambhala.com.

Chapter 4:

Quotation from *The Tao of Physics*, Fourth Edition, by Fritjof Capra © 1975, 1983, 1991, 1999, 2000 by Fritjof Capra. Reprinted by arrangement with Shambhala Publications, Inc., Boston, www.shambhala.com.

Chapter 5:

Quotation from *The Hidden Words*, by Bahá'u'lláh used with permission of the publisher, the Bahá'í Publishing Trust, Wilmette, IL © 1932, 1975, by the National Spiritual Assembly of the Bahá'ís of the United States.

Chapter 10:

Definition of "fight or flight" taken from the *Professional Hypnotism Manual*, by John G. Kappas, is used with permission of George Kappas, Vice President of Panorama Publishing © 1999.

Chapter 11:

The quotation by Richard Wilhelm in *The I Ching Book of Changes* is used with permission of Princeton University Press © 1950.

The quotation by Joseph Needham in *Science and Civilisation in China* is used with permission of Cambridge University Press © 1956.

Chapter 13:

The quotation by Annemarie Schimmel in *The Mystery of Numbers* is used with permission of Oxford University Press © 1993.

Chapter 19:

The photo of the split-level house and the corresponding floor plan is used with permission of Pauline Warren.

Every effort has been made to secure permissions for use of any original work appearing in this book. Please contact the authors with any oversight at GlobalFengShui@aol.com. Thank you.

Trademarks

All terms mentioned in this book that are known to be or are suspected of being trademarks or service marks have been appropriately capitalized. Alpha Books and Penguin Group (USA) Inc. cannot attest to the accuracy of this information. Use of a term in this book should not be regarded as affecting the validity of any trademark or service mark.

Part 1

Let's Get into Feng Shui

Part 1 is an introduction and more. You'll learn what feng shui is and what it isn't. You'll learn who uses this ancient Chinese art and science and how it can benefit you. What do you need to begin your study? Besides your brain and integrity, the most important thing you'll need is a compass. Details about what you'll need are given in Chapter 1.

Part 1 also introduces you to, well, you. Let's face it, Westerners think in a way that's different from our Eastern neighbors. We're a logical lot, preferring rational knowledge over intuitive wisdom. So, before you can embark on a journey into an age-old Eastern tradition—one that requires you to push aside your rational mind-set—you must first understand how you, the Westerner, think. You'll also learn how the Chinese think and discover how both thought processes have come to the same conclusion—that everything and everyone is one interconnected dance of energy.

What Is Feng Shui?

In This Chapter

- ◆ Taking the feng shui IQ test
- ◆ Understanding faux and authentic schools of feng shui
- ◆ Discovering what you need to practice feng shui
- ◆ Learning 20 ways feng shui can improve your life

You're not an idiot if you're confused about feng shui (pronounced *fung schway*). This ancient Chinese tradition has bulldozed its way into the West, becoming the craze du jour. It seems everyone is either doing it or dissing it. Feng shui articles, books, entire magazines, complete schools, and comprehensive websites have crowded the market. Some of these offer advice and varied techniques far removed from the real thing. They all seek to cash in while misleading the unsuspecting, taking full advantage before the uninformed consumer wises up and begins to question the myriad inconsistencies.

Actually, this dilution of the classic tradition can be likened to playing telephone. Remember that childhood game? One kid whispers a sentence into the next kid's ear. Something like, "My 50-foot alligator lives in a black lagoon." By the time the sentence reaches the end of the line, it may have become, "My pin-striped crocodile swims in a pink polka-dot pool."

Get the idea? This book will avoid such silliness and present to you a clear, concise explanation of feng shui. Let's get started by taking a little quiz.

The Feng Shui IQ Test

Before you learn what feng shui actually is (and what it isn't), let's test your feng shui IQ. For each of these questions, pick the answer you believe is correct. (*Hint:* Some questions might have more than one correct answer.) Don't worry, your grades won't be sent home to Mom!

1. What is feng shui?

    a. A specialty of Chinese cuisine

    b. The study of time and space

    c. A belief system of warding off evil spirits using mirrors

2. You should always sleep with your head pointed north.

    a. True

    b. False

3. Which instruments are used by a feng shui practitioner?

    a. A smudge stick

    b. Crystals

    c. A compass

4. You're practicing good feng shui when you …

    a. Open the window to let fresh air in.

    b. Hang a mirror in a small room.

    c. Hang a wind chime in your entrance.

5. Which sort of house promotes a more healthful well-being?

    a. A house made of bricks

    b. A house built on a level lot

    c. A house built on a hilltop

6. You and your significant other have submitted an offer on a new house. At the last minute, you discover the previous two sets of owners divorced while living in the dwelling. Do you withdraw your offer?

    a. Yes

    b. No

7. You should always keep toilet lids down so your money *qi* won't flush away.

    a. True

    b. False

8. Feng shui can help you …

    a. Find love and romance.

    b. Increase your earning potential.

    c. Gain a restful sleep.

9. The object of feng shui is to activate your fame, marriage, children, helpful people, career, knowledge, family, and wealth qi sectors within your home.

    a. True

    b. False

10. Feng shui is practiced by …

    a. Individuals like yourself.

    b. Major corporations.

    c. The Asian population.

> **Wise Words**
>
> Qi (also spelled ch'i and pronounced *chee*) is the life force underlying everyone and everything. It is a field of information connecting us with each other and with our environment. The goal of feng shui is to balance qi in your living and/or working space to promote the likelihood of better health, wealth, and relationships. Qi is the subject of Chapter 4.

Feng shui IQ answers: 1. b; 2. b; 3. c; 4. a; 5. b; 6. b; 7. b; 8. a–c; 9. b; 10. a–c.

So, how did you do? Did the correct answers surprise you? Or maybe you feel more confused than ever. Don't worry; we'll tell you everything you need to know to understand feng shui. It's time to embark on a unique journey that will change the way you view the world. Let's start by discussing what feng shui *isn't*.

What Feng Shui Is Not

From the many questions we receive from readers, clients, and students, great confusion exists about the different schools of feng shui: "They all conflict." "Which one is right?" "How do I activate my wealth corner?" "Where is my wealth corner?" To address these concerns, we have added information to this chapter—information that will help you separate fact from falsehood; information that will help set you on the proper feng shui path.

Unfortunately, feng shui is plagued with many misconceptions. Largely steeped in myth and superstition, a discriminating feng shui enthusiast can easily learn to distinguish faux from authentic schools of feng shui by a number of telltale factors. Here are some attributes associated with faux schools of feng shui:

◆ They often are linked with Life Aspirations or Black Sect (also known as Black Hat Sect Tantric Buddhist feng shui) theory. Developed during the 1970s and 1980s, respectively, these commercialized schools are referred to as "modern," "compass," or "Western" schools of feng shui.

◆ They divide a home into eight "life aspirations" or eight "life stations" of career, knowledge, family, wealth, fame, marriage, children, and helpful people.

◆ They use the location of the front door to determine the orientation of the eight life aspirations/stations. (See the illustrations on the following page.)

◆ They match each of the five phases of qi (fire, earth, metal, water, and wood) with its affiliated direction. Stated another way, fire activates the southern fame aspiration/station; earth activates the northeastern knowledge and southwestern marriage sectors; metal activates the western children and northwestern helpful people sectors; water activates the northern career sector; and wood activates the eastern family and southeastern wealth sectors. The five phases is the subject of Chapter 6.

◆ They also use "cures" such as mirrors, crystals, bamboo flutes, red ribbons, and statues or sculptures of fu dogs, frogs, and cats, among other things, to activate the eight life aspirations/stations. Statements like "A mirror will help to ward off evil spirits," "A fish tank placed in the north will bring prosperity," or "Hanging bells inside your door will ring in joy and happiness" are commonplace among these schools.

It's a pity these inaccuracies have clouded the nature of feng shui. In fact, these widespread assumptions have made the practice seem like a fad reserved for the gullible and eccentric. As you get further along into this book, you'll understand how these misrepresentations have never been part of classical feng shui. For example, 2 + 2 = 4, correct? Could you be convinced otherwise?

Surely not.

Just to set the record straight, feng shui is not a charming Eastern philosophy grounded in superstition. It is not a religion, nor does it derive from any religion. Feng shui does not provide elixirs or cure-alls for your problems. It is not magic. It is not a New Age discovery. Feng shui will not reduce your wrinkles, zap your fat, or help you win the lottery.

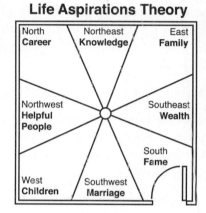

Life Aspirations Theory

The eight life aspirations are correlated with a direction. The magnetic orientation of the main entrance determines the placement of the life aspirations map. In this example, the front door faces south.

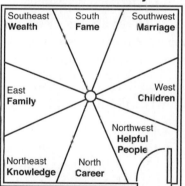

Black Sect Theory

The eight life stations are correlated with a direction. The northern stations always correspond to the wall containing the main entrance even if the door does not face a northerly direction. Whether the doorway is on the left, center, or right side of the wall (if you face the dwelling) will determine whether you enter the knowledge, career, or helpful people sectors, respectively.

What Feng Shui Is

Authentic *feng shui*, which we will hereafter refer to as "traditional" or "classical" feng shui, is an ancient practice first developed some 6,000 years ago by the Neolithic

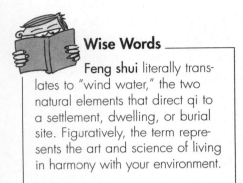

Wise Words

Feng shui literally translates to "wind water," the two natural elements that direct qi to a settlement, dwelling, or burial site. Figuratively, the term represents the art and science of living in harmony with your environment.

Chinese. The early findings blossomed into a sophisticated, well-honed tradition by the Tang dynasty (618–907 C.E.). Essentially, classical feng shui is a system based on keen observation of heavenly (time) and earthly (interior and exterior space) forces and how the qi of each interact. It is a practice of balancing these forces. With balance comes the likelihood of better health, wealth, and relationships. With balance, feng shui gives you the impetus, and the drive, to succeed!

Here are a few distinguishing factors about classical feng shui:

- The principal tool of the practitioner is a compass. Although a Chinese *luopan* compass contains many concentric rings of information, for our purposes a basic protractor compass will suffice. You'll learn more about the type of compass you'll need later in this chapter.

- The magnetic (space) sitting or backside of the dwelling (as opposed to the location of the front door) and the year (time) the building was built are used to draw up an intricate numeric qi map of your dwelling (see the following figure). This technique is called Flying Star, the most sophisticated method of feng shui and the subject of Part 4. For reasons that will be explained in successive chapters, there are 216 types of houses. In other words, a prefabricated, one-size-fits-all qi map composed of eight life aspirations/stations does not exist in classical feng shui. Like a snowflake or a fingerprint, each home is unique and individual.

- The year the occupant(s) was born is an important factor in determining his or her innate compatibility with the house.

- *Only* the five phases of qi (fire, earth, metal, water, and wood) are used to transform the home's qi into a productive cycle, fostering the probability of increased prosperity, better health, and beneficial relationships. Where each phase is placed depends on the number combination in the area in question.

Compasses and number schemes? Yikes! This sounds complex. It seems hard! Will I be able to grasp and implement classical feng shui's fundamentals and techniques? Of course! Don't fear. Forge ahead. Although classical feng shui certainly cannot be fully learned in a weekend seminar or even in this book, you *can* learn the basics of one method (Flying Star) that you *will* employ and from which you will benefit.

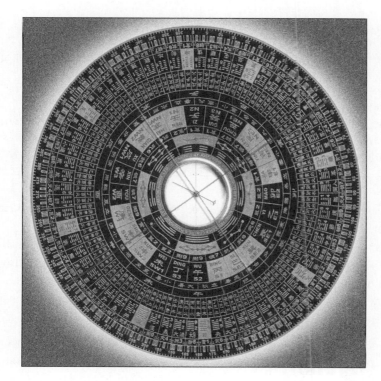

A lupoan compass used by practitioners of classical feng shui.

(Photograph by Master Joseph Vu)

Classical Feng Shui Flying Star Qi Map

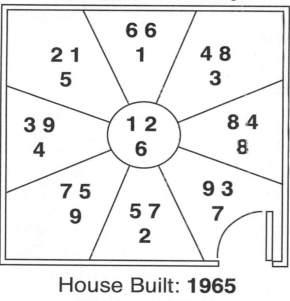

House Built: **1965**
Facing: **10° N**

The year the building was built and its magnetic sitting direction yield a numeric qi map. The classically trained feng shui practitioner studies the individual numbers, combination of numbers, and location of the numbers, among other things, to determine the likelihood of specific events occurring within the home. The practitioner balances the dwelling's qi to enhance its positive aspects and discourage its negative ones.

Master Class _____

The time your house was constructed or "born" and the time you were born are important considerations in a classical feng shui analysis. What does this mean? Well, many Chinese believe the first breath you take at birth marks your innate destiny. In the same way, when the foundation is set, the walls are secured, and the roof is affixed, your house is born. It, too, has a core personality. The central premise of feng shui is to correct and/or enhance your dwelling's personality so that its qi forces nourish your well-being, inspiring you to maximize your potential.

As you will learn in later chapters, classical feng shui is based, in part, on modern scientific reasoning. For example, acclaimed physicist Albert Einstein (1879–1955) proved that matter is an illusion, a masked form of energy. In other words, we, and our living space, are actually bundles of intertwining, connecting energy—all in flux, all confluent, pervading our very being. If not properly or effectively harnessed, human possibility is wasted. Doesn't it make sense to enhance our environment positively and productively?

Who Practices Feng Shui?

You need not be Asian or of Asian descent to practice feng shui. You don't have to be an interior designer, architect, or landscaper. Nor a philosopher, scientist, or celebrity. In fact, no prerequisites are required to practice feng shui. Yet, this is not to say that feng shui practitioners don't share common traits. They do.

Generally feng shui practitioners …

- Have an open mind.
- Are willing to try alternative forms of therapy.
- Believe that the world and its peoples are interconnected.
- Believe in God or a Higher Power.
- Believe harmony and balance are essential to our well-being.
- Believe in a sense of fate or destiny.

Feng shui practitioners are global. They transcend cultural, racial, economic, and political barriers.

Feng Shui's Beginnings in the East

In medieval China, feng shui was a closely guarded secret. Its masters were restricted to the ruling class of emperors, aristocrats, and the privileged elite. By deliberately excluding commoners from feng shui's power, they ensured their stately positions. Feng shui masters were greatly rewarded for their expertise, and severely punished, or even killed, if they were known to aid the public.

Feng Facts

One notable master, Yang Yunsong, managed to escape the Forbidden City (the famous complex of buildings in Beijing so called because at one time, only the emperor, his female entourage, and eunuchs lived there) during the Yellow Bandits Rebellion of 907 C.E. Yang sought refuge in the mountainous area of northwest China. There, he helped the poor by using his skills in feng shui. Nicknamed "Save the Poor," Yang Yunsong is still revered today for being among the first to explain and share some of the shrouded secrets of the tradition.

Today, feng shui is a way of life in many parts of Asia. In Hong Kong, Singapore, Taiwan, and Malaysia, feng shui masters are regularly called upon to bring prosperity, good health, and beneficial relationships to individuals and businesses alike. Meanwhile, feng shui is enjoying a resurgence on mainland China. After being long suppressed by the Communist regime, feng shui—along with many of China's other traditions—is once again being embraced.

Feng Shui Moves West

As Asians move west, so do their traditions. Oriental medicine (such as acupuncture and herbal remedies), Far Eastern cuisine, and the martial arts have all been accepted in our multicultural societies. Following their influences, feng shui is on the verge of being accepted by mainstream America. As we mentioned, feng shui is cropping up everywhere. Adult education courses, magazines, and websites are helping it to become a household word. Indeed, this cultural exchange of ideas will help facilitate communication and better understanding between two divergent peoples. Perhaps a time will come when feng shui will lose its distinctly cultural identity and become a worldwide tradition.

Would you be surprised to learn that some of the Western world's largest corporations use feng shui? Here are a few examples of progressive Western feng shui partisans:

- ◆ Trump Towers in New York City
- ◆ Creative Artists Agency in Beverly Hills, California

◆ MGM Grand Hotel and Mirage Resorts in Las Vegas, Nevada

◆ The Deepak Chopra Center in California

◆ Sydney Harbour Casino and Hotel in Australia

Although myriad Eastern companies adhere to feng shui principles, you might be interested to learn that Hong Kong Disneyland, scheduled to open in 2005, is being constructed according to feng shui principles.

Feng Shui and You

You don't have to be a mover or shaker to partake in feng shui's power. Feng shui is meant for everyone. We have two kinds of clients: those who are seeking desperate measures for desperate times and those who are looking for a winning edge. They share a desire to improve their living and/or working conditions. Do you see yourself in any of the following situations?

◆ Alice is a stockbroker. She's smart, attractive, funny, and single. She has grown tired of blind dates, bad dates, and no dates. She wants to settle down and have a family. We will help her choose an apartment to attract Mr. Right.

◆ John and Jane have two small children. Although they've been living in their split-level home for a couple of years, they just don't feel comfortable in their living space. We'll help them feel at ease and gain a restful sleep.

◆ Mr. Smith owns a small insurance agency. Despite competitive salaries, bonuses, and other incentives not offered by many employers, his staff can't get along. Will the bickering ever end?

The fact that these people will consider feng shui to improve their situations is testimony to their open minds. They will take a leap of faith and extend their common senses to the realm of the invisible, the realm that extends beyond our five senses of sight, touch, hearing, taste, and smell.

But, you might ask, exactly how will these people be helped? Patience, our friends! Later on, after you've learned feng shui's fundamental principles, we'll review these case studies and see how they remedied their situations. Patience, perseverance, and reading to the end will enable you to solve these mysteries.

What Do I Need to Practice Feng Shui?

The most important thing you need is a positive attitude—a willingness to want to improve your life and that of your loved ones. Although feng shui is used to balance your home's space, the onus is on you to create good Man Luck (Ji yin de) by balancing your own space, your own mind and body. By living the Golden Rule, by refraining from gossip, maliciousness, and hate, you will become a more centered being. You will be working with feng shui's power. It's a two-way street, friends! How can you expect feng shui to fully work if you're arguing incessantly, spending beyond your means, or living in a cluttered and disorderly environment? Take charge! Seize the day. Become proactive and not reactive to your own wants and needs and life's situations. Help to create a positive destiny by performing good deeds, uttering good words, and eating healthful food. Balance and harmony begin with you!

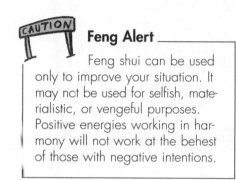

Feng Alert

Feng shui can be used only to improve your situation. It may not be used for selfish, materialistic, or vengeful purposes. Positive energies working in harmony will not work at the behest of those with negative intentions.

Here's a short list of things you'll need to begin your study of classical feng shui:

- Your brain.

- Integrity.

- A clear plastic, 6-inch, 360-degree protractor with half-inch gradations. This can be found in any office supply store. We recommend the Mars College protractor.

- A straight edge ruler.

- A basic protractor compass. This can be found in any outdoor equipment and camping store. A model that graduates in two-degree steps on which directions are clearly marked is best. Also, a compass featuring a line of sight is beneficial. We recommend the Silva Explorer Model 203 compass. It costs about $25 and is shown in the following photo.

The final thing you'll need is patience. To the newcomer, feng shui's principles may seem abstract and difficult to comprehend. Our advice is to take your time. Read each chapter thoroughly. Digest it. Review it again. If you become frustrated, confused, or just plain fed up, relax and take a break. The Great Wall of China wasn't built in a day. Neither was feng shui!

Example of a basic protractor compass.

(Photo courtesy of Johnson Outdoors Inc.)

Twenty Ways to Benefit from Feng Shui

Here are 20 ways feng shui can potentially help you. We'll be covering many of these topics in later chapters:

1. Getting a job, raise, or promotion

2. Improving health

3. Getting married

4. Getting pregnant or preventing miscarriages

5. Guarding against separations or divorce

6. Increasing motivation

7. Creating more harmonious family/work relationships

8. Developing better study habits

9. Increasing creativity

10. Feeling more in control

11. Feeling more comfortable in your home/office

12. Eliminating depression

13. Stimulating social life

14. Spurring better business

15. Preventing lawsuits or malicious influences

16. Preventing accidents

17. Finding an apartment, home, or business

18. Warding off addictions

19. Promoting better sleep

20. Bringing respect and fame

Even if you feel your life is on track, practicing feng shui is fun. Get involved. Enlist your friends and family.

Pinyin and Wade-Giles: Chinese Romanization

In this book, we use the *Pinyin* system of romanization that uses the Roman or Latin alphabet to spell Chinese words. Developed by the Chinese in the mid-twentieth century, Pinyin was accepted as the international standard in 1979. Nevertheless, many Western authors still use the older Wade-Giles system of transliteration, which was developed by two British *sinologists* (a person who studies Chinese culture, customs, language, and the like): Sir Francis Wade (1818–1895) and Herbert Allen Giles (1845–1935). For our readers who have books about feng shui that use Wade-Giles, here's the Pinyin equivalent of some of the words you'll encounter in this book:

Wade-Giles	Pinyin	Meaning
Ch'i	Qi	Life's breath
Lo p'an	Luopan	Chinese compass
Pa-k'ua	Bagua	Eight trigrams
Kua	Gua	Natal trigram number
Ch'ien	Qian	Northwestern trigram
Tui	Dui	Western trigram
Li	Li	Southern trigram
Chen	Zhen	Eastern trigram
Sun	Xun	Southeastern trigram
K'an	Kan	Northern trigram
Ken	Gen	Northeastern trigram
K'un	Kun	Southwestern trigram
I Ching	*Yijing*	*Book of Changes*

Don't worry if you're not familiar with these words. In upcoming chapters, you'll understand all of them!

So, where do we go from here? Before you depart on this journey, you must first understand how you think as a Westerner. Understanding how you are a product of a culture of rational thinkers will enable you to set aside your preconceptions. Only then can you investigate and accept alternative ways of thinking based on intuitive knowledge—a method primarily used by our Eastern counterparts. Yet, regardless of how anyone thinks, we'll all arrive at the same conclusions about the world we live in. What's that? Keep reading!

Wise Words

Hanyu Pinyin Wenzi (the alphabet of Chinese phonetic combinations) is a system of romanization that uses the Roman or Latin alphabet to spell Chinese words. Based on the Peking dialect of Mandarin Chinese, Pinyin was developed by the Chinese after the advent of Communism in 1949. In 1979, it became the international standard and is used in all forms of printed material, television, Braille for the blind, and finger spelling for the deaf. Wade-Giles is an older system of transliteration first developed by a Cambridge University sinologist, Sir Thomas Francis Wade (1818–1895) and improved upon and popularized by another British sinologist, Herbert Allen Giles (1845–1935).

The Least You Need to Know

◆ Feng shui is not a superstition, philosophy, or religion.

◆ Feng shui is the study of time and space. The practice seeks to harmonize nature's forces within your living/working space and surrounding environment.

◆ The use of mirrors, crystals, bamboo flutes, and red ribbons, along with the concept of dividing a home into sections of career, knowledge, family, wealth, fame, marriage, children, and helpful people belong to faux schools of feng shui.

◆ Feng shui can potentially improve your health, wealth, and relationships.

◆ A positive attitude, integrity, patience, and a basic protractor compass are all that you need to begin practicing classical feng shui.

Chapter 2

Western Intellectual Heritage and the Holy Grail

In This Chapter

- How our minds work
- Our scientific legacy
- A holistic universe
- The relationship between nature and mathematics
- A new world vision for the millennium: suggestions to implement global harmony

Pretend the universe is a car. We all know that a car is an intricate mechanism comprised of thousands of pieces, all functioning as parts of the whole. We know that it would be impossible to discern how the car operates by studying, say, a tire. Ironically, this is how most Western scientists study the universe. They focus on one spot or element, disregarding the interconnectedness of that which surrounds and/or encompasses it.

Yet, the *big picture* is now beginning to emerge. As modern scientists delve deeper into the celestial heavens and probe deeper into the infinitesimal, many are becoming aware of the unity of all things. The acceptance of universal wholeness will guide and enable us to define a new world vision—a vision that will change our fundamental moral, social, political, and religious order.

This chapter is about understanding how our minds work and how we have tuned in to nature's truths. This chapter is about our intellectual heritage—how the Western world has become a culture of rational thinkers and how we are becoming a people of united reformers. What does this have to do with feng shui? Our Eastern neighbors have always favored the unity of all things. As you will come to learn, feng shui is about harnessing nature's forces, which connect us all. Understanding and accepting this concept will lead you to better health, wealth, and relationships.

Mind Power 101

The human mind is a powerful tool. Using our minds, we have progressed from being a tribe of hunters and gatherers to a society overly dependent on our inventions and discoveries. Without such conveniences as telephones, computers, automobiles, or microwave ovens, we would feel lost, frustrated, and frazzled. The last 150 years alone have yielded mind-boggling advances in the fields of science, medicine, genetics, and technology, unequaled during any other time in the history of humankind. The endless stream of wonders continues still, each new development vastly increasing our knowledge and capabilities.

Notable Quotables

A mechanism of world inter-communication will be devised, embracing the whole planet, freed from national hindrances and restrictions, and functioning with marvelous swiftness and perfect regularity.

—Shoghi Effendi, *The World Order of Bahá'u'lláh*, 1938

Using our minds, we have ushered in the Information Age: An age in which communication devices like the telephone, cellular phone, fax machine, and especially the computer, have connected people all over the world. An age in which ideas can flow freely, where walls of judgment are breaking down. Using our minds, we have collectively taken a step toward global integration and the unity of all peoples.

Twelve Percent of the Whole

Logic and reason are the bulwarks of Western thinking. But did you know that these abilities compose only 12 percent of our mind's power? Considering the level of intellect, sophistication, and complexity needed to generate such far-reaching advances as satellites and space stations, this is truly remarkable. Yet it is a physiological fact.

The adult mind comprises two contingent but distinctly different components: the *conscious* mind (12 percent) and the *subconscious* mind (88 percent). Separating the realms is the critical area of the mind. Part conscious, part subconscious, the critical area accepts and rejects information based on *knowns*, units of communication that have been learned before.

Imagine that your mind is a computer. The input of information is tremendous. Files are constantly being made: Belief files, feeling files, habit files, and everything else that is a known are filed in your subconscious memory. If a computer encounters instructions or data that are totally foreign to its known programs, they are rejected. Likewise, if your mind receives information unknown to your frame of reference, it is immediately dismissed. For example, if we said you could derive nature's truths by meditating, you would probably reject this idea, if you had an analytical, scientific way of thinking.

Wise Words

The **conscious**, or waking, state of mind gives us logic, reason, and willpower. The **subconscious** realm is the area of the mind that receives and stores information. A **known** is a unit of communication that has been learned before. It can be positive or negative and will be accepted into the subconscious mind. An **unknown** is a unit that is rejected by the critical area of the mind and will not enter the subconscious.

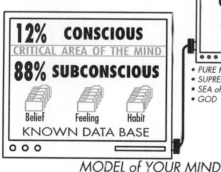

MODEL of YOUR MIND

Our mind accepts and rejects information similar to the way a computer processes data.

As a culture, we have learned to isolate, compartmentalize, and fragmentize information. Only in the West do we tend to separate such things as mind from body and faith from reason. Our separatist notion and the way we view the world stem from our linear scientific heritage. We are comfortable with taking a step-by-step, logical approach to problem solving. Everyday phrases like "Let's be reasonable" and "This is not logical" are testament to our deeply ingrained thought process.

Faux Feng Shui and the Western Mind

The Western mind-set helped, in part, to create faux feng shui! The keen master-minds behind Black Sect and Life Aspirations feng shui (see Chapter 1 for a reminder of faux feng shui) understood that Westerners like things neat and orderly. Westerners need to break things down. Westerners need to label things. Hence, the creation of distinct components or life aspirations/stations of wealth, career, knowledge, and the like.

Remember the television commercial: "Two all-beef patties, special sauce, lettuce, cheese, pickles, onions, on a sesame seed bun"? Quick, was it McDonald's or Burger King? Chances are, you had to think about it. The point is, the savvy production team hired by the owners of McDonald's capitalized on the Western obsession with parts. Little emphasis was placed on the whole burger.

Continuing with our fast-food analogy, Westerners want things bigger-better-faster. We want things now-now-now. Borrowing a term from our friend and feng shui teacher and practitioner Cate Bramble, feng shui has become "McFeng shui." Simply, most Westerners do not have the patience to fully understand a complicated concept. We want the *Reader's Digest* version—only part of the story.

Friends, understand that classical feng shui is the study of qi, the holistic, pervasive, and uniting force underlying everyone and everything. You'll learn all about qi in Chapter 4, but for now understand that qi is not like a pet dog. Qi cannot be commanded and taught to separate into different sociological factions. Wealth qi, over here. Sit and stay. Career qi, over here. Sit and stay. Remember, feng shui is the study of time (heaven qi) and space (earth qi). Each dwelling's space is different, born into different times. Actually, you may have more than one area within your home or office that promotes prosperity and promotion!

The study of classical feng shui will not only free us, allowing for alterations in the way of seeing and thinking, but also help us grow, develop, progress, and succeed. It will help us become more holistic, shedding our separatist ways.

In Search of the Holy Grail

Before we move on to presenting scientific evidence and theories about a holistic universe, it's worth understanding from where our rational and separatist mind-set derives.

Since ancient times, philosophers and scientists have searched for the Holy Grail of Knowledge: the origin, structure, and order of the universe. With each new discovery, myths were dispelled and replaced by new "truths," which often carried over into successive centuries, becoming firmly rooted in our collective consciousness. Over the past 2,500 years, there has been an impressive roster of individuals whose scientific discoveries or philosophical ideas changed the way we view the world. Here is a brief overview of those who have helped to form our rational, separatist mind-set:

◆ **The Greek Age:** The ancient Greeks considered the study of science a noble pursuit. It was not inspired by religion, which at the time was polytheistic—a belief in or worship of more than one god. Science that presents a rational and orderly view of the cosmos developed in ancient Greece around the sixth century B.C.E. with Thales of Miletus. A seafaring and trading people, the Greeks developed an acute sense of time and space, their observations giving birth to the fields of astronomy and geometry. We can credit Pythagoras (560–500 B.C.E.) and Aristotle (384–322 B.C.E.) with instituting scientific methods based on logic and reason. These methods of *deductive* and *inductive reasoning* still play a role today in scientific thinking.

Wise Words

The method of reaching a conclusion by deducing laws through observation is **deductive reasoning**. The method of reaching a conclusion by developing specific cases based on general laws is **inductive reasoning**.

◆ **The Newtonian Age:** English physicist Sir Isaac Newton's (1642–1727) universe was black and white, void of gray. Now called classical or mechanical physics, Newton's belief was that simple and permanent mechanical laws that could be understood by careful observation and experimentation governed the universe. Based on the Greeks' deductive and inductive methodology, Newton explained his theories using mathematics. He maintained that we are separate from nature and, thus, are able to observe the world objectively. Although Newton sought to reconcile his deep religious convictions with science, his ideas set the stage for a break between science and religion, or physics and metaphysics (philosophy).

◆ **The Enlightenment Age:** Coined by German philosopher Immanuel Kant (1724–1804), the term "enlightenment" took God out of the scientific equation, viewing natural phenomena entirely as a mechanical scheme. Kant sought to bring together two divergent philosophical ideas developed during the seventeenth century—the notion that knowledge is derived from observation and experience and not theory (empiricism) and the notion that knowledge is derived from reasoning (rationalism). According to Kant, the concepts of time and space cannot be fully understood using sensory perception. Because of these limitations, the physical world must be studied using a rational system like mathematics. Other enlightened philosophers include Denis Diderot (1713–1784), Julien Offra de la Mettrie (1709–1751), and David Hume (1711–1761).

◆ **The Darwinian Age:** The split between science and religion was fully realized with British naturalist Charles Darwin (1809–1882). Postulated in his book, *On the Origin of the Species by Means of Natural Selection, or the Preservation of Favoured Races in the Struggle for Life* (1859), Darwin's groundbreaking and controversial theory of evolution and natural selection caused much discord between the scientific and religious factions. The schism deeply impacted the Western mind-set.

The preceding examples demonstrate how we have learned to rationalize, separate, and isolate information as a means of understanding the totality of the universe and its inhabitants. As a result, we have effectively disengaged, separating science, religion, mind, and body into distinct and fortified camps—a mind-set that would be shattered with twentieth-century science.

United We Stand

The discoveries made by twentieth-century physicists have rocked the scientific world, crushing long-held traditional views spearheaded by Newtonian mechanics. A unified world picture is emerging that no longer reduces nature (and human nature) to a series of isolated parts. Modern scientists now view the cosmos as a web of interconnected and interrelated events. As you'll soon learn, many modern scientists believe in the existence of God or a Higher Power to which we are connected. The new scientific paradigm—the whole is the sum of its parts—is replacing the common ideology—the parts are the means to the whole.

Although these two ideologies may sound alike, they really are not. The distinction may be subtle but, nonetheless, is significant. We are speaking of ways of thinking, considering, and perceiving the world. Remember the car at the beginning of this chapter? Today, when we look at it, we see more than just a set of tires, a carburetor, or a fuel tank. We see all these things and more: a means of transportation, a status symbol, and a product of a powerful worldwide industry. When we drive this car on a highway, we are involved in more than going from point A to point B; we are using a vast and vital, well-connected national and interstate road system upon which the economic health of our nation depends. When we consider our nation, we do not stop at borders. We belong to a community of nations, diverse peoples all sharing the same planet.

In feng shui, the totality is what is stressed—a rich totality composed of a harmonious unity of parts. This is opposed to a collection of distinct and singular parts (the eight life aspirations/stations) joining together to form a loose federation. So, as scientists continue to search for "pure truth," feng shui helps to provide an alternate path, if you will—new frames of reference to our collective consciousness.

Scientific Holistic Theories

Two influential and revolutionary scientific theories surfaced during the twentieth century that played a leading role in changing how scientists understand the world. On a larger scale, the discoveries enabled us to see the big picture, a holistic reality.

◆ **Theories of relativity:** Postulated by German physicist Albert Einstein (1879–1955), these theories state that mass is nothing more than a different manifestation of energy. It means that the book you're now reading and the chair you are sitting in are forms of energy at rest. Also, Einstein understood that space and time were not separate entities, but are connected to form a fourth dimension called space-time.

Notable Quotables

Everything is determined … by forces over which we have no control. It is determined for the insect as well as for the star. Human beings, vegetables, or cosmic dust—we all dance to the mysterious tune, intoned in the distance by an invisible piper.

—Albert Einstein in *The Saturday Evening Post*, October 26, 1929

◆ **Quantum physics:** Formulated in the 1920s by Niels Bohr (1885–1962), Max Planck (1858–1947), and Werner Heisenberg (1901–1976), among others, quantum physics is the study of subatomic particles such as electrons and atoms. In a nutshell, quantum theory reveals the unity of all things. It shows that we cannot use isolation as a method to gain knowledge of the whole.

If these theories seem like old hat to you, ideas that have lost their power and passion, consider the following theories of which many people are not yet aware.

Theoretical Holistic Theories

Perhaps the most exciting theories cannot be fully scientifically proven. Nevertheless, they cause us to broaden our minds, raising us to new levels of understanding, wisdom, and insight. Here is a short description of the work generated by three innovative and progressive Western scientists.

◆ **David Bohm** (1917–1992): Based in part on his work concerning the behavior of electrons, theoretical physicist David Bohm believed the universe can be likened to a hologram in which each part of the image contains the entire picture. He believed the universe is "an undivided and unbroken whole" and that there exists a hidden primary reality (the quantum potential) that provides information to the totality of humankind and its environment. Bohm's beliefs give a scientific explanation to the phenomenon of synchronicity—a pattern of correlated coincidences (thoughts, objects, numbers, and/or events) linked together to form a theme of meaning to the observer.

◆ **Rupert Sheldrake** (1942–): Biologist Rupert Sheldrake claims that the development and evolution of an organism and human consciousness is guided by a holistic force that he calls the morphic field. Specifically, the morphic field is a phenomenon of nature whereby if a form or thought occurs in nature, it is likely to repeat again in another species; and if a thought occurs, it is likely to be thought again by another person. In nature, the spiral shape of conch shells, hurricanes, and galaxies are examples. In human nature, the independent and almost simultaneous "discovery" of calculus in 1675 by English mathematician and philosopher Sir Isaac Newton (1642–1727) and German mathematician and philosopher Gottfried Leibniz (1646–1716) is an example of humankind tapping into the morphic field.

◆ **Andrew Newberg** (1967–): Neuroscientist Andrew Newberg believes he can prove that a Higher Power exists by the way the brain functions during states of deep concentration, meditation, and prayer. In these states the "line" that separates the self from the world disappears, producing the effect of a mystical union with God (or the Sea of Consciousness, a Higher Power). The question remains: Is God an illusion produced by the brain's activity, or has God wired our brain to experience a holistic reality? These mysteries and many other studies about the convergence of science and religion are being funded by the John Templeton Foundation.

Indeed, the notion of a holistic world order is quite profound and worthy of more study. Please see Appendix C for a list of Bohm's, Sheldrake's, and Newberg's thought-provoking works. Also, see Chapter 11 in *The Complete Idiot's Guide to the I Ching* (Alpha Books, 2002). Here, we give a detailed account of David Bohm's ideas as they relate to the *Yijing*, a book of divination developed at the end of the second millennium B.C.E.

In the meantime, if we can accept their ideas, it means we are able to draw from an infinite well of potential and possibilities. This is the hallmark of feng shui—to harness nature's well (qi) to better our existence.

Feng Facts

First self-published in Japan, Dr. Masaru Emoto's revolutionary book, *The Hidden Messages in Water* (Beyond Words Publishing, 2004) features his discoveries showing how thoughts affect physical reality. Using a high-powered telescope and high-speed film, Emoto captured samples of frozen water changing form when they were exposed to positive and negative thoughts. Positive thoughts directed toward the water sample caused it to crystallize into symmetrical snowflake shapes. Negative thoughts caused the water to crystallize into distorted and chaotic shapes. Emoto also studied how music and the spoken word affects water. Since the world and our bodies are mostly comprised of water, the implications of Emoto's work can create a new understanding of how we can positively influence our environment and our well-being.

Nature Speaks Mathematics, Too

Scientists use mathematics to help explain what we cannot understand using sensory perception. Somehow, this man-made abstraction magically conforms to nature's truths. Put another way, somehow we conform to mathematical principles in the universe. Whether we do it on a conscious or subconscious level is not known, but we've stumbled on mathematical patterns in nature that continue to perplex and inspire, propelling us to new levels of understanding about ourselves and the world in which we live.

Although modern scientists understand that mathematics is the language of the universe, the ancient Chinese understood that mathematics was the language of the gods—that the pantheon of ancestors in heaven "spoke" to their descendants using numbers. The Chinese used the numeric information made apparent in the celestial heavens to improve their well-being. Eventually, their astute knowledge of the cosmos evolved into a system of feng shui called Flying Star, the subject of Part 4.

Fascinating Fibonacci and the Golden Ratio

1, 1, 2, 3, 5, 8, 13, 21, 34, 55, 89, 144, 233, 377, 610 …

This sequence of numbers is called the *Fibonacci Sequence,* named after thirteenth-century mathematician Leonardo of Pisa, also known as Fibonacci. By charting a population of rabbits, Fibonacci stumbled upon a certain numeric pattern as a solution to a story problem: Each number in the series is the sum of the two previous numbers. For example, 3 + 5 = 8; 5 + 8 = 13; 8 + 13 = 21; and so on to infinity.

Pretty neat, but it gets even better. Dividing each number in the series by the one preceding it yields a ratio that stabilizes at 1.618034. For example, 2 ÷ 1 = 2; 3 ÷ 2 = 1.5; 1597 ÷ 987 = 1.618034; 4181 ÷ 2584 = 1.618034; and so on to infinity. This figure has come to be known as the *Golden Ratio.*

Wise Words

The **Fibonacci Sequence** is a series of numbers in which each number in the series is the sum of the two previous numbers. A **Golden Ratio** is a special number approximately equal to 1.6180339887498948482. The digits of the Golden Ratio go on to infinity without any pattern repeating. It's related to the Fibonacci Sequence and is obtained by dividing each number in the series by the one that precedes it.

Big deal, you say? Okay, here's the cool stuff. Fibonacci numbers and the Golden Ratio can be found in nature and our bodies, and have influenced art, architecture, and music. Fibonacci proportions can even be found in everyday items like playing cards, notepads, mirrors, windows, and credit cards. Simply, we are drawn to certain number proportions. Put another way, we, and our surroundings, conform to mathematical principles made manifest in the universe.

Here is a short list of things in which you can find Fibonacci numbers and the Golden Ratio:

- On pinecones, artichokes, pineapples, and sunflowers, the bracts, petals, scales, and seeds, respectively, exemplify Fibonacci ratios. There are 5 steep and 8 gradual spirals on pinecones and artichokes. There are 8 and 13 gradual and 21 steep spirals on a pineapple. The head of a sunflower shows 55 rows of seeds revolving counterclockwise and 89 rows of seeds revolving clockwise.

- We have Fibonacci fingers: 2 hands, each of which has 5 fingers broken into 3 parts of 2 knuckles. Our body and face conform to Fibonacci proportions.

- On a piano keyboard, 13 keys comprise an octave (chromatic scale). These are broken down into 8 white keys and 5 black keys, which are divided into groups of 2 and 3 keys. Moreover, the pentatonic scale is made up of 5 keys, and the diatonic scale with 8 keys.

Fibonacci numbers and the Golden Ratio are manifestations of the innate harmony, symmetry, and balance in the universe. As we stated at the beginning of this section, whether consciously or subconsciously, we have tapped into and benefited by nature's truth. Indeed, we are all part of a cosmic dance in which we affect and are affected by everyone and everything.

For more information about the Fibonacci Sequence, please see Trudi Hammel Garland's inspiring book, *Fascinating Fibonaccis: Mystery and Magic in Numbers* (Dale Seymour Publications, 1987).

Feng Facts

Add up any 10 consecutive numbers in the Fibonacci Sequence and divide the sum by 11. You'll find that not only is the sum always evenly divisible, the sum is a Fibonacci number! For example, $2 + 3 + 5 + 8 + 13 + 21 + 34 + 55 + 89 + 144 = 374 \div 11 = 34$; $8 + 13 + 21 + 34 + 55 + 89 + 144 + 233 + 377 + 610 = 1584 \div 11 = 144$. See Chapter 13 for more interesting information about how the number 11 is mysteriously linked with the catastrophic events surrounding the September 11, 2001, World Trade Center attack. (The number 11 is especially linked with the Towers and not the Pentagon in this case.)

Other Profound Patterns

The Fibonacci Sequence and the Golden Ratio aren't the only number series found in nature. Many other transcendental mathematical examples exist, but space restricts us from presenting them.

As we have mentioned, feng shui is a system of mathematical patterns in nature discovered by the ancient Chinese. In fact, four of feng shui's fundamental principles correspond to numbers in the Fibonacci Sequence: taiji (1); yin and yang (2); heaven, earth, and human qi (3); five phases (5); and eight trigrams (8). Part 2 is devoted to learning the principles of these patterns.

A New World Vision for the Millennium

If we do discover a single unifying force or scientifically prove the existence of God or a Higher Power, how will that affect our everyday life? Will we lay down our warheads and use this knowledge constructively? Will we become united as citizens of planet Earth? Perhaps we earthlings should establish a new vision for the millennium, a set of principles that will unite us on a fundamental human level. These principles will heal cultural and racial tensions resulting from dogmas and superstitions of the past, as well as elevate our awareness so that we can create a harmonious and peaceful world.

If for no other reason, our common purpose of survival will force us to adopt a new world vision for the millennium. Our goals could include, but not be limited to ...

◆ An independent search for truth.

◆ The harmony of science and religion.

- The oneness of all belief systems.
- Equality of men and women.
- The elimination of extremes of wealth and poverty.
- The abolition of prejudices.
- Universal compulsory education.
- A universal language.
- The establishment of a world government.

The implementation of world harmony begins with you. Before we can hope to change our global frame of reference, we must each foster unity and harmony in our own home. We hope that you'll set aside your rational mind-set and opt for a more holistic way of thinking. Feng shui is a powerful tool that can help do this.

In the next chapter, you'll learn how the Chinese have always viewed the world as a holistic reality. Also, you'll learn how feng shui developed.

The Least You Need to Know

- Logic and reasoning constitute just 12 percent of our mind power; the other 88 percent is our subconscious.
- Our logical, rational mind-set stems from the ancient Greeks.
- With the advent of Einstein's theories of relativity and quantum physics, modern science has begun to accept the "oneness" of all things.
- Theoretical scientists like David Bohm, Rupert Sheldrake, and Andrew Newberg propose that the world is a holistic entity from which we can draw information.
- Mathematics is the language of nature.
- A set of principles must be developed to secure harmony on a human level.

Chapter 3

The Great Wall of Knowledge and the Rise of Feng Shui

In This Chapter

- ◆ Chinese inventions
- ◆ How nature has influenced science and philosophy
- ◆ The development of feng shui
- ◆ Form School and Compass School: the two classic schools of feng shui

Dim sum, the Great Wall, kung fu, the Cultural Revolution, scroll painting, mah jongg, the Forbidden City, rice fields, rickshaws, Chairman Mao, the Silk Road, Beijing, terra-cotta warriors, Confucius, acupuncture, Daoism .... What comes to mind when *you* think of China?

No doubt China is an ancient culture whose enduring traditions, colorful symbolism, and systems of government captivate us. Yet, did you know that for 2,000 years, beginning around 500 B.C.E. to 1500 C.E., this Eastern nation's scientific and technological advances exceeded anything found in the West?

The Chinese have always believed in the oneness of all things. The practice of feng shui was born out of China's reverence for nature. The Chinese believed if they could reflect the balance of nature's forces in their daily lives, they could achieve a more harmonious living condition. That assumption was correct. In this chapter, you'll learn how the Chinese developed a thought process based, in part, on intuitive wisdom, and how they derived mathematical truths from nature.

Made in China

A common misunderstanding among Westerners is that the Chinese lack scientific and technological know-how. The ubiquitous "Made in China" label, stuck to the bottom of practically every inexpensive trinket, probably contributes to this stereotype. But the fact is we have the Chinese to thank for inventing many things that have improved our lives and made them more pleasurable. The wheelbarrow, umbrella, animal harness, stirrups, the game of chess, paper money, fishing reels, matches, and kites are all products of Chinese ingenuity. Also, the Chinese developed the first seismograph and planetarium. They created movable sails, the rudder, and the bulkhead. Iron casting and silk harvesting originated in China.

But, surely, China's four most important inventions are the developments of paper-making, printing, gunpowder, and the compass. The compass is the tool of the feng shui practitioner. You'll be learning more about this later.

China's Greater Nature

The ancient Chinese took what they called "Greater Nature" (Da Zi Ran) very seriously. Its forces inspired, awed, and humbled. It was a favorite subject of artisans. Greater Nature even gave rise to earth sciences like geology, cartography, and chemistry. The Chinese believed they were a product of nature's forces. They believed these forces determined their fate. To the farmer, gentle winds meant abundant crops, prosperity, and good health. Conversely, harsh winds, floods, and drought meant devastation, misfortune, and illness.

Natural phenomena were important to the emperor, too. Since the Shang dynasty (c. 1600–1045 B.C.E.), these semi-divine leaders petitioned Shangdi (their high god who ruled over lesser gods and spirits of the departed) on behalf of their kingdom. If Shangdi approved of his leadership, he blessed the kingdom with favorable weather, thus securing the king's position. If Shangdi disapproved of the king's leadership, the lord punished him by sending bad weather and illness. Considered an evil omen, such harsh conditions were a direct communication from above that the king should rectify his poor behavior.

Skywatcher for Hire

When Marco Polo visited China in 1275 C.E., purportedly he described Beijing as a city of 5,000 skywatchers. He was probably right. Some of those skywatchers were astrologers; some were astronomers. Both ran flourishing businesses in interpreting and divulging nature's secrets.

Feng Facts

In her book *Did Marco Polo Go to China?* (Secker & Warburg, 1995), British librarian Frances Wood claims he didn't. This comes as quite a shock to Western minds who believe Polo discovered China. Although Wood makes a compelling case, she can't emphatically prove her claim. If Polo did visit China in 1275 C.E., why is there no court documentation of his governorship of Yangshou or his 17-year relationship with Mongol leader Kublai Kan? In Polo's 1299 epic travelogue, *Divisament dou Monde (Description of the World)*, why doesn't he mention such Chinese peculiarities as chopsticks, tea drinking, and the Great Wall? Wood theorizes that Polo may have taken details from Persian and Arabic guidebooks on China acquired by the Polo family and that Polo never ventured beyond the family's trading posts on the Black Sea and in Constantinople.

The Art of Astrology

Astrologers analyze cycles of time. They study the position and movements of the sun, moon, stars, and planets in association with the consistency of human characteristics and the occurrence of human events on Earth. Based on the position of the heavenly bodies at any given point in time, astrologers can then map your fate. In China, the imperial court relied on a stable of learned astrologers to map out the most auspicious and inauspicious time to do just about everything, including the signing of documents, the construction of buildings, travel, military excursions, and marriage.

Astrology is considered an art because its predictions are based on supposition. Although an astrologer can forecast your fate, the conclusions cannot be scientifically proven. Astrology requires you to believe in a force of destiny predetermined by the cosmos. This is not to say that destiny replaces free will. Astrological calculations can foretell only *possibilities*. The astrologer who foretold accurate possibilities was held in high esteem and paid handsomely. The astrologer who was proven wrong was not so lucky. He was either exiled or executed.

Feng shui derives, in part, from astrological observations. While feng shui studies a building's fate, a synthesis of heaven (time) and earth (space) luck, methods of Chinese astrology like The Four Pillars of Destiny (Ziping Bazi) and Purple Constellation

Fate Computation (Ziwei Doushu) focus on a person's natal character. You'll learn about The Four Pillars of Destiny in Part 6.

Master Class _____

A wide range of divinatory methods was used in China. Besides astrology, the Chinese practiced chronomancy (an astro-calendrical system of determining favorable and unfavorable days), oneiromancy (divination based on dreams), physiognomy (divination based on facial features), scapulimancy and plastromancy (divination based on heating and interpreting the cracks formed on the scapula or shoulder bones of animals and the plastron or bottom shell of turtles), and sortilege (divination by drawing lots). The last method is especially significant to the formulation of the _Yijing (The Book of Changes)_, a book of divination written by King Wen and his son, the Duke of Zhou, about 3,000 years ago.

The Science of Astronomy

Astronomy is based on factual information derived from studying the cosmos. Chinese astronomers dealt with the practical needs of society. They developed almanacs and calendars. Because China's farmers produced food for every stratum of civilization, it was important for them to know the best times to plant and harvest their crops. According to markings found on a bone fragment some 3,500 years ago, Chinese astronomers understood the year is 365¼ days long, a statistic strikingly similar to today's precise measurement of 365.24219.

Aided by astronomical instruments, the Chinese also observed and recorded a number of celestial events:

- They began noting eclipses of the moon in 1361 B.C.E. and eclipses of the sun in 1217 B.C.E.

- They recorded a nova (an exploding star) in the area now known as Antares in 1300 B.C.E.

- They witnessed Haley's comet in 467 B.C.E.

- They documented a supernova (a really big exploding star) in 1054 C.E. Their accurate observation allowed modern astronomers to establish that the supernova was the origin of the Crab Nebula.

By 400 B.C.E., Chinese skywatchers had recorded 1,464 stars, dividing many of them into the 28 constellations of the Zodiac.

Confucianism and Daoism

Beginning in the sixth and fourth centuries B.C.E., respectively, two main schools of philosophy flourished in China: Confucianism and Daoism.

Confucianism, based on the teachings of Confucius (551–479 B.C.E.), was a system of ethics designed to cultivate moral virtues and social values in humankind. It dealt with practical and earthly affairs. Confucius's primary interest lay in proper behavior and social harmony. He emphasized rational knowledge and education. Later, obedience to one's parents became one of the most important virtues of Confucianism. The philosophy became so influential that it was taught in Chinese schools from the advent of the Han reign in 206 B.C.E. to the founding of the People's Republic of China in 1949.

Daoism (also spelled Taoism), on the other hand, was concerned with intuitive insight and heavenly affairs. One could attain intuitive or true knowledge by communing with nature and being at one with it, the Dao (or what Westerns variously call God, the Sea of Consciousness, the Higher Power). To understand the Dao (also spelled Tao) meant to recognize the inherent unity of all things and live your life accordingly. This meant trusting your intuition, your gut instinct, your sixth sense. The person who could cultivate his or her spirituality and develop this kind of character is following the Dao.

Wise Words

Confucianism, based on the sixth-century B.C.E. teachings of Confucius, is a system of ethics designed to cultivate moral perfection. **Daoism** is concerned with intuitive knowledge acquired by communicating with nature and being at one with it, the Dao. The founding fathers of Daoism emerged as a group of like-minded persons who lived and taught from the fourth to the second centuries B.C.E.

There is great debate about who founded the school of Daoism. Although many steadfastly hold the opinion that Laozi (also spelled Lao Tzu) founded the school, many contemporary scholars disagree. In fact, they maintain that Laozi, whom revered scholar Richard Wilhelm describes as a "shadowy figure," is not an individual, but a committee of like-minded people, who lived and taught from the fourth to the second centuries B.C.E.

This can be perplexing. What of Laozi's famous work, the *Daode jing* (also spelled *Tao Teh Ching*)? How this legendary figure is connected to the text is a mystery (and not our concern here). However, we do know that the *Daode jing* was actually written in the

Warring States Period (403–221 B.C.E.), at least 200 years after its purported authorship. We know this because the text is commented on and criticized by various people of that era. Furthermore, the *Daode jing* and another great Daoist work called the *Zhuangzi* (also spelled *Chuang Tzu*) was written by an actual person of the same name before the school of Daoism emerged in the Han dynasty (206 B.C.E.–220 C.E.).

Experience Versus Experiment

To the Daoists, rational thinking and experimentation (hallmarks of the Western mindset) are totally inadequate methods of understanding nature's truths. True knowledge extends beyond sensory perception; it can be experienced only in a meditative state of consciousness. The Daoists quiet their minds to let nature's truths flow into their beings from a supreme force.

Notable Quotables

Without going out of the door
You can know the ways of the world.
Without peeping through the window,
You can see the Way of Heaven.
The farther you go, The less you know.
Thus, the sage knows without traveling,
Sees without looking,
And achieves without ado.

—From the *Daode jing*

The Daoists believe you can't comprehend the Dao, the unnamed and unknowable, by describing it with words. Words were limited; nature was limitless. Words restricted; they barricaded the self from the universe of truth. This is why the Daoists and other Eastern mystics express their teachings in the form of aphorisms (concise statements of a principle or truth), huatou (paradoxical statements meant to be meditated upon to gain sudden intuitive enlightenment), or illustrations. These short verses showed the inconsistencies with rational communication.

Reversal Is the Movement of the Dao

When anything comes to its extreme, be it on the natural or human plane, a reversal to the other extreme takes place. This idea is central to both the Daoists and the Confucianists. But what does it mean?

It means that everything is cyclical, moving through ceaseless cycles of birth, growth, decay, and death. Everything is in a constant state of flux and change. Everything is interrelated and interconnected. With the extreme of winter comes the beginning of spring and renewal. With the extreme of night comes day. With the extreme of war comes peace. With the extreme of despair comes hope, and so forth.

To achieve anything, the general rule of thumb is to acknowledge its opposite. You need not experience it literally. Noting and respecting its possibility will help to keep you aware of sudden shifts of fortune. For example, being content and humble safeguards the possibility that the opposite nature won't be reached. If you have wealth, recognize the possibility that you may lose it. This concept has greatly impacted the Chinese to this day. It's all about balance and harmony.

This polarity of opposites is known as the theory of yin and yang. It is a fundamental principle of feng shui. You'll learn all about yin and yang in Chapter 5, but we'll touch on it in the following sections.

Change Is in the Wind

Generally speaking, the philosophy of the *Yijing*, or *Book of Changes*, is the first known attempt by the Chinese to formulate a system of knowledge around the interplay of opposites (yin and yang). The *Yijing* is a deceptively simple yet complex system of understanding the patterns of change in our universe. The *Yijing* can foretell your present and future prospects made manifest by changes you make in your attitude, actions, and activity. In other words, the *Yijing* suggests the appropriate change to achieve the desired result.

These patterns of change were recorded symbolically in the form of solid (yang) and broken (yin) lines called trigrams and hexagrams. Although we won't concern ourselves with the 64 hexagrams (six-tiered configurations of solid and broken lines) comprising the *Yijing*, the eight fundamental *trigrams* (three-tiered configurations of solid and broken lines) are central to practicing classical feng shui. Simply, the eight trigrams represent transitional stages of all possible natural and human situations.

The eight fundamental trigrams.

You'll be learning all about the meaning of these trigrams in Chapter 7.

The Masked Origin of the Yijing

A lot of misinformation has been written about the origin of the *Yijing*. For the record, here is a short chronology of its origins (part mythical, part historical). For more detailed information, please see our book *The Complete Idiot's Guide to the I Ching* (Alpha Books, 2002).

Initially, the *Yijing* was called the *Zhouyi*, or *The Changes of Zhou*. Initiated by King Wen and completed by his son, the Duke of Zhou of the Zhou dynasty (1045–221 B.C.E.), the *Zhouyi* draws on information gained by some of China's legendary figures. Specifically, the 8 trigrams and 64 hexagrams (composed of 2 trigrams each) are thought to have been devised by Fuxi.

As the story goes, the mythical sage-king Fuxi invented the eight trigrams after observing celestial and terrestrial activity. The idea was to create heaven on earth, to emulate nature's perfection. Perhaps to reward his efforts, Fuxi received a gift from heaven, a diagram of the perfect world, a world that was motionless, void of change. Sometime later, heaven bestowed a gift on another sage-king, Yu the Great. He also received a diagram, but this one represented the world in motion. Called the Luoshu, this diagram (its parts correlated to the eight trigrams) provides the foundation for a classical method of feng shui called Flying Star, the subject of Part 4.

Returning to the development of the *Yijing*, sometime during the Han dynasty (206 B.C.E.–220 C.E.), scholars set about collecting the great texts of their culture. At this time, commentaries, known as the *Ten Wings*, were attached to the *Zhouyi*. Basically, the seven essays "philosophized" the oracle by attempting to give meaning to the arrangement of yin and yang lines composing each hexagram and the archaic text. The new compilation was called the *Yijing*.

Changing Patterns

You might be interested to learn that trigram and hexagram symbols were not part of the *Zhouyi* text. In the 1970s, Zheng Zhenglang, a Chinese scholar of the Chinese Academy of Social Sciences in Beijing, discovered that the symbols were recorded in numeric form, a finding made after examining markings on oracle bones and bronze sacrificial containers dating from 1500–1000 B.C.E. (the late Shang and early Zhou dynastic periods). Zheng's discovery proved that from the beginning, the *Yijing* was based on numerological divination. From the preceding chapter, you'll remember that the Chinese believed their ancestors spoke to them using numbers. In other words, they believed the deceased manipulated the stalks of yarrow (the instruments used in a casting procedure that yields a hexagram, the answer to a question). Over time, the collection and examination of the divinatory records produced a text that matched a question with a numeric answer and an answer with a likely result.

But, although the Chinese believe their forebears were responsible for imparting wisdom and clarity, you might believe the answer is derived from the holistic realm of pure knowledge, a totality that can be analyzed mathematically.

How Does Feng Shui Fit In?

Classical feng shui combines elements of astrology and astronomy, geology, physics, mathematics, philosophy, and intuition—all the stuff you've just read about.

Now that you understand feng shui's components, you can better appreciate what the whole of feng shui means. Feng shui is the art and science of analyzing nature's forces with the intent of influencing its positive manifestations in you. A balanced environment leads to better health, increased prosperity, and beneficial relationships. And who doesn't want that?

Feng Facts

The term "feng shui" was first used in Guo Pu's (276–324 C.E.) *Zangshu (Book of Burial)*, a short text describing the disposition of qi (life's breath) on the earth's plane. Yet, earlier, during the Warring States Period (403–221 B.C.E.), feng shui was known as an art of divination called kanyu. "Kan" means "way of heaven," and "yu" means "way of the earth." Together, kanyu translates as "The way of heaven and earth."

Neolithic Feng Shui

Feng shui is a lot older than you might think. It predates Daoism, and even the *Yijing*. So how old do you think feng shui is—2,000, 4,000, or 6,000 years old? If you guessed the latter, you're right—for the time being, anyway.

In 1988, a Neolithic gravesite was excavated in the Henan province in central China. It revealed that the ancient Chinese were practicing some form of primitive feng shui some 6,000 years ago.

The head of the gravesite is rounded and points toward the south. The grave is squared at the body's feet, facing north. This arrangement conforms to the Chinese view of the cosmos. Symbolically, the sky is represented as round or domed and the Earth as square or flat. On each side of the remains, and outlined with shells, is a representation of two Chinese constellations—the azure dragon and the white tiger. A representation of the Big Dipper (*Beidou*) lies in the center. These artifacts testify to the fact that the Neolithic Chinese were already orienting their graves with the revolution of the Big Dipper around the North Star, the polestar (in Ursa Minor) in the northern hemisphere toward which the axis of Earth points.

These ancient coins reflect the Chinese idea of the cosmos. The central square represents the earth; the circular disc, heaven.

(Image © 1998 Photo Disc, Inc.)

The Form School of Feng Shui

The *Form School* (*Xingfa*) is the first and oldest school of feng shui officially dating to Qing Wuzi's (whom many believe is a fictitious figure) late Han (190–220 C.E.) text, the *Zangjing* or *Classic of Burial*. Some 100 years later, Guo Pu clarified and expanded upon the *Zangjing* in his book, the *Zangshu* or the *Book of Burial*, the same text from where the term feng shui derives.

Even before Daoism and Confucianism, ancestor worship was an intrinsic and important part of the Chinese belief system. They believed the spirits of the deceased directly affected the well-being of the living. Fortunes could be made or lost depending, in some measure, on the favorable location and orientation of their ancestors' tombs. If you think this is an outdated custom, think again. Today, feng shui masters run a brisk business selecting the most auspicious gravesites for their clientele.

The orientation of homes is also a part of Form School feng shui. Landforms and waterways were intensely scrutinized to determine the location of the dragon's lair (long xue), the place on the terrain where qi converges—the place that qi can be carried by the wind (feng) and settle in water (shui). In today's urbanized world, buildings, fences, and hedges represent terrestrial features, and roadways represent watercourses. You'll learn more about this in Chapters 9 and 10. The intuitive approach characterized Form School feng shui.

Wise Words

Form School or Xingfa ("Xing" means form and "fa" means method) is the first and oldest school of feng shui first explained in the late Han (190–220 C.E.) text called the *Zangjing* (*Classic of Burial*). The idea was to locate the place on the terrain where qi converges—the place where qi rides the wind (feng) and settles in water (shui).

The Compass School of Feng Shui

The term *Compass School* is a Western invention. In Chinese, the school that uses a compass and analyzes heavenly (time) and earthly (space) forces is called *Liqi Pai, Patterns of Qi School*. Because the English translation is a mouthful, we'll conform to the Western vernacular.

Formally dating to the Spring and Autumn Period (722–481 B.C.E.) with a simplistic method called Diagramatic Houses for the Five Families (Tuzhai Wuxing), which is no longer used, the Compass School is an umbrella term encompassing a host of more sophisticated techniques that are still widely used today. Flying Star (Xuankong Feixing), Three Harmonies (Sanhe), Mystical Doors (Qi Men), and Changing Trigrams/Eight House/Eight Mansions/The East West System (Yigua) are examples of Compass School methods. For the record, Life Aspirations and Black Sect techniques are not examples of Compass School methods.

The Compass School is based on the concept that each of the eight cardinal directions holds a different type of qi. Around this central premise, other factors are added, including astrology and numerology. The Compass School method is very computational, relying on intellect, observation, and experimentation rather than intuitive insights.

Wise Words

The term **Compass School** is a misnomer, invented by Westerners. It is called *Liqi Pai (Patterns of Qi School)* by the Chinese. It is any classical method that studies the effects of time (heavenly forces) and space (earthly forces) on the well-being of an individual. The tool of the trade is the compass.

Master Class

The ancient Chinese chose to think of a compass needle pointing south because it is the region from which warmth, light, and goodness come; whereas cold, darkness, and barbarian attacks come from the north.

The tool of the trade is, you guessed it, the compass. An early version dating to about 83 C.E. was a two-part, south-pointing instrument—a metal spoon made of magnetic lodestone and a square baseplate called a sinan. This developed into what is now called a luopan compass used by practitioners today. The luopan has anywhere from 4 to 40 concentric rings of information featuring things like the 8 fundamental trigrams, the 28 constellations, the 5 phases of qi, and the 9 stars or numbers of the Luoshu.

But, for your purposes, all you need is a basic protractor compass with clear markings (refer to Chapter 1 for specific guidelines in choosing a compass).

Precursor to the modern luopan compass, this early version dates to about 83 C.E.

(Photo by Val Biktashev)

Feng Shui Today

Today, both Form School and Compass School methods are used to perform an accurate feng shui reading. For the most part, today's practitioners have combined both schools into one system commonly referred to as classical or traditional feng shui.

In the next chapter, you'll learn about qi, the physical and metaphysical life force underlying all things.

The Least You Need to Know

◆ For 2,000 years, beginning in 500 B.C.E., the Chinese led the West in scientific and technological advances.

◆ Feng shui was born out of China's reverence for nature. The practice stems from the Neolithic Chinese.

◆ Form School is a classical method that studies landforms and waterways with the intention of locating the place on the terrain where qi converges.

◆ Compass School, a term invented by Westerners, is called the Patterns of Qi School in China. It studies how time and space impact the livelihood and health of an individual.

◆ Form School and Compass School have merged into one school of thought called classical or traditional feng shui.

Chapter **4**

Qi Wiz! It's Life's Force!

In This Chapter

- ◆ Qi: the life force at the heart of it all
- ◆ How other cultures define qi
- ◆ The three primal forces of qi: heaven qi, earth qi, and human qi
- ◆ Good vibes and bad vibes: types of qi

What we've been describing as nature's forces is what the Chinese call qi (also spelled ch'i). Qi has many meanings. It's described as the air we breathe. It's the Earth's magnetic field, cosmic radiation, and the sun's light. Qi is our spirit. Qi is luck. As you shall soon see, qi underlies all these things and more. Although this may seem somewhat abstract to us Westerners, Eastern cultures believe this holistic force governs our health, wealth, and happiness. Feng shui seeks to harness qi's positive aspects to better our well-being.

Now, to be perfectly clear, the existence of qi can't be fully scientifically proven. In fact, some of qi's more mystical aspects can never be proven using quantitative measurement. For example, can you prove the existence of your sixth sense? Can you prove luck or fate? Can you prove intuition? Surely not. Yet, most of us believe these things exist. Simply, qi's meta-physical or supernatural features defy measurement.

But we shouldn't be too hasty and dismiss this notion of a partly nonmeasurable force. After all, it wasn't so long ago that Benjamin Franklin "discovered" electricity—considered a mysterious force of nature at the time. We certainly have harnessed this energy, making our lives more pleasurable in the process. And what about the discovery of x-rays, radioactivity, and subatomic particles? All have led to a profound revolution in how we view the world.

This chapter is all about understanding qi, the foundation upon which many Eastern practices are based. So, keep your mind open, and let's take a journey into the force unifying us all.

What Is Qi?

Simply, qi (pronounced *chee*) is the underlying quintessence, soul, and substance of all things. It is the all-encompassing, all-permeating, unifying force at the heart of the heavenly, earthly, and human realms. Both physical and metaphysical, qi is the fundamental, vital, nourishing force that drives life forward. It is the field of information connecting us all. Although no direct English translation for qi exists, it can best be called "life's breath."

This definition may seem rather vague and even abstract. But actually, the idea of qi bears a striking resemblance to the quantum field in modern physics. Fritjof Capra in his best-selling book, *The Tao of Physics* (Shambhala Publications, fourth edition, 2000), makes the correlation: "Like the quantum field, qi is conceived as a tenuous and nonperceptible form of matter which is present throughout space and can condense into solid material objects. The field, or qi, is not only the underlying essence of all material objects, but also carries their mutual interactions in the form of waves."

Still need clarification? Qi is the stuff of and behind it all. It's the stuff that breathes life into plants, animals, the mountains, oceans, and us. It's the stuff of dreams, intuition, fate, and luck. It's the stuff at the core of nonliving matter such as airplanes, buildings, and the chair on which you sit. It's the stuff acupuncturists stimulate with their needles. It's the stuff martial artists conjure up to split solid objects. And, it's the stuff feng shui practitioners harness to improve the health, wealth, and relationships of their clients.

> **Feng Facts**
>
> The Chinese concept of qi was first recorded in the *Ten Wings*, a Warring States Period (403–221 B.C.E.) text appended to the *Zhouyi* (*The Changes of Zhou*), which was later renamed the *Yijing* (*The Book of Changes*). For a detailed discussion about the historical development of qi, please consult Chapter 8 of *The Complete Idiot's Guide to the I Ching* (Alpha Books, 2001).

Qi Around the World

The concept of qi is not unique to the Chinese It's also known to other cultures:

- *Ki* to the Japanese

- *Prana* to the Hindus

- *Pneuma* to the Greeks

- *Ankh* to the Egyptians

- *Ruah* to the Hebrews

- *Tane* to the Hawaiians

- *Arunquiltha* to the Australian Aborigine

- *Orenda* to the Iroquois

Whatever you choose to call it, identifying, controlling, and directing this invisible life force for the benefit of your well-being is what feng shui's all about.

Qi on the Move

Qi moves. It is in a perpetual process of change. Qi accumulates, disperses, expands, and condenses. It moves quickly, slowly, in, out, up, and down. Qi meanders and spirals. It flows along straight, angular, and curved pathways. It rides the wind (feng) and is retained in water (shui). There's no escaping qi's influence. We are all products of, and subject to, qi's enormous power.

The Three Forces of Qi Energy

The Chinese believe three primal forces of qi sustain all that exists: heaven qi, earth qi, and human qi. To ignore their effects on your body is like ignoring a virus that weakens and depletes your strength. Viruses and other setbacks (like financial loss, unemployment, and illness) can be directly challenged by harnessing qi's beneficial qualities, leading to a strengthened body, an alert mind, and a full and contented spirit.

What does this mean exactly? As you will come to learn in later chapters, the ancient Chinese have determined how to manipulate qi so that it promotes harmony in your living/working space. When balance and harmony exist in your environment, there's a good chance your being will be in balance, too. Of course, you must also maintain a proper diet and exercise regime. You must get a good night's rest. You must live by the Golden Rule. All of these components foster a healthful whole. Only when you are at your optimum capacity can you be inspired to succeed.

Within these forces, there exists an abundance of other lines of qi that impact every aspect of our lives—as you'll see a little later in this chapter.

We are the balance of heav-enly and earthly forces.

Heaven Qi

What comes from above is known as heaven qi. It's the first force of nature. It's the qi that spirals down from the celestial heavens—the sun, moon, planets, and stars. If you have difficulty believing the idea that heavenly qi can affect us, consider the sun, the central star of our solar system. Without its force, life would cease to exist. Disregard its force, and you might be prone to sunburn, heatstroke, skin cancer, and even death.

And the moon? Well, if the moon can deform the shape of the solid earth and the oceans roughly every 12 hours, doesn't it stand to reason that its forces will, in some measure, affect you? After all, the earth's main component is water—and so is ours. In fact, when the moon is full, we tend to retain water. Also, the migration and reproductive patterns of animals, fish, and birds conform to or are in harmony with the moon's phases. The same applies to vegetation. Studies have shown that planting seeds two days before to seven days after a new moon yields a better crop.

Weather qi is also a component of heaven qi. There's no question that weather phenomena affect our well-being. Extremes of cold "chill us to the bone," while extremes of heat create "dog-day afternoons" and heighten passions. For some people, lack of daylight and long periods of rain cause depression—even suicide. Although this is more common in northern countries, any variant in weather can influence a person's health and mood.

Feng Alert

If you feel different during a full moon, it's not just your imagination! A condition called "Full-Moon Madness" can occur when an excess of fluid accumulates in the skull, causing some of us to feel increased levels of passion, anxiety, and tension. In fact, the word lunatic ("luna" means moon in Latin) derives from the notion that the moon's phases produce lunacy, or insanity.

Another component of heaven qi is associated with time, a factor indubitably associated with change and transformation. The time of day and season changes as a result of celestial activity. The time your home was constructed is essential information, for it determines, in part, the inherent personality of your dwelling.

Finally, heaven qi is associated with destiny (ming) and luck (yun). If life is a road map and your life's purpose is your destination, then destiny is the car in which you are fated to make the journey. The driver represents your free will (your thoughts and actions). For example, if you're destined to drive a Ferrari and then take the vehicle off road onto rugged, rocky terrain, certainly you would agree that you've misused the car, potentially causing irreparable damage to it. Assuming you got to your destination, doing so would have been fraught with obstacles and pitfalls that could have been avoided if you had stayed on surfaces suited to your automobile (unless you're Speed Racer driving the Mach 5!). Understanding what your vehicle can and cannot do is tantamount to arriving at your destination safely and successfully.

Although most Westerners believe luck is random and unpredictable, the Chinese believe luck is measurable and knowable. Continuing with our automobile analogy, good luck would be finding a time-saving shortcut, driving on an open road in fine weather and with no traffic. Good luck is picking up the Pass Go and Collect $200 Monopoly card. Bad luck is puncturing a tire, getting lost, encountering an unexpected detour, and driving in hazardous weather conditions. Bad luck is picking up the "Go to Jail" Monopoly card.

You'll learn to evaluate your heaven qi—your destiny and luck—in Part 6, where you'll use a method of Chinese astrology called The Four Pillars of Destiny (Ziping Bazi).

Earth Qi

The forces of mountains, waterways, deserts, valleys, and plains all carry earth qi currents that can affect our physical health, temperament, and compatibility with others. While mountain ranges protect us from harsh elements, they also provide psychological support. We tend to feel more stable and grounded if there is a mountain to our backs.

In classical feng shui, the mountain force is synonymous with the yin or female force of nature. Like a mother guarding her children from illness caused by gusting winds and torrential rain, the mountain force governs our health and relationships. A feng shui practitioner's goal is to study and direct qi associated with the external mountains (or man-made mountains such as buildings and tall hedges) surrounding the dwelling, and internal mountains made manifest as walls and large furniture so that they bolster good health and relations with other people.

Conversely, watercourses correspond to the yang or male force. Traditionally, the man is responsible for generating wealth. Like water's flow, wealth qi is retained in lakes and oceans. It's carried down rivers, streets, and hallways. It flows through windows and doorways. All of these things must be considered when assessing a person's living and/or working space.

Finding a balance among natural elements is the fundamental premise of classical feng shui. You'll learn more about this in Chapters 9 and 10, as well as in Part 4, where mountain (health and relationship) and water (wealth) qi manifest as number schemes on a qi map.

> **Feng Facts**
>
> Those who live in the mountains tend to be more stubborn, loyal, and honest. Like a mountain, these people are unmovable and steadfast in their values. Those of us who live near water, on the other hand, tend to "go with the flow." Our attitudes and outlooks are fluid and flexible. We are more open to change and even welcome it.

The Earth's magnetic field is also a component of earth qi. Coupled with the time your house was constructed, the magnetic orientation characterizes your home's qi, its innate essence. It's important also to understand that the electromagnetic field influences the quality of qi flowing into and inhabiting your house. There's no question that fields generated by high-voltage power lines and modern-day electrical conveniences affect our health in some way. We must be mindful of such potential and exercise caution when we use electrical appliances and live in close proximity to power plants, electrical transformers, and the like.

Human Qi

You have qi, too. Your own qi is marked at birth, the time when you inhaled your first breath. Like a fingerprint, your qi is singular and unique. In feng shui, the year of your birth is a vital source of information. The energy you were born into (your birth year) determines how your life force is compatible to that of other people and to your home's qi. This notion will become clearer in Chapter 8.

For now, understand that many Western scientists and medical experts are accepting and embracing the idea that some kind of vital and holistic force exists within the body that regulates the totality of our mental and physical well-being. Moreover, this bio-network connects us with the whole of our environment, and on a broader scale, the collective consciousness, the source of pure knowledge. In fact, the force field emanating from your body (what many call an aura) actually can be captured on film. Known as Kirlian photography, the technique was developed by two Russian scientists, Semyon and Valentina Kirlian.

Although the connective force within the human body is known by many names in the West (the odic force, life fields, entelechy, animal electricity, subtle spirit, and pneuma, for example), generally the progressive Western pioneers who have adopted the idea believe the field is electrical in nature. Well, human qi may very well be partly electrical, but let's not lose sight of the fact that aspects of this unifying force cannot be measured or fully understood with our five senses of sight, taste, smell, touch, and hearing. Harkening back to the beginning of this chapter, remember that qi is physical *and* metaphysical (beyond physical or supernatural), the latter including fate, luck, and intuition.

Nevertheless, it seems that experts in divergent fields (physics, biology, psychology, religion, anthropology, neurology, and linguistics, for example) are coming together, realizing that the question about our existence and purpose in life cannot be answered by any one part. Using an analogy, a cake is created by the fusion of distinct and different ingredients. Similarly, the auspiciousness or inauspiciousness of a house is a result of layers of merging information. Get the idea?

Finally, the accumulation of virtuous deeds (ji yin de) and the act of studying (du shu) to acquire greater knowledge are components of human qi, or what is properly called Man Luck. Simply, treating others as you would want to be treated, helping those less fortunate than you, and refraining from gossip will inspire a contented and humbled spirit. By devoting more time to study and less time to watching television and other mindless pursuits, you'll sharpen your wit and wisdom and fortify your brainpower.

Feng Facts

Besides feng shui, which seeks to balance your home's qi, the Chinese also use acupuncture to restore balance to your body's qi. They believe 14 interconnected main qi highways (meridians) exist on each side of the body that surface at some 360 acupuncture points. The meridians correspond to one or more specific areas or organs. When an imbalance or illness occurs, an acupuncturist stimulates the appropriate points with needles. Also, there's The Four Pillars of Destiny. This is a method of Chinese astrology that studies your birth qi. Here, you can learn to calculate your destiny and luck. You can determine the colors, environment, and career best suited to you. We offer the beginning level of The Four Pillars in Part 6.

Feeling Qi's Power

How qi directly or indirectly affects you is vital to your state of being. To illustrate this point, let's do a simple exercise. First, turn off the television and radio and find a quiet place free of distractions. It's important that you actually participate in this exercise to fully understand how qi's flow impacts you.

Ready?

Now, look at the following photo. Imagine you are sitting on the bench facing the waterfall. If we told you that suddenly the falls rushed at you in violent gushes of water, wind, and noise, buffeting and overwhelming your being, how would you feel? Scared, confused, disoriented, or tired perhaps? But what if we told you the water gently sprays in a cool cascade of mist and soft, gentle breezes, soothing and refreshing your body? Does this sensation promote feelings of relaxation, balance, comfort, and security? The feeling is quite different, isn't it?

What we've demonstrated is how the flow of qi can affect your mood—and ultimately your health—over a period of time. Nourishing qi circulates. It gently revolves and curves; it creates a healthful, balanced environment. Strong qi (or what is actually called *sha qi*—a term you'll soon learn) disturbs, especially if you're in its powerful path. Strong qi can cause mental and physical illness. Qi can also be weak. Weak qi is stagnant and sickly. A stuffy, airless room is an example of weak qi.

So, can we control weak or negative qi? Absolutely! If the waterfall featured in the preceding photograph was a flood of gushing water, wouldn't you move? If your house is stuffy, wouldn't you instinctively open a window to let fresh air circulate? Although much of feng shui relies on plain old common sense, some factors are not obvious, such as determining the quality of qi your home innately carries. And, the change in qi ushered in with each new year. You'll learn how to determine these numerological aspects in upcoming chapters.

Cascade Park, Monterey Park, California.

(Photograph by Val Biktashev)

Sheng Qi

Sheng qi is positive qi. It carries auspicious currents that nourish your well-being. We can detect some of sheng qi's aspects with our five senses:

1. **Sight sheng.** Manicured gardens and lawns, neatly painted exteriors, tidy, clean, and organized interiors, and happy and cooperative people. Basically, sight sheng is anything you find pleasing to the eye.

Wise Words _____

Sheng qi is positive qi carrying auspicious currents that can influence your well-being.

Located on the shores of Lake Michigan west of Chicago is the impressive Bahá'í House of Worship. Recognized as a national landmark, the building's circular architecture, nine entrances, and manicured gardens are an exquisite example of sight sheng.

(Photo courtesy of Bahá'í Publishing Trust)

2. **Sound sheng.** Babbling brooks/fountains, chirping birds, wind chimes, cooing babies, certain types of music. It's important to understand, however, that what you might consider soothing to the ear might be an auditory disturbance to someone else. For example, many people prefer quiet solitude or the peace of rural areas or suburbs. Others thrive on the high-intensity atmosphere of cities. Although you might find classical music soothing, your friend might disagree, changing the station to rock-and-roll.

3. **Touch sheng.** Smooth surfaces, pets, a warm bath, a kiss, a massage, silk, satin, and velvet are examples of touch sheng.

4. **Smell sheng.** Flowers, perfume, scented candles, and food inspire smell sheng. Again, what you find a pleasing, fragrant odor, another person might find sickening. Cigarette smoke is an example of subjective smell sheng.

5. **Taste sheng.** Home-cooked meals, comfort food, chocolate, a fine wine or liqueur are all associated with taste sheng. It is anything you find satisfying. If this includes tobacco products, then, for you, these items are taste sheng.

There also exists a sixth sheng qi. Somewhat esoteric and metaphysical, it can be compared to your sixth sense. It is the vibe you feel when you're about to get a raise or a promotion. It's how you feel when you click with someone. It's the feeling of being in love. Sheng qi is the look of confidence and contentment. It's the resonance of helpful and kind people.

Sha Qi

Sha qi is negative qi. It carries inauspicious currents that create negative influences on your body. Sha qi is anything antagonistic to your five senses:

1. **Sight sha.** Glaring lights; dark places; offensive, disturbing art; clutter; trash; dead or dying things; and anything you find threatening or looming. We believe a good example of the latter is the interior of the pyramid-theme Luxor Hotel in Las Vegas. Upon entering the inverted interior, you are at the mercy of over-hanging tiers of floors, which can cause vertigo. It looks and feels as though the upper levels can and will come crashing down on you like a house of cards. (We left with a headache, feeling disoriented and quite off balance!) Sight sha also includes acts of violence, prejudice, or intolerance.

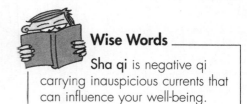

Wise Words

Sha qi is negative qi carrying inauspicious currents that can influence your well-being.

2. **Sound sha.** Noise pollution like traffic, sirens, construction work, loud arguments, screaming babies, and certain types of music are examples of sound sha.

3. **Touch sha.** Grime, filth, dust, and mold; splinters, cracks, and tears. Maneuvering a rickety staircase or bridge, skating on thin ice, and scaling unsteady terrain are examples of touch sha, as are unwanted sexual advances and physical aggression.

4. **Smell sha.** Pollution, exhaust fumes, mildew, rot, pollen, and toxins are examples of smell sha.

5. **Taste sha.** Bitter, sour, or rotten food. Unfamiliar foodstuffs might prove distasteful and unpleasant experiences. Yet, we must remember that raw fish, insects, and seaweed are considered normal foods by many cultures. Vegetarians find animal products unpalatable.

Just like there exists an extrasensory sheng qi, so, too, is there a sixth sha qi. It is the vibe you feel when "Something's in the air," or when "You can cut the tension with a knife." It's the queasy feeling you get when "Something's wrong," or when you feel you are being watched or followed. This sixth sha also takes the form of anger, hate, and jealousy. It can be the resonance of evil spirits.

Poison Arrow Qi

Also called "killing breath," poison arrow qi hits you like a bullet. The offending culprit can be straight roads, opposing doorways or windows; sharp, pointed edges of objects and buildings; and anything else directed at you in a straight line.

Like an arrow pointed at you, the poison arrow sha of the Sony Music building in Santa Monica, California, could cause misfortune to those in its path.

(Photo by Lorraine Wilcox)

A model of the Concorde pointed toward the Condé Nast building in New York City's Times Square may have caused scaffolding to collapse, killing an elderly woman.

(Photo by Arkadiy Yagudaev)

Poison arrow qi is extremely inauspicious and carries misfortune, illness, and even disaster. You will be learning more about poison arrow qi and how to avoid and remedy it in Chapters 9 and 10.

The Holy Trinity, Chinese Style

As you're learning, feng shui is the art and science of living in harmony with your environment and gaining the maximum benefit by being in the right place at the right time. The key phrase being, living in the "right place" (or space), built in the "right time." Simply, with humankind acting as matchmaker, heaven qi and earth qi marry. While the changing forces of heaven qi correspond to the time in which your house was constructed, the stable force of earth qi corresponds to the magnetic space upon which it sits. Viewing it this way, wouldn't it make sense to produce a good marriage, one generating prosperity, compatibility, and good health with its influence affecting your well-being positively and productively?

In the next chapter, you'll learn about yin and yang, the two dynamic qi forces of nature.

The Least You Need to Know

- ◆ Qi is the underlying substance and soul of all things.
- ◆ Heaven, earth, and human qi compose all that is.
- ◆ Sheng qi is positive qi that can influence your well-being.
- ◆ Sha qi is negative qi that can impact your health and livelihood.

Part 2

The Fundamental Principles of Feng Shui

Before you walk, you must crawl. Before you read and write, you must learn the alphabet. Before you practice feng shui, you must learn its fundamental principles—the same principles that form the basis of Chinese medicine, acupuncture, martial arts, and military strategy.

First, you'll learn about *yin* and *yang*, the eternal interplay of opposites governing all that exists. Next, you'll learn about the five phases, the backbone of feng shui, and other Chinese disciplines. (The five phases are particularly important because their principles hold the key to remedying and enhancing *qi*.) Finally, you'll learn about the eight trigrams. These relate to a host of things, such as the magnetic directions, familial relations, and parts of the body.

Chapter 5

The Principle of Yin and Yang

In This Chapter

- ◆ The source of everything
- ◆ Yin: the passive principle
- ◆ Yang: the active principle
- ◆ The correct orientation of the taiji—the composite of yin and yang

Can there be male and no female? Can there be left and no right? Can there be hot and no cold? How about day and no night, or anger and no happiness? Of course not. Although each is a counterpart of the other, each is dependent on the other's existence. Separate but together, yin and yang illustrate the evolution of all things.

The concept of yin and yang is the first principle of feng shui. Initially, yin and yang meant the shady (yin) and sunny (yang) sides of a hill, an idea ascribed to Zhou ancestor Gong Liu when he set about selecting an auspicious site for his people. However, some five centuries later during the mid to late Zhou dynasty (c. 770–481 B.C.E.), yin and yang came to symbolize the two primal forces of qi. Yin was classified as the female principle of nature, and thus, was regarded as passive and weak. Yang was classified as the male principle of nature and was regarded as active and strong.

The yin-yang and wuxing (the five phases of qi that you'll learn about in the next chapter) models were used to explain the structure, order, and change within the universe. Perhaps the primary champion of correlating the cosmological theories was the Naturalist philosopher, Zou Yan (305–240 B.C.E.). A follower of Confucian and Mencian teachings, Zou Yan was given considerable space as a leading intellectual thinker in the *Shiji* (*Records of the Grand Historian*), a Western Han (206–24 B.C.E.) text assembled by Sima Tan and his son, Sima Qian.

The concept of yin and yang is firmly embedded in Chinese philosophy, science, and medicine. In fact, the terms yin and yang originate in the *Dazhuan* or *Great Commentary* of the *Yijing*. The *Dazhuan*, along with six other essays (collectively called the *Ten Wings* or *Shi Yi*, in Chinese), were philosophical theories about the meaning of the divinatory text written some 600 years earlier by King Wen and his son, the Duke of Zhou.

Needless to say, the principle of yin and yang is fundamental to understanding and practicing feng shui. Master the principle, and you will forever change the way you interact with people, your living/working environment, and the outside natural world.

The Big Bang, Chinese Style

Ever since the dawn of humankind we've wondered where we come from. Where did it all begin? Why are we here? What happens when we die? Indeed, the mystery of life intrigues us all, spawning all sorts of theories attempting to answer these age-old questions. Many of us believe an all-knowing, all-seeing presence created everything. In the West, this presence is variously called God, the Supreme Force, or the Sea of Consciousness. Some believe we're a product of pure happenstance. Others even maintain extraterrestrial creatures planted us on planet Earth as colonists. (Of course, there's also the strictly scientific approach, but we won't get into that here.)

No one really knows for sure the true source of existence. Yet, our curiosity and determination drive us forward to investigate and understand the unknown.

The Nothing of Everything

The Chinese Daoists have their own idea. By observing nature's forces and monitoring their effects on our bodies, they've concluded we are a microcosm of the macrocosmic natural world. This means the microcosmic (small) universe within our bodies is a reflection of the macrocosmic (big) universe outside of our bodies. Therefore, a comparison can be drawn between our own birth and the birth of the universe.

The Daoists believe that we come from a great void out of which everything emerges. They call this great void *Wuji*. Wuji is believed to be the fountainhead of creation, the source of pure knowledge. It is expressed as a circle, an unbroken whole.

Symbolizing eternal motion and wholeness, the circle may appear empty, containing nothing. Yet, actually, it's full of possibility. Similar to the womb, it is both empty *and* full. When an egg (yin) is fertilized by a sperm (yang), the unified state is broken. The tranquil nucleus containing ceaseless possibilities is set in motion, ready to give life. Change occurs. The single primordial entity divides, forming the two fundamental qi forces of the universe—yin and yang. They are represented as tadpolelike symbols, with a bulge at the top for the head and a pointed end for the tail. Since fish swim head first, this shape accounts for taiji's (the composite of yin and yang) "movement," or balancing motion.

Yin: The Feminine Side

Yin symbolizes earth's force, which contracts and condenses. Yin represents the passive principle in nature exhibited as darkness, cold, and wetness. On a human level, yin symbolizes femininity and inertia. Other traits of yin are shown in the following figure.

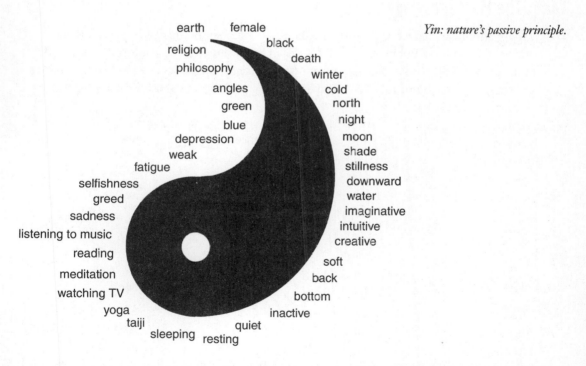

Yin: nature's passive principle.

You may be wondering (especially if you're female) whether yin's dark qualities express the Chinese view of women. No! Even though yin's associated traits may seem offensive, they are not meant to be taken personally. Think about it—yin is quiet and inward.

Traditionally, women stayed at home inside their dwelling. Women receive sperm (inward) and protect the fetus inside. As you shall soon see, yang is associated with the male, activity, and outwardness. Traditionally, men are more active outside of the home. Men send sperm outward.

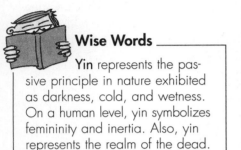

Wise Words

Yin represents the passive principle in nature exhibited as darkness, cold, and wetness. On a human level, yin symbolizes femininity and inertia. Also, yin represents the realm of the dead.

But what does the dot mean, you ask? Well, it's not a dot at all; rather, a knowing awareness. The white eye amid yin's blackness symbolizes the potential for change. Nothing can be wholly yin, just as nothing can be wholly yang. For example, night inevitably changes into day; death and decay always give rise to new life. Even the most heinous criminal and stingiest tightwad have a hint of goodness in them. Just think of Ebenezer Scrooge or the Grinch who stole Christmas!

Yang: The Masculine Side

Yang symbolizes heaven's force that expands. It represents the active principle in nature exhibited as light, heat, and dryness. On a human level, yang represents masculinity and the positive side of our emotions. Yang represents the land of the living; yin the realm of the dead. Other traits of yang are shown in the following figure.

Yang: nature's active principle.

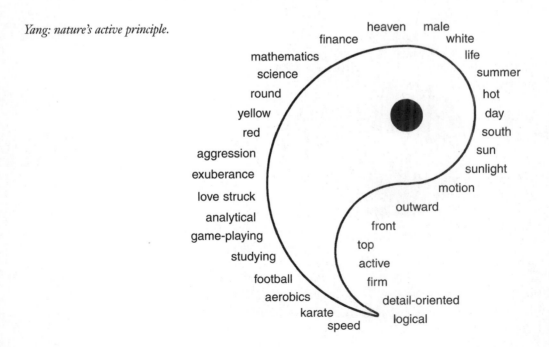

Yang also contains an aspect of its counterpart, giving credence to the phrase, "What goes up, must come down." If the sun didn't rise, we would all die. If you don't give your body a rest after a strenuous workout, you might drop dead from exhaustion. Get the idea?

Wise Words

Yang represents the active principle in nature exhibited by light, heat, and dryness. On a human level, yang represents masculinity and the positive side of our emotions. Also, yang represents the realm of the living.

The Symbol of Taiji—Opposites Do Attract

The taiji symbol illustrates the eternal interaction between yin and yang. Like two sides of a coin, yin can never separate from yang. Together, yin and yang represent the law of nature: perpetual and unceasing change. Time changes; seasons change; qi changes; your environment changes; and *you* change. Indeed, the universe, and everything in it, oscillates from birth to death in a beautiful dance of intertwining and interconnected energy.

The S-like curve separating/connecting yin and yang illustrates that nothing is complete, fixed, or absolute. In other words, life isn't defined by rigid black and white thinking, but rather varying shades of gray. In yin there is the seed of yang, a white tone. In yang there is a seed of yin, a black tone. In the clearest sky, you'll find a cloud; in the darkest night, you'll find a star. On your happiest day, there is a hint of sadness; on your saddest day, there is hope.

The taiji represents the eternal interplay between yin and yang.

Despite how complicated the universe may seem, everything is subject to the laws of yin and yang. Finding a balance between the two is primary to feng shui.

Which Way Is Up?

No doubt you've seen various illustrations of the taiji. But have you ever wondered whether there is a correct orientation? Although an argument can be made that a model in motion cannot possibly have a defined point of reference, we say that if you had to capture the taiji on a two-dimension plane, a certain configuration embodies the inherent meaning of the symbol. Let's take another look at the symbol in the following figure.

The traditional orientation of the taiji.

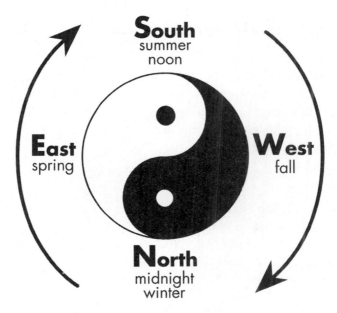

South
summer
noon

East
spring

West
fall

North
midnight
winter

Master Class

How a feng shui practitioner orients the taiji is a strong indication of his or her knowledge of basic feng shui principles. The traditional and correct way to orient the taiji is with the yang white head at the top-left side.

In Chinese cosmology, the south is always situated at the top. This is because it's the direction from which warmth and soft winds come, factors that favorably influence crop yield and good health. As you've just learned, summer and noon are symbolic of yang. Because heat rises, it follows logically that yang's "head" of energy orients at the top-left side of the taiji. The fact that the sun rises in the east further illustrates yang's orientation.

Conversely, north is associated with cold, harsh winds, barbaric attacks, and possible illness. The north is symbolic of yin qi. The "weight" of cold "falls." Summer slides into autumn. The sun sets in the west. Daylight descends to midnight. Get the idea? Logically, then, the black head of yin should rest at the bottom-right side of the taiji.

Yin and Yang Culture Clash

The imbalance of the world's ideas, values, and attitudes can be explained using yin-yang terminology. Perhaps if Eastern and Western cultures recognize that each contains an element of the other, factions and frictions can heal. Only then can we unite in harmony. Only then can we say the Earth is but one country, one people.

Western Yang

Let's face it, we Westerners are yang-oriented. We consistently favor the masculine over feminine; reason over faith; separation over integration; and spending over saving. Our impatience has given rise to fast-food restaurants, microwave ovens, automatic teller machines, self-service gas stations, credit cards, and the ubiquitous remote control. We are besieged with advertisements for all kinds of things, each claiming to be the best. Such thinking filters down to national and individual levels, causing division. When will we realize that we as a culture, and we as individuals, aren't better than our neighbors?

Yet, as the principle of yin and yang teaches, our "yangness" will eventually revolve to yin. Remember, balance must be achieved. As the seasons give way to one another, the day to night, so, too, do yin and yang. In fact, we can witness this evolution now. Holistic health care, strengthening faith, and movements for social equality all embody the yin in our culture. Can we build, construct, and evolve further? Feng shui provides an answer.

Notable Quotables _____

Know ye not why We created you all from the same dust? That no one should exalt himself over the other. Ponder at all times in your hearts how ye were created. Since We have created you all from one same substance it is incumbent on you to be even as one soul, to walk with the same feet, eat with the same mouth and dwell in the same land, that from your inmost being, by your deeds and actions, the signs of oneness and the essence of detachment may be manifest.

—Bahá'u'lláh (1817–1892), the prophet founder of the Bahá'í faith, *The Hidden Words* (1932)

Eastern Yin

Our Eastern counterparts have traditionally been more yin-oriented. They favor philosophy and religion over science; intuitive wisdom over rational knowledge; traditions over progress; family over the individual. Developing the inner spirit has always taken precedence over materialism, technology, and the outer world. Respecting nature's beauty has been far more important than extracting something from it.

However, the seed of yang is growing. Now more than ever, the Chinese are embracing Western ideas. Elevating their national status, economically and progressively, has become paramount. The spirit of yangness that produced the many scientific and technological advances discussed in Chapter 3 is returning. The balance is shifting as yin revolves into yang.

Yin and Yang and Feng Shui

So what do yin and yang have to do with feng shui? A lot. If yin and yang aren't balanced in your environment, their imbalance can produce unwanted emotional and physical effects. We have many clients who complain of fatigue, depression, and lack of motivation. Generally, these people spend much time in dark places. Conversely, we have clients who live in bright, sun-filled homes, offering no relief from the sun's intensity. Is it any surprise these clients complain of headaches?

Much of feng shui relies on plain old common sense. If a room is dark, add more light. If a room is overly bright, add window blinds or curtains. If a room is stuffy, open the window. If it's too warm or too cool, adjust the thermostat. This is the easy stuff. Yet, life is not always easy. Feng shui is here to help us confront and overcome the difficulties.

The Least You Need to Know

- Yin and yang represent eternal change.
- Everything seeks a state of harmony and balance.
- Nothing can be wholly yin or wholly yang.
- The taiji is oriented with its white yang head at the top-left side.

6

The Principle of the Five Phases

In This Chapter

- ◆ Understanding the five phases of fire, earth, metal, water, and wood
- ◆ Learning the cycles of the five phases
- ◆ Balancing qi using the five phases
- ◆ Five phase remedies
- ◆ Mirrors and feng shui

With keen interest the ancients watched, monitored, compared, and contrasted that which occurred in nature to that which was made manifest in our bodies and in our lives. Over time, an accumulation of knowledge and experience produced the principle of the five phases. Based on an acceptance of how the world operated, the principle offered a predictable and systematic solution to how qi moves through the cyclic changes of yin and yang.

In feng shui, the interaction of the five phases is used extensively to enhance positive qi and correct negative qi. Understanding its cycles is what this chapter's all about. The principle of the five phases is the backbone of feng shui. Also, you'll need a solid understanding of the phase relationships in order to make sense of the one method of classical feng shui that we present in this book—Flying Star, as well as a method of Chinese astrology called The Four Pillars of Destiny—something you'll learn about in Parts 4 and 6, respectively.

What Are the Five Phases?

Like yin and yang, the five phases are five characteristics or types of qi that change over time. For example, ice, snow, steam, and fog represent types of water that transform over time. Similarly, the five phases are five physical elements in nature—*fire*, *earth*, *metal*, *water*, and *wood*—that represent different manifestations of qi. The operative word here is *phases*. The movement, transformation, and interaction of each phase are what is studied, not the particular element itself. Remember, a tree, a rock, and a human being are actually bundles of intertwining energy—phases interacting. From creation and birth to maturity and decay, everything revolves around the changes of yin and yang.

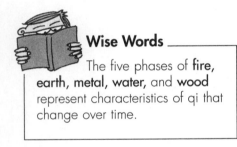

Wise Words

The five phases of **fire, earth, metal, water,** and **wood** represent characteristics of qi that change over time.

The ancient Chinese believed that the interaction of the five phases creates all that exists on the heaven, earth, and human planes. Each phase has its own qi character and, thus, interacts with other phases in different ways. Fire qi radiates; earth qi compacts; metal qi contracts; water qi falls; and wood qi grows upward. How the five phases interact with one another determines the balance of qi in nature, in our living/working space, and in our beings.

If It's Fire, It Must Be Summer

Each phase element is associated with a season, direction(s), weather condition, color(s), number(s), and a trigram (the subject of the next chapter). Referring to the following table, you may question why earth can have three direction values, or how numbers correspond to each element. This is because the five phases, the eight trigrams, and the Luoshu, or magic square, which we'll tell you about in Chapter 11, have been correlated into a nice, neat package.

What does this mean? In the early Warring States period (475–221 B.C.E.), the principles of the five phases, the eight trigrams, and the nine numbers of the Luoshu magic square all existed separately. By the time of the Han dynasty (206 B.C.E.–220 C.E.), the principles combined, correlating into an integrated whole.

Master Class _____

In Chinese, the five phases are known as *wuxing* or technically, *wu zhong liu xing zhi qi*, meaning "the five kinds of qi prevailing at different times." With earth positioned in the center, fire qi (south) dominates in summer, metal qi (west) in autumn, water qi (north) in winter, and wood qi (east) in spring. The earliest documentation of five-phase theory (wuxing) can be found in the Duke Zhao section of Zuo Qiuming's work, the *Zuozhuan* (541 B.C.E.).

First, the five phases were correlated to the four cardinal directions. With the phase earth placed in the center, fire-metal-water-wood readily connected to south-west-north-east. Then, this diagram was correlated to the eight directions, eight trigrams, and nine numbers of the Luoshu. Of course, correlating four- and five-term systems to eight- and nine-term systems posed problems. To solve the matter, the Chinese arbitrarily assigned phases to the four corner directions/Luoshu numbers. All of this may seem confusing. To better grasp what we've described, take a look at the illustration of the nine-celled grid (called the bagua) in Chapter 7.

The Five Phase Associations of Each Element

Element	Season	Direction(s)	Condition	Color(s)	Number(s)	Body Parts
Fire	Summer	South	Heat	Red, purple, dark orange, pink	9	Heart, eyes
Earth	Late summer	Northeast, southwest, center	Wet	Brown, yellow	2, 5, 8	Abdomen, stomach hands, fingers
Metal	Autumn	West, northwest	Dry	White, silver, gold	6, 7	Head, lungs, mouth, chest
Water	Winter	North	Cold	Black, blue	1	Ears, blood, kidneys
Wood	Spring	East, southeast	Wind	Green	3, 4	Feet, legs, liver, lower back

But wait! The preceding table shows five seasons. This is to accommodate the phase earth (remember, initially, earth was placed in the center of the four cardinal directions and corresponding phases). Among other associations, earth now corresponds to late summer, the northeast, southwest, and the center cell of the bagua (a term you'll become familiar with in the next chapter).

> ### Feng Facts
>
> In humans, the five phases correspond to our vital organs, senses, body characteristics, and emotions. For example, fire is associated with the heart/small intestines and joy; earth with the spleen/stomach and intense concentration; metal with the lungs/large intestines and grief; water with the kidney/urinary/bladder and fear; wood with the liver/gallbladder and anger. Considering these relationships, it's not surprising that an overly sad person taxes his lungs to cry and sigh, that intense fear may cause a release of the bladder, or that excessive joy could produce heart ailments. Recently, a friend of ours was playing the slot machines. She won the $5,000 jackpot, but her jubilation triggered a heart attack. Practitioners of acupuncture, acupressure, and herbs use the five phases concept to correct imbalances of qi in our bodies.

The Productive Cycle

The productive cycle, shown in the following figure, is one of balance and creation. Each phase produces, or enhances, the succeeding phase. This progressively producing relationship of the five phases is known as the "mother-son" relationship. Each phase is the "son" of the phase that produces it, and the "mother" of the one it produces.

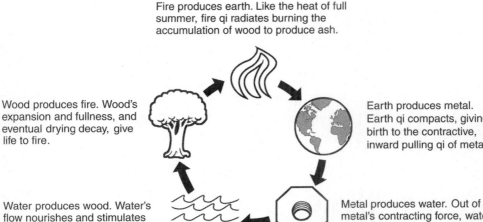

Fire produces earth. Like the heat of full summer, fire qi radiates burning the accumulation of wood to produce ash.

Wood produces fire. Wood's expansion and fullness, and eventual drying decay, give life to fire.

Earth produces metal. Earth qi compacts, giving birth to the contractive, inward pulling qi of metal.

Water produces wood. Water's flow nourishes and stimulates the growth of wood.

Metal produces water. Out of metal's contracting force, water qi condenses and liquefies.

The Productive Cycle

As you can see, each phase follows a natural progression, the sequence of change creating harmony and balance. On paper, this seems logical. It makes sense. Yet, we react much differently when confronted with, say, an out-of-control brush fire threatening to consume our home. We must understand that actually, things are in control. Rainfall produces lush greenery that dries, causing raging fires. End of story. Think about this the next time you're tempted to buy that mountain retreat or beachfront cottage!

The Controlling Cycle

The controlling cycle, shown in the following figure, is just that. Each phase controls its counterpart. It's a cycle of imbalance. The controlling cycle sets into motion weakened and depleted qi, which stagnates the environment and causes illness and other unwanted effects in us.

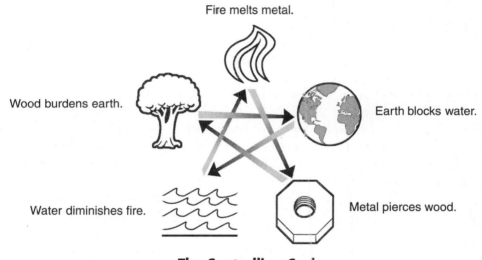

Fire melts metal.

Wood burdens earth.

Earth blocks water.

Water diminishes fire.

Metal pierces wood.

The Controlling Cycle

The controlling cycle describes a battle between confronting qi. On the positive side, qi's counterpart keeps it under control, in check. On the negative side, qi's counterpart suggests unceasing conflict. In the controlling cycle, the phases control or dominate each other. Harmony and order give way to discord and chaos.

The Weakening Cycle

The weakening cycle, shown in the following figure, reduces the power of the controlling phase and restores the sequential balance (the productive cycle) of the phases in question. In feng shui, more often than not, the weakening cycle is used to remedy negative, or controlling, qi. The weakening cycle combines the productive and controlling cycles and is represented by the dotted lines revolving in a counterclockwise motion.

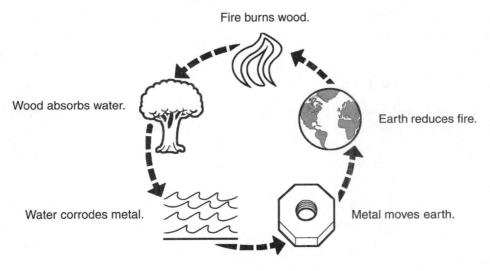

The Weakening Cycle

But, you may ask, how does a reductive phase remedy controlling qi? Good question. Let's look at a few examples. If water controls fire, how would you propose to lessen water's power? Would you add earth, metal, or wood? If you answered earth, guess again. Earth would certainly dominate (controlling cycle) water's power, but it will also reduce (reductive cycle) fire. Earth then would become too dominant over water and fire. If you believe metal will reduce water's control, this, too, is an incorrect assumption. Metal produces (productive cycle) water. You would be adding to water's power. The correct answer is wood. Wood both absorbs (reductive cycle) water's power and fuels (productive cycle) the weakened fire. By adding wood, the natural sequence of qi is restored.

Feng Alert

Many have mistakenly called the controlling cycle "the destruction cycle." Remember, energy cannot be destroyed, it can only change form.

Here's another example. In this situation, let's make earth the controlling agent over water. How would you propose lessening earth's power? Would you add wood or metal? If you answered wood, guess again. Wood diminishes earth and reduces water. It would dominate over two weakened agents—earth and water. If you answered metal, you're getting it! Metal both reduces earth and produces water. For example, if a mudslide dams the little creek in your backyard, you would use a shovel (metal) to clear the earth, allowing the water to flow. Right? If this mudslide blocked a river, you would use a bulldozer (a really big piece of metal). Get the idea?

Master Class

The weakening cycle provides a means to remedy controlling qi.

Generally, if the relationship is productive, a remedy is not needed. If one phase controls another phase, the reductive phase is used to revert the cycle to a productive one. Remember, the weakening cycle creates balance, restoring the productive sequence of qi without creating any side effects. Metal's contractive qi force and wood's expansive qi are balanced with water's downward pull. Fire's rising qi and metal's contractive qi are balanced with earth's compacting force, and so forth.

Although these rules are generalities, please understand there are exceptions that you'll find out about in Part 4. The exceptions have to do with the Luoshu number with which each phase is affiliated. The inherent characteristic of the number, its timeliness, the numbers it is combined with, its correlative effect on our well-being, and the position of the number in the combination are layers of information that must be studied in order to apply the appropriate five-phase remedy. For example, take a 4 (wood) 5 (earth) combination. It is a controlling combination known to bring financial loss and breast tumors. Although you might think to add fire to restore a productive balance (wood-fire-earth), this isn't the proper remedy here. As you will come to learn, the number 5 earth (and 2 earth) are inherently sinister numbers that must be directly dealt with. Moreover, the number 5 (and 2) are dead, making them even more harmful. In this case, the remedy is to add metal. Metal reduces the number 5 earth that will greatly lessen the probability for misfortune.

Here's another example. Take a 1 (water) 8 (earth) combination. You're correct if you've determined that it's a controlling combination (earth blocks water). Although adding metal would certainly restore order (earth-metal-water), at this early stage in the book, you have not yet learned that the number 8 is the king money number for 20 years beginning in 2004. In this case, with the number 8 properly positioned on the right or money side, water is needed to enhance good fortune.

So you see, classical feng shui is not a black and white, one-size-fits-all scheme. This is why it is impossible to provide you with a chart outlining a remedy based solely on the relationships between each phase. Moreover, you must consider other numbers like the time and annual numbers. Again, you'll learn how to analyze number combinations in Parts 4 and 5.

A Spoonful of Sugar

In feng shui, recognizing the correct remedy and selecting the proper remedying agent are key to promoting balance in your home. With balance comes better health, wealth, and relationships.

In our experience, using the actual phase is more effective than using the phase's corresponding color. For example, if a particular area in your home calls for water, a table fountain is much more effective than painting the walls blue. However, sometimes it isn't always possible to use the actual phase. For example, leaving a candle burning or a fire blazing in the fireplace is negligent if left unattended. When using color, it's important that items such as walls, upholstery, carpets, bedspreads, and drapes *be of the same color* for maximum benefit to your well-being. Following are suggested remedies for each of the five phases.

Fire remedies include ...

♦ A burning candle or working fireplace.

♦ Lamps with red shades or red light bulbs burning 24 hours.

♦ The colors red, purple, dark orange, and pink.

Master Class

The vibration of the remedy's qi must be strong enough to balance the controlling agent. Therefore, the size of the remedy must be proportional to the size of the room. You must feel its essence.

A lamp with a red bulb works well as a fire remedy. You can find a lamp like this or a similar one at most lamp stores.

(Photograph by Val Biktashev)

Feng Alert

You cannot mix phase elements. In other words, if the water phase is needed in a particular area, make sure that other phase elements don't conflict with the remedy. In this case, the room mustn't be a red tone (fire). Avoid placing plants (wood) here. An abundance of earthenware may also upset the balance. Although metal produces water, make sure that metal objects don't overwhelm water's essence.

Earth remedies include …

- ◆ Rocks.

- ◆ Ceramic, clay, or cement figurines, sculptures, table bases, or lamps.

- ◆ The colors brown and yellow.

This table base and lamp are ceramic. Taken together, the earth remedy is in proportion to the size of the room.

(Photograph by Val Biktashev)

Metal remedies include …

◆ Brass, steel, silver, gold, copper, or bronze figurines, picture frames, bed frames, planters, exercise equipment, chiming and/or pendulum clocks, filing cabinets, lamps, or fixtures.

◆ The colors white, gold, and silver.

◆ The metallic sound of wind chimes, a chiming clock, or piano playing.

This grouping of heavy metal picture frames (pewter), the bronze wall sculpture, and the brass light fixture serve as a metal remedy.

(Photograph by Val Biktashev)

Water remedies include …

◆ Aquariums, table fountains, a container of clean moving water, or humidifiers. *Note:* Although fish are aesthetically pleasing, they aren't necessary. A waterbed is not a water remedy, because the water is concealed.

◆ The colors black and blue.

Remember, the size of the remedy must be proportionate to the size of the room. Add the color blue if needed. Water must be clean and exposed, such as this inside fountain.

(Photograph by Val Biktashev)

Here's an example of an outside water fountain.

(Photograph by Val Biktashev)

Wood remedies include …

◆ A living plant or tree.

◆ The color green.

Note: Dead wood such as hardwood floors and furniture cannot be used as a remedy. Dried flower arrangements or wreaths also do not count as a remedy.

A bonsai tree makes an excellent wood remedy. It is also pleasing to the eye.

(Photograph by Val Biktashev)

Mirror, Mirror …

Mirrors have never been used as a remedy in classical feng shui. The belief that mirrors can ward off evil omens, absorb, deflect, or stimulate qi's movement is wishful thinking. Mirrors only reflect light hitting its glass surface. So, where does the misconception about mirrors come from? The precursor to the modern Loupan compass was called a shi pan. Made of a round "heaven" disc that swivels on a square "earth" base plate, the shi pan was inscribed with various images of the cosmos, including an image of the Big Dipper (Beidou). Interestingly, the inscribed Dipper is a mirror opposite from its true configuration in the heavens. This is because the shi pan "mirrors" the perfect and ideal world. In the Han dynasty (206 B.C.E.– 220 C.E.), mirrors were made of polished bronze, also illustrating the model world. Both the bronze mirrors and shi pan were considered magical because they reflected an absolute balance between heaven and earth. They were even buried in tombs to help the deceased into the next world.

The Five Phases of Buildings

Building shapes correspond to the five phases, too. Triangular buildings are associated with fire qi. Many churches conform to this shape. So does your local International House of Pancakes! Square and rectangular buildings represent earth qi. Most of our homes are square, allowing qi to meander and spiral from room to room. Round or domed-shaped buildings represent metal qi. Sports arenas, coliseums, and observatories conform to this shape. New York's Guggenheim Museum is an excellent example. Round on the outside, its inner art galleries are spirally arrayed, inviting onlookers to be swallowed along a circular path. Wavy shapes correspond to water qi. Structures with variegated roof/ceiling lines conform to this shape. Finally, tall buildings, like skyscrapers, correspond to wood qi's growth and expansion.

Is one shape better than the other? Do certain shapes promote a healthy well-being while others inspire illness and misfortune? These questions and more will be addressed in Chapter 10.

The Five Phases Quiz

You know this stuff must be important if there's a pop quiz! If you're going to practice feng shui, understanding the five phases is just as important as learning how to tie your shoelaces and drive a car. Give it a try.

1. Stated in this order, fire, wood, water, metal, and earth represent what cycle?

    a. The productive cycle

    b. The controlling cycle

    c. The weakening cycle

2. Fire controls _____.

    Earth controls _____.

    Metal controls _____.

    Water controls _____.

    Wood controls _____.

3. The color white, autumn, and west are associated with which phase?

    a. Fire

    b. Earth

    c. Metal

    d. Water

    e. Wood

4. Which phase acts as the weakening agent for fire's control over metal?

    a. Fire

    b. Earth

    c. Metal

    d. Water

    e. Wood

5. Fire produces _____.

    Earth produces _____.

    Metal produces _____.

    Water produces _____.

    Wood produces _____.

6. Wooden furniture can be used as a wood remedy.

    a. True

    b. False

7. Wood acts as a weakening agent for which controlling relationship?

    a. Fire-metal

    b. Metal-wood

    c. Water-fire

8. The color black, north, and winter are associated with which phase?

   a. Fire

   b. Earth

   c. Metal

   d. Water

   e. Wood

9. You must have fish in your aquarium for the water remedy to work.

   a. True

   b. False

10. The five phases provide the only remedies to correct negative qi.

   a. True

   b. False

Answers: 1. c; 2. Fire controls metal; earth controls water; metal controls wood; water controls fire; wood controls earth; 3. c; 4. b; 5. Fire produces earth; earth produces metal; metal produces water; water produces wood; wood produces fire; 6. b; 7. c; 8. d; 9. b; 10. a.

So, how did you do? Are you ready to move on to some heavier stuff? Bravo! Keep your thinking cap on and let's proceed to succeed!

The Least You Need to Know

- The five phases are five physical elements in nature that characterize different types of qi that change over time.

- The five phases are fire, earth, metal, water, and wood.

- The five phases combine to form a productive or controlling cycle.

- The five phases are used to balance negative qi and enhance positive qi.

- Mirrors are not used as a remedy in classical feng shui.

Chapter **7**

The Principle of the Eight Trigrams

In This Chapter

- ◆ The eight trigrams defined
- ◆ The symbols of the eight trigrams
- ◆ The meaning of the eight trigrams
- ◆ The Before Heaven and After Heaven sequence of trigrams

The eight trigrams are the fundamental building blocks that form the 64 hexagrams of the *Yijing* (*The Book of Changes*). Each trigram expresses patterns of movement and change. Each has been used extensively in the fields of philosophy, astrology, Chinese traditional medicine, numerology, the martial arts, mathematics, and, of course, feng shui.

Understanding the eight trigrams will give you greater insight into the patterns of change inherent in nature and in you.

Motion over Matter—Qi's Pattern of Movement

As you learned in Chapter 4, feng shui is wrapped around the concept of qi—the mysterious underlying force whose existence has yet to be proven scientifically. To the Chinese, whether or not this age-old notion is bolstered by scientific data is irrelevant. In the East, intuitive wisdom has always reigned over rational knowledge. Qi is a fact of life. They know it's here, there, and everywhere. So, how can you study that which cannot be seen?

Simply, the ancient Chinese followed how qi navigates through the cycles of yin and yang. Studying its patterns of movement, transformation, and evolution through nature's elements was considered far more important than studying the isolated element itself. In fact, the whole of nature was seen as a network of interconnected and interdependent events. These events, phases, or patterns were correlated into a symmetrical model representing all possible natural and human situations. This model is called the principle of the *eight trigrams*.

Interestingly, Fritjof Capra, in his thought-provoking book, *The Tao of Physics* (Shambhala, fourth edition, 2000), points out that this Eastern concept bears a striking resemblance to German physicist Werner Heisenberg's (1901–1976) S-Matrix theory. In the theory developed in 1943, Heisenberg described the realm of hadrons (a class of subatomic particles) as a network of inseparable reactions. Reactions connect particles to other reactions. The particle is secondary to its chain of movement and transformation. Like the principle of the eight trigrams, Heisenberg's S-Matrix theory explains all possible reactions relating to hadrons.

In feng shui, the movement, change, and interactions of qi, together with the elements of time and space, determine your state of being. Understanding the eight trigrams and their associations will help you to enhance good qi and correct bad qi.

Wise Words

The **eight trigrams** are symbols representing transitional phases of all possible natural and human situations.

Eight Is Enough

Out of the dynamic interplay of yin and yang, a family of eight trigrams is born. Take a look at the following illustration. As indicated, yang (male) is represented by a solid line, and yin (female) is represented by a broken line. Individually, yang and yin each produce two offspring. How so? Upon closer examination of respective offspring, you'll notice that the bottom line corresponds to the "parent" yang or yin line in question. The addition of the top yang or yin line results in the production of four unique pairs or bigrams (sixiang, in Chinese). Next, each of the four bigrams produces two trigrams each, the bottom two lines identical to the parent pair. Again, only the addition of the top yang or yin line distinguishes the trigram from its "sibling."

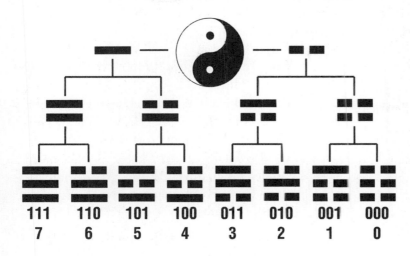

The evolution of the eight trigrams. The three-term numbers on the bottom of each trigram represent its binary correlation.

111	110	101	100	011	010	001	000
7	6	5	4	3	2	1	0

Together, the eight trigrams, or what is known as the *bagua*, represent the maximum number of yang or yin combinations in sets of three. If you continue multiplying the eight trigrams by themselves, you'll end up with the 64 hexagrams of the *Yijing*, but we won't concern ourselves with that here.

How do you interpret the trigram symbols? What do they mean? And what do they have to do with feng shui? You'll soon find out!

Wise Words

The **bagua** are the eight trigrams of the *Yijing*. "Ba" means "eight," and "gua" means "the result of divination." Figuratively, the bagua suggests creating heaven on earth.

Meet the Bagua Family

As you have just learned, the eight fundamental trigrams (and hexagrams) are built from the bottom line up. The bottom line represents earth. The middle line represents humankind, and the top line, heaven. The line that is different determines the trigram's gender (a fuller explanation of this is coming up).

Aside from their gender identity, the trigrams are associated with a host of natural and human phenomena: the seasons, the time of day, magnetic directions, the five phases and their corresponding colors, animals, human personality types (merchants, teachers, thieves, and so on), body parts, related illnesses, and numbers. The trigrams are even given a name appropriate to their qi energy ("the arousing," "the gentle," "the clinging"). Although each association is significant, we've listed only those attributes that will be the most useful to your study and practice of feng shui.

So, let's meet the men in the bagua family. Remember, a male is represented by the solid yang line. Referring to each illustration, watch how line 1 (the bottom line) moves up the trigram, creating each new male family member.

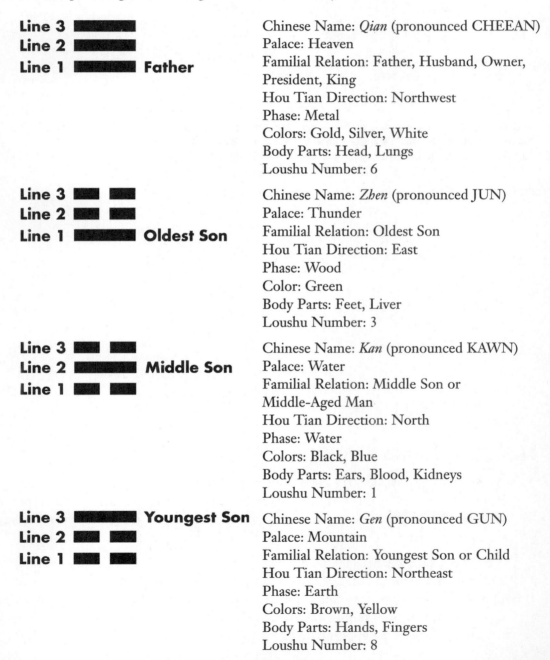

Line 3 ▬▬▬
Line 2 ▬▬▬
Line 1 ▬▬▬ **Father**

Chinese Name: *Qian* (pronounced CHEEAN)
Palace: Heaven
Familial Relation: Father, Husband, Owner, President, King
Hou Tian Direction: Northwest
Phase: Metal
Colors: Gold, Silver, White
Body Parts: Head, Lungs
Loushu Number: 6

Line 3 ▬ ▬
Line 2 ▬ ▬
Line 1 ▬▬▬ **Oldest Son**

Chinese Name: *Zhen* (pronounced JUN)
Palace: Thunder
Familial Relation: Oldest Son
Hou Tian Direction: East
Phase: Wood
Color: Green
Body Parts: Feet, Liver
Loushu Number: 3

Line 3 ▬ ▬
Line 2 ▬▬▬ **Middle Son**
Line 1 ▬ ▬

Chinese Name: *Kan* (pronounced KAWN)
Palace: Water
Familial Relation: Middle Son or Middle-Aged Man
Hou Tian Direction: North
Phase: Water
Colors: Black, Blue
Body Parts: Ears, Blood, Kidneys
Loushu Number: 1

Line 3 ▬▬▬ **Youngest Son**
Line 2 ▬ ▬
Line 1 ▬ ▬

Chinese Name: *Gen* (pronounced GUN)
Palace: Mountain
Familial Relation: Youngest Son or Child
Hou Tian Direction: Northeast
Phase: Earth
Colors: Brown, Yellow
Body Parts: Hands, Fingers
Loushu Number: 8

Do you see how each family member is created? Now, let's meet the women of the bagua family. Again, watch how the bottom yin line moves up the trigram, creating each new female family member.

Line 3 ▬ ▬
Line 2 ▬ ▬
Line 1 ▬ ▬ **Mother**

Chinese Name: *Kun* (pronounced KUEN)
Palace: Earth
Familial Relation: Mother, Wife, Grandmother, Old Woman
Hou Tian Direction: Southwest
Phase: Earth
Colors: Brown, Yellow
Body Parts: Abdomen, Stomach
Loushu Number: 2

Line 3 ▬▬▬
Line 2 ▬▬▬
Line 1 ▬ ▬ **Oldest Daughter**

Chinese Name: *Xun* (pronounced SHUEN)
Palace: Wind
Familial Relation: Oldest Daughter
Hou Tian Direction: Southeast
Phase: Wood
Color: Green
Body Parts: Thighs, Buttocks, Lower Back
Loushu Number: 4

Line 3 ▬▬▬
Line 2 ▬ ▬ **Middle**
Line 1 ▬▬▬ **Daughter**

Chinese Name: *Li* (pronounced LEE)
Palace: Fire
Familial Relation: Middle Daughter or Middle-Aged Woman
Hou Tian Direction: South
Phase: Fire
Colors: Red, Purple, Burnt Orange, Pink
Body Parts: Eyes, Heart
Loushu Number: 9

Line 3 ▬ ▬ **Youngest**
Line 2 ▬▬▬ **Daughter**
Line 1 ▬▬▬

Chinese Name: *Dui* (pronounced DWAY)
Palace: Lake
Familial Relation: Youngest Daughter or Young Girl
Hou Tian Direction: West
Phase: Metal
Colors: Gold, Silver, White
Body Parts: Mouth, Teeth, Tongue, Chest
Loushu Number: 7

These are the eight members of the bagua, or trigram, family. Although the symbols might seem abstract and their configurations daunting, don't worry. In time you'll come to recognize each trigram and its corresponding associations. It's similar to learning to understand road signs. After a while, the abstract symbols for Yield, No Entry, and No Passing become absorbed into your subconscious realm of knowns. So will the trigrams, if you give them a chance.

The Cyclic Pattern of the Bagua

Although the eight trigrams can be arranged in many different ways, only two configurations really make sense. The first arrangement, shown in the following illustration, is called the *Before Heaven* sequence. "Before Heaven" is an interpretive translation of the Chinese term *Xian Tian*, which means "prior to the appearance of the phenomenal world." The Before Heaven sequence denotes perfect balance and harmony.

The Before Heaven sequence of the eight trigrams.

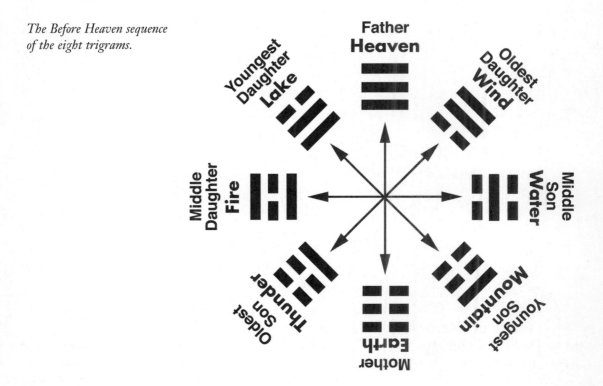

All eight qi forces are balanced by their counterparts: Heaven is balanced by earth, water by fire. Or, father is balanced by mother, and middle son by middle daughter.

In essence, this arrangement represents the ideal world, the underlying reality. The problem with the Before Heaven sequence is that it's motionless, a study of still life. It doesn't move, transform, or interact. Let's move on.

The second arrangement, shown in the following illustration, is called the *After Heaven* sequence. Translated from the Chinese term *Hou Tian*, it means "after the appearance of the phenomenal world." The After Heaven sequence follows the cyclic changes of yin and yang. Each trigram evolves in a natural sequence of events in a lifelike world. In feng shui, we use the After Heaven sequence to analyze how the movement of qi's forces affects you.

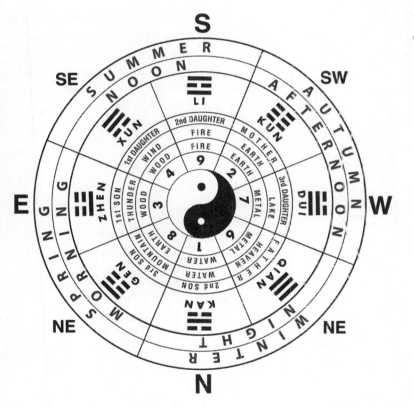

The After Heaven sequence of the eight trigrams.

Beginning with the Zhen trigram to the east and moving in a clockwise motion, spring arrives with a clap of thunder. Next, the Xun trigram's gentle winds nourish the growth and development of summer's expansion. Li follows. The intensity of Li's brightness gives rise to early autumn's soft light. In human consciousness, Li is a time of love and curiosity. You are the middle daughter exploring new concepts.

Next comes Kun, early autumn. You are maturing and receptive to new ideas. But it is in Dui that you turn inward, harvesting what you've learned. It's a time of reflection and self-assessment. With Qian's emergence comes the beginning of winter. Intuitive wisdom takes over as you develop your inner spirit. In Kan, you submerge yourself even further into the profundities of life, deep meditation. You are still and quiet as midnight. Your inward journey is now completed. In Gen, clouds form over winter's repose, and thunder heralds a new cycle of growth and development.

Wise Words

The **Before Heaven** sequence of trigrams, called the *Xian Tian* in Chinese, represents an ideal reality where natural and human qi forces are in perfect balance. The **After Heaven** sequence of trigrams, called the *Hou Tian* in Chinese, denotes motion, transformation, and the interaction of natural and human qi forces.

As shown in the next illustration, the eight trigram circle is squared off to form a grid of eight place values (with the center representing Earth). This allows the principle of the eight trigrams (along with the yin and yang and five phase theories) to correlate to the Luoshu, also known as the magic square, which you'll learn about in Chapter 11.

The bagua grid.

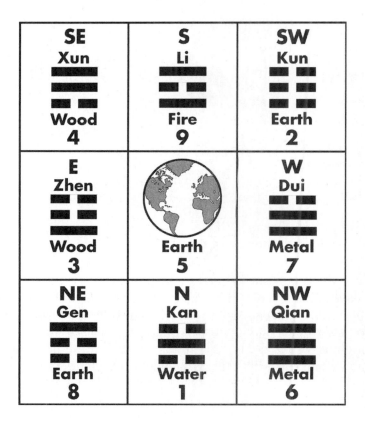

Patterns of Numbers

The combination of solid and broken lines forming the trigrams and hexagrams corresponds to the binary system of mathematics—the same system used today in computer programming. Every function your computer performs—calculations, graphics, and word processing—uses binary numeration. The system uses 01 for the number 1 and 10 for the number 2. The succeeding numbers compute as shown in the following table.

1	=	01	6	=	110	11	=	1011
2	=	10	7	=	111	12	=	1100
3	=	11	8	=	1000	13	=	1101
4	=	100	9	=	1001	14	=	1110
5	=	101	10	=	1010	15	=	1111

In the same way, if you let yang (solid line) represent the number one and yin (broken line) represent zero, you can see that the combinations follow the rules of binary numeration. For example, reading the trigrams from the bottom line up, trigram ☷ , or 001, represents binary number 1.

Trigram ☶ , or 010, represents binary number 2.

Trigram ☵ , or 011, represents binary number 3, and so forth.

Get the idea? Flip back a couple of pages to the illustration of the bagua family tree. We've included the binary code for all eight trigrams.

How this mathematical interpretation of the trigrams and hexagrams was discovered is an interesting story. It began with German philosopher and mathematician Gottfried Wilhelm von Leibnitz (1646–1716), who believed the mathematical system proved God's creation of the world: Everything was created by God (1) from nothing (0).

As the story goes, Leibnitz was corresponding with a Jesuit missionary in China, Father Joachim Bouvet, at the time. In 1701, hoping to persuade the Chinese to accept the Christian doctrine with his mystical calculations, Leibnitz sent Bouvet a copy of his published work on binary numeration. Bouvet recognized a connection between the binary system and the *Yijing*'s symbols and sent him a circular arrangement of the hexagrams composed by Song dynasty philosopher Shao Yong. Remarkably, Yong's arrangement was a mirror image of the base-two system from 0 to 63.

Can the fact that the East and West independently invented binary mathematics serve as an example for our ability to subconsciously tap into the Sea of Consciousness?

Notable Quotables

The nature of the Ultimate Supreme [Taiji] is total balance. When motion is initiated, it generates spirituality. Spirituality generates numbers. Numbers generate emblems. Emblems generate vision. Vision generates transformation, everything returning to spirituality.

—Cosmological philosopher Shao Yong (1011–1077 C.E.)

Well, in this case, no. As we mentioned in Chapter 3, the original *Yijing*, the *Zhouyi*, was strictly a system of numerological divination in which sequences of odd and even numbers had significance. A Chinese scholar named Zhang Zhenglang made this discovery in the 1970s, theorizing that over time the odd numbers became the solid yang lines and the even numbers, the broken yin lines as we know them. Moreover, at the time the *Yijing* was assembled at the end of the second millennium B.C.E. by King Wen and the Duke of Zhou, the concept of zero was not yet known. (For a detailed account of Leibnitz, binary numeration, and the *Yijing*, see Chapter 10 of *The Complete Idiot's Guide to the I Ching*.)

So the real question is, what is the meaning of the patterns of numbers underlying the trigrams and hexagrams? Although we might never learn their meaning, clearly the ancient Chinese recognized correlative mathematical patterns made manifest in nature and human nature/events. They recorded how these macrocosmic events affected our microcosmic beings. You'll study one such number-based system in Part 4. Until then, you must first learn about your ming gua, or guardian star, which influences your character.

The Least You Need to Know

◆ The eight trigrams represent transitional phases in nature and in humans.

◆ The eight trigrams are associated with things such as magnetic directions, colors, body parts, illness, and numbers.

◆ The eight trigram symbols are read from the bottom line up. The bottom line represents earth; the middle line, humankind; and the top line, heaven.

◆ The Before Heaven sequence of trigrams represents the perfect world where nature and human qi are balanced. The After Heaven sequence of trigrams represents motion and the interaction between natural forces and human qi.

Chapter 8

What's Your Gua?

In This Chapter

- ◆ Calculate your ming gua
- ◆ What your ming gua says about you
- ◆ Figure out your gua compatibility
- ◆ Determine your best sitting directions
- ◆ Determine your best sleeping directions

In this chapter, you learn about your guardian star or what is also known as your ming gua, or simply, gua. It is a number affiliated with a five-phase element (fire, earth, metal, water, wood) and one of the eight trigrams (Kan, Kun, Zhen, Xun, Qian, Dui, Gen, Li). Your ming gua says a lot about your character and how you relate to others. People with the same ming gua will, therefore, share similarities in their behavior, likes, and dislikes. Your ming gua also determines your best sleeping and working/studying directions. For example, a male born in 1954 should sleep with his head pointed north. This will bring him peace and stability. His worst sleeping direction is the southwest. Sleeping toward this direction might cause him to lose his job.

Sharpen your pencil—you're about to learn some basic feng shui mechanics. You'll also be putting to good use everything you've learned thus far.

Determining Your Gua

There's a special formula that determines your *ming gua*. You need only to know two things: your year of birth and gender. After you figure out your ming gua, you then can learn about your innate character, which we think will be strikingly similar to what you already know about yourself. You'll also understand how you affect—and are affected by—other people. Are you the controlled or the controller? Do you support, or are you supported?

Generally, those of the same gender born in a given year will share the same ming gua—but there's an exception to this rule. If you were born between January 1 and February 2 of a given year, you'll use the year prior to your birth year to determine your ming gua. If you were born on February 3, 4, or 5, you must consult the table in Chapter 21, to determine to which year you belong (instructions and examples are provided to ensure an accurate calculation). Why all the fuss? This is because feng shui uses the Chinese solar calendar, which variously marks February 3, 4, or 5 as the first day of the new year, the midpoint between the winter solstice and spring equinox. For example, let's take a woman born on January 3, 1962. She would use the year 1961 to calculate her ming gua.

Wise Words

Your **ming** (personal or birth) **gua** (trigram) is the guardian star (or number) you are born under. Depending on your gender and your year of birth, you are assigned a number from 1 to 9 (excluding the number 5) that is affiliated with a five-phase element and a trigram.

Ming Gua Formula: Male

Use the following formula to determine a male's ming gua. The blank spaces after each sample calculation are for you to calculate your own gua. If you're a female, use the formula for female in the following section. Use the following formula to calculate the guas of the men in your family. Why are there different formulas for a male and female? Because yang (male) and yin (female) qi tend to flow in opposing directions. Although it is beyond our scope to investigate this further, know that each formula is determined by movement of qi.

1. Add the digits in your birth year. As an example, let's use a male born in 1954.

   $1 + 9 + 5 + 4 = 19$

   _____ + _____ + _____ + _____ = _____

2. Add the resulting number until you get a single-digit number.

   $1 + 9 = 10; 1 + 0 = 1$

   _____ + _____ = _____

3. Subtract the resulting number from 11. If the result is 10, add the digits until you get a single-digit number.

   $11 - 1 = 10; 1 + 0 = 1$

   _____ − _____ = _____

The resulting number is your ming gua, your guardian star or personal trigram, which is matched with a number from the Luoshu magic square (something you'll learn about in Chapter 11).

In the example's case, the number 1 is his ming gua. Gua 1 is associated with the Kan trigram and the water phase. The example is a gua 1 water person.

Note: If your ming gua works out to the number 5, use the number 2 as your gua. Because the number 5 earth is located in the central palace and, thus, is not associated with a direction or a trigram, it will migrate to the earth palace located in the southwest. The southwest is affiliated with the number 2.

Master Class

Yang (male) qi moves forward (1, 2, 3, 4...), and yin (female) qi moves backward (3, 2, 1, 9). However, if you look at the Ming Gua Quick Reference Chart in Appendix F, you'll notice that the male numeric sequence runs backward, and the female sequence runs forward. This is because each is seeking balance in the other.

Ming Gua Formula: Female

Use the following formula to determine a female's ming gua. The blank spaces are for you to calculate your own gua, assuming, of course, that you're female.

1. Add the digits in the birth year. As an example, let's use the woman born on January 3, 1962 mentioned earlier in this chapter. She would use the year 1961 to calculate her ming gua.

   $1 + 9 + 6 + 1 = 17$

   _____ + _____ + _____ + _____ = _____

2. Add the resulting number until you get a single-digit number.

   1 + 7 = 8

   _____ + _____ = _____

3. Add 4 to the resulting number.

   8 + 4 = 12

   _____ + _____ = _____

4. The resulting number is your ming gua. Because the example's resulting number is a two-digit number, she must add up the digits. The sum is the example's ming gua. Therefore:

   1 + 2 = 3.

Master Class

Remember, if you were born between January 1 and February 2, use the year prior to your birth year to determine your ming gua. If you were born on February 3, 4, or 5, you must consult the table in Chapter 21 to determine your Chinese birth year.

In the example's case, the number 3 is her ming gua. Gua 3 is associated with the Zhen trigram and the wood phase. The example is a gua 3 wood person.

Note: If your ming gua works out to the number 5, use the number 8 as your gua. Because the number 5 earth is located in the central palace and, thus, is not associated with a direction or a trigram, it will migrate to the earth palace located in the northeast. The northeast is affiliated with the number 8.

Now you know your ming gua.

The Ming Gua Quick Reference Chart

Anxious that you may have made a mistake? Don't worry. The following quick reference chart gives you everything you need to know right at your fingertips.

Before you proceed with this chapter, you must determine your ming gua. Take a moment to calculate it now if you haven't already done so.

Table 1 - Ming Gua Quick Reference Chart

Year	Male	Gua	Phase	Female	Gua	Phase	Year	Male	Gua	Phase	Female	Gua	Phase
1924	Xun	4	Wood	Kun	2	Earth	1964	Li	9	Fire	Qian	6	Metal
1925	Zhen	3	Wood	Zhen	3	Wood	1965	Gen	8	Earth	Dui	7	Metal
1926	Kun	2	Earth	Xun	4	Wood	1966	Dui	7	Metal	Gen	8	Earth
1927	Kan	1	Water	Gen	8	Earth	1967	Qian	6	Metal	Li	9	Fire
1928	Li	9	Fire	Qian	6	Metal	1968	Kun	2	Earth	Kan	1	Water
1929	Gen	8	Earth	Dui	7	Metal	1969	Xun	4	Wood	Kun	2	Earth
1930	Dui	7	Metal	Gen	8	Earth	1970	Zhen	3	Wood	Zhen	3	Wood
1931	Qian	6	Metal	Li	9	Fire	1971	Kun	2	Earth	Xun	4	Wood
1932	Kun	2	Earth	Kan	1	Water	1972	Kan	1	Water	Gen	8	Earth
1933	Xun	4	Wood	Kun	2	Earth	1973	Li	9	Fire	Qian	6	Metal
1934	Zhen	3	Wood	Zhen	3	Wood	1974	Gen	8	Earth	Dui	7	Metal
1935	Kun	2	Earth	Xun	4	Wood	1975	Dui	7	Metal	Gen	8	Earth
1936	Kan	1	Water	Gen	8	Earth	1976	Qian	6	Metal	Li	9	Fire
1937	Li	9	Fire	Qian	6	Metal	1977	Kun	2	Earth	Kan	1	Water
1938	Gen	8	Earth	Dui	7	Metal	1978	Xun	4	Wood	Kun	2	Earth
1939	Dui	7	Metal	Gen	8	Earth	1979	Zhen	3	Wood	Zhen	3	Wood
1940	Qian	6	Metal	Li	9	Fire	1980	Kun	2	Earth	Xun	4	Wood
1941	Kun	2	Earth	Kan	1	Water	1981	Kan	1	Water	Gen	8	Earth
1942	Xun	4	Wood	Kun	2	Earth	1982	Li	9	Fire	Qian	6	Metal
1943	Zhen	3	Wood	Zhen	3	Wood	1983	Gen	8	Earth	Dui	7	Metal
1944	Kun	2	Earth	Xun	4	Wood	1984	Dui	7	Metal	Gen	8	Earth
1945	Kan	1	Water	Gen	8	Earth	1985	Qian	6	Metal	Li	9	Fire
1946	Li	9	Fire	Qian	6	Metal	1986	Kun	2	Earth	Kan	1	Water
1947	Gen	8	Earth	Dui	7	Metal	1987	Xun	4	Wood	Kun	2	Earth
1948	Dui	7	Metal	Gen	8	Earth	1988	Zhen	3	Wood	Zhen	3	Wood
1949	Qian	6	Metal	Li	9	Fire	1989	Kun	2	Earth	Xun	4	Wood
1950	Kun	2	Earth	Kan	1	Water	1990	Kan	1	Water	Gen	8	Earth
1951	Xun	4	Wood	Kun	2	Earth	1991	Li	9	Fire	Qian	6	Metal
1952	Zhen	3	Wood	Zhen	3	Wood	1992	Gen	8	Earth	Dui	7	Metal
1953	Kun	2	Earth	Xun	4	Wood	1993	Dui	7	Metal	Gen	8	Earth
1954	Kan	1	Water	Gen	8	Earth	1994	Qian	6	Metal	Li	9	Fire
1955	Li	9	Fire	Qian	6	Metal	1995	Kun	2	Earth	Kan	1	Water
1956	Gen	8	Earth	Dui	7	Metal	1996	Xun	4	Wood	Kun	2	Earth
1957	Dui	7	Metal	Gen	8	Earth	1997	Zhen	3	Wood	Zhen	3	Wood
1958	Qian	6	Metal	Li	9	Fire	1998	Kun	2	Earth	Xun	4	Wood
1959	Kun	2	Earth	Kan	1	Water	1999	Kan	1	Water	Gen	8	Earth
1960	Xun	4	Wood	Kun	2	Earth	2000	Li	9	Fire	Qian	6	Metal
1961	Zhen	3	Wood	Zhen	3	Wood	2001	Gen	8	Earth	Dui	7	Metal
1962	Kun	2	Earth	Xun	4	Wood	2002	Dui	7	Metal	Gen	8	Earth
1963	Kan	1	Water	Gen	8	Earth	2003	Qian	6	Metal	Li	9	Fire

continues

continued

Table 1 - Ming Gua Quick Reference Chart

Year	Male	Gua	Phase	Female	Gua	Phase	Year	Male	Gua	Phase	Female	Gua	Phase
2004	Kun	2	Earth	Kan	1	Water	2014	Xun	4	Wood	Kun	2	Earth
2005	Xun	4	Wood	Kun	2	Earth	2015	Zhen	3	Wood	Zhen	3	Wood
2006	Zhen	3	Wood	Zhen	3	Wood	2016	Kun	2	Earth	Xun	4	Wood
2007	Kun	2	Earth	Xun	4	Wood	2017	Kan	1	Water	Gen	8	Earth
2008	Kan	1	Water	Gen	8	Earth	2018	Li	9	Fire	Qian	6	Metal
2009	Li	9	Fire	Qian	6	Metal	2019	Gen	8	Earth	Dui	7	Metal
2010	Gen	8	Earth	Dui	7	Metal	2020	Dui	7	Metal	Gen	8	Earth
2011	Dui	7	Metal	Gen	8	Earth	2021	Qian	6	Metal	Li	9	Fire
2012	Qian	6	Metal	Li	9	Fire	2022	Kun	2	Earth	Kan	1	Water
2013	Kun	2	Earth	Kan	1	Water	2023	Xun	4	Wood	Kun	2	Earth

Your Ming Gua Personality

What follows are the characteristics of each of the eight guardian stars or ming gua numbers. Note that there are two types of wood (gua 3 and 4), two types of earth (gua 2 and 8), and two types of metal (gua 6 and 7) people.

The question often arises: "Does wearing the color or decorating my room in the color associated with my ming gua bring me good luck?" For example, if you're a gua 3 wood person, is green your best color? Or, if you're a gua 1 water person, are blue and black your best colors? The answer is not necessarily. The colors that represent your innate qi can be determined only by calculating your Four Pillars, a method of Chinese astrology that you'll learn about in Part 6.

Gua 1 Water

Belonging to the Kan trigram, gua 1 water people go with the flow. They're flexible, able to shift courses at a moment's notice. Although water people appear to be quiet and stable on the outside, they are actually quite restless on the inside. Like a river that carries boats from one place to another, water people like to travel. They're good networkers and communicators, making them astute diplomats and leaders. Be it on the home front or at work, the water person's mediation skills are finely tuned. They can successfully navigate through white water rapids and strong currents. Of course, smooth sailing is always preferable! Overall, water people are charming, courageous, persistent, confident, and liberal-minded. Like the depths of the ocean, water people are deep thinkers. Diving too deeply may cause sadness and depression.

Gua 2 Earth

Belonging to the Kun trigram, gua 2 earth people are generally traditionalists. They tend to be stable and conservative, mulling things over before making a final decision. Earth people are the most loyal of all the guas. Often, they are self-sacrificing, putting the needs of others before themselves. There are two types of earth people: Soft earth (like soil) and hard earth (like a rocky mountain). Gua 2 people fall into the latter group. Hard earth people are strong-minded, giving credence to the phrase, "When I want your opinion, I'll give it to you." Like a mountain, they are unmovable. Their stubbornness is their biggest foible. Hard earth people need to realize that their way isn't necessary the only way or the best way. Hard earth people can either be your best friend or your biggest foe.

Gua 3 Wood

Belonging to the Zhen trigram, gua 3 wood people are determined, fearless, and persistent. A new generation is born in gua 3, the first of the two wood phases. Gua 3 wood people shoot through the soil, letting nothing stand in their way. Exuberant and confident, they're champions of living life to its fullest. Like a clap of thunder announcing spring's arrival, gua 3 people like others to know that they're a force to be seen and heard. Like an oak tree (hard wood), they tower over others. Although some people feel overwhelmed by them, other people feel sheltered in their domineering presence. And like a tree's branches, gua 3 people have many interests and friends. They become bored easily, causing them to change careers over their lifetime. Overall, gua 3 people are impulsive and stubborn. They have a good sense of humor.

Gua 4 Wood

Belonging to the Xun trigram, gua 4 wood people are much more compromising than their unbending gua 3 counterparts. Whereas a hard wood (gua 3) person resembles an oak tree, a soft wood (gua 4) person resembles a birch tree. Willowy and flexible, a birch tree bends and rustles in the wind. Whereas hard wood people are vibrant and impulsive, soft wood people are more subdued and hesitant. Instinctively, soft wood people know when to proceed and when to retreat. They're cautiously optimistic and take great care in how

> **CAUTION**
>
> **Feng Alert**
>
> Determining your ming gua and learning about the associated personality traits is a far more accurate prognostication than what is prescribed under your animal sign (the subject of Chapter 21). The Chinese Zodiac should be used for entertainment purposes only.

they present themselves. Romantic and social, gua 4 people are good communicators. They are also academic-minded, always striving to learn new things. Like hard wood people, the soft wood types have varied interests and a diverse network of friends. They like to be independent and, thus, make good entrepreneurs. On the downside, gua 4 people are emotional, their moods blowing with the wind. Owing to their flexible spirit, gua 4 people tend to bend the rules to suit their needs.

Gua 6 Metal

Belonging to the Qian trigram, gua 6 people might appear to be hard and rigid like iron, but they are actually calm. Similar to a commander and chief of the army, gua 6 people will lead, but they won't follow. There's just no arguing with them. Headstrong and obstinate, hard metal people are strict disciplinarians. They make the rules, and they enforce them. Like their hard counterparts (gua 2 earth and gua 3 wood), gua 6 people are uncompromising and, thus, can be hard to get along with. They're goal-oriented perfectionists. They are extremely focused. Shoulders back, stomach in, head up, gua 6 people are very proud. They will not air their dirty laundry in public or do anything to mar their stellar reputations. Unfortunately, their hardness can cause loneliness and depression. Gua 6 people need to learn not to take things so seriously.

Gua 7 Metal

Belonging to the Dui trigram, gua 7 people appear soft (like gold and silver) on the outside, but their behavior is deceiving. They are actually quite stern on the inside. Nevertheless, they have a sparkling vivaciousness that is contagious. They're also easy on the eye. Unfortunately, their outward beauty causes them to be egotistical and snobbish. Gua 7 people are good speakers, getting the point across effectively and efficiently. They are also very argumentative. However, their words are like a double-edged sword. They can be both soothing and slicing. Like the proverbial "kiss and a slap," it is hard to know whether you were just complimented or condemned! To say the least, gua 7 people are quite cunning. They're hard to get to know. In fact, gua 7 people are very private. They keep their cards close and will offer only "need to know" information. Their lives are often challenging.

Gua 8 Earth

Belonging to the Gen trigram, gua 8 earth people are much softer than their hard earth gua 2 counterparts. Whereas gua 2 people are like rocky mountains, gua 8 people are like soil or rolling hills. Gua 8 people are nurturers. They're down-to-earth, practical, and very reliable. Supportive and good-natured, gua 8 people are compatible with most people. Gua 8 people like to be hands-on. They're doers rather than thinkers.

No beating around the bush! Why wait when it could be done now? Gua 8 people are also confident, firm in their convictions, and quite learned. Because their ego doesn't get in the way, they can be a leader or a follower. They are also good money managers. Because earth is the mother of metal (money), gua 8 people can accumulate money better than any of the other guas. On the downside, gua 8 people are super-sensitive, internalizing everything. They must learn to express their emotions.

Gua 9 Fire

Belonging to the Li trigram, fire people are warm-hearted, energetic, and affectionate. They are very happy people who have an unparalleled zeal for life. Spontaneity is their *modus operandi*. They're passionate people. Out of all of the guas, gua 9 people are the most enlightened and spiritual-minded. In fact, their deep desire to find truth and meaning in their lives inspires others to do the same. Like a torch, their radiance enables them to see clearly all options. They're quick thinkers and are able to grasp difficult concepts easily. Needless to say, gua 9 people are highly intelligent and have little patience for those who are not up to their standards. They also seek fame and respect, which can make them vain. On the down side, fire people are hot-headed. Like fire, they need to control their emotion before it rages out of control.

Take this time now to absorb the personality traits associated with your guardian star along with the stars belonging to your family, friends, co-workers, and superiors.

Are You Compatible?

Having a firm understanding of the relationships between the five phases will help you better grasp how you relate to others. It may be a good idea to paper-clip Appendix F. Referring to it will help reinforce the phase relationships.

Here's how compatible gua 1 water people are with each other and with other guas:

- ◆ WATER and WATER: Water people get along quite well with each other. Because they're easygoing to begin with, there is no cause for concern.

- ◆ WATER and WOOD: Because water nourishes wood's growth, water people innately seek to support a wood person. It's a productive and stable relationship.

- ◆ WATER and FIRE: Water controls fire. How it is done determines the quality of the relationship. Douse the fire with water, and you'll saturate its spirit. Sprinkle water on fire, and you'll keep it in check.

- ◆ WATER and EARTH: Water people are afraid of earth's damming power. Water people need an escape route. If there's nowhere to go, water's spirit will stagnate. Innately, water and earth people do not make good partners.

◆ WATER and METAL: Water and metal people understand each other. Both yin in nature, a water person depends on a metal person's support. It is a productive relationship.

Here's how compatible gua 2 and gua 8 earth people are with each other and with other guas:

◆ EARTH and EARTH: Born of the same cloth, earth people recognize their own. It's often easier to be with your own kind than to venture into the unknown.

◆ EARTH and METAL: Yin by nature, earth and metal people make compatible mates, siblings, and business partners even if the hard types (gua 2 earth and gua 6 metal) sometimes lock horns.

◆ EARTH and WATER: Earth people will try to control a water person's every move. To keep the peace, it's best to give water an outlet.

◆ EARTH and WOOD: Earth people do not like to be dominated at all, much less by a wood person! Although it's probably best to steer clear of one another (particularly between hard earth gua 2 and hard wood gua 3 people), learning tolerance is the best advice.

◆ EARTH and FIRE: An earth person's biggest fan is a fire person. They are allies. Except for another earth person, fire people best understand (and will often egg on) an earth person's invincible spirit.

Here's how compatible gua 3 and gua 4 wood people are with each other and with other guas:

◆ WOOD and WOOD: Like attracts like. Expect spirited conversation around the dinner table. Wood people respect each other. Count on him or her to help elevate your status.

◆ WOOD and FIRE: A wood person is a fire person's best friend. Both yang in nature, they are very compatible friends, co-workers, bosses, business partners, and mates.

◆ WOOD and EARTH: Trouble! Especially between hard wood (gua 3) and hard earth (gua 2) people. Generally, this is not an auspicious relationship.

◆ WOOD and METAL: Wood people do not like to be bossed around by metal people. Hard wood (gua 3) and hard metal (gua 6) relationships are problematic. This is a controlling relationship.

◆ WOOD and WATER: Wood people love to lap up water's support. They favor the constant nourishment. A wood person can always rely on a water person.

Here's how compatible gua 6 and gua 7 metal people are with each other and with other guas:

♦ METAL and METAL: They see eye-to-eye. Strong-willed and determined, metal people stick up for each other.

♦ METAL and WATER: Being natural-born leaders, metal people love to be anyone's rock. Particularly, they relish supporting a water person. It's an auspicious partnership.

♦ METAL and WOOD: You can either use an ax to unceremoniously chop off wood's branches, or you can use pruning sheers to gently trim them. If you were wood, what would you prefer? Be mindful of your tone.

♦ METAL and FIRE: Metal is being melted by fire's heat. Although hard metal people are thick-skinned, soft metal people will be quick to quiver.

♦ METAL and EARTH: This is a favorable partnership. Both yin in nature, a metal person can lean on earth for support.

Here's how compatible gua 9 people are with each other and with other guas:

♦ FIRE and FIRE: Enthusiastic and bubbly, a fire person will naturally gravitate toward one of his own. They listen to each other, taking them to new heights.

♦ FIRE and EARTH: A born cheerleader, fire people like best to encourage an earth person's endeavors. It's a very compatible relationship.

♦ FIRE and METAL: A fire person can quickly melt a metal person's spirit. Become a candle flame instead of blowtorch, and you'll improve your relations with metal.

♦ FIRE and WATER: Fire people are afraid of water's dampening force. Take it down a notch, and water won't extinguish your flame.

♦ FIRE and WOOD: A wood person is a fire person's best friend. They feed off of each other. It's a favorable pairing.

So, have you figured out where you stand in your family? Are you the supporter or the controller? Are you being supported or are you being controlled? We believe this section will prove to be very helpful in how you interact with your mate, children, siblings, co-workers, and the like.

The Eight Wandering Stars

Collectively, the eight guardian stars (or ming gua numbers) are called the Eight Wandering Stars (You Xing). Individually, gua 1 is called the white water star; gua 2 is called the black earth star; gua 3 is called the jade wood star; gua 4 is called the green wood star; gua 6 is called the white metal star; gua 7 is called the red metal star; gua 8 is called the white earth star; and gua 9 is called the purple fire star. Each guardian star (or ming gua number) is a special type of qi unique to the person under which it is born.

Referring to the following table, we've included each star's Chinese name and English translation, its associated phase, a level of fortune, and a description of its qi. The letter F stands for Fortunate Qi, with F1 being the most favorable star and F4 being the fourth most favorable star. Conversely, the letter H stands for Harmful Qi, with H1 representing the least harmful star and H4 the most harmful star. Depending on which trigram you belong to, each of the eight directions is either fortunate or harmful to you in varying degrees. So how can you determine which direction corresponds to Sheng Qi (F1)? Keep reading!

Table 2 - The Eight Wandering Stars

Star	English Translation	Phase	Level of Fortune	Auspice
Sheng Qi	Life Qi	Wood	F1	Prosperity & Respectability
Yan Nian	Prolonged Years	Metal	F2	Longevity & Romantic Relationships
Tian Yi	Heavenly Doctor	Earth	F3	Good Health & Harmonious Relationships
Fu Wei	Stooping Position	Wood	F4	Peace & Stability
Huo Hai	Misfortune	Earth	H1	Accidents, Arguments, & Injury
Liu Sha	Six Devils	Water	H2	Malicious Encounters & Failed Relationships
Wu Gui	Five Ghosts	Fire	H3	Litigation, Accidents, Injury, & Fire
Jue Ming	Ultimate End of Life	Metal	H4	Disease, Misfortune, & Unproductive Careers

Changing Your Fortune

To determine your most favorable directions, you need your ming gua's symbol (see Chapter 7). Again, follow along and compute your own favorable directions using a separate sheet of paper.

Your F1 direction corresponds to Sheng Qi, the qi energy that brings about heightened prosperity and respectability. It's your most favorable magnetic direction for conducting business, studying, or anything else of importance. To determine your F1 direction, change line 3. Let's take the gua 1 water male example who belongs to the Kan trigram. In this case, line 3 of the Kan trigram is yin (broken line). He would then change it to yang (solid line).

<table>
<tr><td rowspan="2">

Feng Facts

</td></tr>
<tr></tr>
</table>

> **Feng Facts**
>
> Remember, trigrams are read from the bottom line up.

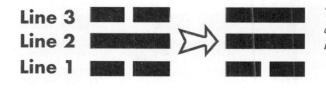

The example's Kan trigram changes to the Xun trigram, located in the southeast.

Your F2 direction corresponds to Yan Nian, the qi energy that brings about longevity and romantic relationships. The F2 direction is your second most favorable direction. To determine your F2 direction, change all three lines.

The example's Kan trigram changes to the Li trigram, located in the south.

Your F3 direction corresponds to Tian Yi, the qi energy that brings about good health and harmonious relationships. The F3 direction is your third most favorable direction. To determine your F3 direction, change lines 1 and 2. In the example's case, line 1 is yin, which now changes to yang; line 2 is yang, which becomes yin.

The example's Kan trigram changes to the Zhen trigram, located in the east.

Your F4 direction corresponds to Fu Wei, the qi energy that brings about peace and stability. F4 is your fourth most favorable direction. You will get your best sleep if the crown of your head points toward F4. To determine your F4 direction, no lines are changed.

The example's Kan (north) trigram remains the same.

Your H1 direction corresponds to Huo Hai, the qi energy that is considered the first least harmful. If located at your entrance or bedroom, H1 qi has been known to cause accidents, arguments, and injury. To determine your H1 direction, change line 1. The example's yin line becomes a yang line.

The example's Kan trigram changes to Dui, located in the west.

Your H2 direction corresponds with Liu Sha, the qi energy that is considered the second least harmful. H2 qi has been known to cause malicious encounters or sexual entanglements and failed relationships. To determine your H2 direction, change lines 1 and 3. In the example's case, lines 1 and 3 are yin, which now becomes yang.

The example's Kan trigram changes to Qian, located in the northwest.

Your H3 direction corresponds with Wu Gui, the qi energy that is the third least harmful. H3 qi has been known to cause fires, accidents, and abandonment of friends and family. To determine your H3 direction, change lines 2 and 3. The example's line 2 becomes yin; line 3 becomes yang.

The example's Kan trigram changes to Gen, located in the northeast.

Your H4 direction corresponds with Jue Ming, the qi energy that is the most harmful and dangerous. You should spend the least amount of time in or avoid this area altogether. H4 qi brings about disease, misfortune, and unproductive careers. Using entrances or bedrooms with H4 qi will weaken your health, wealth, and relationships. To determine your H4 direction, change line 2. The example's line 2 now becomes yin.

The example's Kan trigram changes to Kun, located in the southwest.

If you're wondering how a particular star is associated with the changing trigram formula, there is a reason behind the methodology. For example, why is a person's Sheng Qi (F1) and not, say, the qi associated with the star Huo Hai, determined by changing line 3 of his or her trigram? Unfortunately, space prevents us from offering an explanation here. However, one explanation can be found in Chapter 14 of *The Complete Idiot's Guide to the I Ching*.

> **Master Class**
>
> The Eight Wandering Stars are matched with the nine stars of the Big Dipper as follows: Sheng Qi is matched with Tan Lang (Ravenous Wolf); Yan Nian is matched with Wu Qu (The Military); Tian Yi with Ju Men (Great Gate); Fu Wei with the two stars comprising the Big Dipper's handle, Zuo Fu and You Bi (Left and Right Assistants); Huo Hai with Lu Cun (Prosperity Reserved); Liu Sha with Wen Qu (The Scholars); Wu Gui with Lian Zhen (Chastity); and Jue Ming with Po Jun (Destructive Army). Although it is not clear how the concept of the Nine Stars developed, many scholars believe the names comprising the seven stars of the Big Dipper (excluding the two stars forming its handle) came from India.

Wandering Star Auspice

How can you be sure you've calculated your favorable and unfavorable directions correctly? Have no fear; another quick reference table is here! (The Wandering Star Auspice Chart can also be found in Appendix F.) The following table shows how each of the eight Wandering Stars affects the ming gua/trigram in question. For example, take the Kun trigram (gua 2 earth). A Kun person's favorable directions are northeast (F1), northwest (F2), west (F3), and southwest (F4). Conversely, the Kun person's unfavorable directions are east (H1), south (H2), southeast (H3), and north (H4). Before you proceed, learn the directions that are beneficial and detrimental to your well-being.

The eight ming gua and their corresponding good and bad directions.

WANDERING STAR AUSPICE

D I R E C T I O N S

		1	2	3	4	6	7	8	9
		Water	Earth	Wood	Wood	Metal	Metal	Earth	Fire
		Kan	Kun	Zhen	Xun	Qian	Dui	Gen	Li
Great Prosperity & Respectability	**F1**	SE	NE	S	N	W	NW	SW	E
Longevity & Romantic Relationships	**F2**	S	NW	SE	E	SW	NE	W	N
Good Health & Harmonious Relationships	**F3**	E	W	N	S	NE	SW	NW	SE
Peace & Stability	**F4**	N	SW	E	SE	NW	W	NE	S
Accidents, Arguments, & Injury	**H1**	W	E	SW	NW	SE	N	S	NE
Possible Malicious Encounters & Failed Relationships	**H2**	NW	S	NE	W	N	SE	E	SW
Litigation, Accidents, Injury, & Fire	**H3**	NE	SE	NW	SW	E	S	N	W
Possible Disease, Misfortune, & Unproductive Careers	**H4**	SW	N	W	NE	S	E	SE	NW

At this point you may be thinking, "Okay, I understand this table. But how can the letter designations help to improve my health, livelihood, and relationships?" Well, you can benefit from the auspicious qi (designations F1 to F4) appropriate to your ming gua by making simple adjustments now. Referring to the illustration that follows, it is most advantageous to face your F1 direction, followed by your F2 and F3 directions. Although F4 is more favorable than H1 to H4, you might experience drowsiness or a sense of procrastination.

Facing your favorable directions F1 to F3 will promote good fortune and productivity.

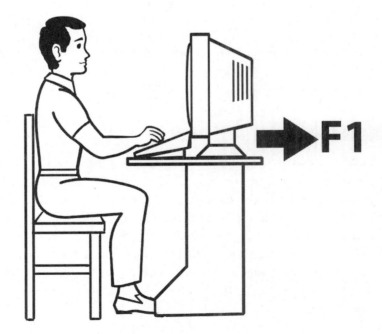

F1

Now, let's discuss your most favorable sleeping directions. Referring to the following illustration, the position promoting the most restful night's sleep is to have the crown of your head pointing toward your F4 direction. This is followed by F3 (your second choice) and F2 (your third choice). Although F1 is more favorable than H1 to H4, sleeping toward your F1 direction may cause insomnia. This is because your subconscious mind will continue to work at the same pace as when you are awake. The inability of the subconscious mind to relax often causes insomnia.

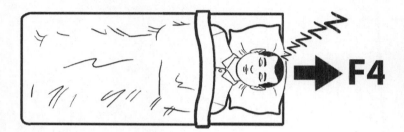

To promote a restful night, sleep with your head pointed toward your F4 direction ideally, and then the F3, F2, and F1 directions in order of decreasing preferences.

Now that you understand how to determine the directions most beneficial to you, feel free to don your work gloves and move your bed and desk positions accordingly. But be careful! You must also consider door and window alignment. You'll learn more in Chapter 10.

In Part 3 you'll learn how your home's external and internal environments play a significant role in how you think, feel, and relate.

The Least You Need to Know

♦ Your ming gua is determined by your birth year and gender.

♦ Your ming gua reflects how you affect—and are affected by—other people.

♦ Your ming gua determines your favorable and unfavorable directions.

♦ Your ming gua can determine which direction is best for work, study, and sleep.

Part 3

Understanding Your Environment

Did you know that landforms, building shapes, rivers, and roads influence your well-being? That living near places of worship, hospitals, and schools governs how you think, feel, and relate? That your front yard, backyard, window and door alignment, ceiling beams, and furniture placement affect your prosperity? Indeed, there's much to consider when analyzing your external and internal environments.

Part 3 is all about recognizing these natural and man-made factors. You'll learn how to distinguish that which brings favorable qi from that which brings unfavorable qi. Moreover, you'll learn how to remedy inauspicious situations. The simplest modifications can turn a bullfrog into a prince and your home into a comfortable, prosperous, and healthful haven.

Chapter 9

Turtles, Tigers, and Dragons, Oh My: Evaluating Your Environment

In This Chapter

◆ The Four Celestial Palaces: totems worshipped by the ancient Chinese

◆ The four terrestrial animals: landform and building shapes that affect your well-being

◆ River and road patterns

◆ The importance of where your home is placed

Feng shui's all about living in harmony with your environment. It's about harnessing sheng, or positive qi, to promote better health, wealth, and relations with others. It's about avoiding or correcting sha, or negative qi, a detriment to your well-being. In this chapter, you'll learn about ancient Chinese cosmology—how four celestial deities (the crimson bird, azure dragon, white tiger, and black turtle) worshipped by the Chinese transformed into terrestrial landforms. You'll discover how to recognize these landforms and how they offer protection and security. Also, we'll show you how neighboring buildings, river courses, and roadways play a role in your life and livelihood.

We guarantee you'll see your neighborhood, city—heck, even the world—with new vision. Can a film editor watch a film without critiquing its edits and pace? Can a fitness professional look at a body without assessing the person's physique? Certainly not.

Here a Totem, There a Totem

All ancient societies worshipped the heavens, envisioning their gods, guardians, and clan ancestors as configurations of celestial bodies. For the most part, these star-patterned deities were represented in animal form. Called *totems*, the animals were worshipped in exchange for protection. Originating from the Algonquin tribe of North America, the word "totem" describes a clan's emblem—an animal or natural object with which a group feels a special affection or attachment.

Wise Words

Totem is an Algonquin word describing an animal or natural object with which a clan feels a special attachment. Symbolizing group membership, the totem is worshipped by the members of the clan bearing its name.

Why the affinity with a particular animal? This is a mystery. Although we'll probably never know why a tribe chose a particular animal as its emblem, the geographic region of the culture in question might provide important clues. Also, it's reasonable to assume the animal embodied positive attributes (like courage, strength, or loyalty) with which the tribe wanted to associate itself. But, before we get into these aspects, let's first define the totems worshipped by the ancient Chinese. Then we can learn how these totems relate to the art and science of feng shui.

Circus of the Stars

In China, four celestial deities revered by ancient tribes combined to help form the culture we know today. What would come to be known as the *Four Celestial Palaces*—the *crimson bird*, *azure dragon*, *mysterious black turtle*, and *white tiger*—are actually macroconstellations, or an enormous stellar division, composed of seven independent constellations each. Together, the 4 macroconstellations make up the 28 constellations of the Chinese Zodiac.

Signaling the arrival of the solstices and equinoxes, each macroconstellation represents a quarter of the night sky, each visible in its entirety only in the season with which it's associated (you'll learn more about this later in this chapter). As an aside, it's important to understand that the Chinese use the *celestial equator* to track stellar positions. In China's mountainous regions, it makes more sense to base observations on the times when the heavenly bodies come into view overhead. In the Western world, emphasis is placed on the rising and setting of celestial bodies on the terrestrial horizon. Called the *ecliptic* system, it originated in subtropic regions where the land is flat and the view unobstructed.

Wise Words

The **celestial equator** is the circular path the constellations traverse perpendicular to an imaginary line joining the celestial north pole to Earth's North Pole. The ancient Chinese called the celestial equator the Red Path. Westerners developed an **ecliptic** system. It traces the path of the sun through the sky. The ancient Chinese called this system the Yellow Path.

Read All About It: Heaven Falls to Earth!

You might be wondering how ancient cosmology relates to feng shui, how celestial deities are associated with harnessing positive qi. Unfortunately, like many ancient traditions, the answers are swathed in myth. Sometime between the 6000 B.C.E. Neolithic tomb (described in Chapter 3) and the writing of the fourth century C.E. *Book of Burial*, the bird, dragon, turtle, and tiger deities came down to earth to represent four unique types of landforms associated with Form School feng shui—the practice of locating the most auspicious sites on which to construct a building or bury the dead.

As the story goes, the circular (or domed) heaven and square (or flat) earth were once perfectly balanced, eight majestic mountains (corresponding to each of the eight directions) separating the two realms. However, this ideal and perfect world came to an end when the water demon Gong Gong battled the fire god Zhu Rong. During the battle, Mount Buzhou, the northwest pillar, collapsed. As a consequence, heaven came crashing down, causing the earth plane to rise in the southeast and fall in the northwest. Somehow, the four macroconstellations transformed into terrestrial shapes, each associated with one of the four cardinal directions: the crimson bird to the south, the white tiger to the west, the black turtle to the north, and the azure dragon to the east.

Although an exciting tale, we all know this primeval battle didn't really occur. How the star-patterned deities entered the earth plane is anyone's guess. Nevertheless, their shape and proximity to one another help to describe the disposition of qi, ultimately providing the foundation of Form School (Xingfa) feng shui. It was the task of the master to find the place, nestled between the creatures that represented heaven on earth. He did this using a shipan (described in Chapter 6). Over time, this divine instrument was replaced by the luopan, the compass used by feng shui masters today.

In Search of the Dragon's Lair

The earliest textual documentation underlying the theories of Form School feng shui surface in the fifth century B.C.E. in *Guanzi*, purportedly written by Guan Zhong, the prime minister of the state of Qi. However, a fully developed theory discussing the relationship of the terrestrial plane and qi isn't seen for another six centuries. As we already mentioned, the fourth century C.E. *Book of Burial* (*Zhangshu*) was the bible of landforms, the text describing in detail how to locate the *dragon's lair* (long xue). This is the place where qi converges, the common point of intersection between the southern landform of the crimson bird, the eastern landform of the azure dragon, the northern black turtle, and the western white tiger. The dragon's lair is considered the most auspicious site on which to build a home or to bury the dead.

Many scholars believe Guo Pu's (276–324 C.E.) *Book of Burial* clarifies the *Classic of Burial*, a text purportedly dating to the Han dynasty. It states: "Qi flows according to the shape of the earth. With qi's nourishment, all living things come into existence. Qi flows within the ground. Its motion follows the shape of the terrain, accumulating where the terrain stops."

Locating the cave of the lair, a metaphor for the place where sheng qi pools, is what Form School feng shui is about. When the deceased are buried in this spot, the yin (dead) bones are activated by or charged with yang (living) qi. When a home is built on this auspicious site, the occupants are blessed with good health and wealth.

Climb Every Mountain

Besides being associated with a direction, the bird, dragon, turtle, and tiger landforms correspond to a season, a five-phase color, and a yin and yang polarity, as shown in the following illustration.

Beginning with the *crimson bird* and traveling clockwise, the bird represents the south, summer, the color red, and yang qi. Because birds are more abundant in warmer climates, it makes sense why the bird deity was placed in the southern sky. Terrestrially, the bird's features must be lower than the others. The bird doesn't have to be a landform; it can also represent a body of water.

The *white tiger* represents the west, autumn, the color white, and yin qi. The tiger is indigenous and plentiful the farther west toward India you travel. Terrestrially, the tiger's peak is traditionally longer and lower than its eastern counterpart, the dragon.

Master Class

What type of feathered friend is the crimson bird? In its earliest version, it was a sparrow. However, later on, the sparrow was replaced by an antlered phoenix.

North

Black Turtle

West

White Tiger

Azure Dragon

East

Crimson Bird

South

The terrestrial configurations of the four celestial deities.

The *black turtle* represents the north, winter, the color black, and yin qi. Not to be confused with the amphibious tortoise, the land creature boasts the highest terrestrial landform feature. Why a turtle? Why the north? Well, all we know is that turtle shell divination was a northern tradition. In fact, divination using the plastrons or bottom shells of turtles (plastomancy) led to a type of divination called sortilege, in which a person drew lots (stone, sticks, or straws, for example) to determine his or her fate. The ancient Chinese used stalks from the yarrow plant, a method directly tied to the development of the *Yijing*, considered the oldest system of divination still in use today.

Wise Words

The lowest of the land-forms, the southern **crimson bird** can also represent a body of water. This is balanced by the highest northern landform, the **black turtle**. To the east, the high **azure dragon** is balanced by the long and low **white tiger** of the west.

Finally, the *azure dragon* represents the east, spring, the color green, and yang qi. Traditionally, the dragon's terrestrial features are higher than the western tiger. Meteorologically, the azure dragon is equivalent to the Greco-Roman constellation Scorpious.

Together, the crimson bird, white tiger, black turtle, and azure dragon form the dragon's lair. Regardless of their stature, each component plays a vital role in nourishing the land of the living and the realm of the dead. Let's find out what role each plays.

Situated between Aberdeen Harbor (representing the crimson bird) and Victoria Peak (representing the black turtle), Hong Kong offers its residents both psychological and physical security and protection.

(Image © 1998 PhotoDisc, Inc.)

Have a Seat

Imagine the lair as an armchair. The tiger and dragon represent the arms; the turtle is the back; and the bird is the foot stool. The fortunate site for a grave, building, or settlement rests in the middle, the seat of the chair. Now, imagine sitting in the chair. How would you feel if the left (azure dragon) or right (white tiger) arm was missing? Would you feel uncomfortable? Exposed? Unbalanced, perhaps? In feng shui, the dragon and the tiger protect the lair just as the arms of the chair protect your body.

The black turtle provides support and protection. In China, the turtle blocked bitter Arctic winds and helped to battle against barbaric attacks. Continuing with our chair analogy, don't you feel safer and more secure with your back supported? Of course you do! This idea also gives rise to the phrase "Watch your back."

Master Class

Traditionally, the Chinese believe the left is more important than the right. For this reason, the highest-ranking prime minister always appeared on the left side of the emperor. In part, this has to do with how our brain functions. For people who are right-handed, the left side of the brain controls the right side of the body. The ancient Chinese understood this, honoring the brain's importance by ranking its officials accordingly.

What about the crimson bird? Although not offering protection, this low-lying landform or body of water buffers you from incoming forces. Also, this area provides an unobstructed view of the site in question.

Although traditionally the four terrestrial creatures correspond to one of the four directions, we mustn't be so strict when we judge our home's location. Regardless of magnetic orientation, just know it's most favorable to have the landforms of the turtle supporting your back, the dragon on your left, the white tiger on your right, and the crimson bird in front.

City Slickers

Let's say you live on flat terrain with no dragon, turtle, or tiger landform in sight. Does this mean your home brings you misfortune? Absolutely not! Symbolically, the four terrestrial creatures can represent buildings. For example, most of us have neighboring structures on the left and right sides of our home. Looking outside from within our dwelling, these structures represent the dragon (left side) and tiger (right side). To determine which side bears the greatest strength you must consider …

◆ The size of the buildings: the bigger and more imposing, the stronger.

◆ The proximity of each to your home: the closer, the more powerful.

◆ The density on each side: the side with a greater number of buildings has more influence.

If the neighboring buildings on the left side are more prominent than on the right side, your home favors the male occupants. This is because the left side, the dragon side, corresponds to yang (male) qi. If the neighboring buildings on the right side are more prominent, your home favors the yin female occupants.

The back side of your home can also be supported by a building. While offering security and protection, the structure in question must not overwhelm your home. Also, it must not block sunlight.

Suitably placed and appropriately sized trees, hedges, bushes, or even fences are a valid substitute for landforms and buildings. If your home backs onto a park, for example, you could plant a grove of trees or a hedge to protect your back side. A fence will also do.

Rolling on the River or Easing on Down the Road

In feng shui, river courses and roadways are evaluated in the same way. A meandering river is similar to a winding road. A sharp current is like heavy rushing traffic. Depending on their patterns, rivers and roads can bring you benevolent sheng qi, inspiring good fortune, or malicious sha qi, causing misfortune and illness.

Notable Quotables

Qi rides the wind and disperses until it encounters water.
—Guo (276–324 C.E.), *Book of Burial*

So, if you're in the market to buy a new home or would just like to assess your current situation, what we offer here should be considered. In some measure, our health and livelihood depend on the very paths we take for granted.

Consider the following illustrations. Before reading our analysis, try to form your own conclusion. Staying oblivious to all other factors, consider only how the road's contour makes you feel.

In feng shui, river courses and roadways are evaluated the same way.

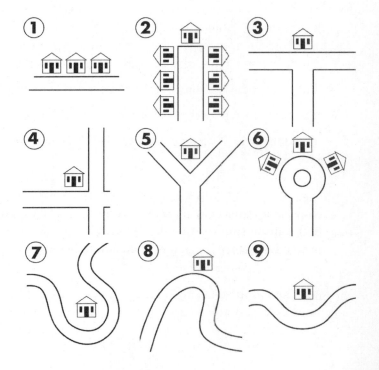

Let's consider each illustration separately:

1. **A straight road.** Generally, most homes are positioned along this type of road pattern. Is this a bad thing? Only if the road is a main thoroughfare, where you're subjected to extra noise, dirt, and other things possibly causing fatigue and illness. Is it more peaceful listening to sirens or song birds? If you live along a straight roadway, the most auspicious house is in the middle supported by the tiger and dragon. In the same vein, if you live alongside an aqueduct or river rapids, you might feel out of control, as if you're being buffeted downstream. Now, if the straight road in question is not frequented by traffic, it resembles a lazy stream—quiet, peaceful, balanced.

2. **A dead-end street.** Here, this dwelling is a recipient of poison arrow qi rushing up the street into the occupant's front door. Most inauspicious, indeed. It's also unfavorable to live in an apartment or work in an office at the end of a long hall.

3. **A T-junction.** Once again, poison arrow qi intrudes. Like a runaway locomotive, it will stop only on impact, enveloping your home in its destructive forces. If you live at a T- or Y-junction (see #5), can anything be done to protect you from the affects of poison arrow qi? Install a high fence or plant a wall of shrubbery to block qi's destructive path. However, it's best to avoid choosing locations requiring such action.

4. **A corner lot.** You may feel unbalanced living on a corner lot. This is because one side of your dwelling's protection is separated by the street. Also, traffic, noise, and glaring headlights are a consideration. In feng shui, the corner dwelling (or the one at the end of the lane) is considered unfavorable because the qi has dispersed. Also the house's support is unbalanced with the street coming between the protection of the tiger/dragon.

5. **A Y-junction.** Similar to a dead-end and T-junction pattern, a home residing in a Y-junction is subjected to two torrents of unfavorable qi. Further, this configuration is cause for accidents due to cars careening off the path into your home.

6. **A cul-de-sac.** Unlike the dead-end street depicted in illustration 2, a house situated on a cul-de-sac containing an island is fortunate. Why? If you imagine the street as a water course, the island (in this situation) is the crimson bird—the buffer dispersing sha qi's ill effects. What about a cul-de-sac that doesn't have a protective island? This, too, is favorable because qi can flow, moving in a circular motion, dispersing its benevolent energy.

7. **A U-shape.** It stands to reason you may feel suffocated living in a house positioned inside a noose! Although atypical to city streetscape, avoid purchasing a country or mountain home where this type of pattern is more common.

8. **A sharp bend.** Maneuvering a car around sharp bends is tricky business. The screech of brakes and the glare of headlights add extra anxiety. Would you want to live on such a danger-prone street?

9. **A meandering path.** Cradled inside an open U-junction, you are protected from the threat of accidents, glaring lights, and poison arrow qi. A house situated here is considered lucky—the benevolent, winding qi bringing prosperity, good health, and promotion.

Some final points: Although not illustrated here, living on the same level or below a freeway is inauspicious. So is living between parallel roads. So, what then are the most favorable locations? Simply, a meandering path (9), followed by a cul-de-sac (6), and a straight road (1) not frequented by traffic. Remember, when evaluating your situation, roadways and water courses are equivalent.

The Least You Need to Know

◆ The foundation of Form School feng shui stems from ancient cosmology.

◆ In feng shui, landforms are referred to as the bird, dragon, turtle, and tiger shapes.

◆ Buildings, trees, and fences can represent the four terrestrial creatures.

◆ Rivers and roads are evaluated in the same way.

◆ The patterns of river courses and roadways can bring either fortune or misfortune to your dwelling.

Chapter 10

Home Sweet Home: Evaluating Your House and Its Surroundings

In This Chapter

- ◆ How neighboring facilities can be a health risk
- ◆ Recognizing favorable lot shapes
- ◆ Houses of all shapes and sizes
- ◆ Laying out your bedroom and office

This chapter continues where Chapter 9 left off. Here, you'll learn more about your environment, and how the proximity of a school, church, or power plant—among other things—affects how you feel, relate, and even sleep. You'll discover how the land your house is built on plays a role in your well-being.

This chapter is also about practical application—things you can do now to improve your living space, such as the best way to position your bed to gain a restful night's sleep, or where to station your desk to increase your productivity. By making simple adjustments and being mindful of potential qi-inspired hazards, you'll feel more balanced and centered. You'll feel strong and in control instead of butting heads with the elements.

Church Bells and Power Poles

A host of man-made factors can influence your health and livelihood. Although some are obvious hazards, others are less so. Take living next to a school. Would you think its proximity poses a health risk? Aside from the school bus exhaust fumes, the area is charged with the high energy of youth. Just being in your own children's presence can wear you out. Now, multiply this by say, a thousand. Over time, the voltage of kid qi may cause insomnia, anxiety, and muscle tension.

Conversely, how about living next to a hospital, funeral parlor, or even a place of worship? Here, you're enveloped with trauma, depression, sorrow, illness, and death. But wait, aren't churches, synagogues, and the like peaceful places? They can be. However, you're still subjected to the maladies of others. Here are more sites you should avoid living in close proximity to:

- Garbage dump
- Landfill
- Cemetery
- Police station
- Fire station
- Airport
- Railroad
- Factory
- Military camp
- High-tension power lines

If you live next to one of these places, can a five-phase remedy offer protection? Unfortunately, no. The presence is simply too overwhelming. If you're a soldier stationed in a military camp or a minister living in the parsonage next to the church, take extra precautions to safeguard your health. A proper diet and exercise will help to defend against the inherently inauspicious site in which you must live. However, it's best to try to avoid it altogether.

Land Sakes Alive!

There's much to consider when choosing or evaluating a house. You've already learned you can create a veritable heaven on earth just by identifying and situating yourself in an area that protects your back and left and right sides. Even if you don't live in a mountainous region, you can still find security and protection among neighboring structures. Also, don't forget the fourth component—river and/or road patterns (and foothills, if applicable). Do the river courses and roadways surrounding your house bring sheng qi, promoting good health, wealth, and happiness? Or is your house the object of sha qi, bringing potential money loss, illness, and failed relationships?

Let's examine the land on which your house is situated. Later, we'll look at other favorable and unfavorable factors that influence your state of being.

Over Hill, Over Dale

Where's the best place to live? On top of a hill? On a steep incline? How about on sloping land or flat terrain? Look at the following illustration. What do you believe to be the most favorable terrain?

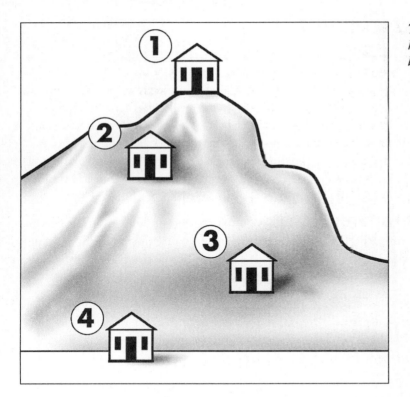

The geophysical plane your house sits on can affect your livelihood.

1. **A hilltop.** While offering a spectacular view, this is not an auspicious site. Left unprotected, you're subjected not only to nature's forces but also to psychological vulnerability. People who live on hilltops are known to feel insecure and exposed. Often, these individuals are prone to insomnia and nervousness.

Imagine yourself camping out on a hilltop. It's just you and your sleeping bag. You have an unobstructed view of the stars. After a while, you doze off. But your sleep is not restful. On guard, you summon up the *fight or flight instinct* understood by primitive man. Although the inhabitants of Masada and Machu Picchu might have been skilled at sleeping with one eye open, ultimately, they did not withstand the test of time. Again, choose a secure haven over a scenic view.

Wise Words

According to the *Professional Hypnotism Manual* by John G. Kappas, the **fight or flight instinct** is a primitive and involuntary reaction triggered during moments of danger or anxiety. As humankind (and animals) evolved, some developed greater strength and aggressiveness (fight), while others developed agility, speed, and a sensitivity to the senses of smell, sight, and hearing (flight). Those who remained passive eventually became extinct.

2. **A steep incline.** A mountain view in back, a panoramic view in front. Sound ideal? Imagine standing on a vertical incline. Naturally, you tend to lean back and widen your stance—anything to offer stability to prevent you from toppling over. Psychological effects aside, how about the threat of landslides? In feng shui, those who live on a steep incline are unable to retain wealth. Like a house on top of a hill, a house on a steep incline does not allow sheng qi to accumulate and settle. It's carried downhill. So is your hard-earned money.

   Although generally it's favorable to have a natural mountain formation supporting your back and a body of water in front, in some circumstances this configuration can be detrimental to your health and livelihood. You'll learn more about this in Part 4.

3. **A sloping hill.** Classical feng shui doctrines tell us that living on a gently sloping hill is ideal. This is because the soil on this terrain is fertile and rich. Here, your house is less likely to flood. Depending on the grade of the slope, the upward incline can represent the black turtle, protecting and supporting your back.

4. **Flat terrain.** Although the ancient Chinese classics tell us flat, low-lying areas are best avoided (because of the threat of flooding and poor soil quality), these texts spoke to an agricultural society. Today, most urban dwellers live on flat terrain. Offering a solid foundation and security, this type of site is favorable.

Armed with this information, you'll think twice before purchasing your dream house on a hilltop or steep incline. As mama says, "It's better to be safe than sorry!"

Lots of Plots

Now that you understand what kind of terrain is considered favorable, let's see how the shape of your lot affects your well-being. Much of what we have presented so far relies on plain old common sense, a factor we're more accustomed to dealing with than complicated environmental concerns. We've discussed where you should seek a lot, now let's talk about the individual lot itself. Disregarding all other external details, look at the following illustrations. Which lots do you think are most favorable?

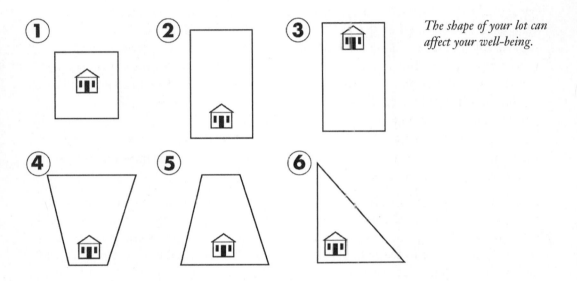

The shape of your lot can affect your well-being.

1. **Square lot.** In feng shui, a square shape, be it a lot, a room, or a table, denotes stability and balance. Qi is able to flow freely, unobstructed. Ideally, your house should be situated in the center of a lot, allowing qi to circulate around the structure and through its windows and doors, nourishing the occupants.

2. **Rectangular lot.** In this example, the dwelling is positioned at the front of the lot. Qi flows in and accumulates in the back, your wealth and health safeguarded. It's similar to a wealthy individual having "deep pockets." Investors have *backers*—ensuring support behind them.

3. **Deep front yard, shallow backyard.** In feng shui, if the space behind your house is significantly less than the space in front, you will have difficulty retaining money.

4. **Trapezoid lot.** Here, sheng qi inspiring good health and monetary gain must squeeze in. Like a bottleneck, the object in question must maneuver through the tight opening in order to accumulate in back. Because qi will have difficulty entering, this shape is not considered favorable.

5. **Inverted trapezoid lot.** In this example, qi has no trouble entering, but a difficult time staying. Imagine a cone-shaped paper cup. Flatten the bottom so that it's able to stand on its end, then fill it with water. More than likely, before the water reaches the rim, the cup will fall over. Its support base is too weak to retain the liquid. Similarly, sheng qi is unable to collect and settle.

6. **Triangular lot.** This is the most unfavorable of all the lot shapes. Simply, angular lots are disorienting.

Most likely, the shape of your lot corresponds to one of the illustrations just offered. Of course, there are other shapes like an L configuration. This shape is considered unfavorable because qi has a difficult time maneuvering around corners. Also, the junction of walls and/or fences produces angle sha, which impacts negatively on the well-being of the occupants. But, what if you live on a lot with no visible boundaries? Common in the Midwest, this situation features adjoining multiple lots with little, if any, visible division. The suggestion here is of one great yard. As long as qi is able to flow unobstructed, nourishing each structure, this housing configuration does not pose a problem. However, do be mindful of wind tunnels. We suggest planting shrubs and trees to prevent possible negative effects.

Regarding apartment-dwellers, although the external lot the building sits on is certainly a consideration, the shape of your unit within the building takes precedence. In other words, think of the floor your unit is located on as the lot. Where your unit is situated plays a role in the overall auspiciousness of your dwelling. Traditionally, side and back units don't receive as much light as front units. To offset the lack of yang qi, make sure that your unit is amply lit.

House of Shapes

As we mentioned in Chapter 6, each of the five phases corresponds to a shape: fire is triangular, earth is square, metal is round, water is wavy, and wood is rectangular. How does the shape affect qi's course? Consider each individually:

◆ **Triangle.** Most of us don't live in a teepee or a church. But some of us live in A-framed houses, or have some rooms whose walls are angular. Attic rooms are a good example. What does this mean? Well, again, you may feel disoriented, out of control, as if the room might cave in on you. Some people feel claustrophobic. Also, if two protruding walls come together to form an angle, this troublesome juncture creates sha qi.

Regarding qi's flow in a triangular dwelling, imagine bouncing a Super Ball in this room. What happens? The angular walls cause it to bounce in a crazy, haphazard fashion. It is the same with qi. After a while, this dizzying effect will take its toll on your well-being.

- **Square.** This shape is your best friend. Square lots, square house, square rooms. No fuss, no muss. Here, qi flows freely. So abstain from an architecturally challenged structure in favor of something nice and normal. You'll be better off.

- **Circle.** This shape is ideal for sports coliseums, but would you want to be caught up in a whirlwind of qi? Imagine how water drains. Imagine the power a hurricane or tornado creates. Caught in the path, it's nearly impossible to free yourself. People who live in circular houses or who spend a lot of time in domed or circular rooms have trouble concentrating and sleeping.

- **Wavy.** A house conforming to this horizontal shape has variegated roof/ceiling lines. Like a ship at sea, the up-and-down motion of qi waves can cause you to feel unstable. Many castles and modern houses correspond to this shape.

- **Rectangle.** Symbolic of wood's expansion and growth, living in this type of structure is considered favorable. Like a square shape, rectangles don't present any odd angles to which qi will have difficulty maneuvering. Ranch houses and trailers are examples of rectangular dwellings. Now, a rectangle standing on its end is also considered a wood shape. High-rise buildings are good examples.

> **CAUTION**
>
> **Feng Alert**
>
> Many modern houses are designed in a W- or lightning-bolt shape. Although these houses may be the subject of interesting conversation, the sharp angles created by the juncture of these walls can cause misfortune and illness.

What about other configurations? Although there are myriad different shapes, here are two common ones that, from our experience, affect the occupants differently:

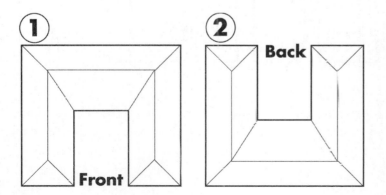

Two common shapes that affect the occupants differently.

1. People who live in a house with a receding central section are known to be of humble means and content. But in this case, you can't judge a book by its cover. Although subconsciously they might appear to others to lack wealth, it's more likely the owners are financially secure. This is because the back of their house is solid, providing support and security.

2. People who live in a house that forms a U-shape, its central back section missing, subconsciously appear to others to be well off. In fact, these people are subjected to possible divorce, money loss, and other misfortune. This is because the sitting side of their dwelling does not provide uniform protection. Occupants feel as though they're exposed.

When judging a structure's form and layout, disregard furniture, doors, and windows, concentrating only on the shape of the dwelling and rooms. How do they make you feel? Remember, the external and internal environment should nurture, not deplete, you.

A Grand Entrance

As you'll soon find out in upcoming chapters, the most important part of a house is the entrance. It represents who we are. Similar to the car we drive or the clothes we wear, much can be said about the outward appearance of the main entrance. Yet, aside from visual factors, the front door is the primary location for the invisible qi force to enter. Later, you'll learn to determine whether the entrance is inherently auspicious. But for now, let's concentrate on factors that can influence how you and your guests feel.

The size of the entrance affects occupants.

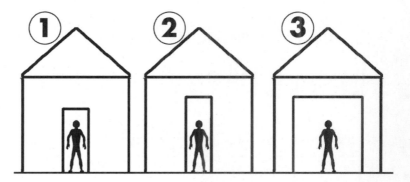

The size of your front door should be proportionate to the size of an average person (see illustration 1). Illustrations 2 and 3 show an entrance that is too tall and too large, respectively. Doors of this size encourage valuable qi to escape. In feng shui, it is believed you may experience financial loss by having such a grand entrance.

Conversely, if your entrance is too small (not illustrated here), you are restricting qi from entering. Here are some other considerations:

♦ The front door should not be impeded by things like a single tree or utility pole placed curbside in direct alignment with your entrance.

♦ The front door should be protected against any poison arrow qi coming from T-junctions, Y-junctions, or other sha qi emitted by neighboring structures.

♦ The path leading to your front door should be curved, forming a right angle just before the door.

♦ Ideally, the main entrance should be at the top of a flight of stairs. Subconsciously, the occupants feel safer above street level.

Feng Alert

Many public buildings, places of business, houses of worship, and large residential houses feature impressive double doors. If you're the owner of such a dwelling and are experiencing financial troubles, the size of the door may be a contributing factor to your hardship. We suggest using only one side of the door, disabling qi from gushing out.

♦ The main entrance should not be below street level. Qi is not able to enter easily; the occupants feel trapped.

♦ The main entrance should be inviting. Your front lawn should be mowed and bushes trimmed. In general, you should feel good about entering your own house; your guests should feel welcome. Your house shouldn't be an eyesore of weeds, overgrown plants, and peeling paint!

♦ The front entrance should not open onto a stairway positioned directly opposite the door. Similar to living on a hilltop or a steep incline, your potential to accumulate wealth will flow out the door.

♦ The front door and back door should not be in alignment. Literally, qi will enter in one door and exit from the other. Unfortunately, many houses are constructed such that a long hallway connects the front and back doors. Considering the appropriate five-phase remedy (and space provided), block negative qi's path by placing a screen, piece of furniture, or plant near the main entrance.

♦ The front entrance should be well lit. By protecting the main entrance, you'll be promoting better health, wealth, and happiness.

You may be wondering whether these considerations apply to only your main entrance. They apply to the front door and any other door (such as the back or side entrances) you use most often.

Room for Improvement

You may have heard that you should sleep with your head positioned toward the north. But as you'll soon learn, the direction you should sleep is determined by your ming gua—knowledge you acquired in Chapter 8. This same method will also describe which directions are best for work and study. But until then, other factors contribute to the quality of your sleep, work, and study. Even though auspicious bed and desk positions are evaluated in the same way, we will separate the two to facilitate easier learning.

Now I Lay Me Down to Sleep

It stands to reason we should do everything possible to ensure a restful sleep. After all, we spend a third of our lifetime in our bedroom. Disregarding factors such as the shape of the room and the color of the room, here are some bed positions you should avoid:

1. The foot of your bed should not face the door. Qi's flow will disrupt your sleep.

2. For the same reason, your bed should not be placed on the same wall as the door.

3. Your bed should not be positioned under a window. The elements will prevent a peaceful rest.

4. Your bed should not be positioned between a doorway and window, or a combination thereof. The wind tunnel will cause a disturbance.

Unfavorable bed placement.

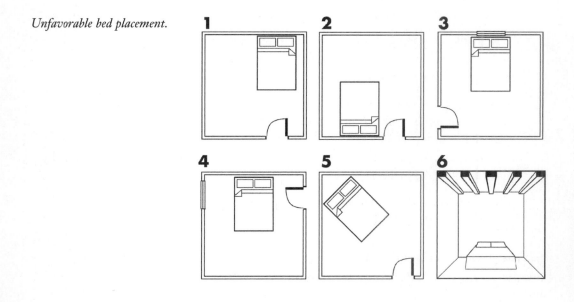

5. Your bed should not be placed on an angle. Having the solid support of the black turtle will make you feel more secure, preventing the bogeyman from lurking in the black crevices.

6. You should not sleep under ceiling beams. The beams cause qi to create a ripple effect, the downward pressure impacting not only your sleep but also your health.

So, where is the ideal place to position your bed? Referring to the following illustrations, the bed should be placed on an unobstructed wall diagonally across from the door and far enough away from the window so that you aren't bothered by the direct hit of incoming qi. Also, the bed should be accessible from both sides.

Feng Alert _____

Although bunk beds save space, they don't promote quality sleep. The occupant on the bottom feels threatened by the looming top bunk; the occupant on top feels unconsciously susceptible to an inevitable fall. If a room is too small for two beds, consider a trundle bed (a bed that slides out from under a bed).

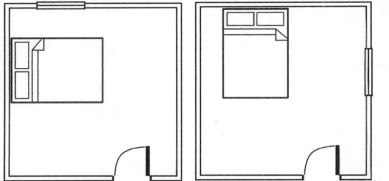

Favorable bed placement.

Now, before you begin to move furniture, you first must learn to determine which directions favor you (an important factor you'll learn about in the next chapter). Only then can you make a competent evaluation.

Working Nine to Five

The time we spend in our bedrooms may reign, but the time we spend at our desks follows closely. So, again, it behooves us to harness sheng qi to promote a better livelihood. Look at the following illustrations:

Unfavorable desk placement.

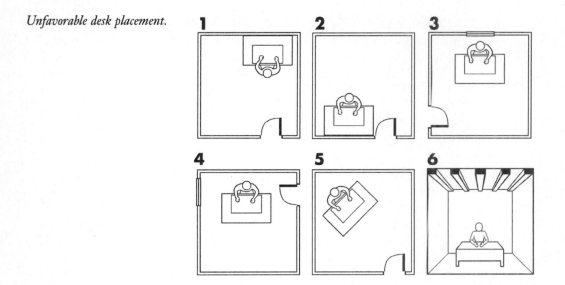

1. Your back should not face a doorway. It's important that you see anyone who enters. More importantly, your back must be supported by a wall.

2. The desk must not be placed on the same wall as the doorway. Qi flows directly toward you, causing a lack of concentration.

3. Your back must not be exposed to a window. Again, you need support. Besides, incoming sunlight will cause a glare on your computer screen.

Master Class

If you are seated facing a wall, the wall will effectively block your ideas and concentration. You can dramatically improve your productivity if you turn your desk around so that you face the room. This is especially important for children.

4. The desk should not be positioned between two doors or two windows, or a combination thereof. The wind tunnel creates a lack of concentration and need for paperweights.

5. The desk should not be placed on an angle. You need support to get the job done.

6. The desk should not be positioned under overhead beams. The bombardment of the hammerlike qi pattern created by the beams will negatively affect you over time.

Now for the favorable positions. The following illustrations show a desk placed so that the person's back is supported by a wall. How close should your back be to the wall? Close enough so that you feel its solidity. Also, you must be far enough away from qi's direct path entering through the window and door. And, the occupant must have a clear view of anyone entering.

Again, don't move anything just yet. First, you must learn how to determine your favorable directions. When all factors are considered, then you can begin the laborious task of rearranging the furniture. Hey, while you're at it, why not apply a fresh coat of paint (using the appropriate color, of course), and get rid of clutter? Qi will flow more smoothly. You'll feel more organized, confident, and motivated.

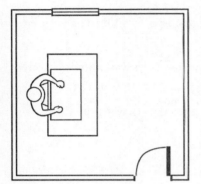 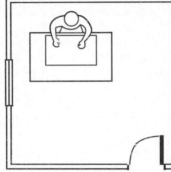

Favorable desk placement.

Moving Day

What about the rest of your house? What about arranging your living room, den, and kitchen according to feng shui principles? Follow these simple guidelines, and you'll be on your way to achieving harmony, balance, good health, and prosperity:

- The furniture in the room should be a mixture of yin and yang. Balance dark with light; angled corners with round.
- The furniture should be proportionate to the room. The pieces should be arranged evenly to facilitate easy access.
- Sofas are best placed against a wall.
- The backs of sofas or chairs should not face any entrances.
- All areas should be free of clutter.
- Objects d'art should be balanced.

It's a good idea to plot out different furniture arrangements on graph paper. Study each design and choose the one best corresponding to our suggestions. Sometimes change can be difficult. So, have a friend or family member help you. A well-informed, objective opinion can present options you might not have considered.

In the next part, we'll introduce you to one method of classical feng shui called Flying Star.

The Least You Need to Know

- ◆ Living next to a place of worship, school, hospital, or fire station can cause health risks.

- ◆ Living on gently sloping or flat terrain is better than living on a hill or a steep incline.

- ◆ The shape of your lot and house affects how vital sheng qi is able to accumulate and settle.

- ◆ To ensure a restful sleep, your bed should be supported by a wall and positioned away from doors and windows.

- ◆ To increase productivity, your back should be supported by a wall; the desk should be stationed away from doors and windows.

Part 4

Feng Shui Mechanics

A bit more complex, but well worth your while, Part 4 teaches you the Flying Star System. Here you'll use those mysterious numbers correlated to the five phases and eight trigrams. Although numerology is the gist of this method, mathematics isn't involved. So put away your calculator and put on your thinking cap. Understanding a number's inherent nature and its life cycle, among other things, can be a tricky business.

Part 4 also gives you step-by-step instructions about performing a Flying Star analysis. You'll learn what the number combinations mean and how you can remedy or enhance the qi in a particular area to encourage favorable events and discourage unfavorable ones. You'll find this sophisticated technique interesting and enlightening.

The Flying Stars, Part 1

In This Chapter

- ◆ It's all in the stars: introducing the Flying Star system
- ◆ The Hetu and Luoshu diagrams and what they mean to you
- ◆ The Magic Square of Three
- ◆ The significance of the number nine in cultures throughout the world

You've come this far. You've learned the three fundamental principles governing feng shui: yin and yang, the five phases, and the eight trigrams. You've learned about your ming gua—your innate character. You've learned how to evaluate the area surrounding your house, apartment, and office. You've learned how to properly situate your bed to gain a restful sleep. And you've learned how to situate your desk to inspire productivity.

Now you're ready to learn Flying Star, a sophisticated technique that uses factors associated with both time and space to describe your dwelling's qi. Yet, before you apply this method, you first must acquire some background knowledge. This will help you to better understand this complex, yet fascinating system of feng shui. This chapter's all about learning the history behind the stars, or numbers, that govern your well-being.

What Is the Flying Star System?

Flying Star feng shui studies how time and space affect your health, wealth, and relationships with others. In fact, time and space are like two sides of a coin. One cannot exist without the other. For example, your body (your own personal space) changes over time. Everyone and everything moves through ceaseless cycles of birth, growth, decay, and death. The time your home was born and the time you were born are important considerations in a Flying Star analysis. The Chinese believe the first breath you take at birth determines your character and destiny. In the same way, when the foundation is set and the roof is affixed, your home is born. It, too, has a core personality. But remember, despite your inherent character, you still change! Therefore, an inherently good home will encounter times of misfortune. An inherently inauspicious home will encounters times of fortune. We all go through lucky and unlucky times!

Flying Star is a mathematical technique that uses the numbers 1 to 9. The magnetic orientation (space) of the dwelling and the time it was built yield a numeric qi map. The combination of numbers is interpreted. Favorable number combinations are enhanced (a 4-1 and a 9-8 combination brings romance and marriage, for example), and unfavorable number combinations are discouraged (a 7-5 brings financial loss and a 2-1 brings divorce, for example). Liken the process to an astrological reading of your home. Besides the time dimension of the stars, space also plays an important role in an analysis. Although you'll learn to install one of the five phases of qi (fire, earth, metal, water, and wood) to enhance or correct a specific number combination, you must also consider how the exterior environment, layout of the home, and furniture placement (among other things) influence the building's destiny and character. The mechanics of Flying Star feng shui with become clearer with each succeeding chapter.

In Chinese, Flying Star is called Xuankong Feixing, which means "Time and Space Flying Stars." Although there exists no textual evidence to support the system's authorship, Flying Star was probably developed during the Tang dynasty (618–907 C.E.) and no later than the Song dynasty (960–1279 C.E.). Jiang Da Hong, an officer in the Ming dynasty (1368–1644 C.E.), is credited as being the first feng shui master on record to use Flying Star.

Wise Words

Flying Star is a sophisticated and complex system of analyzing how time and space affect a building. The magnetic orientation of the dwelling, along with the year the home was built, are important factors that determine the innate character of the house.

Ancient Beginnings

You might be wondering about the word "star" in Flying Star. Are the numbers 1 to 9 affiliated with nine celestial stars? Yes and no. The stars in question are the seven stars that form the Big Dipper (Beidou), plus the two adjacent stars at its handle. Like the principle of the five phases, it's not the object (the stars) that is important but the movement and transformation of its associated qi.

The Flying Star system is based on mathematical patterns in nature, the macrocosmic world directly influencing us, the microcosmic world. As above, so below. These observations gave rise to two specific mathematical diagrams of the universe, as you are about to learn.

The Hetu River Map

The fifth century B.C.E. text called the *Shangshu* (*Classic of History*) tells how Fuxi, one of China's legendary figures who is credited with inventing the bagua (the eight fundamental trigrams), among other things, received a gift from heaven. But, it was no ordinary gift, for it described an ideal world where all is in perfect harmony. According to legend, the gift appeared as a pattern of black and white dots on the flank of a mystical dragon-horse emerging from the Yellow River. Hence, the diagram is also known as the *Hetu* (also spelled Ho-t'u) or *River Map*. In the following diagram of the Hetu, the markings illustrate structure and balance, with the white dots representing yang, and the black dots representing yin. This scheme becomes clearer when numbers are applied to the dot patterns. For example, the 7 white dots found at the top of the diagram correspond to the number 7 in the numeric structure of the Hetu. The 2 black dots beneath the 7 white dots correspond to the numeric value of 2, and so forth. Disregarding the central 5 white dots and surrounding 10 black ones, you can see how the odd (yang) numbers are perfectly balanced by an opposing even (yin) number: 1 (yang) is opposite 2 (yin); 3 (yang) is opposite 4 (yin); 6 (yin) is opposite 7 (yang); and 8 (yin) is opposite 9 (yang).

Upon closer examination (again, disregarding the central 5), notice how all of the odd (yang) numbers and even (yin) numbers add up to 20: $1 + 3 + 7 + 9 = 20$; $2 + 4 + 6 + 8 = 20$.

Wise Words

The **Hetu** or **River Map** is a pattern of black (yin) and white (yang) dots purportedly found on a fantastic dragon-horse emerging from the Yellow River. The Hetu symbolizes the ideal world.

The Hetu River Map.

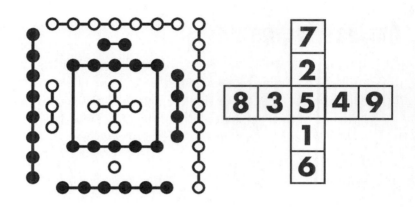

Does this diagram of an ideal, perfect, and sedentary world remind you of anything? Perhaps the Before Heaven sequence of trigrams that we discussed in Chapter 7? Although the Hetu diagram was correlated with the trigram sequence in the Song dynasty (960–1279 C.E.), there is much debate about whether this correlation is meaningful. In fact, some contemporary scholars believe there is no connection between the Hetu number sequence and the Before Heaven trigram sequence.

So, you might ask, what's so special about the Hetu diagram? The answer is its link with the turtle's offering, the Luoshu diagram.

The Luoshu Writing

A second gift was bestowed on Yu the Great, founder of China's first dynasty Xia (c. 2100–1600 B.C.E.) This one was another pattern of black (yin) and white (yang) dots inscribed on a turtle's shell, an arrangement that came to be known as the *Luo River Writing*. Simply called the Luoshu (also spelled Lo-shu), this diagram was correlated to the After Heaven sequence of trigrams (again see Chapter 7 for a reminder) conceivably as early as the Han dynasty (206 B.C.E.–220 C.E.), some 2,000 years after its purported discovery by Yu. As a reminder, the After Heaven sequence of trigrams denotes motion, transformation, and interaction of natural and human qi forces. The Luoshu/After Heaven sequence is the antithesis of the motionless Hetu and Before Heaven sequence of trigrams.

Wise Words

Also known as the **Luo River Writing,** the **Luoshu** is a pattern of black (yin) and white (yang) dots said to be inscribed on a turtle's shell. The Luoshu correlates to the After Heaven sequence of trigrams denoting motion, transformation, and interaction of natural and human qi.

We all know these diagrams couldn't have really appeared on the backs of two animals. So what's the real story? The fact is, the origins of the Hetu and Luoshu sequence of numbers are unknown. Although their antiquity is unquestioned, contemporary scholars can't prove the Luoshu existed before the time of Confucius (551–479 B.C.E.). This is because the Luoshu is first mentioned in the *Confucian Analects* (sayings of Confucius compiled by his students). The origin of the Hetu diagram, on the other hand, is a bit more mysterious. It isn't mentioned until the early Han dynasty, some 400 years after Confucius. And, the configuration of numbers it represents can't be dated until the Song dynasty (960–1279 C.E.), some 1,000 years later. So, until new discoveries are made, or scholars put forth new evidence, we will never know the diagrams' true inventor(s) or date of origin.

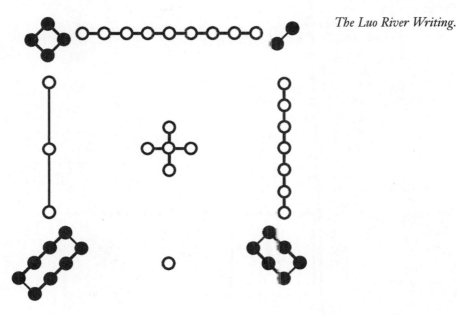

The Luo River Writing.

Despite the mysterious origins of the Hetu and Luoshu diagrams, we can surmise they were a product of astute observations by the ancients—that they recognized and recorded patterns made manifest in the celestial heavens, patterns that revealed the secrets of the universe. The legend of the miraculous appearance of the Hetu and Luoshu points to their power. The fact that the ancient Chinese had forgotten what they meant by the time scholars began to analyze the diagrams increases their mysterious nature. Nevertheless, because they are considered magical and because their meanings were elusive, they were thought to be divine in origin.

The Magic Square of Three

Just as the black (yin) and white (yang) dots of the Hetu correspond to a numeric value, so, too, do the Luoshu's dots. Referring back to the illustration of the Luo River Writing, look at the top configuration of dots: A pattern of 4 black dots and 2 black dots is separated by a pattern of 9 white dots. Numerically, the dot values equal 4, 9, and 2, respectively—a factor that is illustrated in the following diagram of the Magic Square of Three. Before you continue, take a minute to consider how all the other dot patterns correspond to the numbers in the following illustration.

Wise Words

The **Magic Square of Three** is considered magical because 3 cells along any diagonal, vertical, or horizontal line add up to 15. The Magic Square of Three represents the numeric value of the black (yin) and white (yang) dots of the Luoshu.

The Luoshu is also known as the *Magic Square of Three*. This is because 3 cells add up to 15 along any diagonal, vertical, or horizontal line:

Diagonally	4 + 5 + 6 = 15
	2 + 5 + 8 = 15
Vertically	4 + 3 + 8 = 15
	9 + 5 + 1 = 15
	2 + 7 + 6 = 15
Horizontally	4 + 9 + 2 = 15
	3 + 5 + 7 = 15
	8 + 1 + 6 = 15

The Magic Square of Three.

4	9	2
3	5	7
8	1	6

The magic doesn't stop here. Like the After Heaven trigram sequence, the Luoshu diagram moves, symbolizing a world in flux, in constant transformation. Although the diagram is square, it is also inherently cyclic. How so, you ask? First, connect the 2 pairs of odd (yang) numbers: 1 and 9 and 3 and 7. Next, draw a line through the 2 northern cells 6 and 1. In the same fashion, draw lines through the 2 eastern cells 8 and 3, the 2 southern cells 4 and 9, and the 2 western cells 2 and 7. The end result should look similar to the following illustration, a counterclockwise swastika—each arm connecting the 9 cells of the Magic Square.

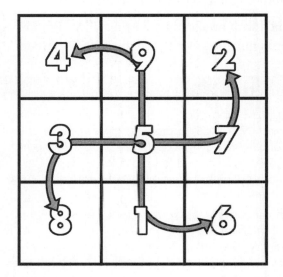

The cyclic nature of the Magic Square of Three.

Notice how the odd (yang) numbers forming the cross and the 4 extending arms of even (yin) numbers add up to 10: 9 + 1 = 10, 3 + 7 = 10, 4 + 6 = 10, and 2 + 8 = 10. The sums differ by a factor of 5, the number of the central cell. Impressed? There's more. Upon closer examination, you'll notice that central number 5 is the factor that links the extending pairs:

> 1 (north) and 6 (northwest), or 1 + 5 = 6
>
> 3 (east) and 8 (northeast), or 3 + 5 = 8
>
> 4 (southeast) and 9 (south), or 4 + 5 = 9
>
> 2 (southwest) and 7 (west), or 2 + 5 = 7

Finally, you'll notice these directional pairs are none other than the arms forming the Hetu cross! This connection suggests the Hetu is probably a by-product of the Luoshu diagram.

You might be wondering why the swastika revolves counterclockwise. This is because the clockwise movement expresses passing time, whereas the counterclockwise movement expresses future time. Richard Wilhelm in his preface to the *I Ching or Book of Changes* (Princeton University Press, 1950) explains it this way: "The usual clockwise movement, cumulative and expanding as time goes on, determines the events that are passing; an opposite, backward movement, folding up and contracting as time goes, through which the seeds of the future take form. To know this movement is to know the future. In figurative terms, if we understand how a tree is contracted into a seed, we understand the future unfolding of the seed into a tree."

Feng shui is concerned with predicting the probability of future events. Moreover, feng shui seeks to promote good events and dissuade bad events.

Feng Facts

Today, the swastika is a symbol widely associated with anti-Semitism and Hitler's Third Reich. But did you know the swastika predates Hitler's empire of evil? That it is one of the oldest symbols of humankind? Virtually every ancient culture has a remarkably similar version of what is generally accepted to be a solar emblem. The swastika has been used by the indigenous peoples of North, Central, and South America, and the French, Greek, Swiss, Japanese, and Irish.

However, many scholars believe the swastika was probably first used by the Hindus. In fact, the word swastika comes from the Sanskrit *svastika* meaning "lucky" and "fortunate." The most distinctly identifiable ancient use of the swastika was by the Jains, a Hindu religious doctrine closely resembling Buddhism, founded about 500 B.C.E. The Jains used the symbol as an emblem of Buddha. Always represented with its arms in a counterclockwise fashion, the swastika was introduced to China in about 200 B.C.E. The Chinese called the swastika Lei Wen, meaning "thunder scroll," a name suggesting it was a symbol associated with celestial activity.

How did Hitler contaminate such a kindly sign? Actually, the Viennese racial theorist and founder of the Order of the New Templars, Dr. Jorge Lanz von Liebenfels (a.k.a. Adolf Lanz), adopted the swastika in 1907. Symbolizing his irrational belief in establishing a pure master race, the swastika was probably mistaken by Lanz to be a symbol of Germanic origin. The clockwise version adopted by Hitler in 1920 was designed by a dentist, Dr. Freidrich Krohn.

The Nine Imperial Palaces

The nine cells, or nine halls, of the Magic Square describe the layout of the Imperial Palace in China, what venerated scholar Joseph Needham in *Science and Civilization in China* (Cambridge University Press, 1956) calls "the mystical temple-dwelling which the emperor was supposed to frequent, carrying out the rites appropriate to the season."

What does this mean exactly? Well, the emperor, the Son of Heaven, petitioned heaven (composed of a group of his illustrious forebears) on behalf of his people, rendering thanks and appreciation for fine weather, good health, and prosperity. It was also his duty to ask heaven to continue its benevolence. Specifically, requests were made for the upcoming year. Each rite would be carried out in the appropriate hall of the emperor's palace. Each hall corresponded to the one of the twelve lunar months. Each lunar month lasted approximately 29½ days; each lunar year, 360 days.

But there are 9 cells and 12 months. How does this figure? Good question. Basically, it worked like this. The emperor would live in each of the central rooms (north, south, east, and west) for one month. Because the corner rooms corresponded to two directions (for example, southeast = south and east), the emperor would live in these rooms for two months. So, during the spring, he would presumably live in the northeast room for one month, the east room for one month, and the southeast room for one month. In the summer, he would spend one more month in the southeast room, followed by a month in the south room, and a month in the southwest room, and so forth. Thus, the emperor was able to complete a tour of the lunar calendar, cycling around each of the nine halls.

As if this wasn't enough, the emperor also had to symbolically harmonize with each season's distinct affiliations (color, animal, smell, sound, cereal, and so on). For example, in summer, the emperor donned red garments and feasted on peas and chicken. In autumn, he dressed in white and ate sesame and dog. In winter, he wore black and ate millet and pork. And, in spring, the emperor chose green clothing and ate mutton and wheat. Sounds exhausting, doesn't it? Such were the duties and obligations of imperial privilege.

Here's to the Nines

Before we move on to providing step-by-step instructions for performing a Flying Stars audit, let's explore for a moment the significance of the number nine, the highest single-digit number. Interestingly, nine is revered globally, its symbology strikingly similar. It symbolizes completeness, the end of a cycle before returning to number one. To the Chinese, the number nine represents heaven and perfection. It is the supreme yang (male) number. But, that's not all. Here are a few more examples of how the number nine has been incorporated into Chinese culture:

◆ In early Chinese mythology, the number nine figures often: nine fields of heaven, nine terraces of the sacred mountain Kunlun, and nine songs of heaven.

◆ *The Book of Rituals*, compiled in the later Han dynasty, speaks of nine ceremonies: puberty rite for men, wedding, audience, ambassadorship, burial, sacrifice, hospitality, drinking, and military.

- The center of Peking (now Beijing) has eight roads leading to the collective ninth, the city.

- The Forbidden City is said to have 9,999 rooms.

- Nine dragons are incorporated into the emperor's throne.

- Nine mythical animals adorn palace and temple buildings.

- Many pagodas have nine stories.

The number nine is significant in other cultures, too: In Egypt, nine, or the higher power of three, was very important to the religious and cosmological order. A group of nine gods was called a pesedjet, or ennead. Flip back a couple of pages to the illustration of the swastika formation inside the Magic Square. The cross connecting the odd numbers (1 and 9, 3 and 7), together with the "X" connecting the even numbers (4 and 6, 8 and 2), forms the 3000 B.C.E. Egyptian hieroglyph for "heaven."

To the Hebrews, the ninth letter of their alphabet is Tet. Tet symbolizes completeness. At the next level, the Zadi (90) represents righteousness, and the completeness of the human spirit. The final Zadi (900) represents the outer world.

In Christianity, hell has nine gates (three of brass, three of iron, and three of adamantine). Furthermore, the hierarchy of hell is divided into nine sections. Also, there are nine choirs of angels in heaven. Christ died at the ninth hour.

To the Bahá'í, nine represents culmination, comprehensiveness. In the numerology connected with the Arabic alphabet, nine is the numeric value of the letters making up the name "Baha," the revealer of the Bahá'í faith—considered by its followers to be the ninth existing independent religion.

Western numerologists believe if the total number of letters in your first name is nine, you are a person of great talent. You possess global consciousness.

In sorcery, a magic circle must be nine feet in diameter. Magical formulas generally must be repeated nine times. The human gestation period is nine months. Cats are said to have nine lives. We dress to the "nines." Mathematicians check their calculations by "casting out nines." There are nine judges on the Supreme Court, nine players on a baseball team. Shopkeepers will forever charge $9.99. Finally, who can forget the Beatles' song, "Revolution 9"?

Feng Shui and Nine

In feng shui, the nine cells of the Luoshu are connected by the counterclockwise swastika. Also, the number nine enhances the number it's combined with, as you shall soon see. What does this mean? If the number nine combines with an auspicious number (you'll learn all about favorable and unfavorable numbers in Chapter 13), expect the possibility of promotion, financial gain, and happy events. However, if nine combines with an inauspicious number, beware! The threat of eye disease, fire, litigation, and insanity is likely.

In the next chapter, you'll learn how to determine the sitting and facing sides of your dwelling. You'll also create a to-scale floor plan that you'll divide into eight equal wedges.

The Least You Need to Know

- Flying Star is a system that calculates the qi pattern of a building according to the way the dwelling is oriented and the date of construction.

- The Hetu diagram of black and white dots represents the ideal world.

- The Luoshu diagram of black and white dots represents motion, transformation, and the interaction of qi.

- The Chinese believe the Magic Square of Three is a divine gift. Each number along any diagonal, vertical, or horizontal line adds to 15.

- The number nine is significant in many cultures around the world.

Chapter 12

The Flying Stars, Part 2

In This Chapter

- Using a compass to determine your dwelling's sitting and facing directions
- Understanding the 24 mountains or directions
- Assembling a floor plan of your dwelling
- Dividing your dwelling into eight equal sections

In this chapter, you'll learn how to locate your home or apartment's sitting and facing side. Once you determine where your dwelling sits, you'll take a compass reading to determine the trigram and mountain to which your dwelling belongs. Don't worry, it's not as complicated as it seems. We'll provide step-by-step instructions, making the process a snap!

Next, you'll learn to divide your living and/or working space into eight equal portions that are then subdivided into three additional portions. Have ready your compass, your protractor, and your ruler. Please see Chapter 1 for more information about these items.

Determine Your Home's Sitting and Facing Directions

Your house's trigram is determined by its sitting direction. The sitting direction is the direction your house leans against. Imagine your house sitting in an armchair. Now, what direction corresponds with its backside? This is pretty easy to figure out. It's the side corresponding to the backyard or alley.

Once you've located the sitting or backside of your dwelling, the facing side is magnetically opposite. Don't allow the position of the front door to cloud your judgment. In classical feng shui, the front door plays no role in determining the sitting and facing sides of the building or unit in question. Using the chair analogy again, if you're sitting in a chair, your back represents the sitting direction and your chest represents the facing direction, right? Now, say that your face represents the main entrance. Although the main entrance usually correlates with the facing side, in some cases, the front door might represent neither the sitting nor the facing side. For example, if you turn your head (front door) to the right, your chest or facing side hasn't changed. Get the idea?

There are many factors to consider when determining your home's orientation, but again, the fundamental rule to remember is that the *sitting and facing directions are magnetically opposite*. Here are some general guidelines to keep in mind as you determine your home's orientation:

- The backyard corresponds to the sitting direction.

- A back alleyway usually corresponds to the sitting direction.

- The main entrance is usually on the facing direction.

- The street address corresponds to the facing direction.

- Traffic is heaviest on the facing direction.

- Large windows might indicate the facing direction.

- Room location may help determine the sitting and facing directions. Usually, the living/family rooms (the yang areas) are located on the facing side, while the bedrooms and kitchen (the yin areas) are located on the sitting side.

Understanding how to locate the sitting and facing directions is the most important aspect of performing a precise feng shui reading. But try not to overanalyze each situation. Instead, *feel* how the dwelling is oriented. Use your common sense. Go with your gut. Determining your home's sitting and facing directions requires keen observation, practice, groundwork, and patience.

Determine Your Apartment's Facing Direction

For an apartment, determining the sitting side is a little tricky because the sitting and facing sides of the unit might differ from the sitting and facing sides of the building. Some apartments might share the same facing side as the building. Others might face the backside of the building. Some apartments might face an inner courtyard. Others might face a neighboring building.

We suggest you imagine that your apartment is a stand-alone house. Disregarding the location of your entry door, where would you place the front yard and street? Where would the backyard be located? Now, with this imaginary picture in mind, focus on finding the facing side of your unit-cum-house. If you have large windows and/or a view, this usually corresponds to the front or facing side. For most apartment-dwellers, this area is the living room—the yang side of the unit where a lot of activity takes place. The area magnetically opposite the facing side is the sitting side. Although it's irrelevant what rooms are located there, usually the sitting or backside contains the bedrooms—the yin areas of the unit.

The same guidelines apply for finding the facing side of an office unit.

Using a Compass to Determine Your Dwelling's Trigram

You can obtain an accurate reading of your home and apartment unit's sitting and facing directions using an ordinary Western-style compass. For our purposes here, we'll use the Silva Explorer Model 203 compass that's pictured in Chapter 1. (See that chapter for more detailed instructions regarding compass selection.) If you are unfamiliar with using a compass, spend a few minutes to become comfortable with it. Although it will probably be obvious to you, a little patience and caution will prevent inaccurate readings.

To determine your dwelling's trigram, refer to the following illustration as you follow these simple procedures.

To determine the facing and sitting direction:

1. Stand in front of your house, the side corresponding to the facing side. Make sure that your back is perfectly square

Master Class

To ensure an accurate compass reading, remove any metal adornments—including watches, cufflinks, belt buckles, and jewelry—that may influence the compass's magnetic arrow. Also, make sure that you distance yourself from parking meters, cars, and even the building itself. Generally, a distance of 5 feet should be sufficient to ensure an accurate reading.

with the house. If you live in an apartment, you must take a compass reading *outside* the apartment building. Stand on the sidewalk in front of the building. If the front side of your unit shares the same facing as the building, stand with your back perfectly square with the building (as shown in the following illustration). If the front side of your unit faces a neighboring building or an inner courtyard, stand perpendicular to your apartment building. If your unit faces the backside of the building, stand facing the apartment building.

2. Holding your compass at waist level, rotate the compass dial until the red portion of the magnetic arrow aligns with north.

3. Read the compass grade at the index line (labeled the "bearing" line on the Silva Explorer Model 203). This is the facing direction. The grade magnetically opposite is the sitting direction.

4. Repeat steps 1, 2, and 3, taking a reading at two other locations parallel to the sitting side of your home as indicated by B and C in the following illustration. (If you live in an apartment, you might not be able to do this—especially if you live in a densely populated area like New York City.) Your compass reading should be the same. If it fluctuates, which can happen particularly in urban areas where metal parking meters, street signs, building material, and automobiles hinder an accurate reading, we suggest using two different compasses. If your building is on a parallel line with a neighboring one, take a reading of that building, too. Go with the common compass reading.

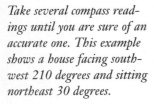

Take several compass readings until you are sure of an accurate one. This example shows a house facing southwest 210 degrees and sitting northeast 30 degrees.

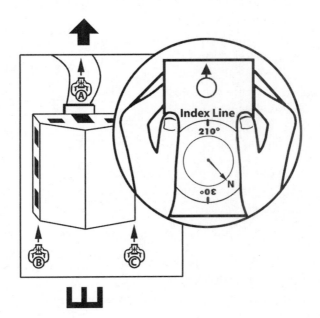

Space: The 24 Mountains

As you learned in Chapter 7, each of the eight trigrams and their correlative directions hold a different kind of qi that describe a building's inherent personality. In Flying Star methodology, the 8 fundamental directions are divided into 3 components each for a total of 24 directions (8 trigrams × 3 parts = 24 directions). Called the *24 mountains*, these finer directional distinctions, coupled with the time your home was constructed, hold a lot of valuable information, as you shall soon learn.

Wise Words _____

The **24 mountains** or directions of a luopan compass derive from the 8 fundamental trigrams: Each trigram constitutes 45 degrees of the compass (8 trigrams × 45 degrees = 360 degrees). Each trigram is subdivided into 3 equal parts of 15 degrees each (3 parts × 15 degrees = 45 degrees). The total number of subdivided parts (3 parts × 8 trigrams) comprises the 24 mountains, each of which has a Chinese name.

A simplified luopan compass.

Referring to the illustration of a simplified luopan compass, let's take a closer look. Beginning with the Kan trigram at the bottom, notice that this northern trigram is divided into three mountains: Ren (north 1) at 337.5 degrees to 352.5 degrees, Zi (north 2) at 352.5 degrees to 7.5 degrees, and Gui (north 3) at 7.5 degrees to 22.5 degrees. Moving clockwise around the luopan, the northeastern trigram Gen follows. It's comprised of Chou (northeast 1) at 22.5 to 37.5 degrees, Gen (northeast 2) at 37.5 degrees to 52.5 degrees, and Yin (northeast 3) at 52.5 degrees to 67.5 degrees. The 24 mountains and their magnetic affiliations continue around the luopan in this fashion.

But why are some mountains black and some white? Simply, the mountains in black are yang; the white ones are yin. We include these designations for the sake of completeness.

Do You Know Where Your House Is?

In the system of the Flying Stars, it is not enough to determine to which trigram your home belongs. Here, we need to be more exact. Referring to the first illustration in this chapter of the figure taking a compass reading of his home, the house sits ⊔⊔ 30 degrees northeast and faces ⬆ 210 degrees southwest. Based on the sitting direction, the house belongs to the Gen trigram. Next, you need to determine what type of Gen house you have: Chou, Gen or Yin. In this case, the mountain is Chou, sitting ⊔⊔ NE1 and facing ⬆ SW1. Let's take another example. Say your home sits at 330 degrees. It belongs to the Qian trigram. The dwelling's mountain is Hai (322.5 degrees to 337.5 degrees), sitting ⊔⊔ NW3 and facing ⬆ SE3. Get the idea?

Feng Alert _____

If the compass reading corresponding to your home is on the boundary between two mountains (at 292.5, 307.5, or 322.5, for example), you might want to find a digital compass that can provide a more precise reading. If the reading is still on the line, then you cannot proceed. In these cases, there is a special treatment that is beyond the scope of this book.

The Luopan Charted

The following table shows a charted version of the luopan compass. You might find it easier on your eye than the circular representation.

Before we proceed, please determine to which mountain your home sits in and faces toward. For our purposes, after you have determined to which mountain your home corresponds, the magnetic designations are no longer needed. Record your information as follows:

Example: My home belongs to the Dui trigram. It sits 🔲 in W2 and faces ⬆ toward E2.

My home belongs to the _____ trigram. It sits 🔲 in ____ and faces ⬆ toward ____.

You have now determined the magnetic space your home occupies.

Trigram	Mountain	Sitting Direction	Compass Designation	Facing Direction	Compass Designation
KAN	REN	N1	337.5° - 352.5°	S1	157.5° - 172.5°
	ZI	N2	352.5° - 7.5°	S2	172.5° - 187.5°
	GUI	N3	7.5° - 22.5°	S3	187.5° - 202.5°
GEN	CHOU	NE1	22.5° - 37.5°	SW1	202.5° - 217.5°
	GEN	NE2	37.5° - 52.5°	SW2	217.5° - 232.5°
	YIN	NE3	52.5° - 67.5°	SW3	232.5° - 247.5°
ZHEN	JIA	E1	67.5° - 82.5°	W1	247.5° - 262.5°
	MAO	E2	82.5° - 97.5°	W2	262.5° - 277.5°
	YI	E3	97.5° - 112.5°	W3	277.5° - 292.5°
XUN	CHEN	SE1	112.5° - 127.5°	NW1	292.5° - 307.5°
	XUN	SE2	127.5° - 142.5°	NW2	307.5° - 322.5°
	SI	SE3	142.5° - 157.5°	NW3	322.5° - 337.5°
LI	BING	S1	157.5° - 172.5°	N1	337.5° - 352.5°
	WU	S2	172.5° - 187.5°	N2	352.5° - 7.5°
	DING	S3	187.5° - 202.5°	N3	7.5° - 22.5°
KUN	WEI	SW1	202.5° - 217.5°	NE1	22.5° - 37.5°
	KUN	SW2	217.5° - 232.5°	NE2	37.5° - 52.5°
	SHEN	SW3	232.5° - 247.5°	NE3	52.5° - 67.5°
DUI	GENG	W1	247.5° - 262.5°	E1	67.5° - 82.5°
	YOU	W2	262.5° - 277.5°	E2	82.5° - 97.5°
	XIN	W3	277.5° - 292.5°	E3	97.5° - 112.5°
QIAN	XU	NW1	292.5° - 307.5°	SE1	112.5° - 127.5°
	QIAN	NW2	307.5° - 322.5°	SE2	127.5° - 142.5°
	HAI	NW3	322.5° - 337.5°	SE3	142.5° - 157.5°

Assembling a Simple Floor Plan

If you're lucky enough to have a to-scale floor plan of your home, you're ahead of the game. But most of you probably don't. Assembling one is no big deal. Your goal is to draw a *simple* plan with the sitting direction oriented on the *bottom* of the page. To get a better idea of your task at hand, refer to the following illustration. Your floor plan should include the following:

- All exterior and interior entrances and doorways
- All windows
- All beds
- All desks

To avoid wasting time, don't try to eyeball the measurements. Why not? Because ultimately, you're going to divide the whole of your dwelling into eight equal wedges. An inaccurate measurement will ensure an incorrect analysis of which areas hold positive and negative qi. Instead, spend an extra 15 minutes to measure the length and width of your dwelling. You can do this in a few ways:

- Get one of those nifty electronic measuring devices found in most hardware or building supply stores. The one we use is the Starrett DigiTape, which costs about $24. All you have to do is run the tape measure. The measurement will illuminate in the display window.

- Use a plain old tape measure or ruler. It'll take a couple more minutes, but what's the hurry?

- Use the tried-and-true, one-foot-in-front-of-the-other method. It's a little less exact, but it gets the job done. Counting one step as a measurement of one foot in length, just place your right heel parallel to the wall, then place your left foot at the right's toe. Continue walking, heel to toe, counting the number of steps to the end of the wall.

We suggest first measuring the length of each room. Begin with the back wall connected to the sitting side of your dwelling. Jot down its measurement. Next, measure the room adjacent to the length of the wall you just measured. (Don't forget to consider the wall space separating each room.) Jot down its measurement. Continue this procedure until the last room adjacent to the length of the wall in question is measured. Repeat this procedure to obtain the width of each room. Based on these measurements, you now can draw a simple to-scale floor plan. We suggest using a pencil as you might have to make changes.

If your home is more than one story or if it is a split-level home, you must draw a plan for each floor or level. Any part of your dwelling that falls under the roof and is contained within the main frame of the house is considered part of the house and should be included in your floor plan. This includes an attached garage and an enclosed porch. If you have an outside porch or a balcony, you can include these areas in your floor plan, but they do not count when you proceed to determine the center of your home.

The next step is to find the center of the house by dividing the total length and width by two. For example, if the total length is 60 feet, the midpoint is 30 feet. If the total width is 45 feet, the midpoint is 22½ feet. The point where the midsections converge corresponds to the center of your dwelling. Mark the center of your home. Now, orient your floor plan so that the sitting side is flush with the bottom of the page (as shown in the following illustration). Note the sitting and facing directions using the sitting **⊔⊔** and facing ⬆ symbols. Note the sitting and facing degrees (as illustrated). Your final step is to label the plan. Inside, label each room. Outside, label each of the eight directions (not shown in this illustration).

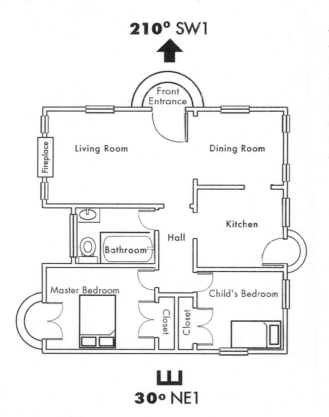

210° SW1

A simple floor plan. Note the sitting direction is oriented on the bottom of the page; and the plan is labeled both inside and outside. This is a Gen house, belonging to the mountain Chou. It sits NE1 (30 degrees) and faces SW1 at 210 degrees.

⊔⊔
30° NE1

If you're having trouble finding the center of your dwelling because it is an odd shape, keep reading! If you found your dwelling's center, skip the next section. It's now time to divide your home into eight equal sections. You'll need a clear plastic 6-inch, 360-degree protractor with half-inch gradations to help with this task. We recommend the Mars College protractor, found in any office supply store.

Great Grids!

But, you ask, what if my house isn't square? What if it's a rectangle, an L-shape, or it has some funky alcoves? What if my house is missing a section? The following illustrations show some examples of irregularly shaped houses divided properly.

In the following figure, illustration A shows a house with a missing section. Is this bad luck? No! A missing section is a missing section. It is not unlucky. End of story.

Illustration B also has sections missing to varying degrees. Again, you can't make something out of nothing. To find the center of a house with a trapezoid shape, connect the midpoint of the upper and lower sides. Because the house is broader at the base (or sitting side), the center is one third to halfway from the base.

Proper division of irregularly shaped houses.

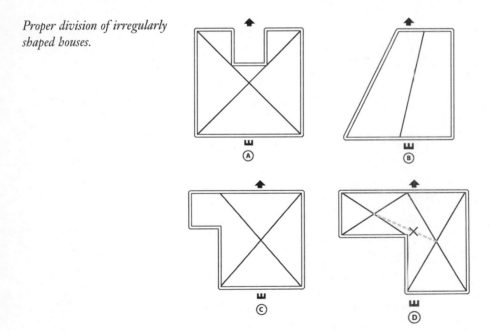

Illustration C shows a house with a small extension. If an extended area is one quarter or less than the main body of the house, then the extension becomes part of the wedge in question, as in illustration C. However, if an extended area is greater than one quarter of the main body of the house, then it is representative of an L-shaped house. Follow the instructions provided for illustration D below.

Illustration D shows an L-shaped house. To locate the center of the house, first find the center of each wing. The center of the house will be along the line joining the centers of the wings. But be careful. If the two wings comprising the L-shape are equal, the center would be the exact midpoint of this line. However, in this example, the north-south wing is bigger than its smaller east-west counterpart. Therefore, the center will be closer to center of the larger rectangle. Represented by an "x," the point marks the center for the whole house.

Master Class

Some feng shui masters divide a house by creating a grid of nine equal cells—an idea that conforms to the nine-celled Luoshu numeric diagram. Although this is an acceptable practice, we believe the pie-shaped wedges conform to the movement of qi through the perpetual cycle of nature (birth, growth, decay, and death). Also, as you'll learn in Chapter 13, the Chinese believe time is cyclic rather than linear.

A Pie Is Eight Slices

The next step is to divide your floor plan into eight equal sections corresponding to the eight fundamental directions (trigrams):

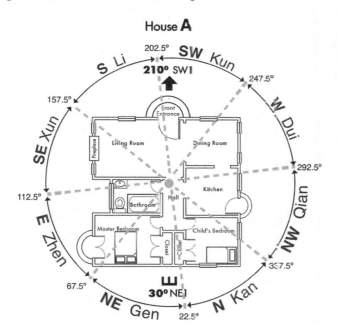

A properly divided Gen dwelling ☶ *NE1 and* ⬆ *SW1 at 210 degrees.*

1. Overlay your protractor onto your newly created floor plan. Reading the inside grades that ascend around the circular instrument, align the facing degree with the facing of your dwelling (as shown in the House A illustration).

2. With a pencil, mark the point where each of the eight directions begin and end (as illustrated). Label each direction. It is not necessary to notate each direction's corresponding trigram or the degrees dividing each wedge. We include this information for learning purposes only. Before you proceed, it might be a good idea to compare the protractor with the figure of the simplified luopan compass presented earlier in this chapter. (If you want to purchase a luopan, please go to Joseph Yu's website at www.astro-fengshui.com.)

3. Now, connect the dots to form eight equal wedges.

The House B illustration shows the same house sitting NE2 and facing SW2 at 225 degrees.

A properly divided Gen dwelling ⼭ *NE2 and* ⬆ *SW2 at 225 degrees.*

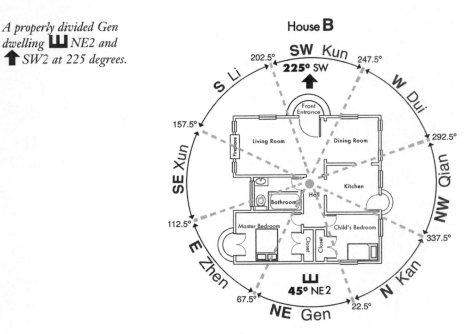

The House C illustration shows the same apartment sitting NE3 and facing SW3 at 240 degrees.

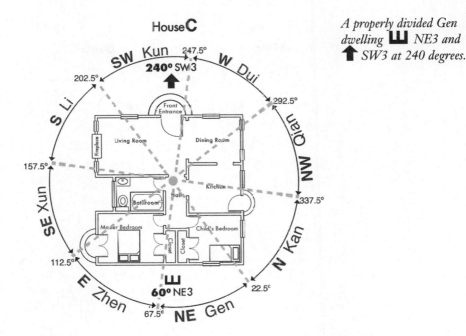

House **C**

A properly divided Gen dwelling 山 *NE3 and* ↑ *SW3 at 240 degrees.*

Taken together, you can see that depending on the facing degree, the sections are oriented somewhat differently for each of the three types of Gen dwellings (mountains Chou, Gen, and Yin).

Now that you've properly divided and labeled your house or apartment unit, we bet you're eager to analyze and remedy your dwelling's qi! Well, not just yet. In the next chapter, you'll learn about the Chinese concept of time—specifically, how it relates to human events, characteristics, and health.

The Least You Need to Know

- A dwelling's sitting and facing directions can sometimes be difficult to ascertain.

- A dwelling's trigram is determined by its sitting direction. The facing direction is magnetically opposite the sitting direction.

- The sitting direction is determined by a compass reading.

- In a Flying Star reading, 24 mountains or directions are considered.

- Creating a to-scale floor plan ensures an accurate analysis.

The Flying Stars, Part 3

In This Chapter

◆ Time: nine periods of 20 years each

◆ The personalities of the nine stars

◆ The ruling number

◆ What we can expect from Period 8 (2004 to 2024)

In this chapter, you'll learn about time. You'll understand that the nine stars or numbers of the Luoshu relate to specific periods of time. And that, like a person, each star has a personality that changes over time. Also, new to this edition of the book, you'll learn how Period 8, a 20-year cycle of time that began on February 4, 2004, impacts your destiny.

Time: Three Cycles and Nine Periods

To Westerners, the Chinese concept of time may seem very peculiar. Time isn't linear, but spiral-shaped. Following the laws of yin and yang, time repeats itself. Because time repeats, events are also likely to repeat. This idea is the central premise of the *Yijing*, considered the oldest book of divination still in use. Basically, when you ask the oracle a question, you are projecting your situation into a time-space model, the *Yijing*. Because your situation has occurred before, the *Yijing* can foretell a probable solution.

To learn more about the *Yijing* and how you can use it to help you solve a dilemma, concern, or problem, please see *The Complete Idiot's Guide to the I Ching* (Alpha Books, 2002).

Referring to the following table, the largest unit of time consists of 180 years. Called the *Great Cycle* (Da Yun), February 4, 1864, marked the beginning of the 180 cycle we are currently in. The cycle officially ends on February 4, 2044, with the new one beginning immediately thereafter.

CYCLE	UPPER			MIDDLE			LOWER		
PERIOD	1	2	3	4	5	6	7	8	9
YEAR BEGIN	Feb. 4 1864	Feb. 4 1884	Feb. 4 1904	Feb. 5 1924	Feb. 5 1944	Feb. 5 1964	Feb. 4 1984	Feb. 4 2004	Feb. 4 2024

The Great Cycle is divided equally into 3 cycles of 60 years each: the Upper Cycle (1864–1924), the Middle Cycle (1924–1984), and the Lower Cycle (1984–2044). The Great Cycle is also divided into 9 luck periods composed of 20 years each. Notice that the Upper Cycle consists of Period 1 (1864–1884), Period 2 (1884–1904), and Period 3 (1904–1924). The Middle Cycle consists of Period 4 (1924–1944), Period 5 (1944–1964), and Period 6 (1964–1984). Finally, the Lower Cycle consists of Period 7 (1984–2004), Period 8 (2004–2024), and Period 9 (2024–2044). Can you guess what period we are in now? Period 8 began on February 4, 2004.

So, where is all this leading, you ask? The year the construction of your house was completed determines which 20-year period it was "born into." For example, if your house was completed in 1902, it falls in Period 3 of the Upper Cycle. If your house was completed in 1927, it falls in Period 4 of the Middle Cycle. If your house was completed in 1985, it falls in Period 7 of the Lower Cycle. Finally, if your house was completed in 2004, then it shares the period we are currently in—Period 8 of the Lower Cycle.

The key words here are "construction completed." This is because construction may have begun in one year and ended in the next, a factor that becomes especially crucial if the 20-year period is changing. How can you find out when your house was built? What if you live in an apartment complex? No sweat. This information is a phone call away. The county recorder's office, the tax assessor's office, your building supervisor, or rental office should be able to help you.

Before we proceed, determine to which 20-year period your home was built. Record the information here:

My home was built in Period _____.

Now, let's step back for a minute and talk more about numbers and their characteristics as they relate to human events. The idea behind this concept is central to evaluating your numeral-based Flying Star chart.

It's All in the Numbers

As you're coming to learn, numbers express more than their values—they express ideas and beliefs. And, somehow, nature and humankind conform to this man-made abstraction, an idea we talked about in Chapter 2. In classical feng shui, numbers also express probabilities: the probability an event may happen within a given time and space. It could be a good event, such as a promotion or wedding, or a bad event, suggesting misfortune or illness. But how can these events be determined?

In the West, we've learned to determine the outcome of events by applying the laws of cause and effect. This has been the basis of Western scientific thinking for centuries. Causality is the name of the game—nothing is left to chance, a very unscientific process. The Chinese, on the other hand, are concerned with acausal probabilities, chance happenings and coincidences that are connected by seemingly unrelated events. Nature, or more precisely, the macrocosm, plays a starring role in their acausal theory. They believe human events aren't necessarily caused by natural phenomena, only connected in an acausal relationship. Countless hours through countless centuries were spent correlating acausal events between the outer world and our well-being. Numbers became a method of recording and predicting, forming the basis of the *Yijing*, from which feng shui is partially derived.

In Sync with Greater Nature

This acausal connecting principle is actually known as *synchronicity*, a word coined by renowned Swiss psychologist Carl Jung (1875–1961). Simply, synchronicity can be described as a pattern of coincidences in which thoughts, ideas, objects, and events (or a combination) are linked to form a theme of meaning to the observer(s).

Wise Words _____

Developed by Swiss psychologist Carl Jung (1875–1961), **synchronicity** expresses the connection of acausal (random) events within a limited time frame. The Chinese believe human events are linked with nature in an acausal relationship. Feng shui seeks to determine probabilities of synchronistic events within a certain time period. Numerology is one method classical feng shui uses.

We've all experienced synchronicity. For example, we (Elizabeth Moran and Val Biktashev) experienced a meaningless type of synchronicity, a happening that was more of an oddity than a life-altering event. Late one night we were driving home. The street was quiet; the road was empty; the radio was off. Suddenly, at the same time, we started to sing the same line from the Elton John song "Goodbye Yellow Brick Road." Shocked at this unlikely incident, we stared at each other. Then, I (Elizabeth) turned on the radio. Guess what was playing? We and the radio station were "in sync." What's the probability of this happening? What caused this striking coincidence? While we won't get into the why here, we talk at great length about the scientific reasoning behind synchronicity in Chapter 11 of *The Complete Idiot's Guide to the I Ching*.

The Attack on America

Yet, there are synchronistic events that are meaningful to the observer(s). For instance, take the September 11, 2001, terrorist attack on New York City's World Trade Center and the Pentagon, the governmental complex for the Department of Defense, located just outside Washington, D.C. A number of seemingly unrelated facts came together on this particular day within a specific space. The synchronicities involve the number 11. They are downright chilling:

- The attack occurred on 9/11: 9 + 1 + 1 = 11

- September 11 marks the two hundred fifty-fourth day of the year: 2 + 5 + 4 = 11.

- After September 11, 111 days are left in the year.

- From afar, the Twin Towers (part of the World Trade Center complex) resembled a gigantic number 11.

- The first airplane that crashed into the North Tower was American Airlines Flight 11.

- In 1788, New York was the eleventh state to join the Union.

♦ The words "New York City" contain 11 letters.

♦ The words "The Pentagon" contain 11 letters.

♦ The word "Afghanistan" contains 11 letters.

Pretty amazing, huh? You may wonder what the number 11 means. According to retired Harvard professor Annemarie Schimmel, as she states in her well-researched book, *The Mystery of Numbers* (Oxford University Press, 1993), "Larger than 10 and smaller than 12, it stands between two very important round numbers and therefore, while every other number had at least one positive aspect, 11 was always interpreted in medieval exegesis *ad malam partem*, in a purely negative sense. The sixteenth-century numerologist Petrus Bungus went so far as to claim that 11 'has no connection with divine things, no ladder reaching up to things above, nor any merit.' He considered it to be the number of sinners and penance."

> **Feng Facts**
>
> Consider another coincidence involving the number 11: The April 19, 1995, explosion devastating the A. P. Murrah Federal Building in Oklahoma City happened at 9:02 A.M.: 9 + 2 = 11. The evildoer behind this tragic event was Timothy McVeigh. He was executed on June 11, 2001. If you add up the digits to this date, they total 11: 6 + 1 + 1 + 2 + 0 + 0 + 1 = 11.

We need not dwell on the symbolic meaning of the number 11 and the extraordinary facts linking it with the attacks of September 11. You can formulate your own conclusion. Here, our point is to illustrate a recent, albeit catastrophic, example of numeric synchronicity.

In classical feng shui, the combination of numbers generated by a Flying Star qi chart represents synchronistic probabilities. For example, the Chinese recognized that a 2-1 combination was often linked with spousal conflict, separation, or divorce. An 8-9 combination spawned the likelihood of weddings and pregnancy. A 5-1 combination meant the probability of ear, kidney, or genital disorders. Get the idea? You'll be learning more about interpreting number combinations in later chapters.

A Number Is Worth a Thousand Words

Each number of the Luoshu (please refer to Chapter 11 for a reminder) reflects a certain kind of qi. It's important to understand that numbers, too, follow the laws of yin and yang. No number can be favorable or unfavorable all the time. Rather, the auspiciousness of each number is cyclic. But before you learn how to determine a number's timeliness, you first must understand the inherent nature of each number. Remember, we're talking about the numbers comprising a Flying Star qi map, which is generated by the period (time) your home was built in along with its magnetic (space) orientation. Other numbers such as those signifying your birth date, address, age, and the like, have no significance in feng shui. The following are the nine numbers of the Luoshu and their innate characteristics.

Luoshu Number	Inherent Characteristics
1	Wisdom, fame, and fortune
2	Fertility and health (favorable and unfavorable)
3	Misfortune, quarrels, and robbery
4	Writing, academic achievement, creativity, romance, and low morals (extramarital affairs)
5	Power, catastrophe, death, lawsuits, and illness
6	Authority and respect
7	Competition and destruction
8	Happiness and wealth
9	Enhances accompanied number whether favorable or unfavorable

In general, the numbers 1, 6, and 8 are considered good-natured and auspicious. The numbers 2, 3, and 7 are harmful and inauspicious. The number 4 is neutral. The number 5 shows its power by being sinister, by hurting others. Yet, during Period 8 (2004–2024), the number 5 will be tempered. This is because the ruling number 8 (a benevolent earth number) will help keep its naughty earth brother in check. Because they speak the same earth language, they can communicate better and reach an understanding.

Master Class

In Val's experience, the number 2 star is perhaps the most virulent, causing stomach, digestive, and reproductive problems in women (and even in female pets). If you're female and the number 2 star is on the mountain or health side (the subject of Chapter 16) of your bedroom, reposition your bed or switch places with your mate so that 2 won't negatively impact your health. Even if a metal remedy is installed (metal reduces 2 earth), 2's propensity for causing health problems is still strong. Regarding pets, a client's female dog slept against a wall containing the 2 mountain star. As result, the dog was plagued with chronicle stomach problems. When the dog's bed was moved to another wall, her stomach ailments disappeared.

The Ruler Principle

In the Luoshu, the number 5 occupies the central square of the nine-part grid. It rules the Earth. Thus, the number 5 represents the stable matter of earth qi and its gravitational force, pulling everything toward the center.

Conversely, there's heaven qi. It moves and changes over time. Each of the nine stars or numbers takes turns to rule heaven. Each star rules for 20 years or for one period. As you learned earlier on in this chapter, we are now in Period 8, with the number 8 ruling from 2004 to 2024. The ruling star is the most powerful star, followed by the star that is next in line. Using an analogy, think of number 8 as the current president of the United States or Britain's prime minister. Although we don't yet know who the president/prime minister-elect will be, the stars are more orderly. The successor of number 8 is number 9, the next ruling star for the time period 2024 to 2044.

What about the immediate past ruler, the number 7 governing 1984 to 2004? Consider this star like the most recent former president of the United States. While he is no longer president, he is still influential.

Wheel of Fortune

Looking at the following illustration, notice how the life cycle wheel revolves in a counterclockwise fashion: that which rules retires and then dies, only to grow again. Numerically, 8 rules; 7 is retired; 6, 5, 4, 3, and 2 are dead; 1 is growing into the apprentice ruler; and 9 is the future ruler.

The life cycle of numbers.

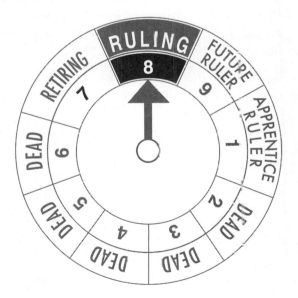

To determine the ruling star for the 20-year period beginning on February 4, 2024, simply turn the wheel one position to the left. The number 9 now rules, and 8 retires. The other numbers follow suit.

Master Class _____

Numbers should be defined in terms of the aging process with their inherent characteristics taken into consideration. For example, the number 1 is inherently a good number representing fame and fortune. If we let number 1 represent Miss America, her reign marks the height of her glory. When she has completed her term, she retires. She is still attractive, but as she ages, she becomes prone to illness and hardship. In other words, when a star ages and then dies, it no longer has the strength to help you.

In Sickness and in Health: The Timeliness of the Stars

How does each number individually embody a ruling, retired, dead, or apprentice/future ruler star? Consult the following table. Pertaining to the previous Period 7 (1984–2004), take the number 1. An inherently favorable number, it has been dead for 100 years since Period 3 (1904–1924). In its death cycle, the number 1 has been known to cause marital troubles. Referring to the illustration of the life cycle, you'll see that number 1 rose from the dead and became the apprentice future ruler in 2004, when number 8 became the ruler. During its productive years, the number 1 promotes wisdom, fame, and fortune. Let's take the number 8. Currently, it's the ruling star. Referring to the chart, when the number 8 is in its ruling or apprentice/future ruler cycle, it ushers in the possibility of financial gain, happiness, and overall good fortune. However, beginning on February 4, 2024, it retires. It exhibits both its good and bad qualities (just like the number 6 does during Period 7).

We suggest placing a paper clip on the following page. Until you have memorized each number's inherent nature and life cycles, you'll be referring to this table often.

The Nature of Timely and Untimely Stars for the
20 Year Period, Feb. 4, 2004 - Feb. 3, 2024

NUMBER	TIMELY CHARACTERISTICS	NUMBER	UNTIMELY CHARACTERISTICS
1	Wisdom, Fame, & Fortune	1	Spousal Conflict, Separation, & Divorce
	Good Health & Fertility	2	Sickness & Miscarriage
	Abundance of Wealth	3	Lawsuits, Robbery, & Asthma
	Academic Achiement, Creativity, Writing, & Romance	4	Affairs & Sexual Entanglements
	Success, Power, & Prosperity	5	Catastrophes, Casualties, Lawsuits, & Sickness
	Great Authority, Dignity, & Fame	6	Loneliness & Lawsuits
7	Financial Gain & Fertility	7	Fire, Theft, & Casualties
8	Steady Progress in Finance, Happiness, & Good Fortune		Harmful to Youth & Solitude
9	Success & Promotion		Eye Desease, Fire, Litigation, & Insanity

Hail Period 8

Classical feng shui practitioners worldwide stood up and cheered when Period 8 was ushered in on February 4, 2004. Harkening back to what you learned earlier in this chapter, remember the number 8 (along with the numbers 1 and 6) is inherently good-natured, bringing happiness, prosperity, and all-around good luck. Who doesn't want that? Now that the number 8 is the ruler, its innate goodness magnifies for 20 years ending on February 3, 2024. So, what can you expect during this auspicious period of time? Well, let's back-peddle for a moment to discuss how Period 7 (1984–2004) impacted us.

Innately, the number 7 (along with the numbers 2 and 5) is harmful. Its timely characteristics are only made manifest when it's the ruler. During this time, the number 7 is outwardly beautiful. Associated with the Dui trigram (youngest daughter), Period 7 proved especially favorable for women. During Period 6 (1964–1984), women planted the seed to win more authority and respect—timely characteristics of the period—with the women's liberation movement. During

> **Feng Facts**
>
> During Period 7, women advanced. Even feng shui, an industry dominated by men, has seen many more female practitioners than male practitioners.

Period 7, women harvested their fruits. Out of the kitchen and into the workforce, more women were made company executives and corporate and governmental leaders than at any other time in history.

Associated with the mouth area, 7 shined on people or industries that relied on their voice to gain a leg up. Singers, especially female performers, took stage. Just think of the success of Madonna, Celine Dion, and Britney Spears, for example. Lawyers became celebrities (Leslie Abramson, Gloria Allred, and Johnnie Cochran, for example); litigiousness became rampant—particularly in America. The expressions, "I'll sue you" and "So, sue me!" became commonplace. Gossip or tabloid magazines and talk shows glittered in Period 7. Advertising dazzled. Yet, let's not forget number 7's inward ugliness. Characterized primarily by fire and casualties, the wrath of 7 reared its ugly head with terrorism, something Americans had not witnessed on their own soil. The 1993 World Trade Center bombing, the 1995 A. P. Murrah Federal Building bombing, and the catastrophic events of September 11, 2001, are recent examples.

Although Period 7's timely characteristics primarily revolved around the advancement of women and talkers, Period 8 focuses on the doers of the world. Associated with the Gen trigram (youngest son), it's a time of action and fresh energy. The phrase "All bark and no bite" will not apply. Activists will take center stage, motivating others to roll up their sleeves and help out. Associated with the hand, Gen also represents something being stopped. What will be stopped is still in question. Stopping terrorism and war is a probability. Stopping the destruction of our planet (pollution, ravaging rain forests, for example) might move to the forefront. To stop, we use the hand and not the mouth.

Because the number 8 is related to the earth, industries that combine the hand and earth will prosper. These include land development, construction, farming, and mining. Yet, let's not forget 8's timely characteristics ushering in happiness and financial gain. You'll learn about enhancing the number 8's goodness in successive chapters.

In the previous chapter and in this chapter, you've determined the two most important factors that will generate a numeric qi pattern of your home—the magnetic orientation (space) and the period (time) it was born into. In the next chapter, you'll learn how to "fly" the stars to create the numeric qi pattern.

The Least You Need to Know

♦ The Chinese view time as cyclic. The largest unit of time is made up of 180 years. Called the Great Cycle, it is divided into three equal parts of 60 years each. Each 60-year cycle is subdivided into three equal parts of 20 years each.

♦ Each of the nine stars or numbers of the Luoshu has distinct personalities that change over time.

♦ In Flying Star methodology, numbers and combinations of numbers express the probability of events occurring.

♦ Currently, we are in Period 8 (2004–2024) of the Lower Cycle, which ushers in a cycle of happiness, prosperity, and all-around good luck.

The Flying Stars, Part 4

In This Chapter

- ◆ Flying the period or time star
- ◆ Flying the stars forward
- ◆ Flying the stars backward
- ◆ Applying the stars to your floor plan

Flying Star is a very challenging system. It's a bit technical so we suggest you undertake this chapter and successive ones regarding the mechanics of the Flying Star system only when you are energetic, clearheaded, and free of time constraints. An alert mind, a positive attitude, and an insatiable curiosity are all it takes to advance toward more sophisticated feng shui techniques.

To "fly" a star means to move numbers around the nine cells of the Luoshu in a specific sequence. What you're actually doing here is calculating the movement of qi; determining the qi pattern made manifest by the building's construction date (time) and its magnetic orientation (space). So, instead of saying, "I'll run the numbers," you say, "I'll fly the numbers." In doing so, you'll sound cool using feng shui lingo!

Oh, My Flying Stars!

In the last chapter, you learned about the Chinese concept of time—that the construction year of your home relates to a specific 20-year period. For example, if your home was completed in 1985, it belongs to Period 7 (1984–2004). If your home was completed in 1950, it belongs to Period 5 (1944–1964). Whatever period your home belongs to is the number that represents the star that ruled when your home was born. In other words, if your home was built between 1984 and 2004 (Period 7), the number 7 prevailed; it ruled heaven's qi. If your home was built after February 4, 2004, the number 8 prevails. It now rules heaven's qi.

Also called the *time star*, the ruling or period number is placed in the central palace of the nine-part Luoshu grid. In an ascending manner, the other numbers will fill the remaining eight cells by following a precise directional sequence: NW, W, NE, S, N, SW, E, SE. For example, let's take a house built during Period 4 (1924–1944). Placing the time star number 4 in the center, the other numbers fly as shown in the following figures.

Example of flying the time star for a house built in Period 4. Note: Although technically the Luoshu diagram is a square configuration, we have rounded the diagram to match the circular Hou Tian (After Heaven) sequence to which the Luoshu numbers are correlated.

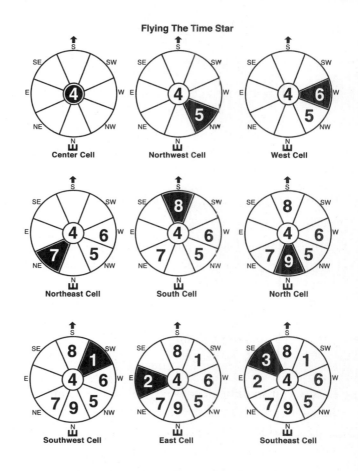

Next, check your work. An easy way to determine whether the numbers have been flown correctly is to check the number in the last, or southeast cell. If it precedes the number in the center palace, there should be no mistake. In this example, the number 3 is in the southeast cell. Three precedes four.

As the saying goes, "Practice makes perfect." To fully comprehend Flying Star, it's best that you take an active role. Participate. Be proactive and not passive. What follows are eight empty charts (representing Period 2 through Period 9) for you to complete. At this stage, the directions corresponding to your home's sitting and facing sides are not a consideration. This aspect comes into play later on in this chapter. Here, we're only concerned with your dwelling's construction date. To give you a head start, we've filled out the first chart (Period 1) for you. Remember, the sequence is:

Center, NW, W, NE, S, N, SW, E, SE

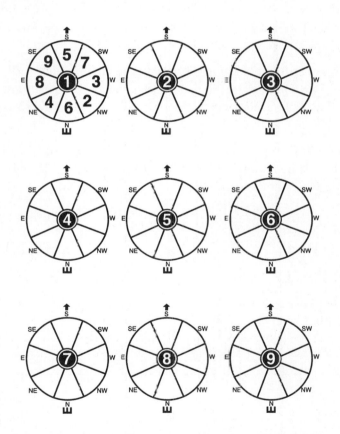

That wasn't so difficult, was it? Did you remember to check the southeast cell? Does the number in this cell precede that which is in the center palace? See. What seemed complicated is, in fact, simple—a piece of cake, a walk in the park.

Constructing a Flying Star Chart

You've just completed step one of constructing a Flying Star chart, manifesting the heaven or time qi governing your home. Now, things get more complicated.

Step two is to calculate the house's qi pattern, which relates to its magnetic space. Let's take a house built in Period 7, sitting N1 and facing S1. Referring to the following illustration of House 1, the star (or number) corresponding to the sitting direction (number 3) is copied and moved to the top, left side of the central palace. This star is called the *sitting star*. Next, the *facing star*, the number corresponding to the dwelling's facing direction, is copied and moved to the top, right side of the central palace. In this example, number 2 represents the facing star.

Let's take another example. House 2 represents a dwelling built in Period 4, sitting SW2 and facing NE2. As indicated, the sitting star 1 is copied and moved to the top, left side of the central palace. The facing star 7 is copied and moved to the top, right side of the central palace.

Finally, one more example. House 3 represents a dwelling built in Period 1, sitting E1 and facing W1. Here, the sitting star 8 is copied and moved to the top, left side of the central palace. The facing star 3 is copied and moved to the top, right side of the central palace.

Using the preceding empty chart (My House), fly the time star (period or ruling star) affiliated with your own home. Then transfer the sitting and facing stars to their appropriate positions in the central palace.

Wise Words _____

The **time star** (period star) is the number that ruled when your house was built. The **sitting star** (zuo xing) is the number that corresponds to your dwelling's sitting direction. The **facing star** (xiang xing) is the number that corresponds to your dwelling's facing direction. These numbers fly to the top left and top right of the central palace, respectively. The sitting star is also called the mountain star (shan xing) or people star (ding xing). The facing star is also called the water star (shui xing) or money star (cai xing).

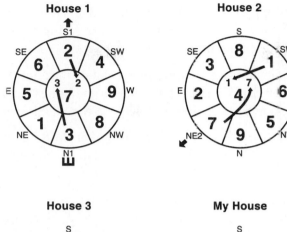

After you have determined to which period your home belongs, the next step is to transfer the sitting and facing stars to the left and right sides of the central cell, respectively. The empty chart is for you to record the information appropriate to your own home.

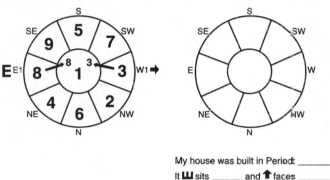

My house was built in Period: _____.

It **Ш** sits _____ and **↑** faces _____.

Flying Forward, Flying Backward

Step three requires you to fly the sitting and facing stars either forward (just like you did for the time star) or backward. Logically, if flying forward (1, 2, 3, 4, 5, 6, 7, 8, 9) means the numbers ascend, then flying backward (9, 8, 7, 6, 5, 4, 3, 2, 1) means the numbers descend while following the directional sequence (center, NW, W, NE, S, N, SW, E, SE). Whether the sitting and facing star flies forward or backward depends on two factors:

♦ If the star in question is odd or even

♦ If the mountain the house sits in and faces toward is the first, second, or third mountain of the trigram in question

Now, following these next five rules, determine whether the sitting and facing stars in the center palace fly forward or backward:

Rule 1: If your house sits in and faces toward the first mountain (N1 to S1; NE1 to SW1; E1 to W1, for example) and if the sitting or facing star is odd (except the number 5), then the star in question flies forward.

Rule 2: If your house sits in and faces toward the first mountain (N1 to S1; NE1 to SW1; E1 to W1, for example) and if the sitting or facing star is even, then the star in question flies backward.

Rule 3: If your house sits in and faces toward the second or third mountains (N2 to S2; N3 to S3; W2 to E2; W3 to E3, for example) and if the sitting or facing star is odd (except the number 5), then the star in question flies backward.

Rule 4: If your house sits in and faces toward the second or third mountains (N2 to S2; N3 to S3; W2 to E2; W3 to E3, for example) and if the sitting or facing star is even, then the star in question flies forward.

Rule 5: The number 5 flies forward or backward according to whether the ruling star in the center palace is odd or even. In other words, if the ruling star is 1, 3, 7, or 9, the number 5 in the sitting or facing position flies according to Rule 1 or Rule 3. If the ruling star is 2, 4, 6, or 8, the number 5 in the sitting or facing position flies according to Rule 2 or Rule 4.

Referring to the following examples, let's look at House 1. Built in Period 7, it sits N1 and faces S1. According to Rule 1, the sitting star 3 (located in the top, left position of the central cell) flies forward: 3 (center), 4 (NW), 5 (W), 6 (NE), 7 (S), 8 (N), 9 (SW), 1 (E), and 2 (SE). According to Rule 2, the facing star 2 (located in the top, right position of the central cell) flies backward: 2 (center), 1 (NW), 9 (W), 8 (NE), 7 (S), 6 (N), 5 (SW), 4 (E), and 3 (SE). Referring to House 2, it sits N3 and faces S3. According to Rule 3, the sitting star 3 flies backward. According to Rule 4, the facing star 2 flies forward. Get the idea?

According to Rule 1, the sitting star 3 flies forward. According to Rule 2, the facing star 2 flies backward.

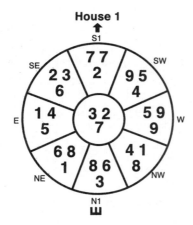

House 1

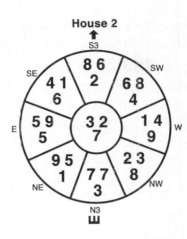

House 2

According to Rule 3, the sitting star 3 flies backward. According to Rule 4, the facing star 2 flies forward.

Now, it's your turn. Take this time to complete your chart (My House) by flying the sitting and facing stars in the central cell.

Master Class

Another method similar to Xuankong Feixing (Time and Space Flying Stars), which we present here, is called Zibai Feigong or Purple-White Flying Palace. Basically, this technique flies the Luoshu number that correlates to your dwelling's sitting trigram and then compares the eight other numbers to the central one. Dating to the Ming dynasty (1368–1644), the system is also called Zibai Jiuxing or Purple-White Nine Stars. Why purple-white? Because each number is associated with a color. The colors white (1, 6, 8) and purple (9) are considered auspicious numbers. Because the colors were used as mnemonics to aid learning, we will not discuss the Zibai Feigong colors, which are not related to the five phase colors.

More Flying Forward, More Flying Backward

To facilitate learning, let's review this intricate procedure one more time. House 3 (following) sits at W2 and faces E2. It was built in 1950. Take this time now to fly the stars. To help you, check off each task as you complete it:

❑ Using the sitting **山** and facing **↑** symbols, notate the directional orientation of the dwelling.

❑ Determine the 20-year period the home was constructed in. Consult Chapter 13 for a reminder. Write this number (the time star) in the central palace.

❑ Fly the time star forward. Remember, the directional sequence is: Center, NW, W, NE, S, N, SW, E, SE.

❏ Copy and move the sitting star to the top, left side of the central palace. Copy and move the facing star to the top, right side of the central palace.

❏ Refer to the five rules to determine whether the sitting and facing stars fly forward or backward. Fly the stars.

House 3

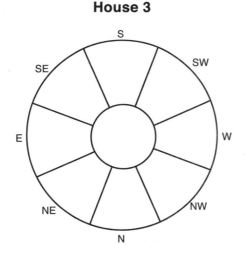

So, how did you do? Compare your result to the answer at the end of the chapter.

Great Charts!

Once you've created a Flying Star chart appropriate to your home, you must transfer the numbers comprising the numeric qi map onto your floor plan. But be careful! *Make sure that you match each number combination with the correct direction on your floor plan.* If you found that flying the stars is a laborious task, don't fear—we've done all the work for you. In fact, we've even oriented the charts so that the sitting is at the bottom of the page and the facing is at the top of the page. All you need to do is look up the chart corresponding to your home! First, find the period in which your house was constructed. Then, find the chart correlating to its sitting direction.

In the next chapter, you'll learn how the position of the sitting and facing stars affects the auspiciousness of a house.

Feng Facts
There are 216 types of houses. How did we come to this conclusion? There are 24 mountains × 9 periods = 216.

Houses Built in Period 1 (Feb. 4, 1864 - Feb. 3, 1884)

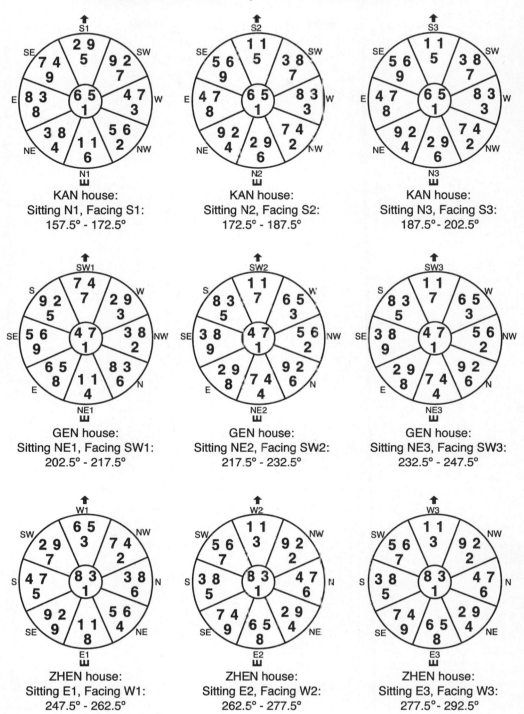

KAN house:
Sitting N1, Facing S1:
157.5° - 172.5°

KAN house:
Sitting N2, Facing S2:
172.5° - 187.5°

KAN house:
Sitting N3, Facing S3:
187.5° - 202.5°

GEN house:
Sitting NE1, Facing SW1:
202.5° - 217.5°

GEN house:
Sitting NE2, Facing SW2:
217.5° - 232.5°

GEN house:
Sitting NE3, Facing SW3:
232.5° - 247.5°

ZHEN house:
Sitting E1, Facing W1:
247.5° - 262.5°

ZHEN house:
Sitting E2, Facing W2:
262.5° - 277.5°

ZHEN house:
Sitting E3, Facing W3:
277.5° - 292.5°

Houses Built in Period 1 (Feb. 4, 1864 - Feb. 3, 1884)

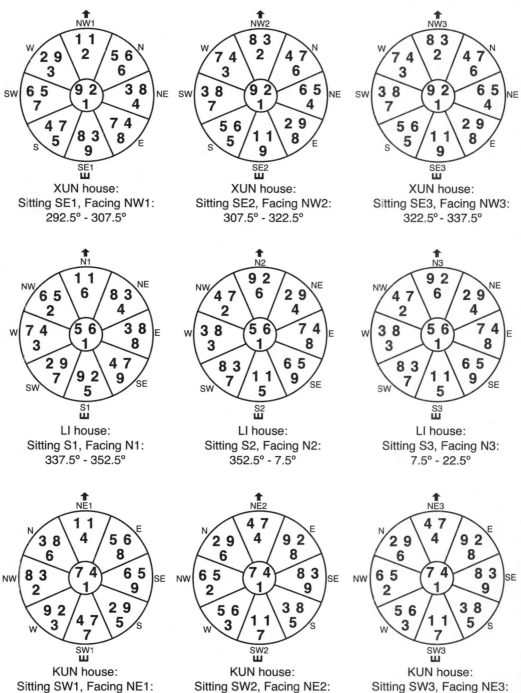

XUN house:
Sitting SE1, Facing NW1:
292.5° - 307.5°

XUN house:
Sitting SE2, Facing NW2:
307.5° - 322.5°

XUN house:
Sitting SE3, Facing NW3:
322.5° - 337.5°

LI house:
Sitting S1, Facing N1:
337.5° - 352.5°

LI house:
Sitting S2, Facing N2:
352.5° - 7.5°

LI house:
Sitting S3, Facing N3:
7.5° - 22.5°

KUN house:
Sitting SW1, Facing NE1:
22.5° - 37.5°

KUN house:
Sitting SW2, Facing NE2:
37.5° - 52.5°

KUN house:
Sitting SW3, Facing NE3:
52.5°- 67.5°

Houses Built in Period 1 (Feb. 4, 1864 - Feb. 3, 1884)

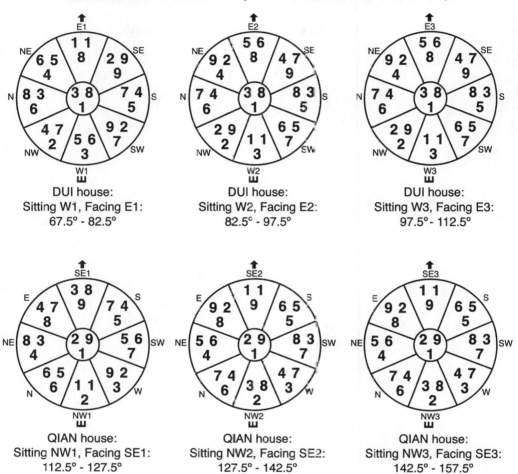

DUI house:
Sitting W1, Facing E1:
67.5° - 82.5°

DUI house:
Sitting W2, Facing E2:
82.5° - 97.5°

DUI house:
Sitting W3, Facing E3:
97.5° - 112.5°

QIAN house:
Sitting NW1, Facing SE1:
112.5° - 127.5°

QIAN house:
Sitting NW2, Facing SE2:
127.5° - 142.5°

QIAN house:
Sitting NW3, Facing SE3:
142.5° - 157.5°

Houses Built in Period 2 (Feb. 4, 1884 - Feb. 4, 1904)

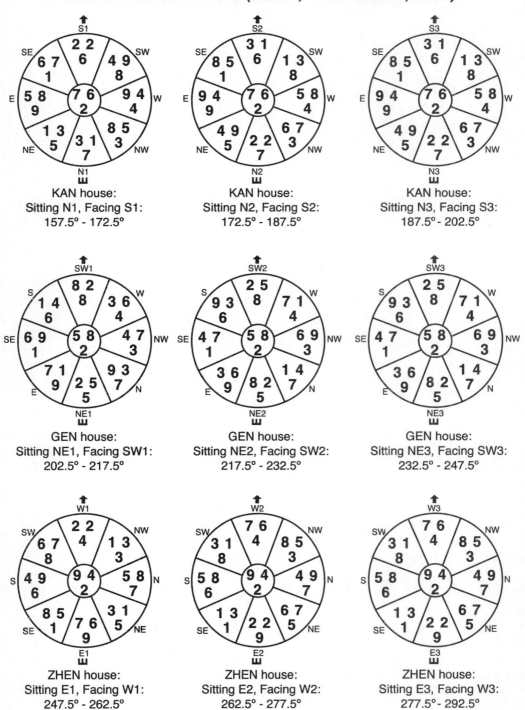

KAN house:
Sitting N1, Facing S1:
157.5° - 172.5°

KAN house:
Sitting N2, Facing S2:
172.5° - 187.5°

KAN house:
Sitting N3, Facing S3:
187.5° - 202.5°

GEN house:
Sitting NE1, Facing SW1:
202.5° - 217.5°

GEN house:
Sitting NE2, Facing SW2:
217.5° - 232.5°

GEN house:
Sitting NE3, Facing SW3:
232.5° - 247.5°

ZHEN house:
Sitting E1, Facing W1:
247.5° - 262.5°

ZHEN house:
Sitting E2, Facing W2:
262.5° - 277.5°

ZHEN house:
Sitting E3, Facing W3:
277.5° - 292.5°

Houses Built in Period 2 (Feb. 4, 1884 - Feb. 4, 1904)

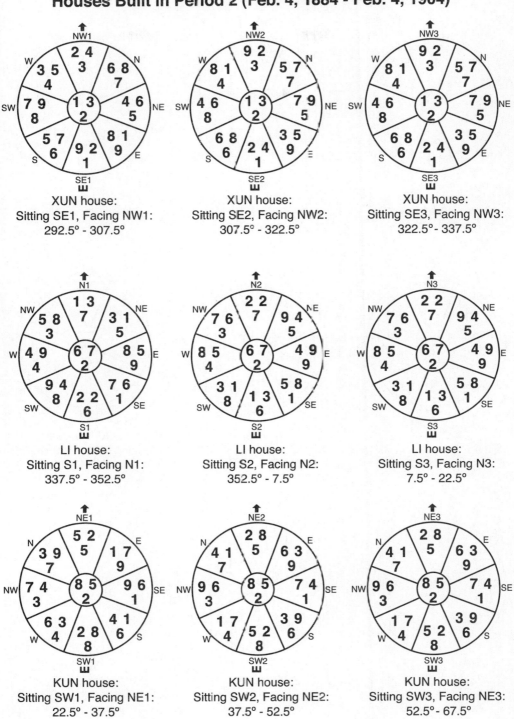

XUN house:
Sitting SE1, Facing NW1:
292.5° - 307.5°

XUN house:
Sitting SE2, Facing NW2:
307.5° - 322.5°

XUN house:
Sitting SE3, Facing NW3:
322.5° - 337.5°

LI house:
Sitting S1, Facing N1:
337.5° - 352.5°

LI house:
Sitting S2, Facing N2:
352.5° - 7.5°

LI house:
Sitting S3, Facing N3:
7.5° - 22.5°

KUN house:
Sitting SW1, Facing NE1:
22.5° - 37.5°

KUN house:
Sitting SW2, Facing NE2:
37.5° - 52.5°

KUN house:
Sitting SW3, Facing NE3:
52.5° - 67.5°

Houses Built in Period 2 (Feb. 4, 1884 - Feb. 4, 1904)

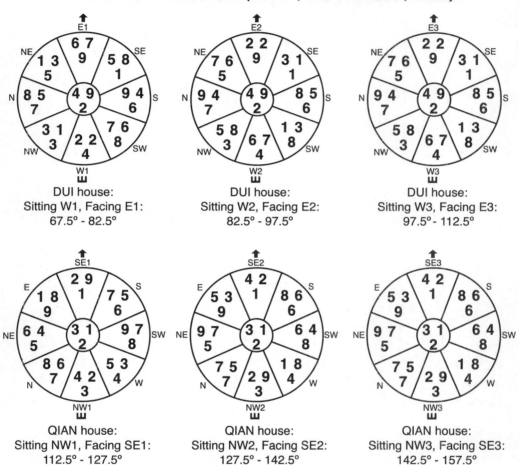

DUI house:
Sitting W1, Facing E1:
67.5° - 82.5°

DUI house:
Sitting W2, Facing E2:
82.5° - 97.5°

DUI house:
Sitting W3, Facing E3:
97.5° - 112.5°

QIAN house:
Sitting NW1, Facing SE1:
112.5° - 127.5°

QIAN house:
Sitting NW2, Facing SE2:
127.5° - 142.5°

QIAN house:
Sitting NW3, Facing SE3:
142.5° - 157.5°

Houses Built in Period 3 (Feb. 5, 1904 - Feb. 4, 1924)

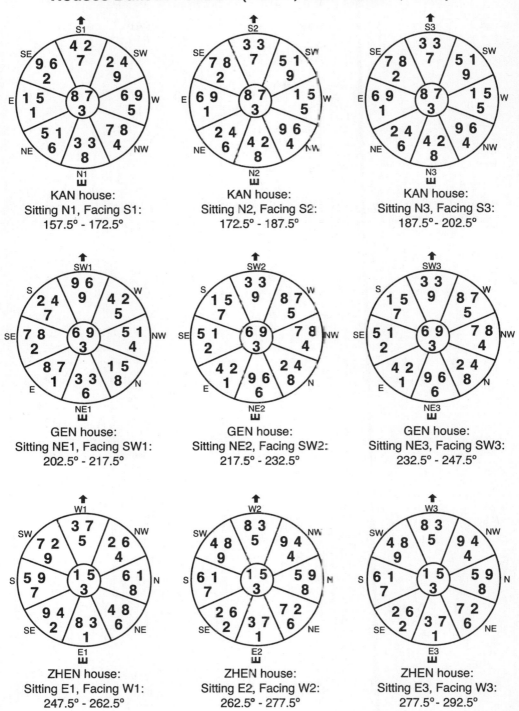

KAN house:
Sitting N1, Facing S1:
157.5° - 172.5°

KAN house:
Sitting N2, Facing S2:
172.5° - 187.5°

KAN house:
Sitting N3, Facing S3:
187.5° - 202.5°

GEN house:
Sitting NE1, Facing SW1:
202.5° - 217.5°

GEN house:
Sitting NE2, Facing SW2:
217.5° - 232.5°

GEN house:
Sitting NE3, Facing SW3:
232.5° - 247.5°

ZHEN house:
Sitting E1, Facing W1:
247.5° - 262.5°

ZHEN house:
Sitting E2, Facing W2:
262.5° - 277.5°

ZHEN house:
Sitting E3, Facing W3:
277.5° - 292.5°

Houses Built in Period 3 (Feb. 5, 1904 - Feb. 4, 1924)

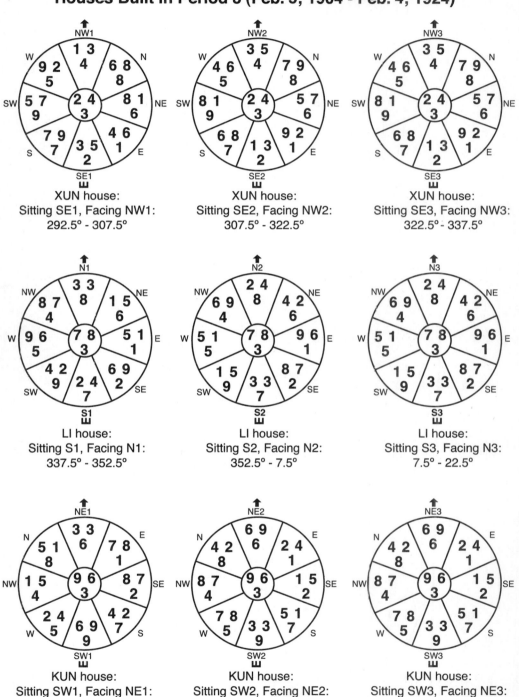

XUN house:
Sitting SE1, Facing NW1:
292.5° - 307.5°

XUN house:
Sitting SE2, Facing NW2:
307.5° - 322.5°

XUN house:
Sitting SE3, Facing NW3:
322.5° - 337.5°

LI house:
Sitting S1, Facing N1:
337.5° - 352.5°

LI house:
Sitting S2, Facing N2:
352.5° - 7.5°

LI house:
Sitting S3, Facing N3:
7.5° - 22.5°

KUN house:
Sitting SW1, Facing NE1:
22.5° - 37.5°

KUN house:
Sitting SW2, Facing NE2:
37.5° - 52.5°

KUN house:
Sitting SW3, Facing NE3:
52.5° - 67.5°

Houses Built in Period 3 (Feb. 5, 1904 - Feb. 4, 1924)

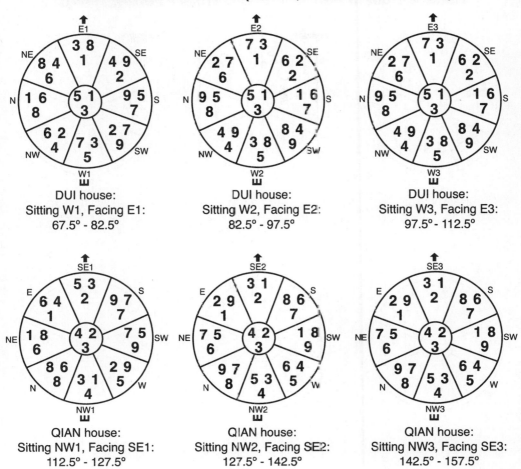

DUI house:
Sitting W1, Facing E1:
67.5° - 82.5°

DUI house:
Sitting W2, Facing E2:
82.5° - 97.5°

DUI house:
Sitting W3, Facing E3:
97.5° - 112.5°

QIAN house:
Sitting NW1, Facing SE1:
112.5° - 127.5°

QIAN house:
Sitting NW2, Facing SE2:
127.5° - 142.5°

QIAN house:
Sitting NW3, Facing SE3:
142.5° - 157.5°

Houses Built in Period 4 (Feb. 5, 1924 - Feb. 4, 1944)

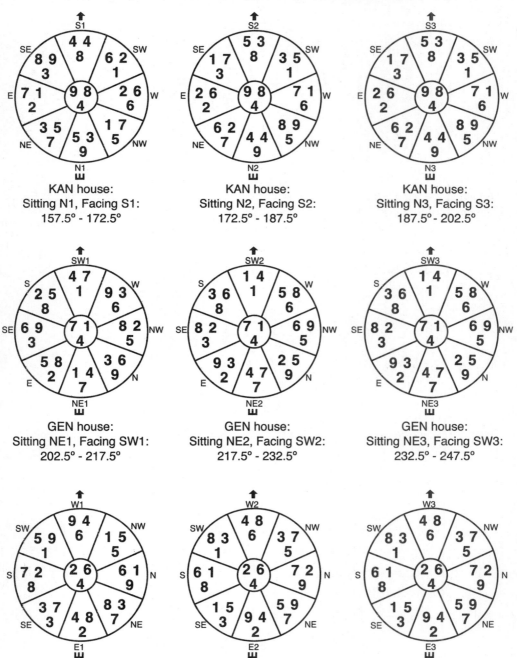

KAN house:
Sitting N1, Facing S1:
157.5° - 172.5°

KAN house:
Sitting N2, Facing S2:
172.5° - 187.5°

KAN house:
Sitting N3, Facing S3:
187.5° - 202.5°

GEN house:
Sitting NE1, Facing SW1:
202.5° - 217.5°

GEN house:
Sitting NE2, Facing SW2:
217.5° - 232.5°

GEN house:
Sitting NE3, Facing SW3:
232.5° - 247.5°

ZHEN house:
Sitting E1, Facing W1:
247.5° - 262.5°

ZHEN house:
Sitting E2, Facing W2:
262.5° - 277.5°

ZHEN house:
Sitting E3, Facing W3:
277.5° - 292.5°

Houses Built in Period 4 (Feb. 5, 1924 - Feb. 4, 1944)

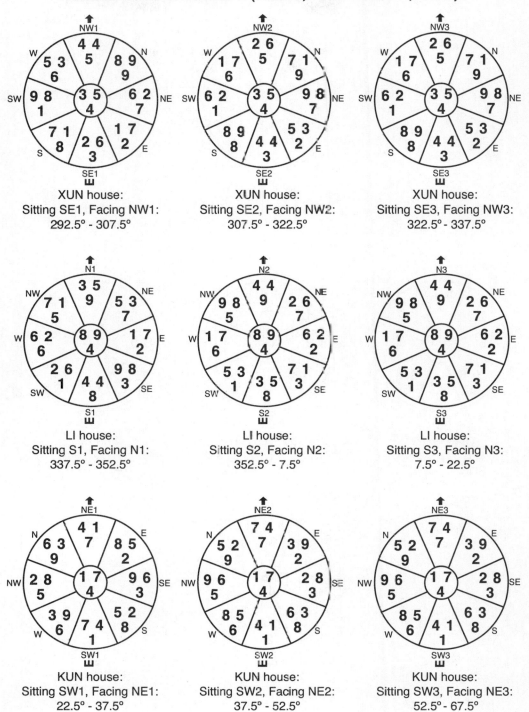

XUN house:
Sitting SE1, Facing NW1:
292.5° - 307.5°

XUN house:
Sitting SE2, Facing NW2:
307.5° - 322.5°

XUN house:
Sitting SE3, Facing NW3:
322.5° - 337.5°

LI house:
Sitting S1, Facing N1:
337.5° - 352.5°

LI house:
Sitting S2, Facing N2:
352.5° - 7.5°

LI house:
Sitting S3, Facing N3:
7.5° - 22.5°

KUN house:
Sitting SW1, Facing NE1:
22.5° - 37.5°

KUN house:
Sitting SW2, Facing NE2:
37.5° - 52.5°

KUN house:
Sitting SW3, Facing NE3:
52.5° - 67.5°

Houses Built in Period 4 (Feb. 5, 1924 - Feb. 4, 1944)

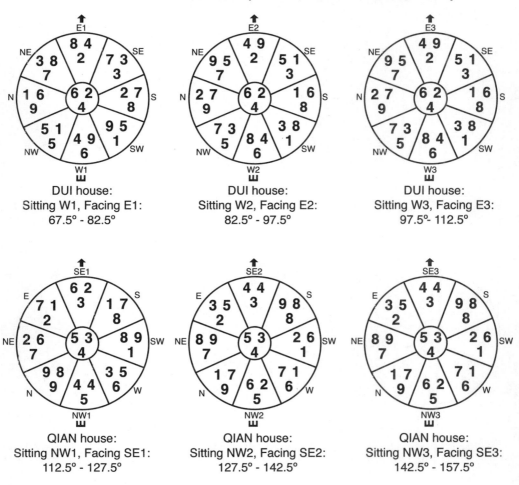

DUI house:
Sitting W1, Facing E1:
67.5° - 82.5°

DUI house:
Sitting W2, Facing E2:
82.5° - 97.5°

DUI house:
Sitting W3, Facing E3:
97.5°- 112.5°

QIAN house:
Sitting NW1, Facing SE1:
112.5° - 127.5°

QIAN house:
Sitting NW2, Facing SE2:
127.5° - 142.5°

QIAN house:
Sitting NW3, Facing SE3:
142.5° - 157.5°

Houses Built in Period 5 (Feb. 5, 1944 - Feb. 4, 1964)

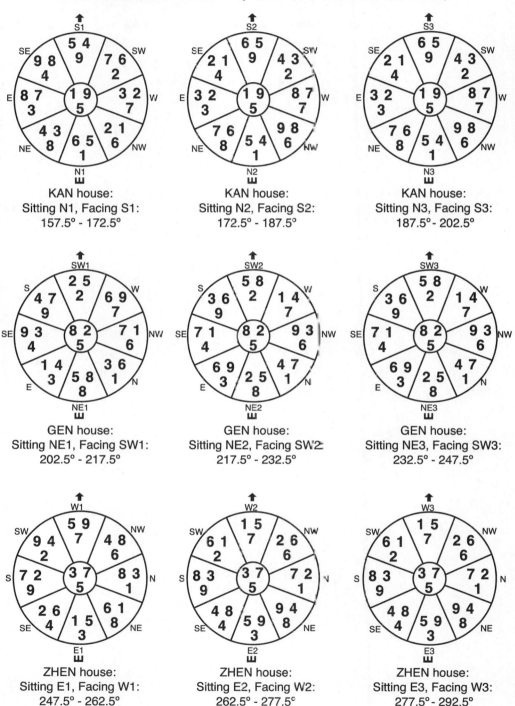

KAN house:
Sitting N1, Facing S1:
157.5° - 172.5°

KAN house:
Sitting N2, Facing S2:
172.5° - 187.5°

KAN house:
Sitting N3, Facing S3:
187.5° - 202.5°

GEN house:
Sitting NE1, Facing SW1:
202.5° - 217.5°

GEN house:
Sitting NE2, Facing SW2:
217.5° - 232.5°

GEN house:
Sitting NE3, Facing SW3:
232.5° - 247.5°

ZHEN house:
Sitting E1, Facing W1:
247.5° - 262.5°

ZHEN house:
Sitting E2, Facing W2:
262.5° - 277.5°

ZHEN house:
Sitting E3, Facing W3:
277.5° - 292.5°

Houses Built in Period 5 (Feb. 5, 1944 - Feb. 4, 1964)

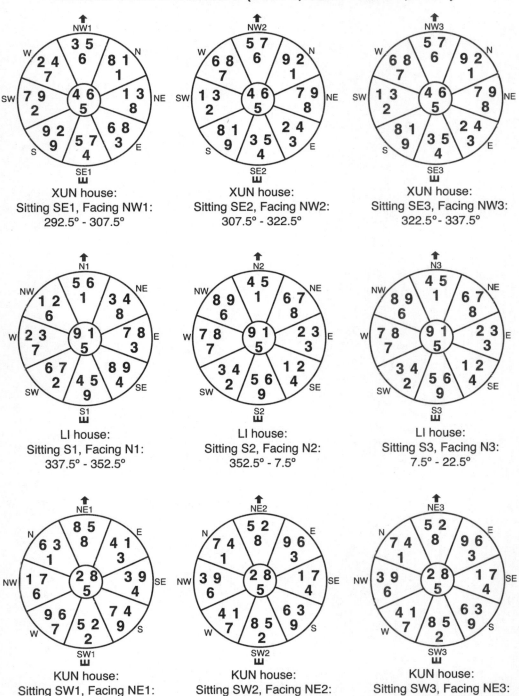

XUN house:
Sitting SE1, Facing NW1:
292.5° - 307.5°

XUN house:
Sitting SE2, Facing NW2:
307.5° - 322.5°

XUN house:
Sitting SE3, Facing NW3:
322.5° - 337.5°

LI house:
Sitting S1, Facing N1:
337.5° - 352.5°

LI house:
Sitting S2, Facing N2:
352.5° - 7.5°

LI house:
Sitting S3, Facing N3:
7.5° - 22.5°

KUN house:
Sitting SW1, Facing NE1:
22.5° - 37.5°

KUN house:
Sitting SW2, Facing NE2:
37.5° - 52.5°

KUN house:
Sitting SW3, Facing NE3:
52.5° - 67.5°

Houses Built in Period 5 (Feb. 5, 1944 - Feb. 4, 1964)

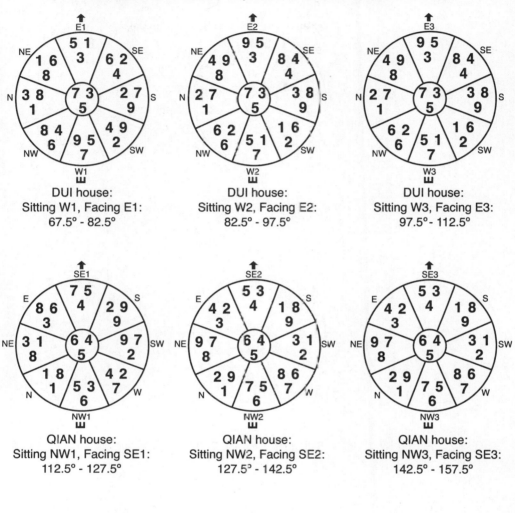

DUI house:
Sitting W1, Facing E1:
67.5° - 82.5°

DUI house:
Sitting W2, Facing E2:
82.5° - 97.5°

DUI house:
Sitting W3, Facing E3:
97.5°- 112.5°

QIAN house:
Sitting NW1, Facing SE1:
112.5° - 127.5°

QIAN house:
Sitting NW2, Facing SE2:
127.5° - 142.5°

QIAN house:
Sitting NW3, Facing SE3:
142.5° - 157.5°

Houses Built in Period 6 (Feb. 5, 1964 - Feb. 3, 1984)

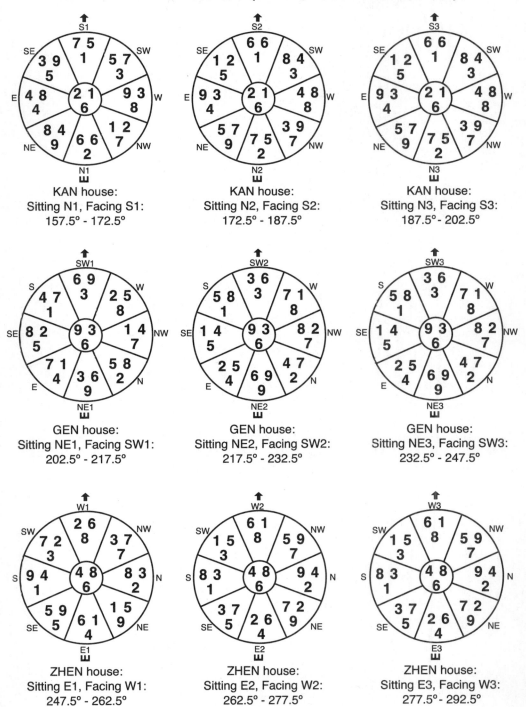

KAN house:
Sitting N1, Facing S1:
157.5° - 172.5°

KAN house:
Sitting N2, Facing S2:
172.5° - 187.5°

KAN house:
Sitting N3, Facing S3:
187.5° - 202.5°

GEN house:
Sitting NE1, Facing SW1:
202.5° - 217.5°

GEN house:
Sitting NE2, Facing SW2:
217.5° - 232.5°

GEN house:
Sitting NE3, Facing SW3:
232.5° - 247.5°

ZHEN house:
Sitting E1, Facing W1:
247.5° - 262.5°

ZHEN house:
Sitting E2, Facing W2:
262.5° - 277.5°

ZHEN house:
Sitting E3, Facing W3:
277.5° - 292.5°

Houses Built in Period 6 (Feb. 5, 1964 - Feb. 3, 1984)

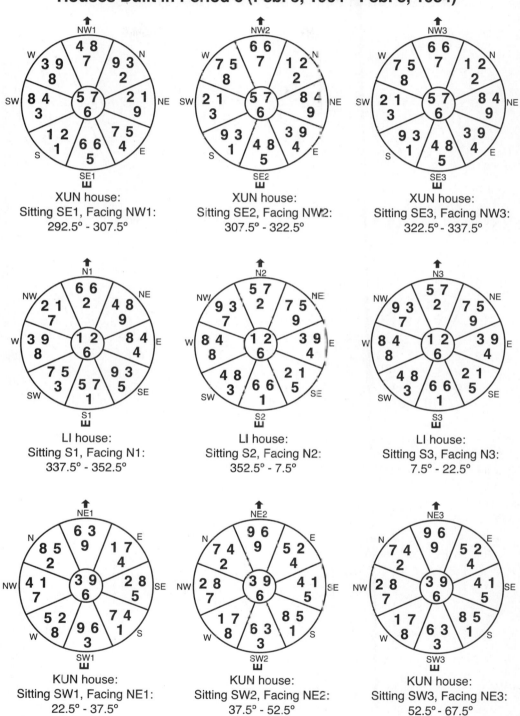

XUN house:
Sitting SE1, Facing NW1:
292.5° - 307.5°

XUN house:
Sitting SE2, Facing NW2:
307.5° - 322.5°

XUN house:
Sitting SE3, Facing NW3:
322.5° - 337.5°

LI house:
Sitting S1, Facing N1:
337.5° - 352.5°

LI house:
Sitting S2, Facing N2:
352.5° - 7.5°

LI house:
Sitting S3, Facing N3:
7.5° - 22.5°

KUN house:
Sitting SW1, Facing NE1:
22.5° - 37.5°

KUN house:
Sitting SW2, Facing NE2:
37.5° - 52.5°

KUN house:
Sitting SW3, Facing NE3:
52.5° - 67.5°

Houses Built in Period 6 (Feb. 5, 1964 - Feb. 3, 1984)

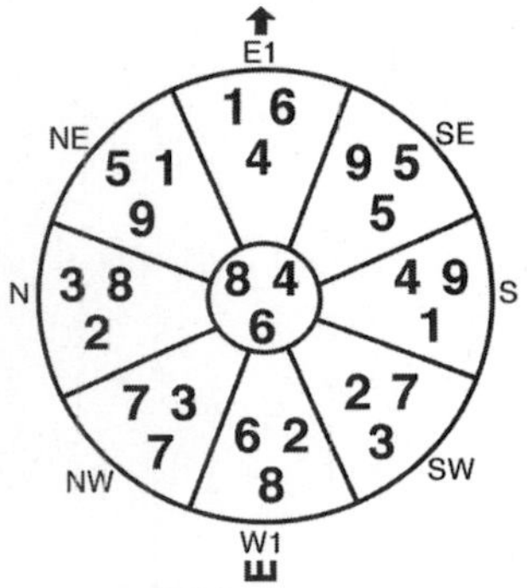

Chart 1 (top left)

E1 ↑

	1 6 4	
NE 5 1 9		SE 9 5 5
N 3 8 2	8 4 6	S 4 9 1
NW 7 3 7	6 2 8	SW 2 7 3

W1

DUI house:
Sitting W1, Facing E1:
67.5° - 82.5°

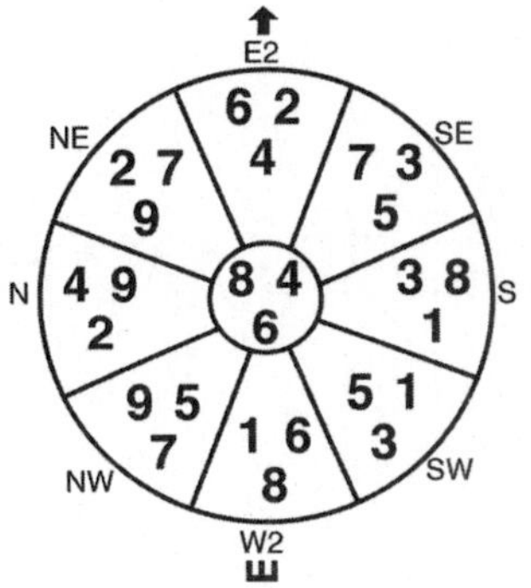

Chart 2 (top middle)

E2 ↑

	6 2 4	
NE 2 7 9		SE 7 3 5
N 4 9 2	8 4 6	S 3 8 1
NW 9 5 7	1 6 8	SW 5 1 3

W2

DUI house:
Sitting W2, Facing E2:
82.5° - 97.5°

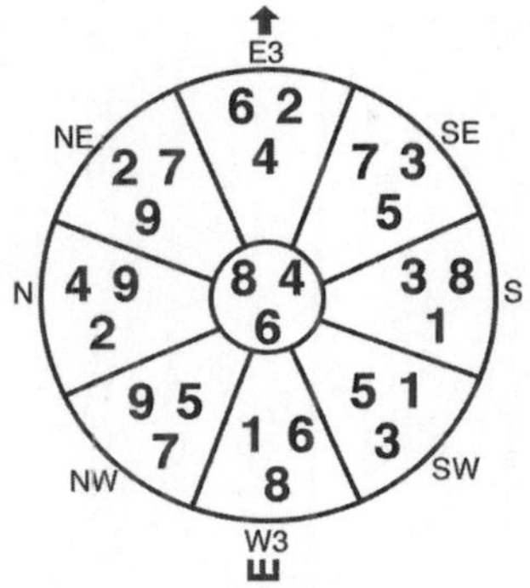

Chart 3 (top right)

E3 ↑

	6 2 4	
NE 2 7 9		SE 7 3 5
N 4 9 2	8 4 6	S 3 8 1
NW 9 5 7	1 6 8	SW 5 1 3

W3

DUI house:
Sitting W3, Facing E3:
97.5 - 112.5°

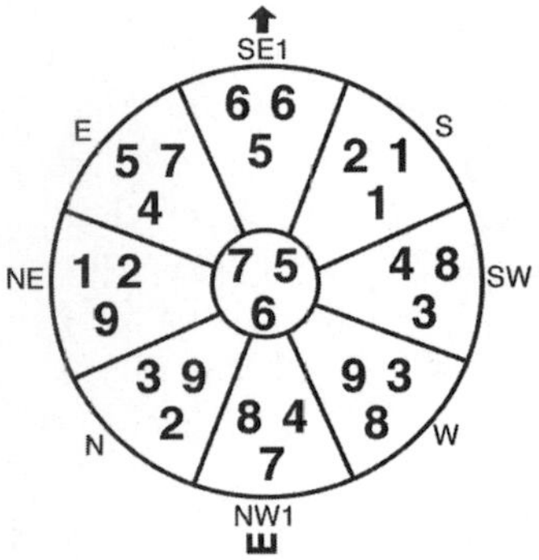

Chart 4 (bottom left)

SE1 ↑

	6 6 5	
E 5 7 4		S 2 1 1
NE 1 2 9	7 5 6	SW 4 8 3
N 3 9 2	8 4 7	W 9 3 8

NW1

QIAN house:
Sitting NW1, Facing SE1:
112.5° - 127.5°

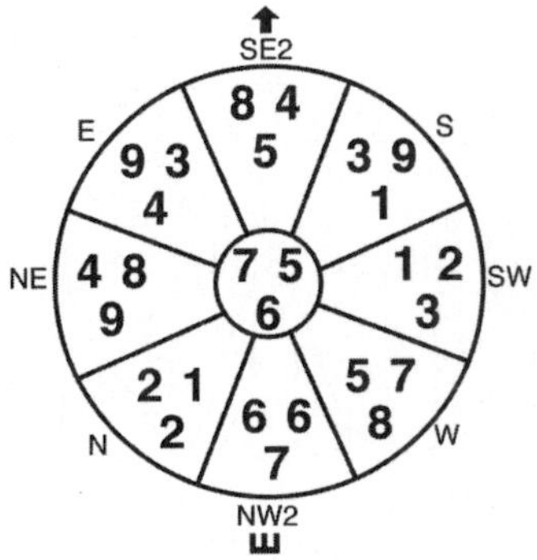

Chart 5 (bottom middle)

SE2 ↑

	8 4 5	
E 9 3 4		S 3 9 1
NE 4 8 9	7 5 6	SW 1 2 3
N 2 1 2	6 6 7	W 5 7 8

NW2

QIAN house:
Sitting NW2, Facing SE2:
127.5° - 142.5°

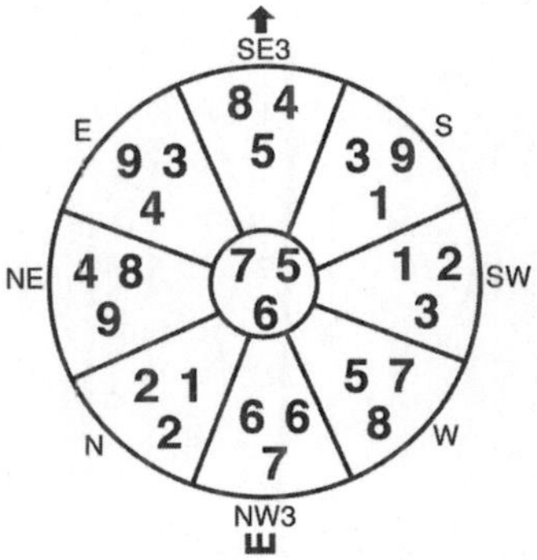

Chart 6 (bottom right)

SE3 ↑

	8 4 5	
E 9 3 4		S 3 9 1
NE 4 8 9	7 5 6	SW 1 2 3
N 2 1 2	6 6 7	W 5 7 8

NW3

QIAN house:
Sitting NW3, Facing SE3:
142.5° - 157.5°

Houses Built in Period 7 (Feb. 4, 1984 - Feb. 3, 2004)

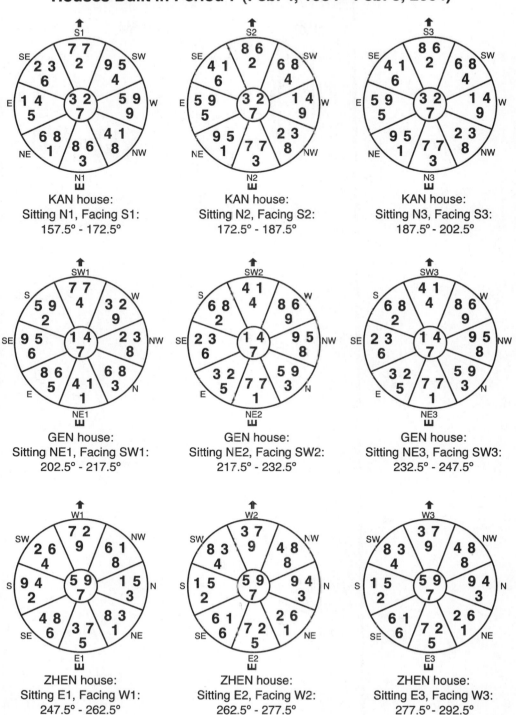

KAN house:
Sitting N1, Facing S1:
157.5° - 172.5°

KAN house:
Sitting N2, Facing S2:
172.5° - 187.5°

KAN house:
Sitting N3, Facing S3:
187.5° - 202.5°

GEN house:
Sitting NE1, Facing SW1:
202.5° - 217.5°

GEN house:
Sitting NE2, Facing SW2:
217.5° - 232.5°

GEN house:
Sitting NE3, Facing SW3:
232.5° - 247.5°

ZHEN house:
Sitting E1, Facing W1:
247.5° - 262.5°

ZHEN house:
Sitting E2, Facing W2:
262.5° - 277.5°

ZHEN house:
Sitting E3, Facing W3:
277.5° - 292.5°

Houses Built in Period 7 (Feb. 4, 1984 - Feb. 3, 2004)

XUN house:
Sitting SE1, Facing NW1:
292.5° - 307.5°

XUN house:
Sitting SE2, Facing NW2:
307.5° - 322.5°

XUN house:
Sitting SE3, Facing NW3:
322.5° - 337.5°

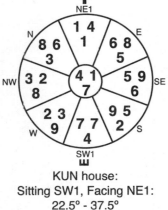

LI house:
Sitting S1, Facing N1:
337.5° - 352.5°

LI house:
Sitting S2, Facing N2:
352.5° - 7.5°

LI house:
Sitting S3, Facing N3:
7.5° - 22.5°

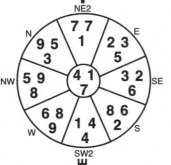

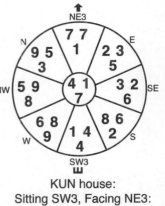

KUN house:
Sitting SW1, Facing NE1:
22.5° - 37.5°

KUN house:
Sitting SW2, Facing NE2:
37.5° - 52.5°

KUN house:
Sitting SW3, Facing NE3:
52.5° - 67.5°

Houses Built in Period 7 (Feb. 4, 1984 - Feb. 3, 2004)

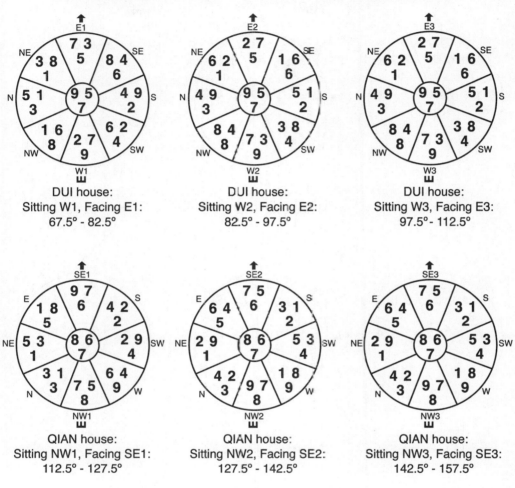

DUI house:
Sitting W1, Facing E1:
67.5° - 82.5°

DUI house:
Sitting W2, Facing E2:
82.5° - 97.5°

DUI house:
Sitting W3, Facing E3:
97.5° - 112.5°

QIAN house:
Sitting NW1, Facing SE1:
112.5° - 127.5°

QIAN house:
Sitting NW2, Facing SE2:
127.5° - 142.5°

QIAN house:
Sitting NW3, Facing SE3:
142.5° - 157.5°

Houses Built in Period 8 (Feb. 4, 2004 - Feb. 3, 2024)

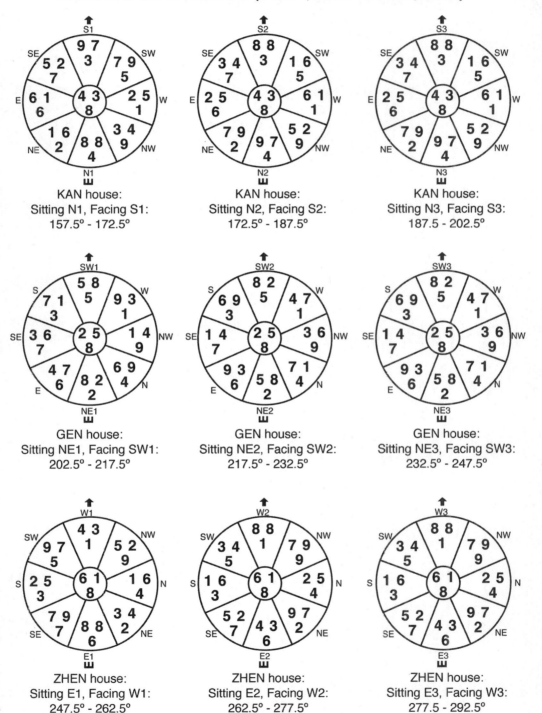

KAN house:
Sitting N1, Facing S1:
157.5° - 172.5°

KAN house:
Sitting N2, Facing S2:
172.5° - 187.5°

KAN house:
Sitting N3, Facing S3:
187.5 - 202.5°

GEN house:
Sitting NE1, Facing SW1:
202.5° - 217.5°

GEN house:
Sitting NE2, Facing SW2:
217.5° - 232.5°

GEN house:
Sitting NE3, Facing SW3:
232.5° - 247.5°

ZHEN house:
Sitting E1, Facing W1:
247.5° - 262.5°

ZHEN house:
Sitting E2, Facing W2:
262.5° - 277.5°

ZHEN house:
Sitting E3, Facing W3:
277.5 - 292.5°

Houses Built in Period 8 (Feb. 4, 2004 - Feb. 3, 2024)

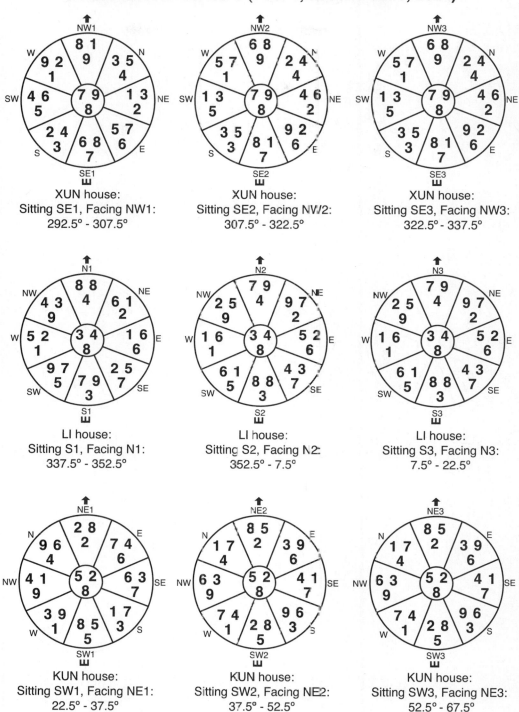

XUN house:
Sitting SE1, Facing NW1:
292.5° - 307.5°

XUN house:
Sitting SE2, Facing NW2:
307.5° - 322.5°

XUN house:
Sitting SE3, Facing NW3:
322.5° - 337.5°

LI house:
Sitting S1, Facing N1:
337.5° - 352.5°

LI house:
Sitting S2, Facing N2:
352.5° - 7.5°

LI house:
Sitting S3, Facing N3:
7.5° - 22.5°

KUN house:
Sitting SW1, Facing NE1:
22.5° - 37.5°

KUN house:
Sitting SW2, Facing NE2:
37.5° - 52.5°

KUN house:
Sitting SW3, Facing NE3:
52.5° - 67.5°

Houses Built in Period 8 (Feb. 4, 2004 - Feb. 3, 2024)

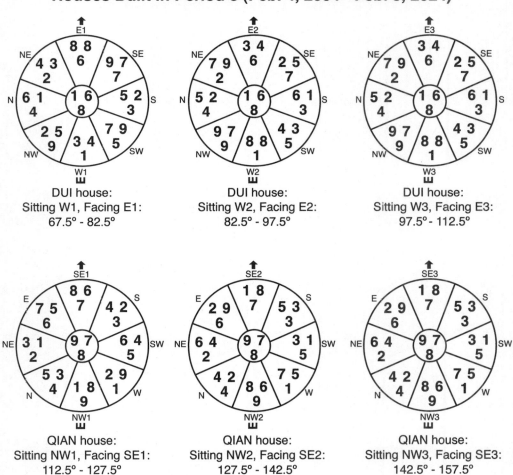

DUI house:
Sitting W1, Facing E1:
67.5° - 82.5°

DUI house:
Sitting W2, Facing E2:
82.5° - 97.5°

DUI house:
Sitting W3, Facing E3:
97.5° - 112.5°

QIAN house:
Sitting NW1, Facing SE1:
112.5° - 127.5°

QIAN house:
Sitting NW2, Facing SE2:
127.5° - 142.5°

QIAN house:
Sitting NW3, Facing SE3:
142.5° - 157.5°

Houses Built in Period 9 (Feb. 4, 2024 - Feb. 4, 2044)

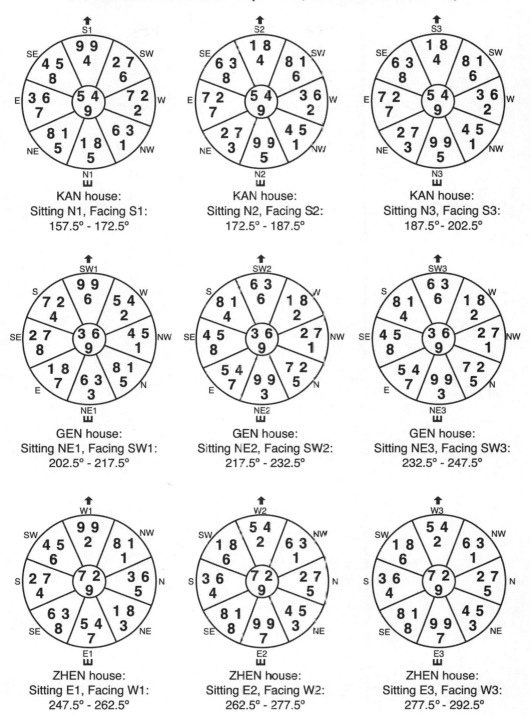

KAN house:
Sitting N1, Facing S1:
157.5° - 172.5°

KAN house:
Sitting N2, Facing S2:
172.5° - 187.5°

KAN house:
Sitting N3, Facing S3:
187.5° - 202.5°

GEN house:
Sitting NE1, Facing SW1:
202.5° - 217.5°

GEN house:
Sitting NE2, Facing SW2:
217.5° - 232.5°

GEN house:
Sitting NE3, Facing SW3:
232.5° - 247.5°

ZHEN house:
Sitting E1, Facing W1:
247.5° - 262.5°

ZHEN house:
Sitting E2, Facing W2:
262.5° - 277.5°

ZHEN house:
Sitting E3, Facing W3:
277.5° - 292.5°

Houses Built in Period 9 (Feb. 4, 2024 - Feb. 4, 2044)

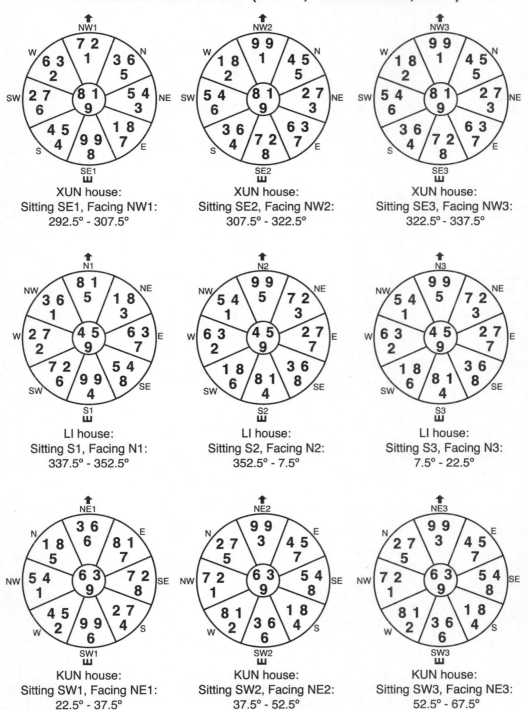

XUN house:
Sitting SE1, Facing NW1:
292.5° - 307.5°

XUN house:
Sitting SE2, Facing NW2:
307.5° - 322.5°

XUN house:
Sitting SE3, Facing NW3:
322.5° - 337.5°

LI house:
Sitting S1, Facing N1:
337.5° - 352.5°

LI house:
Sitting S2, Facing N2:
352.5° - 7.5°

LI house:
Sitting S3, Facing N3:
7.5° - 22.5°

KUN house:
Sitting SW1, Facing NE1:
22.5° - 37.5°

KUN house:
Sitting SW2, Facing NE2:
37.5° - 52.5°

KUN house:
Sitting SW3, Facing NE3:
52.5° - 67.5°

Houses Built in Period 9 (Feb. 4, 2024 - Feb. 4, 2044)

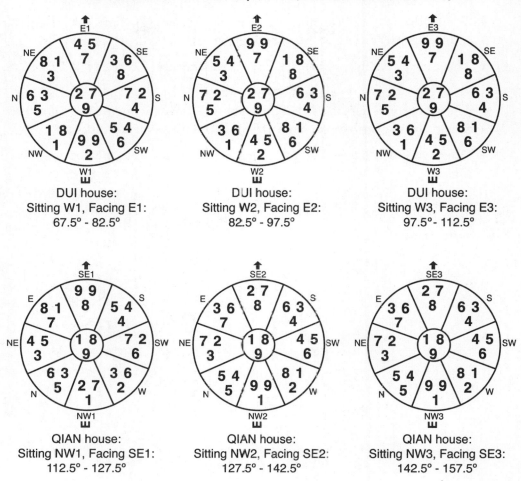

DUI house:
Sitting W1, Facing E1:
67.5° - 82.5°

DUI house:
Sitting W2, Facing E2:
82.5° - 97.5°

DUI house:
Sitting W3, Facing E3:
97.5°- 112.5°

QIAN house:
Sitting NW1, Facing SE1:
112.5° - 127.5°

QIAN house:
Sitting NW2, Facing SE2:
127.5° - 142.5°

QIAN house:
Sitting NW3, Facing SE3:
142.5° - 157.5°

The Least You Need to Know

♦ The set of three stars (numbers) in the central palace (the time star, sitting star, and facing star) dictate where the other stars are located.

♦ The stars always fly in a specific directional sequence: Center, NW, W, NE, S, N, SW, E, SE.

♦ The set of three stars in each of the eight cells surrounding the central cell represents the qi distribution coming from the eight cardinal directions.

♦ Orient your dwelling so that the sitting side corresponds to the bottom of the page.

To double-check your work, consult the appropriate chart we've provided in this chapter.

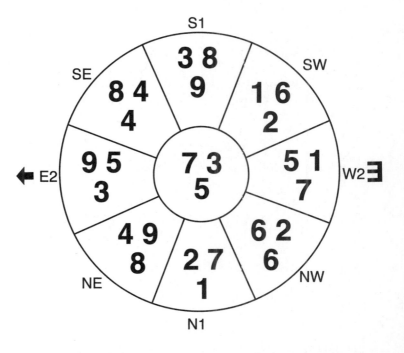

A house built in period 5 (1944-1964)
Ш sitting W2, ⬆ facing E2.

The Flying Stars, Part 5

In This Chapter

- ◆ Identifying a Fortunate Mountain Fortunate Water house
- ◆ Identifying a Reversed Mountain and Water house
- ◆ Identifying a Double Facing star house
- ◆ Identifying a Double Sitting star house
- ◆ Identifying a Locked for Prosperity house

Now that you've assembled a Flying Star chart appropriate to your home, it's time to begin interpreting the patterns of numbers that relate to your wealth, health, and relationships. In this chapter, you'll learn that your home may have special characteristics, a type of personality that can favorably or unfavorably affect the quality of your health and livelihood.

This chapter is especially important if you plan to purchase or build a home. Surely you don't want to buy or build a home that is locked for money for 20 years ending in 2024!

Yin and Yang, Mountain and Water

As you learned in Chapter 5, yin and yang are two dynamic and opposing forces of nature. The premise of feng shui is to study how these qi forces affect the quality of your health, livelihood, and relations with other people.

In Flying Star methodology, yin qi and everything it represents is expressed as the *mountain force*, the qi force that oversees a person's health and relationships. If you think about it, this idea makes perfect sense. Yin qi, associated with the female, is nurturing. Yin qi is quiet, restful, still, and stable—qualities encouraging rejuvenation, a peaceful spirit, and harmonious interaction with other people. Like a mother's yearning to protect her children, yin qi or mountain qi, shields its inhabitants from strong winds and harsh rains. Without this protective shield, you are prone to sickness and subject to arguments and disagreements.

Although the landscape surrounding your house is certainly an important consideration in a feng shui evaluation, in your home the walls are the mountains that govern your health. The walls not only contain valuable qi, but they also allow yin qi coming from the eight fundamental directions to penetrate through them, infusing the occupants with its essence. We'll be talking more about this idea in the next chapter.

Conversely, yang qi governs a person's wealth. Associated with the male, yang qi is equated with the *water force*. It's on the move. Like the streams, rivers, and seas, water qi nourishes the soil, bringing life to vegetation. Water is also an effective mode of transport. Indeed, before the advent of airplanes, societies were economically dependent on the flowing substance to help foster the exchange of goods and services. Likewise, although watercourses and streets (virtual watercourses) are important factors in an accurate feng shui assessment, in Flying Star methodology, water qi is that which flows into your dwelling through windows and doors. Again, this idea will be discussed in more detail in the next chapter.

For now, understand that the mountain force is embodied in the *mountain star*, which is identical to the sitting star (the number affiliated with the sitting direction of your home) and all of the other stars (numbers) occupying the top, left side of each cell. On the other hand, the water force is embodied in the *water star*, which is identical to the facing star (the number affiliated with the facing direction of your home) and all of the other stars occupying the top, right side of each cell. To be perfectly clear, the mountain stars govern your health and relationships; the water stars govern your finances.

Wise Words _____

Associated with yin, the **mountain force** administers a person's health and relationships. Its qi enters a home through the walls, the building's mountainlike structures protecting the occupants. Associated with yang, the **water force** governs a person's wealth. Its qi enters a home through the windows and doors, the building's free-flowing waterlike edifices. In classical feng shui terminology, the **mountain star** is synonymous with the sitting star and the stars on the top, left side of each cell. The **water star** is synonymous with the facing star and the stars on the top, right side of each cell.

Fortunate Mountain Fortunate Water

On February 4, 2004, we entered Period 8 with the number 8 ruling until February 3, 2024. You learned in Chapter 13 that the ruling star reigns supreme. It is the king star, the president, and prime minister. It rules over all other stars for a 20-year period. The ruling star is timely, bestowing its auspicious characteristics onto its subjects, the occupants.

When a ruling mountain star is located in the top, left position of the sitting cell and a ruling water star is located in the top, right position of the facing cell (the mountain and water positions respectively), it is most fortunate. This type of house or apartment unit is called *Fortunate Mountain Fortunate Water*, or Wang Shan Wang Shui in Chinese. Basically, it means the occupants have the highest probability of attaining good fortune, good health, and beneficial relationships. They have a leg up, if you will.

To illustrate this idea, look at the following figure of a Fortunate Mountain Fortunate Water Gen dwelling constructed in Period 8, sitting NE1 and facing SW1.

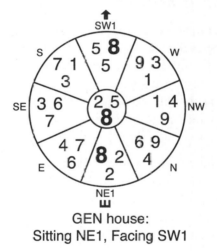

Example of a Fortunate Mountain Fortunate Water dwelling for Period 8.

GEN house:
Sitting NE1, Facing SW1

However, regardless of the auspicious positions of the mountain and water stars in the sitting and facing cells, the stars must be supported environmentally. A mountain or a man-made "mountain" such as a building, tall hedge, or forest must support the ruling mountain star in the sitting or back side of the house or apartment unit. A watercourse (ocean, river, swimming pool, fountain, for example), or a virtual waterway like a road, must support the water star in the facing or front side of the house or apartment unit. How close should these supporting structures be to the dwelling so that it still qualifies as Fortunate Mountain Fortunate Water? The general rule of thumb is that the supporting structure must be in eyesight distance. You must "feel" its essence. For most urban dwellers these factors are easily satisfied. But, what if the converse is true? What if a body of water is located on the sitting or backside and a mountain is located on the facing side or front side of the dwelling? In this case, the house is not considered Fortunate Mountain Fortunate Water. It loses its special quality, its leg up.

Master Class

Fortunate Mountain Fortunate Water dwellings built in Period 8 (February 4, 2004–February 3, 2024) include the Gen dwelling sitting NE1; the Xun dwellings sitting SE2 and SE3; the Kun dwelling sitting SW1; and the Qian dwellings sitting NW2 and NW3.

When Period 9 arrives on February 4, 2024, and the ruling star 8 leaves office, star charts with the Fortunate Mountain Fortunate Water configuration are rendered invalid. The house or apartment unit no longer possesses that extra edge, that something special because the ruling mountain star 8 is not at the sitting, and the ruling water star 8 is not at the facing.

Reversed Mountain and Water

When the ruling mountain and ruling water star in question (the number 8 for Period 8) are improperly placed, the star chart is called *Reversed Mountain and Water*, or *Shang Shan Xia Shui* in Chinese. It is most unfortunate. Stated another way, if the ruling water star (governing wealth) is located on the water (top, right) side of the sitting cell and the ruling mountain star (governing health and relationships) is located on the mountain (top, left) side of the facing cell, the house or apartment unit is potentially less fortunate in wealth and health for the 20-year period.

Simply, the stars are misaligned. Mountain's yin force is preventing your finances from growing, and water's yang force is causing a whirlwind of heightened activity resulting in anxiety, sleeplessness, and illness. Like living in close proximity to a freeway, the overabundance of yang qi embodied by the heavy traffic can wear you out.

Master Class

Reversed Mountain and Water dwellings built in Period 8 (February 4, 2004–February 3, 2024) include the Gen dwellings sitting NE2 and NE3; the Xun dwelling sitting SE1; the Kun dwellings sitting SW2 and SW3; and the Qian dwelling sitting NW1.

Here is an example of a Reversed Mountain and Water dwelling built in Period 8. It sits SE1 and faces NW1.

Can anything be done to remedy the dire prospects? Yes! In this case, a mountain or mountainlike structure (tall hedge, forest, building) must support the misaligned mountain star on the facing or front side of the house or apartment unit. Likewise, a body of water or a roadway must support the misaligned water star on the sitting or back side of the house or apartment unit.

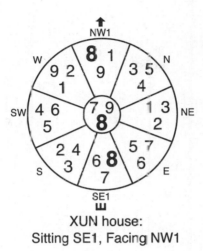

Example of a Reversed Mountain and Water dwelling for Period 8.

XUN house:
Sitting SE1, Facing NW1

When Period 9 arrives on February 4, 2024, and the ruling star 8 leaves office, star-crossed charts will be relieved from their hazardous duties. The havoc they wreaked will be thwarted.

The Double Facing Star Chart

When both the ruling mountain and the ruling water stars are located in the facing cell, the chart is called *Double Ruling Star at Facing*, or Shuang Ling Xing Dou Xiang in Chinese. In this case, the ruling water star (governing wealth) situated in the top, right side of the facing cell is in its proper place. Because of this, the house or apartment unit inspires financial gain. However, the ruling mountain star (governing health and relationships) is improperly placed. Here, it is located in the yang or facing side of the dwelling. Because of the misalignment, the house or apartment unit brings the likelihood of poor health and difficult relationships.

Here is an example of a Double Facing star chart that shows a dwelling built in Period 8, sitting W1 and facing E1.

To remedy a Double Facing situation, a body of water or virtual waterlike a roadway must support the facing or front side of the house or apartment unit. The facing side must also contain a mountain or a man-made mountain structure such as a tall hedge or building to support the misaligned mountain star. That which exists at the sitting or backside of the dwelling is not considered.

Example of a Double Ruling Star at Facing dwelling for Period 8.

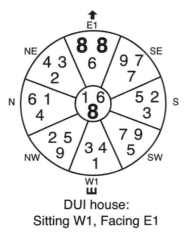

DUI house:
Sitting W1, Facing E1

When Period 9 arrives on February 4, 2024, and the ruling star 8 leaves office, the charts of houses or apartment units conforming to a Double Facing configuration are rendered invalid.

The Double Sitting Star Chart

When both the ruling mountain and the ruling water stars are located in the sitting cell, the star chart is called *Double Ruling Star at Sitting* or Shuang Ling Xing Dou Zuo, in Chinese. In this case, the ruling mountain star (governing health and relationships) situated in the top, left side of the sitting cell is in its proper place. Because of this auspicious orientation, the house or apartment unit inspires robust health and productive relations with other people. However, the ruling water star (governing wealth) is improperly placed. Here, it is located in the yin or sitting side of the dwelling. Because of the misalignment, the house or apartment unit brings the probability of money loss.

Here is an example of a Double Sitting star chart that shows a dwelling built in Period 8, sitting E1 and facing W1.

To remedy a Double Sitting situation, a mountain or a man-made mountain such as a tall hedge or building must support the sitting or back side of the dwelling. The sitting side must also contain a body of water or a roadway to support the misaligned water star. That which exists at the facing or front side of the dwelling is irrelevant.

When Period 9 arrives on February 4, 2024, and the ruling star 8 leaves office, charts of houses or apartment units conforming to a Double Sitting configuration will be rendered invalid.

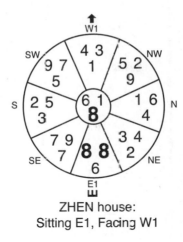

Example of a Double Ruling Star at Sitting dwelling for Period 8.

ZHEN house:
Sitting E1, Facing W1

CAUTION

Feng Alert _____

It's important to understand that the four types of dwellings described in this chapter are only valid if the period the house or apartment unit was constructed in matches the ruling period. For example, take a house constructed in Period 4 (1924–1944). Even if the number configurations conform to a Fortunate Mountain and Water, Reversed Mountain and Water, Double Facing, or Double Sitting situation, the house wouldn't qualify as one of the four special cases until Period 4 arrives again in the year 2104.

Locked for Prosperity House

When a dwelling's facing or water star (on the right side) in the central palace is the same as the period star (the number 8 for Period 8), the chart is called *Locked for Prosperity*, or Ling Xing Ri Qui in Chinese. The ruling water (wealth) star is imprisoned. It is like a country without a ruler. There is discord; money is stuck; occupants will struggle to make ends meet; career advancement is difficult. However, the locked water star doesn't only apply to a person's finances. Anything that brings you good fortune—happiness, romance, and robust health—will be hampered. The dwelling is said to have bad feng shui. The lock will be released when Period 8 ends on February 3, 2024.

Here are two examples of Locked for Prosperity houses. House 1 was built in Period 4, sitting N1 and facing S1. House 2 was built in Period 7, sitting SE1 and facing NW1.

Examples of Locked for Prosperity dwellings built in Period 4 and Period 7.

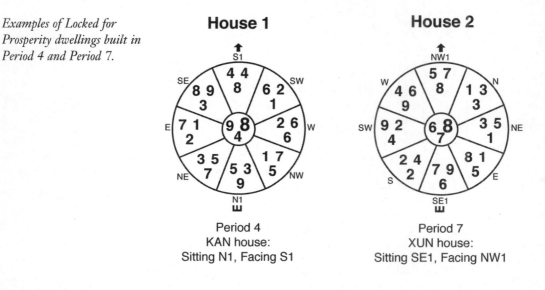

House 1

Period 4
KAN house:
Sitting N1, Facing S1

House 2

Period 7
XUN house:
Sitting SE1, Facing NW1

To set the imprisoned money star free and unlock the house, the central part of the house must be open to all directions. If there's a body of water, virtual water (like a roadway), or a wide-open space at the facing side of the dwelling, the number 8 water star is released. It can flow out of and into the dwelling freely, improving the luck of the occupants. Although central courtyards are common in China, it is not a common feature in Western homes. What to do? We have three suggestions:

◆ Work extra hard to prevent misfortune.

◆ Move. Use Flying Star to find an auspicious dwelling. Remember to consider the forms, too. See Chapters 9 and 10 for a reminder.

◆ Change the period of your house by opening up the roof so that heaven qi and earth qi combine to bring new life. Obviously, this suggestion is radical and expensive, and complex if your house is multilevel. (It is impossible to perform this procedure for an apartment unit.) The opening must be proportional to the space in question, allowing heaven qi to permeate the house for at least one month. If you install a central skylight, the door must be *open*. For example, a Period 4 N1 Kan house becomes a Period 8 N1 Kan house. Beware! Before you proceed, study the Flying Star maps of the existing house and prospective new house. Are the new number combinations more auspicious than the old combinations? You'll learn about the meaning of number combinations in the next chapter. Changing the period of a house is the last resort. Seek a classical practitioner for advice.

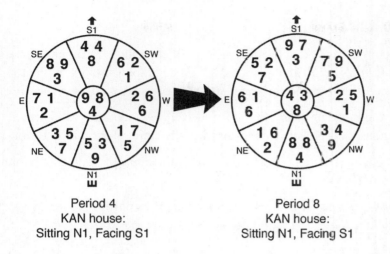

Period 4
KAN house:
Sitting N1, Facing S1

Period 8
KAN house:
Sitting N1, Facing S1

A Period 4 Kan house becomes a Period 8 Kan house if the center is opened.

When Period 9 arrives on February 4, 2024, and the ruling star 8 leaves office, charts of houses and apartment units that are Locked for Prosperity will be rendered invalid. What happens if the ruling mountain star matches the period star? Is the house locked for health and relationships? No, this rule does not exist.

Period 1 houses and apartment units that are Locked for Prosperity in Period 8 include the Dui dwellings sitting W1, W2, and W3. Period 2 dwellings that are locked include the Gen dwellings sitting NE1, NE2, and NE3. Period 3 dwellings that are locked include the Li dwellings sitting S1, S2 and S3. Period 4 houses that are locked include Kan dwellings sitting N1, N2, and N3. Period 5 houses that are locked include Kun dwellings sitting SW1, SW2, and SW3. Period 6 houses that are locked include Zhen dwellings sitting E1, E2, and E3. Period 7 houses that are locked include Xun dwellings sitting SE1, SE2, and SE3. Period 8 dwellings are not Locked for Prosperity.

In the next chapter, you'll learn how to interpret and remedy the number combinations made manifest in the central palace and the remaining eight cells.

The Least You Need to Know

♦ The numbers located on the top, left side of each cell are called the mountain stars. They govern a person's health and relationships. The numbers located on the top, right side of each cell are called the water stars. They govern a person's wealth.

♦ There are four types of star charts that hold special characteristics valid only if the period the house was constructed in matches the ruling period in question.

♦ The auspicious characteristics manifest only when the appropriate forms (mountain, building, water, road) support the stars.

♦ The inauspicious characteristics manifest only when the appropriate forms (mountain, building, water, road) do not exist to thwart the ill affects.

♦ If the top, right number in the central palace matches the period number, your house or apartment unit is Locked for Prosperity.

Chapter 16

The Flying Stars, Part 6

In This Chapter

- ◆ More about the mountain, water, and time stars
- ◆ The stars in the central palace
- ◆ A Flying Star chart analysis
- ◆ Star combinations and their meanings

Congratulations for assembling a Flying Star chart appropriate to your home! Give yourself a round of applause, a pat on the back for a job well done.

In this chapter, you'll learn how to interpret your star chart. Don't be intimidated by the 27 stars (9 cells × 3 stars each) composing a chart. Understanding their meanings, enhancing their positive aspects, and discouraging the negative ones will lead to a productive environment fostering better wealth, good health, and beneficial relationships.

Understanding the Water, Mountain, and Time Stars

Before you proceed with understanding and remedying the number combinations, let's take a moment to fully comprehend the three stars comprising each cell—the water, mountain, and time stars.

The Water Star

Governing wealth, the water star is located on the top, right side of each cell. If your home conforms to one of the four special cases discussed in the previous chapter, follow the advice to activate the ruling star for the chart in question. If your home does not belong to one of the four special cases, locate the ruling water number in your chart (the number 8 for Period 8). Support the star environmentally, allowing the yang qi essence of the nearby water/roadway to flow into the house through an open window or door. Use the space containing the ruling money star for a home office—any area where you conduct money-related business.

Regarding the remaining nonruling money stars, *timely* stars (the numbers 1, 9, and 8 for Period 8) located only in *active* areas can bolster financial gain. Because of their negative characteristics, untimely (retired/dead) stars (the numbers 7, 6, 5, 4, 3, and 2 for Period 8) cannot foster wealth. Diminish an untimely water star's negative aspects by keeping the windows and doors closed in the area in question, at least during the night. Also, as you'll soon learn, employ a five-phase remedy to ward off an unfavorable projection.

In an active (yang) area within a home (family room, home office, kitchen), focus on the water star and how it reacts with the mountain star. If the time star is productive to or belongs to the same phase as the water star, the possibility of financial gain is even greater. In an inactive (yin) area (bedroom, guest bedroom, living room), focus on the mountain star and how it reacts with the water star. If the time star is productive to or belongs to the same phase as the mountain star, the probability of good health increases. Why not remedy the entire dwelling for wealth? Because poor health leads to a poor financial outlook! Remember, feng shui is about balancing the yin and yang qi forces.

The Mountain Star

Governing health and relationships, the mountain star is located on the top, left side of each cell. If your home conforms to one of the four special cases discussed in the previous chapter, follow the advice to activate the mountain star for the chart in question. If your home does not belong to one of the four special cases, locate the ruling mountain number in your chart (the number 8 for Period 8). Support the star, allowing the yin qi essence of the nearby mountain/building to enter the house by infusing and charging the walls. Windows should be kept closed, particularly if the water (yang) star is not favorable. If the water star is favorable, make sure that the wind does not disperse yin's (health and relationship) qi. Use the space containing the ruling health and relationship star for your bedroom and other areas promoting rest and relaxation.

Regarding the remaining nonruling mountain stars, *timely* stars (the numbers 1, 9, and 8 for Period 8) located only in *inactive* areas can foster good health and beneficial relationships. Because of their negative characteristics, untimely (retired/dead) stars (the numbers 7, 6, 5, 4, 3, and 2 for Period 8) cannot bolster your health and relations. In this case, diminish an untimely mountain star's inauspicious aspects by employing a five-phase remedy.

The Time Star

The time star provides a base for the mountain and water stars. Using an analogy, the water star is like steak, the protein fortifying your strength and determination to succeed. The mountain star is like a vegetable, the vitamins nourishing your health. The time star is the plate on which your dinner is served. You do not eat the plate, do you? Yet, the plate must be clean and beautiful; otherwise, you cannot enjoy the meal. Although the time star itself does not foster fortune or misfortune, it either supports or does not support the water and mountain star. It depends on the phase (fire, earth, metal, water, and wood) relationship between the time star and the mountain star and the time star and the water star. If the relationship is productive, the water or mountain star in question is enhanced. If the time star controls or reduces the water or mountain star's power, the star in question loses its zeal.

Before you proceed, it's a good idea to have the Flying Star chart corresponding to your home, which you worked on in Chapter 14, in front of you.

Master Class

Flying Star is about balancing the mountain (yin) and water (yang) forces. External to a house, there are mountains, buildings, rivers, lakes, and streets. Inside a house, there are also mountains and waterways. Walls and large furniture are interior mountains. Doors, windows, and hallways are interior watercourses. When activating a yang area for wealth, keep windows open and make sure that the hallways are unobstructed. When activating a yin area for health and relationships, make sure that the qi is not dispersed by wind. High-back chairs and a bed with its headboard against a solid wall are ways to make good use of a timely mountain star.

The Central Palace

Now that you understand more thoroughly what the water and mountain stars represent and how you can use them to your advantage, let's take a look at the central palace. A feng shui assessment begins here. Heaven's qi (associated with the time the

Feng Alert

Don't forget to consider the exterior and interior environment. What can be done to allow qi to flow productively, easily, and uninhibited? Consult Chapters 9 and 10 about assessing the surrounding terrain, the lot on which your house sits, the alignment of roads and watercourses, and the orientation of furniture.

dwelling was "born" into) and earth's qi (associated with the magnetic orientation of the building) merge to produce a house with a specific type of personality made manifest by the numbers in the central palace. When the sitting (mountain) and facing (water) stars are compatible, chances are the innate essence fosters harmony. However, when the sitting and facing stars conflict, chances are the innate essence fosters discord. Because the central palace does not represent an area, the stars here cannot be balanced with one of the five phases of qi. Great care must be taken, then, to balance the stars comprising the surrounding eight cells.

It's All in the Stars: The Star Combination Chart

The following number combinations reflect the possibility that the favorable or unfavorable event in question may occur if proper remedies/enhancements are *not* installed. As you become more familiar with each number combination, you'll notice that some combinations contain both good and bad aspects. You may be wondering, then, how to promote the good and dissuade the bad? Although space doesn't permit us to get into a detailed analysis of the number combinations, remember that timely stars bring out the good characteristics and untimely stars bring out the bad ones. A general rule of thumb is to enhance timely stars and weaken untimely stars. You might want to review Chapter 13 about the characteristics of untimely and timely stars. The following effects are valid for the Lower Cycle (1984–2044).

The Effects of Combinations of Stars (Numbers)

Mountain Star	Phase	Water Star	Phase	Effect
1	Water	1	Water	Academic, artistic, and monetary achievement. Ear-, blood-, and kidney-related diseases caused by alcohol.
1	Water	2	Earth	Spousal conflict, separation, or divorce. Miscarriage and abdominal pain. Traffic accident likely.
1	Water	3	Wood	Theft and legal entanglements. Exhaustion due to competition.

Mountain Star	Phase	Water Star	Phase	Effect
1	Water	4	Wood	Gaining fame through writing or artistic work. Romance.
1	Water	5	Earth	Illness of the ears, kidney, and genital organs.
1	Water	6	Metal	Promotion and career success. Probability of nervous breakdown.
1	Water	7	Metal	Financial gain. Injury by knife. Flirtation.
1	Water	8	Earth	Health and wealth. Dispute among siblings and colleagues.
1	Water	9	Fire	Career advancement and financial gain. Eye disease.
2	Earth	1	Water	Spousal conflict, separation, or divorce. Miscarriage and abdominal pain. Traffic accidents.
2	Earth	2	Earth	Sickness and injury due to an accident.
2	Earth	3	Wood	Conflict, gossip, litigation, and accidents.
2	Earth	4	Wood	Romance. Woman harassing her mother. Abdominal disease.
2	Earth	5	Earth	Bankruptcy, serious illness, and possible death.
2	Earth	6	Metal	Wealth and power. Abdominal disease.
2	Earth	7	Metal	Financial gain. Abdominal and mouth-related illness.
2	Earth	8	Earth	Great wealth. Frequent minor illness.
2	Earth	9	Fire	Stupidity and mental disorder. Bad for a bedroom.
3	Wood	1	Water	Theft and legal entanglements. Injury due to an accident.
3	Wood	2	Earth	Conflict, gossip, lawsuits, and accidents.

continues

The Effects of Combinations of Stars (Numbers) (continued)

Mountain Star	Phase	Water Star	Phase	Effect
3	Wood	3	Wood	Arguments, disagreements, and assault. Robbery.
3	Wood	4	Wood	Creativity and romance. Unruly behavior.
3	Wood	5	Earth	Financial delinquency. Liver disease and leg injury.
3	Wood	6	Metal	Gaining recognition. Leg injury for a man.
3	Wood	7	Metal	Financial success. Injury by a metal object. Lawsuit.
3	Wood	8	Earth	Monetary gain. Limb injury, especially for children.
3	Wood	9	Fire	Birth of intelligent son. Man easily loses temper. Financial gain through career promotion.
4	Wood	1	Water	Gaining fame through writing or artistic work. Romance.
4	Wood	2	Earth	Woman harassing her mother. Abdominal disease.
4	Wood	3	Wood	Robbery and litigation. Disruptive behavior.
4	Wood	4	Wood	Great artistic achievement. Inappropriate romance.
4	Wood	5	Earth	Loss of wealth. Breast tumor. Plagiarism.
4	Wood	6	Metal	Gaining recognition. Physical injuries for a woman.
4	Wood	7	Metal	Financial gain. Flirtation. Injury to a woman.
4	Wood	8	Earth	Financial success. Injury to children.
4	Wood	9	Fire	Birth of an intelligent child. Failure in examination.
5	Earth	1	Water	Illness of the ears, kidney, and genital organs.

Mountain Star	Phase	Water Star	Phase	Effect
5	Earth	2	Earth	Bankruptcy, serious illness, and possible death.
5	Earth	3	Wood	Financial delinquency. Liver disease and leg injury.
5	Earth	4	Wood	Breast tumor. Entangled in plagiarism. Failed relationship.
5	Earth	5	Earth	Disastrous in wealth and health.
5	Earth	6	Metal	Gaining power, but at the expense of headaches.
5	Earth	7	Metal	Gaining wealth. Food poisoning and mouth-related disease.
5	Earth	8	Earth	Financial gain. Broken bones and injured tendon.
5	Earth	9	Fire	Confusion of the mind. Financial and health hazard due to impulsive behavior.
6	Metal	1	Water	Promotion and career success. Possibility of nervous breakdown.
6	Metal	2	Earth	Financial loss due to sickness.
6	Metal	3	Wood	Robbery resulting in injury. Accident causing leg injury.
6	Metal	4	Wood	Troubled relationship. Woman hurt by a metal object.
6	Metal	5	Earth	Financial loss due to loss of power.
6	Metal	6	Metal	Gaining power. Lawsuit and arguments.
6	Metal	7	Metal	Conflicts, disagreements, and fighting. Injury by a metal object.
6	Metal	8	Earth	Financial success. Promotion. Obstinacy.
6	Metal	9	Fire	Financial gain. Lung and head disease. Authority challenged.
7	Metal	1	Water	Flirtation. Bleeding. Success by traveling overseas.
7	Metal	2	Earth	Financial loss. Physical fitness.

continues

The Effects of Combinations of Stars (Numbers) (continued)

Mountain Star	Phase	Water Star	Phase	Effect
7	Metal	3	Wood	Robbery. Litigation over money.
7	Metal	4	Wood	Flirtation. Injury to a woman.
7	Metal	5	Earth	Financial disaster. Food poisoning.
7	Metal	6	Metal	Conflicts and fighting. Injury by a metal object.
7	Metal	7	Metal	Wealth through competition. Good health.
7	Metal	8	Earth	Great wealth and blossoming romance.
7	Metal	9	Fire	Gaining recognition and wealth. Fire hazard.
8	Earth	1	Water	Health and wealth. Disputes among siblings and colleagues.
8	Earth	2	Earth	Healthy but not quite wealthy. Good for bedroom.
8	Earth	3	Wood	Robbery and arguments. Injury to children.
8	Earth	4	Wood	Inappropriate romance. Injury to children.
8	Earth	5	Earth	Financial loss. Good health.
8	Earth	6	Metal	Gaining authority. Good for a bedroom.
8	Earth	7	Metal	Great monetary gain. Successful romance.
8	Earth	8	Earth	Good for wealth and health. Loneliness.
8	Earth	9	Fire	Happy events, wedding and birth of a child.
9	Fire	1	Water	Career advancement and financial gain. Eye disease.
9	Fire	2	Earth	Stupidity and mental disorder. Financial loss due to illness.
9	Fire	3	Wood	Birth of an intelligent child. Bad temper.
9	Fire	4	Wood	Birth of an intelligent child. Failure in examination.

Mountain Star	Phase	Water Star	Phase	Effect
9	Fire	5	Earth	Confusion of the mind. Financial and health hazard due to impulsive behavior.
9	Fire	6	Metal	Lung and head disease. Authority challenged.
9	Fire	7	Metal	Financial gain. Fire hazard. Arguments and fighting.
9	Fire	8	Earth	Happy events, wedding, and birth of a child.
9	Fire	9	Fire	Celebrations for success in career and romance.

In order to begin analyzing and remedying/enhancing the number combinations, make sure that you fully understand the relationships between the five phases. If the productive, controlling, and weakening cycles aren't firmly embedded into your mind, review Chapter 6.

A Simple Analysis

Considering only the stars, let's examine a Flying Star chart for a Dui house built in Period 7, sitting W2 and facing E2. We'll begin with the central palace, then move up to the facing cell, and travel clockwise around the chart. *Note:* M stands for mountain star; W for water star; and T for time star.

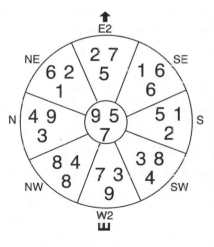

DUI house:
Sitting W2. Facing E2

Center: 9M (fire) 5W (earth) 7T (metal)

Fire produces earth. Although a productive relationship, it is not a healthy one. The number 9 is encouraging the inauspicious number 5's proclivity for misfortune. (Remember, the number 9 enhances any number with which it's paired.) On the up side, the number 9 is also melting the potential harmful affects of the retired star 7. Although the numbers comprising the central palace cannot cause fortune or misfortune, they represent the innate nature of the dwelling. In this case, it is inharmonious, causing the possibility of financial and health hazards.

East: 2M (earth) 7W (metal) 5T (earth)

Earth produces metal. Metal is needed to lessen the negative affects brought on by the innately evil numbers 2 and 5. Be mindful of abdominal and mouth-related disorders.

Southeast: 1M (water) 6W (metal) 6T (metal)

Metal produces water. This is a productive combination heralding prospects for promotion and career success. Thus, no remedy is needed. However, the stress associated with more responsibility might cause an abundance of nervousness. This is because the number 1's water is draining the 6's energy, a number associated with the head.

South: 5M (earth) 1W (water) 2T (earth)

Earth blocks water. This is a controlling relationship, with the combination bringing the possibility of ear-, kidney-, and genital-related disorders. Moving metal (a chiming clock with a metal pendulum or playing the piano) is needed here to thwart the occurrence of an ailment. Metal will reduce the effects of the untimely and inherently inauspicious numbers 2 and 5. Metal will bridge earth and water, reverting the cycle to a productive one. Because the water (wealth) star is also untimely, this area should be avoided.

> **Feng Facts**
>
> Remember how each number affects parts of the body. Here are the number/body correlations: 1) ears, blood, kidneys; 2) abdomen, stomach; 3) feet, lower leg, liver; 4) thighs, buttocks, lower back; 5) N/A; 6) head, lungs; 7) mouth, teeth, tongue, chest; 8) hands, fingers; 9) eyes, heart. A disorder arises only if the number in question is untimely or if it is being attacked by another phase.

Southwest: 3M (wood) 8W (earth) 4T (wood)

Wood burdens earth. The highly favorable number 8 is located on the water or wealth side, making this area terrific for a home office. To increase the chance for financial success, activate the money star by opening a window in this area. Install a water feature so that the water/wealth qi has somewhere to accumulate. The possibility of limb injuries for a child makes this area unsuitable for a playroom or child's bedroom.

West: 7M (metal) 3W (wood) 9T (fire)

Metal pierces wood. To remedy the possibility of robbery and legal entanglements, earth is needed to restore the cycle to a productive one: Wood produces fire; fire produces earth; earth produces metal.

Northwest: 8M (earth) 4W (wood) 8T (earth)

Wood burdens earth. The advantageous number 8 is situated on the mountain (health and relationships) side, making the area favorable for a bedroom. Support the health and relationship star by keeping the windows closed, particularly at night. To thwart possible spousal affairs (brought on by the untimely number 4), install the fire phase to revert the cycle to a productive one. The combination is unfavorable for young children.

North: 4M (wood) 9W (fire) 3T (wood)

Wood produces fire. The auspicious combination 4-9 is known as "fire makes wood glowing and glamorous." In other words, fire brightens 4's romantic nature, making the area good for a bedroom (particularly for a couple seeking a pregnancy). Because 9 is a timely money star, the area also makes a favorable home office. No remedy is needed.

Northeast: 6M (metal) 2W (earth) 1T (water)

Earth produces metal. Although this is a productive relationship, metal is needed to suppress the unfavorable and untimely number 2's promotion of illness and money loss. Metal will also strengthen 6's inherently auspicious quality of bringing authority and fame, which is being corroded by the time (water) star.

What's the bottom line? Although the dwelling's innate personality is inharmonious, several favorable star combinations, if properly remedied, can offset the inauspicious combination in the central palace. The areas that should be actively used and that inspire financial gain are the east, southeast, southwest, and north. The areas promoting good health and good relations are located in the west, north, northwest, and northeast. In this case, the south is an inauspicious area.

Take this time now to evaluate and remedy the eight cells comprising your living and/or working space. However, things might change when we add the annual star. This is the subject of the next chapter.

The Least You Need to Know

♦ Begin a feng shui assessment by studying the numbers comprising the central palace. They represent the dwelling's inherent essence.

♦ Locate the areas containing the ruling and timely water (wealth) stars. If needed, remedy or enhance the area in question with one of the five phases to increase the possibility of financial success.

♦ Locate the areas containing the ruling and timely mountain (health and relationship) stars. If needed, remedy or enhance the area in question with one of the five phases to ensure good health and beneficial relations with other people.

♦ A Flying Star chart must be supported by the proper forms (mountains, buildings, water, and the like) outside.

The Flying Stars, Part 7

In This Chapter

- Determining the annual star
- Using the annual star chart
- Flying the annual star: how the annual star affects the mountain, water, and time stars
- Looking at the annual star for 2006, 2007, and 2008

This is the final chapter about the Flying Star system. Here, you'll receive the last piece of the puzzle—the annual star. After you've incorporated the annual star into your chart, you can fully evaluate your chart to create a productive atmosphere fostering better well-being.

The Annual Star

Each year, the nine heavenly stars visit earth. One of the stars is the leader and is stationed in the central palace along with the mountain, water, and time stars governing the chart. Who's the leader of the annual stars? The nine stars take turns being leader, with the term of office being one solar year beginning variously on the third, fourth, or fifth day of February. Because there are nine stars, it takes nine years to complete a cycle. The cycle we're currently in began in the year 2000, with the number 9 as leader. In 2006, the leader is the number 3; in 2007, the leader is the number 2; in 2008, the leader is the number 1. The year 2009 marks a new 9-year cycle. The other numbers follow suit in a descending order.

To determine the annual star for any particular year, use this simple formula:

1. Add up all the digits for the year in question. For example, let's calculate the annual star for 2009: 2 + 0 + 0 + 9 = 11.

2. Add the resulting number until you get a single-digit number. Continuing with our example: 1 + 1 = 2.

3. Subtract the resulting number from 11. The answer is the annual star number. In the case of 2009, 11 − 2 = 9.

Let's calculate another year. How about 2013?

2 + 0 + 1 + 3 = 6

11 − 6 = 5

The number 5 is the annual star for 2013.

Get the idea? What star prevailed during your birth year?

The Annual Star Chart

For your convenience, we've assembled the following quick-reference table. Notice how the numbers descend with the progression of years.

Year	Star	Year	Star	Year	Star	Year	Star
1991	9	2000	9	2009	9	2018	9
1992	8	2001	8	2010	8	2019	8
1993	7	2002	7	2011	7	2020	7
1994	6	2003	6	2012	6	2021	6
1995	5	2004	5	2013	5	2022	5
1996	4	2005	4	2014	4	2023	4
1997	3	2006	3	2015	3	2024	3
1998	2	2007	2	2016	2	2025	2
1999	1	2008	1	2017	1	2026	1

To figure out the annual stars previous to 1991, count up. To figure out the annual stars beyond 2026, count down.

Flying the Annual Star

The annual star, or number, flies in exactly the same manner as the time star (the period star). It flies forward, the ascending numbers filling the remaining eight cells by following the directional sequence: NW, W, NE, S, N, SW, E, SE.

When a star occupies the central palace, it's less influential than the other stars because it's "locked" or "imprisoned" in the chart. However, if the design of the house leaves the center open (if there's an atrium, patio, or courtyard in the center, for example), then the numbers are freed. The heaven qi from the facing palace (the water star) will positively or negatively affect the numbers situated in the facing cell, and the heaven qi from the sitting palace (the mountain star) will positively or negatively affect the numbers situated in the sitting cell.

As a visiting star, an annual star can affect a house in three ways:

- ◆ An annual star can act on its own to affect the relationship between the mountain, water, and time stars in question. If an annual star is timely, it will affect the area positively. If the annual star is untimely, it will affect the area negatively.

- ◆ An annual star can activate a combination (mountain-water, mountain-time, water-time) if the phase it's correlated with produces the phase attached to the mountain or water star in question.

- ◆ An annual star can activate a combination (mountain-water, mountain-time, water-time) if the number is the same as the mountain or the water star in question. In this case, the annual star assists the mountain and/or time star.

We will demonstrate this idea by carrying over the example from the previous chapter of the house built in Period 7, sitting W2 and facing E2. If you're uncertain about the relationship between the phases and to which number each phase corresponds, it's a good idea to use the first illustration in Appendix F for a handy reminder.

The Annual Star for 2006

Beginning in the central palace, moving up to the facing cell, and traveling clockwise around the chart, let's take a look at how the annual star affects the other stars. Again, M stands for mountain star, W for water star, T for time star, and A for annual star. The number in bold adjacent to the time star corresponds to the annual star.

The annual star 3 (2006) and how it relates to a Dui house built in Period 7, sitting W2 and facing E2.

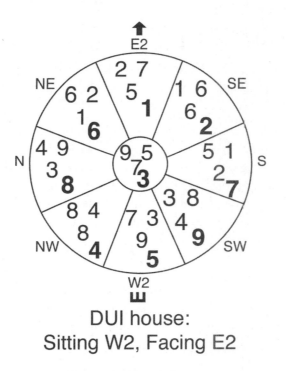

DUI house:
Sitting W2, Facing E2

Center: 9M (fire) 5W (earth) 7T (metal) 3A (wood)

Fire (9M) produces earth (5W). Although a productive relationship, it is not a healthy one. Here, the number 9 is encouraging the highly inauspicious number 5's proclivity for misfortune. It's also melting the recently retired number 7's metal—a number that's still useful for the remainder of the Lower Cycle ending February, 2044. Although the numbers comprising the central cell cannot cause fortune or misfortune, they represent the innate nature of the dwelling. In this case, it is inharmonious. In this example, the 3 wood annual star, which fuels 9 fire, is a bad omen. Fortunately, its influence is minimal within the confines of the central cell.

East: 2M (earth) 7W (metal) 5T (earth) 1A (water)

Earth (2M) produces metal (7W). Although productive, it's a nasty combination. Inherently ugly numbers 2 and 5 must be dealt with so that the number 7 water (money) star can bring financial gain. Metal will not only reduce the threatening earth stars, it will strengthen the number 7 star, which in 2006 is being weakened by water.

Southeast: 1M (water) 6W (metal) 6T (metal) 2A (earth)

Metal (6W) produces water (1M). This productive combination heralds the possibility of promotion and career success. However, the stress associated with more responsibility may cause an abundance of nervousness. This is because 1's water is draining 6's energy, a number associated with the head. The annual 2 earth (an inherently auspicious number) activates the 1M-6W and 6W-6T combinations. Add metal this year to lessen the harmful impact of the number 2 annual star.

South: 5M (earth) 1W (water) 2T (earth) 7A (metal)

Earth (5M) blocks water (1W). This is a controlling relationship, the combination bringing the probability of ear-, kidney-, and genital-related disorders. The annual 7 metal activates the 5M-1W combination, increasing the dire probability. Moving metal is needed here to thwart the untimely and inherently inauspicious numbers 2 and 5. Also, metal will bridge earth and water, reverting the cycle to a productive one.

Southwest: 3M (wood) 8W (earth) 4T (wood) 9A (fire)

Wood (3M) burdens earth (8W). The highly favorable number 8 is located on the water or wealth side. To increase the chance for financial success, install a water remedy here. But remember, a window must be open in this area to allow the water qi to enter. The visiting 9 activates the 3M-8E combination, effectively brightening the auspicious 8 earth star's benevolence. Also, 9 bridges wood and earth, restoring balance to the sequence.

West: 7M (metal) 3W (wood) 9T (fire) 5A (earth)

Metal (7M) pierces wood (3W). In the last chapter, we determined earth was needed to diminish the possibility of robbery and legal entanglements. Earth would restore the cycle to a productive one: wood produces fire; fire produces earth; earth produces metal. However, in 2006, the unfavorable 5 earth visits. It activates the 7M-3W combination, making the disastrous prospects even stronger. Moving metal is needed to repress 5 earth.

Northwest: 8M (earth) 4W (wood) 8T (earth) 4A (wood)

Wood (4W) burdens earth (8M). Because the advantageous number 8 is situated on the mountain (health and relationships) side, we must thwart the possibility of spousal affairs (brought on by the untimely number 4) by installing the fire phase. Fire will revert the cycle to a productive one. Fire will also reduce the visiting 4 wood, which activates the unfavorable 8M-4W combination. Strengthen 8's mountain by keeping the windows closed, especially at night.

North: 4M (wood) 9W (fire) 3T (wood) 8A (earth)

Wood (4M) produces fire (9W). In the previous chapter, we determined that a remedy is not needed because 9's fire would intensify 4's romantic nature, making the area good for a couple seeking a pregnancy. Because 9 is a timely money star, the area also makes a favorable home office. In 2006, the annual 8 acts on its own to bring good fortune. This year add fire to fuel 8's auspiciousness.

Northeast: 6M (metal) 2W (earth) 1T (water) 6A (metal)

Earth (2W) produces metal (6M). Although this is a productive relationship, in the previous chapter, we determined metal is needed to suppress the unfavorable and untimely number 2's promotion of illness and money loss. Metal will also strengthen 6's inherently auspicious quality of bringing authority and fame. Although the annual 6 brings metal, overall, a metal remedy is still needed to strengthen the innately favorable numbers 6 and 1 and to weaken the innately unfavorable 2.

The bottom line: In 2006, the annual star affects the southeast, west, and northern areas of this house. Now, let's see how the annual star 2 for the year 2007 affects the same home.

The Annual Star for 2007

Beginning in the central palace, moving up to the facing cell, and traveling clockwise around the chart, let's take a look at how the annual star affects the other stars. Again, M stands for mountain star, W for water star, T for time star, and A for annual star. The numbers in bold adjacent to the time star correspond to the annual star.

The annual star 2 (2007) and how it relates to a Dui house built in Period 7, sitting W2 and facing E2.

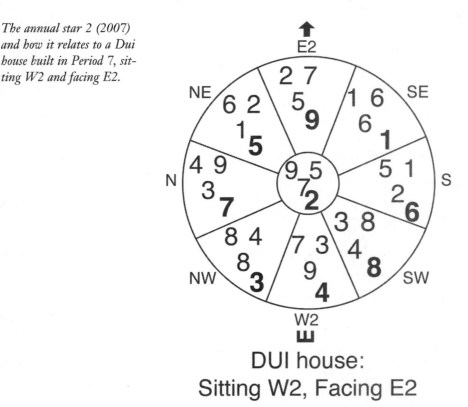

DUI house:
Sitting W2, Facing E2

Center: 9M (fire) 5W (earth) 7T (metal) 2A (earth)

Fire (9M) produces earth (5W). Although a productive relationship, it is not a healthy one. The number 9 is not only encouraging the highly inauspicious number 5's penchant for misfortune, it is also melting the recently retired and still useful star 7's benevolence. Although the numbers comprising the central cell cannot cause fortune or misfortune, they represent the innate nature of the dwelling. In this case, it's inharmonious. For 2007, the sinister visiting 2 star activates, and thereby strengthens, the combinations 9M-5W and 5W-7T. Don't take any unnecessary risks this year. Be mindful of your health, wealth, and spirit. The imprisoned number 2 will soon go.

East: 2M (earth) 7W (metal) 5T (earth) 9A (fire)

Earth (2M) produces metal (7W). In 2007, the annual 9 fire activates the 2M-7W and 2M-5T combinations, making the probability for monetary gain even brighter. Metal is needed to strengthen the money star 7 and to reduce the numbers 2 and 5 that cause misfortune and illness.

Southeast: 1M (water) 6W (metal) 6T (metal) 1A (water)

Metal (6W) produces water (1M). This is a productive combination, fostering the likelihood of promotion and career success. No remedy is needed. However, the stress associated with more responsibility may be accompanied by a nervous breakdown. This is because 1's water is draining 6's energy, a number associated with the head. The visiting and inherently good-natured 1 activates the 1M-6W combination, making the likelihood of good fortune more probable.

South: 5M (earth) 1W (water) 2T (earth) 6A (metal)

Earth (5M) blocks water (1W). This is a controlling relationship, the combination bringing the possibility of ear-, kidney-, and genital-related disorders. Moving metal is needed here to thwart the untimely and inherently inauspicious numbers 2 and 5. Also, metal will connect earth and water, reverting the cycle to a productive one. The annual 6 activates the 5M-1W combination. More metal is needed here to revert these cycles to productive ones: Earth produces metal; metal produces water.

Southwest: 3M (wood) 8W (earth) 4T (wood) 8A (earth)

Wood (3M) burdens earth (8W). The highly favorable number 8 is located on the water or wealth side. To increase the chance for financial achievement, install a water feature and open the window in this area, allowing good fortune to flow in. The visiting annual 8 star activates the 3M-8W and 8W-4T combinations, making this room especially good for a home office.

West: 7M (metal) 3W (wood) 9T (fire) 4A (wood)

Metal (7M) pierces wood (3W). It's a controlling combination bringing the possibility of robbery and lawsuits. Unfortunately, the annual 4 star strengthens this dire possibility. Yet, the annual 4 also activates the 3W-9T combination, bringing career promotion. Add earth to restore the cycle to a productive one: Wood produces fire; fire produces earth; earth produces metal.

Northwest: 8M (earth) 4W (wood) 8T (earth) 3A (wood)

Wood (4W) burdens earth (8M). The advantageous and ruling star 8 is situated on the mountain (health and relationships) side. To create a mountainlike affect, keep the windows closed in this area, especially at night. The visiting 3 wood activates the 8M-4W and 4W-8T combinations. Fire is needed to thwart spousal affairs brought on by the untimely number 4. Fire will revert the cycle to a productive one: Wood produces fire; fire produces earth.

North: 4M (wood) 9W (fire) 3T (wood) 7A (metal)

Wood (4M) produces fire (9W). The number 9's fire intensifies 4's romantic nature, making the area good for a couple seeking a pregnancy. Because 9 is a timely money star, the area also makes an auspicious home office. Although the annual number 7 doesn't activate a combination, it acts on its own to chop the wood stars (3 and 4). Add fire to brighten the romantic 4 and to melt the annual 7 metal star.

Northeast: 6M (metal) 2W (earth) 1T (water) 5A (earth)

Earth (2W) produces metal (6M). Although this is a productive relationship, metal is needed to suppress the unfavorable and untimely number 2's promotion of illness and money loss. Metal will also strengthen 6's inherently auspicious quality of bringing authority and fame, which is being corroded by the time (water) star. The menacing number 5 visits this year, activating the 6M-2W and 2W-1T (divorce) combinations. More metal, or moving metal, will mitigate its nasty effects. If possible, relocate your master suite to a more auspicious area this year.

The bottom line: In 2007, things change in the southeast and west sections.

The Annual Star for 2008

Beginning in the central palace, moving up to the facing cell, and traveling clockwise around the chart, let's take a look at how the annual star affects the other stars. Again, M stands for mountain star, W for water star, T for time star, and A for annual star. The numbers in bold adjacent to the time star correspond to the annual star.

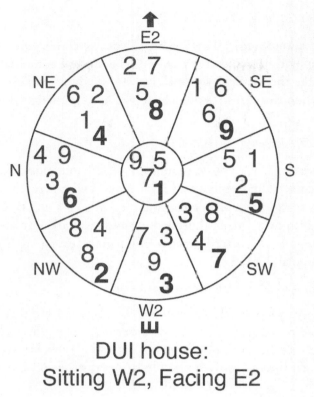

The annual star 1 (2008) and how it relates to a Dui house built in Period 7, sitting W2 and facing E2.

DUI house:
Sitting W2, Facing E2

Center: 9M (fire) 5W (earth) 7T (metal) 1A (water)

Fire (9M) produces earth (5W). Although a production relationship, it's an unfavorable one bringing financial and health hazards. The number 9 fire star is spurring 5's innate ugliness. The number 9 is also melting the number 7, which is trying to reduce the sinister earth star. Fortunately, the number 1 annual star doesn't activate a combination. However, it does work on its own to corrode the benevolent metal time star and extinguish the mountain fire star.

East: 2M (earth) 7W (metal) 5T (earth) 8A (earth)

Earth (2M) produces metal (7W). Although the combination promotes the probability for financial gain, the number 5 time star activates its equally sinister earth brother—2M. Fortunately, the annual and ruling 8 star is able to communicate with 2 and 5 by using their shared earth language. Nevertheless, add metal to lessen possible harm brought on by the evil numbers 2 and 5. Metal will also strengthen the money star 7.

Southeast: 1M (water) 6W (metal) 6T (metal) 9A (fire)

Metal (6W) produces water (1M). This is a very favorable combination bringing career success. Although the annual fire star doesn't activate a combination, it works on its own to brighten the auspicious probability. Although no remedy is needed, be mindful of an overabundance of stress and anxiety. This is a good area for a home office.

South: 5M (earth) 1W (water) 2T (earth) 5A (earth)

Earth (5M) blocks water (1W). This is an unfavorable combination bringing ailments related to the ears, kidneys, and genital area. The annual and inherently mean-spirited number 5 is making matters worse by activating the 5M-1W and 5M-2T combinations. Heavy metal or moving metal is needed to thwart 2 and 5's dreadful impact. This is not a good area for a master bedroom. If possible, relocate to another room this year until the annual 5 leaves.

Southwest: 3M (wood) 8W (earth) 4T (wood) 7A (metal)

Wood (3M) burdens earth (8W). This is a controlling relationship that brings financial gain. Because the ruling 8 star is on the wealth side, activate financial success by opening a window to let the money qi flow in. Also, add a water feature. Although the annual 7 metal star doesn't activate a combination, it works on its own to foster good fortune.

West: 7M (metal) 3W (wood) 9T (fire) 3A (wood)

Metal (7M) chops wood (3W). This combination, bringing possible robbery and litigation over money, is being strengthened or brightened by the number 9 fire star. The visiting star 3 wood, which activates the 7M-3W and 3W-9T (temper tantrums) combinations, is encouraging the inauspicious forecast. Add earth to restore balance: Wood produces fire; fire produces earth; earth produces metal.

Northwest: 8M (earth) 4W (wood) 8T (earth) 2A (earth)

Earth (8M) burdens wood (4W). This is a controlling relationship promoting spousal affairs brought on by the untimely number 4. Because the ruling number 8 is on the mountain side, keep the windows closed in this area, especially at night. The visiting and menacing number 2 activates the 8M-4W and 8M-8T combinations. No harm is done because the benevolent ruling stars overrule 2's naughty behavior. Add fire to reduce 4 wood and strengthen the good earth stars, restoring flow to the sequence: Wood produces fire; fire produces earth.

North: 4M (wood) 9W (fire) 3T (wood) 6A (metal)

Wood (4M) produces fire (9W). This is a favorable combination for a couple seeking to get pregnant. This is because the 9 fire star is brightening 4's romantic nature. However, in 2008, you might have to try harder because the annual 6 metal is chopping 4's wood. Add fire to increase your chances of becoming pregnant. Fire will also melt the visiting star's metal.

Northeast: 6M (metal) 2W (earth) 1T (water) 4A (wood)

Earth (2W) produces metal (6M). An unfavorable combination bringing possible financial disaster, metal is needed to reduce the threatening number 2. Metal will also fortify the inherently good number 6, which is being corroded by the water time star. The annual 4 wood does not activate a combination.

The bottom line: In 2008, things do not change.

Okay, feng shui enthusiasts, go to it! You now have all the tools. You understand how to use them. Take this time now to review your own chart. Implement the appropriate five-phase remedy to balance your dwelling's qi.

In the next part, we'll present three case studies to help facilitate your comprehension of Flying Star.

The Least You Need to Know

- The annual star changes each year beginning variously on the third, fourth, or fifth of February.

- The annual star's reign lasts for one solar year.

- The annual star can activate a combination by sharing the same number as the mountain or water star or by producing the mountain or water phase in question.

- You must consider the annual star to ensure a proper Flying Star analysis.

Part 5

Practical Application

Part 5 puts you in the driver's seat, offering you the chance to test-drive your feng shui skills. You'll meet folks just like you who seek to benefit from feng shui. Using Flying Star, you'll examine an apartment, a split-level home, and a business, each with a unique situation and a particular solution. Also, we'll show you how simple modifications, such as repositioning beds and desks, can make a big difference in how you feel.

We'll be there to assist you every step of the way. So buckle up and enjoy the fruits of your labors. This is one ride you don't want to miss!

Apartment Hunting We Will Go

In This Chapter

- Doing your homework before choosing an apartment
- Finding an apartment that inspires romance
- Using your ming gua to orient your bed and desk
- Using Flying Star to remedy the dwelling's qi

It's taken 17 chapters, but you've made it! You've learned the fundamental components of feng shui (yin and yang, the five phases, and the eight trigrams). You learned how to analyze your interior and exterior environment. You even gained considerable knowledge about the most sophisticated method of classical feng shui—Flying Star.

Before you don your graduation cap, test yourself by applying your new-found knowledge to an analysis of an apartment. It's an open-book test, and cheating is encouraged! (*Pssst:* Appendix F makes the best crib sheet.) The answers follow immediately, so you can grade yourself.

Doing Your Homework

If buying your first apartment (or renting one) is stressful, the process of looking for an apartment is even worse. Unlike shopping for a car where you can take a test drive and get to know the car's design features and flaws before plunking down your hard-earned cash, shopping for an apartment often doesn't present such luxuries.

The search for an apartment (or house) begins at home. Before you scrutinize the Open House listings, you must determine your favorable directions (as well as those of each family member, if applicable). This information will come in handy when judging the bedrooms and home office of prospective units. If the bedroom(s) in question does not have a wall that corresponds to a favorable direction, then there's no suitable place to orient your bed. The same applies for situating your desk. Therefore, the unit under consideration does not fit your needs. There's no need to conduct a Flying Star analysis.

For example, take Alice. She is single and is looking for a mate. Before we help her find an apartment that inspires romance, let's determine her favorable and unfavorable directions:

Name		Alice
Birthdate		1970
Gua		3
Phase		Wood
Trigram		Zhen
F1	G O O D	S
F2		SE
F3		N
F4		E
H1	B A D	SW
H2		NE
H3		NW
H4		W

Alice is a gua 3 wood person. Her most favorable directions are S (F1), SE (F2), N (F3), and E (F4). Her unfavorable directions are SW (H1), NE (F2), NW (F3), and W (F4).

There's No Place Like Home

Of course, environmental factors must be considered even before stepping foot inside the prospective apartment unit. There's no point in examining closet space if the apartment building rests on a steep slope or is the subject of sha qi (refer to Chapters 9 and 10 for a reminder of these negative influences). Move on. Don't waste your valuable time. The external environment is just as important as the internal space. Say that 10 times before you fall in love with the unit on the hill enveloped by potentially cancerous electromagnetic fields emitted by the power plant next door.

So, did Alice find her dream apartment? Well, she found a building that has two units for sale. Built in 1986, the building falls in Period 7. It belongs to the trigram Kan and mountain Ren, sitting N1 and facing S1 at 165°. Innately, the building brings arguments and lawsuits (a 3M-2W combination), but the negative forecast is remedied by the central elevators (moving metal).

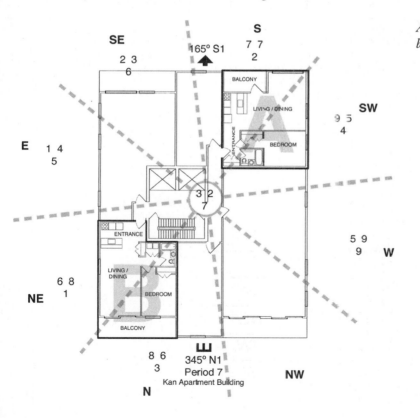

An S1 facing apartment building built in Period 7.

The building's main entrance is in the south. The south contains the number combination 7M-7W, bringing good wealth and health. However, Alice will primarily use the garage entrance (not illustrated) in the east, where she'll park her car and take the elevators up to one of the two prospective fourth floor units. The east contains the number combination 1M-4W, which brings romance—just what Alice is looking for. She must now decide which unit is right for her: the unit in the SW corner (that shares the same sitting and facing as the building) or the unit in the NE corner (a Li dwelling facing N1 at 345°).

Eenie, Meenie, My Unit!

Let's run the numbers and compare the two apartment units. Until she selects which unit best suits her, we'll leave out the time star in this cursory evaluation.

A comparison of the qi distribution for the Kan and Li units.

Kan Unit A			
		ш N1	↑ S1
Entrance	NE	6M 8W	Financial Success
Kitchen	E	1M 4W	Writing, Creativity, & Romance
Dining Room	SE	2M 3W	Conflict, Gossip, Litigation, & Accidents
Living Room	S	7M 7W	Wealth and Good Health
	SW	9M 5W	Financial & Health Hazard
	W	5M 9W	Financial & Health Hazard
Bedroom	NW	4M 1W	Writing, Creativity, & Romance
Bathroom	N	8M 6W	Authority

Li Unit B			
		ш S1	↑ N1
Entrance	S	7M 7W	Wealth and Good Health
Kitchen	SE	3M 2W	Conflict, Gossip, Litigation, & Accidents
Dining Room	E	4M 1W	Writing, Creativity, & Romance
Living Room	NE	8M 6W	Authority
	N	6M 8W	Financial Success
Bedroom	NW	1M 4W	Writing, Creativity, & Romance
	W	9M 5W	Financial & Health Hazard
Bathroom	SW	5M 9W	Financial & Health Hazard

For a preliminary check, first study the numbers occupying the entrances, bedrooms, and living rooms. The remaining areas are not important.

Unit Entrances: The number combinations in both unit A and unit B are auspicious. However, the ruling money star 8 occupying unit A's entrance cannot be activated. It needs to be supported environmentally by water (or virtual water like a roadway), its qi flowing through an open window and into the dwelling. Regarding the layout of the two units, unit A has an immediate feng shui concern. The entrance and the bathroom entrance are aligned. The bathroom should not be the first thing you see! Although the door could be kept closed, the bathroom's location is still a drawback.

Bedrooms: Unit A brings romance and authority. Alice could orient her bed to the south (F1) or to the north (F3). Unit B brings romance and financial and health hazards. Here, Alice can orient her bed to the west (H4) or to the east (F4).

Living Rooms: Even though unit A comprises three number combinations, they are not as favorable as the two number combinations inhabiting unit B's living room. In unit B, the ruling mountain star 8 and the ruling water star 8 occupy this area. We'll discuss how they can be activated later on in this chapter.

All things considered, Alice chooses unit B— the Li apartment.

> **Master Class**
>
> Referring to the illustration of the apartment building, half of unit A inhabits an inauspicious section of the *building* containing the number combination 9M-5W. Unit B inhabits the most auspicious side of the building, with number combinations 8M-6W in the north and 6M-8W in the northeast. The bottom line? Unit B wins over unit A.

The Analysis

Alice uses Flying Star methodology to remedy and enhance the stars in her new apartment unit.

The floor plan is oriented so that its sitting side is flush with this page. Beginning in the center, moving up to the facing cell, and then traveling clockwise around the floor plan, let's examine the number combinations and possible remedies. *Note:* M stands for Mountain Star; W for Water Star; and T for Time Star.

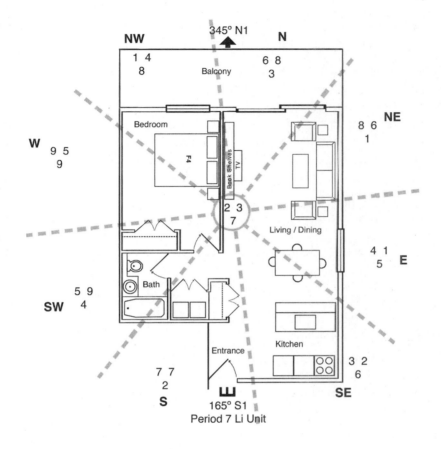

Center: 2M (earth) 3W (wood) 7T (metal)

Wood (3W) burdens earth (2M). Innately, the unit brings conflict, litigation, and accidents. No matter. We'll balance the qi in the entire unit alleviating the negative forecast. Alice's grandfather's clock should be placed on the western wall near the unit's center. Its metallic chime and swinging metal pendulum will help dispel the combination's effects.

North/Northeast Living Room: 6M (metal) 8W (earth) 3T (wood) and 8M (earth) 6W (metal) 1T (water)

Earth (8W) produces metal (6M). These productive relationships bring authority and financial success. It's a great area to spend time in. Activate the ruling water (wealth) star in the north by adding a table fountain on the balcony. Keep the sliding door leading to the balcony open, when possible. Inside, install a water feature in the northern area, too (a fish tank or another table fountain). Activate the ruling mountain star (health and relationships) by keeping the northeastern window closed.

Environmentally, the ruling water star is supported by virtual water (the roadway four floors below); the ruling mountain star is supported by the neighboring building. Regarding furniture layout, orient the couch against the east wall, offering support and security.

East Dining Room: 4M (wood) 1W (water) 5T (earth)

Water (1W) produces wood (4M). A very favorable combination bringing creativity, fame through writing, and romance. No remedy is needed. Alice should enjoy romantic dinners here.

Southeast Kitchen: 3M (wood) 2W (earth) 6T (metal)

Wood (3M) burdens earth (2W). This is an inauspicious combination ushering in the probability of conflict, arguments, and lawsuits. The kitchen appliances remedy the situation. Adding a metallic wall clock above the window is also a good idea.

South Entrance: 7M (metal) 7W (metal) 2T (earth)

Metal (7M) assists metal (7W). The recently retired number 7 star is still benevolent until the Lower Cycle ends in February 2044. The combination brings good health and wealth. No remedy is needed.

Southwest Bathroom: 5M (earth) 9W (fire) 4T (wood)

A remedy is not necessary. Bathrooms (garages and basements) are not important. Nevertheless, we suggest Alice keep the bathroom door closed.

West/Northwest Bedroom: 9M (fire) 5W (earth) 9T (fire) and 1M (water) 4W (wood) 8T (earth)

Fire (9M) produces earth (5W). The western half of the room is inauspicious, bringing financial and health hazards. The number 9 fire time star strengthens the dire forecast. Metal is needed to thwart problems. An arrangement of metallic frames and metal wall art will remedy the situation (see Chapter 6 for an example). However, the northwest section is very auspicious. Water (1M) produces wood (4W), bringing more romantic opportunities to Alice. Although a remedy is not needed, Alice should position her bed against the east wall (as illustrated). For her, east corresponds to her F4 direction, bringing peace and stability.

The bottom line? Alice selected a fine apartment. As you're learning, no home can be completely good—or is completely bad. Following the concept of yin and yang, in one there's always the hint of the other! Of course, before putting the remedies in place, Alice must consider how the annual stars affect the number combinations.

In the next chapter, we'll examine a split-level house.

The Least You Need to Know

◆ First determine your ming gua and its corresponding favorable and unfavorable directions.

◆ If the surrounding environmental factors are favorable, examine the stars in the areas you'll most use: the entrance, bedrooms, living room or den, and home office.

◆ Remedy or enhance the qi in each section of the dwelling.

◆ Use your ming gua to properly orient your bed and desk.

Home Is Where the Hearth Is

In This Chapter

◆ Dividing a split-level house

◆ Analyzing the ming gua family dynamics

◆ Using Flying Star to harmonize the house

◆ Studying and remedying interior forms

John and Jane Ward, along with their two young children Timothy and Mary, live in a split-level house in a quiet, family-oriented neighborhood. The rectangular house is properly located in the middle of a block, with comparable-sized houses flanking theirs. The house is not overly dark (yin) nor overly bright (yang). In fact, the outside forms are ideal. Yet inside, the family doesn't feel comfortable. They can't sleep. They argue. The kids avoid the family room.

In this chapter, we'll examine the Ward's house with feng shui eyes. Regarding the Flying Star number combinations, give yourself a pop quiz by determining the remedy before you read our suggestions.

Divided We All

Built in 1959, the house falls in Period 5 (1944-1964). Belonging to the Kan trigram and mountain Ren, it sits N1 and faces S1 at 167°.

A split-level house.

Looking at the front of the house, the left side comprises one floor. The right side is split-level, comprising two floors. We often are asked how to divide a split-level house. Do you divide each floor separately? No! One pie chart covers the entire house. Let's take a closer look.

Orienting the floor plan so that its sitting side is flush with the bottom of this page, the right side (it's the left side if you're looking at the front of the house from the outside) comprises the living room and kitchen. Near the center of the house is one set of stairs that leads down to the family room, guestroom/office, and bathroom. The adjacent set of stairs leads up to the master bedroom, children's bedrooms, and bathroom. If you overlay the mark designating the center of the house on the upper floor plan with the mark designating the center of the house on the lower floor plan, the division lines perfectly align.

The family room, guestroom/office, and bathroom comprise the lower floor. The bedrooms comprise the upper floor.

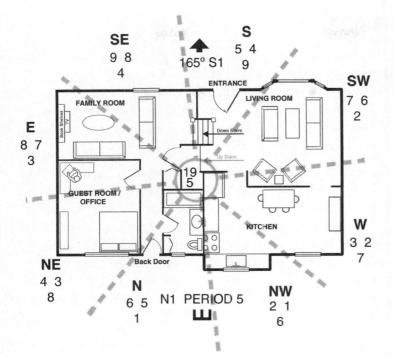

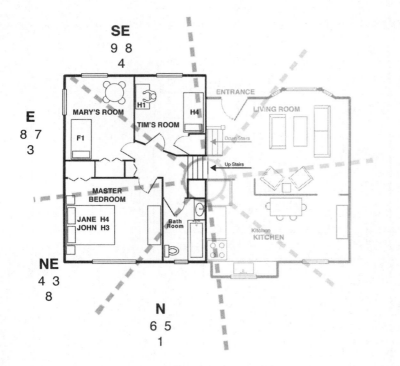

Ward Family Dynamics

Before we analyze the Ward's house, let's analyze how they relate to each other. John Ward is a gua 7 metal person. Being the head of household suits his authoritative nature. Although others see him as rigid and stern, he's actually quite flexible and calm. He relates best with his wife, Jane, who's a metal gua 6 person. Conversely, although others see her as amiable and cooperative, she has an inner sternness. Nevertheless, they're very compatible, even if they're stubborn!

Regarding their relations with their children, John and Jane need to learn that adopting a sweet rather than a spicy tone will yield more positive results. This advice will prove helpful when relating to their gua 4 wood daughter Mary. Their relationship with her is combative. John and Jane innately seek to control her every move. While they are chopping Mary's tree, Mary is busy controlling her brother Tim—a gua 2 earth person. Even though his relationship with his parents is generally agreeable (earth produces metal), his stubbornness gets him in trouble. Basically, John and Jane need to harness their inward and outward softness to successfully mediate disputes and restore harmony to their family unit.

Name	JOHN	JANE	TIM	MARY
Birthdate	1967	1965	1995	1998
Gua	6	7	2	4
Phase	Metal	Metal	Earth	Wood
Trigram	Qian	Dui	Kun	Xun
D i r e c t i o n s				
F1	W	NW	NE	N
F2	SW	NE	NW	E
F3	NE	SW	W	S
F4	NW	W	SW	SE
H1	SE	N	E	NW
H2	N	SE	S	W
H3	E	S	SE	SW
H4	S	E	N	NE

(F rows labeled GOOD; H rows labeled BAD)

Referring to the chart, John, Jane, and Tim share the same favorable directions, but in different orders: W, SW, NE, and NW. What's good for them is not good for Mary. Her favorable directions are N, E, S, and SE. We'll put this information to good use later on in this chapter.

Flying the Stars

Beginning in the center, traveling up to the facing cell, we'll move clockwise around the floor plan as we examine the number combinations and possible remedies. *Note:* M stands for Mountain Star; W for Water Star; and T for Time Star.

Center: 1M (water) 9W (fire) 5T (earth)

Water (1M) controls fire (9W). Although it's a controlling relationship, it is a favorable combination bringing career advancement and monetary gain. This is the innate fortune of the house. Interestingly, however, the Period 5 house was born Reversed Mountain and Water, with the ruling water star 5 (governing wealth) located on the mountain side of the facing cell and the ruling mountain star 5 (governing health and relationships) located on the water side of the sitting cell. The misalignment most likely brought misfortune and illness to the dwelling's first occupants, the inauspiciousness ending when Period 6 arrived on February 5, 1964.

South Entrance 5M (earth) 4W (wood) 9T (fire)

Wood (4W) controls earth (5W). This is a dominating relationship bringing the possibility of breast tumors and troubled relationships. The number 9 time star activates the combination, making it especially inauspicious. Moving metal is needed to lessen 5's naughtiness. A wind chime in the outside entryway or bells hanging on the inside door will work well.

Southwest Living Room 7M (metal) 6W (metal) 2T (earth)

Metal (7M) assists metal (6W). Although productive, the combination brings disagreements. The innately ugly number 2 earth star strengthens the inauspicious forecast. Unfortunately, a five-phase remedy will not help remedy the problematic qi. The Ward family should not hold family discussions here. However, rearranging the furniture will help the family and their guests feel more comfortable in this room. We suggest moving the love seat to the north wall (see the "after" floor plan in the next illustration). As you learned in Chapter 10, a person sitting with his back exposed feels insecure. The love seat was positioned very inauspiciously with its back to the main entrance and to the staircases leading to the upper and lower floors. The new arrangement is open and inviting.

West/Northwest Kitchen 3M (wood) 2W (earth) 7T (metal) and 2M (earth) 1W (water) 6T (metal)

Wood (3M) burdens earth (2W), and earth (2M) blocks water (1W). These are controlling relationships bringing conflict, accidents, and abdominal pain. The kitchen is the most unfavorable area in the house. Moving metal is needed to ward off trouble. The appliances take care of the remedy in the northwest section. In the west, we advise installing a chiming pendulum clock. Regarding the dining table, notice that it's stationed against the south wall. Because the room is narrow, it is not practical to pull out the table for each meal. Repositioning it near the west wall is also inconvenient. Therefore, we suggest the Wards frame the children's report cards and art on the wall they will be facing during mealtime. Mary and Timothy can look at their accomplishments instead of staring at an uninspiring blank wall.

Downstairs:

North Bathroom 6M (metal) 5W (earth) 1T (water)

A remedy is not necessary. Bathrooms (garages and basements) are not important. Nevertheless, we suggest the Wards keep the bathroom door closed.

Northeast Guestroom/Office 4M (wood) 3W (wood) 8T (earth)

Wood (4M) assists wood (3W). The combination attracts burglars. To discourage theft, the Wards must take preventative measures by keeping the backdoor locked at all times. The window in the guestroom/office must also be securely locked, especially when they are not home. Adding the fire phase will also help. A red floor runner for the hallway and a red rug in the guestroom/office room will work. Installing a lamp with a red light bulb or red shade (see Chapter 6) is another option. Regarding the layout, the Wards could make better use of this space. We suggest they remove the double bed, replacing it with a sofa bed. Removing the bed will open up the space. Next, the desk must be relocated. Again, sitting with your back exposed is a feng shui no-no! Also, facing a wall blocks creativity and concentration. Reposition the desk to the opposite side of the room (see the "after" floor plan).

East/Southeast Family Room 8M (earth) 7W (metal) 3T (wood) and 9M (fire) 8W (earth) 4T (wood)

Earth (8M) produces metal (7W), and fire (9M) produces earth (8W). This is the best area in the house, bringing financial gain and happiness. The area also hosts the ruling mountain and water stars for Period 8 (February 4, 2004 to February 3, 2024). In the east section of the room, fire is needed to activate the benevolent 8 mountain star. Fire will also melt the inherently unfavorable number 7. In the southeast, a water feature (a table fountain or a fish tank) will activate the ruling 8 money star. However, the water star must also be supported environmentally. Keep the window open to allow the water (wealth) star to flow into the dwelling. Outside, virtual water (the street) activates the money star. It is strengthened even more when the Wards pull into their driveway and walk to the front door. We suggest installing a fountain or a bird bath in this area. Regarding the room's layout, move the entertainment center to the south wall, reposition the couch against the north wall, and add another couch on the east wall. The room is open and inviting. There's even space for a game table (see the "after" floor plan).

Upstairs:

North Bathroom 6M (metal) 5W (earth) 1T (water)

A remedy is not necessary. Bathrooms are not important. Nevertheless, we suggest the Wards keep the bathroom door closed.

Northeast Master Bedroom 4M (wood) 3W (wood) 8T (earth)

Wood (4M) assists wood (3W). The combination brings disruptive behavior. Fire is needed to brighten 4's romantic propensity and burn 3's bad nature. Currently, the Wards' bed rests against the east wall. For John, east corresponds to his H3 direction. For Jane, east corresponds to her worst direction—H4. Flip-flop the bed to the west wall. For John, west is his F1 direction. For Jane, it's her F4 direction. At night, the bedroom door should be kept partially closed.

East Mary's Bedroom 8M (earth) 7W (metal) 3T (wood)

Earth (8M) produces metal (7W). This is a highly auspicious combination bringing romance and financial gain. If this room were bigger, we would relocate John and Jane here. Fire is needed to ensure Mary's good health. However, the 8 mountain star must be supported environmentally. Therefore, the eastern window must be kept closed, especially at night. Currently, her bed rests against the north wall. For Mary, north corresponds to her F1 direction. Although favorable, it is a highly charged direction, which might cause insomnia. Move her bed to the south—her F3 direction bringing good health and harmonious relations.

> **Feng Facts**
>
> If possible, a bed and desk should be placed against an uninhibited wall—one that doesn't have anything else against it.

Southeast Timothy's Bedroom 9M (fire) 8W (earth) 4T (wood)

Fire (9M) produces earth (8W). Timothy's room promotes happiness and financial success. Although it is not necessary to activate the money star in a child's room, adding a fish tank soothes the soul. Currently, his bed rests against the north closet wall. For Tim, north corresponds to H4. South corresponds to H2. West (F3) is the only other option. However, positioned this way, there isn't room for his desk. Therefore, we suggest that Tim and Mary switch bedrooms (see the "after" floor plan).

Like all houses, there are innately good areas and innately bad areas. By balancing the qi in each area, the Wards will encourage good prospects and discourage bad ones. And by making simple adjustments to each room's layout, they will foster harmony—the tenant of feng shui.

The "after" floor plan.

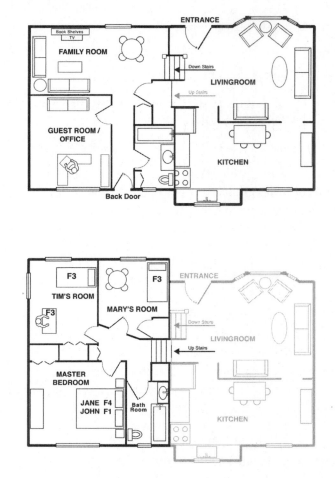

In the next chapter, we'll examine an office.

The Least You Need to Know

- Split-level homes require one pie chart.

- You can improve family dynamics by understanding each person's ming gua.

- Rearranging existing furniture will foster harmonious relations.

- Be open to switching bedrooms, if need be.

20

Does Your Office Measure Up?

In This Chapter

- ◆ Gaining a competitive edge is easier than you think
- ◆ Reorganizing your office space
- ◆ Studying the ming gua staff dynamics
- ◆ Incorporating Flying Star methodology

Whether you own a large corporation or a small business, your primary goal is to generate revenue. Yet, to do this, you must first create a welcoming and comfortable working environment: a place where employees will be driven to succeed and that encourages camaraderie and teamwork. Often, we set aside this notion, viewing the design and layout factors as incidental and low priority.

In this chapter, you'll understand how quite the opposite is true—promoting a harmonious environment is an essential consideration, a positively golden means to a lucrative end.

Labor Pains

Mr. Smith owns and operates a small insurance agency. He has nine full-time employees on his payroll: five sales associates, one accountant, two secretaries, and a receptionist. All are paid competitive salaries. After six months of service, each is eligible to participate in a retirement program and receive medical and dental benefits. Also, Mr. Smith rewards each member of his staff with a three-week paid vacation per year. He reimburses accrued sick days not taken at the end of the year. He provides holiday parties, tickets to sporting events, and other niceties. By most company standards, Mr. Smith offers a very generous package.

So why is his staff listless? Why does Mr. Smith himself feel sluggish? Why must he mediate frequent arguments among his staff? Why, despite all the incentives, is his staff unmotivated and unhappy? Desperate and frustrated, Mr. Smith seeks your advice.

First Things First

Even before you can determine favorable directions and appropriate remedies, you must first walk around the outside of Mr. Smith's facility. Determine the building's sitting direction. Take a compass reading. Evaluate the environment. In this case, no external factors are influencing the owner and his staff. Now, go inside. Scope it out. Draw up a simple floor plan and divide it into eight equal sections. Ask yourself whether the layout is partially responsible for poor performance and troublesome relations.

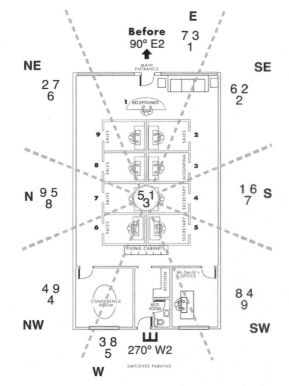

Mr. Smith's previous floor plan. Built in 1920 (Period 3), the Dui building sits W2 and faces E2 at 90 degrees.

Disregarding the numeric qi map for the moment, focus on the floor plan. Upon entering through the eastern main entrance, you are greeted by a receptionist. Is there a problem here? Well, as you learned in Chapter 10, you should not sit directly opposite a door. Here, the receptionist is subjected to a surge of qi hitting her each time the door opens. Take a closer look. The wall in back of the receptionist, formed by two adjoined cubicles, prevents qi from circulating throughout the interior. No wonder Mr. Smith and his staff feel stagnant and tired. They aren't being nourished by life's breath.

Furthermore, the eight cubicles are set up so that the desks face each other. Even though the cubicle walls offer the staff privacy, they still, in effect, are "in each other's face." Also, is it good feng shui to sit with your back exposed to a doorway? Of course not! Plus, despite the close proximity, the staff is dissuaded from interacting with each other, with their cubicle entrances on opposing sides of the room. These factors could quite possibly contribute to the bickering and tension.

Regarding the western areas of the business, Mr. Smith's desk is seemingly situated in an advantageous position against an unobstructed wall (we'll examine this later). The back entrance, adjacent to the employee parking lot, opens into a tidy restroom/kitchen area. The conference room? It holds a proportionate oval table and chairs.

Feng Alert

It is not favorable to sit with your back exposed to a door. You are subjected to a surge of qi, which can cause a lack of concentration, nonproductivity, and illness. This position offers only unfavorable psychological and physical effects. Ideally, your back, like your home, must be supported by a wall or a mountain.

Dui Have a Match?

Born on April 2, 1948, Mr. Smith's ming gua is Dui 7 metal. His west-sitting building also corresponds to Dui. An exact match, Mr. Smith and his structure are compatible. Referring to the ming gua chart presented later in this chapter, Mr. Smith's best directions are the NW (F1), NE (F2), SW (F3), and W (F4). Notice that the agency's main entrance is in the east. For Mr. Smith, east just happens to be his worst direction (H4), bringing unproductive careers and misfortune. The western entrance in the back of the structure is favorable. For Mr. Smith, west is his F4 direction, bringing peace and stability. Finally, his SW-W office (also located in back) corresponds to his F3 and F4 directions. So far, Mr. Smith's office and the back entrance favor his qi.

Won't You Please Come In?

Before we make any changes, let's consider what the Flying Stars have to say. Beginning in the center, traveling up to the facing cell, we'll move clockwise around the floor plan as we examine the number combinations and possible remedies. *Note:* M stands for Mountain Star; W for Water Star; and T for Time Star.

Center: 5M (earth) 1W (water) 3T (wood)

Earth controls water. A dominating relationship promoting the likelihood of ear-, kidney-, and genital-related illness. Install a golden (metal) rug along the central pathway (see the "after" floor plan later in this chapter). This will weaken the ill-natured 5 earth star (metal reduces earth) and strengthen the 1 water star (metal produces water), an innately auspicious number.

East: 7M (metal) 3W (wood) 1T (water)

Metal controls wood. A dominating combination bringing potential robberies and litigation. Although you might think adding water restores balance, and thus, diminishes the unfavorable forecast, the reductive phase water isn't strong enough to thwart the untimely and inherently bad number 3. Here, metal is needed to control the water star and assist the mountain star.

Southeast: 6M (metal) 2W (earth) 2T (earth)

Earth produces metal. Although productive, the relationship fosters financial loss due to illness, an unfortunate mishap that is being encouraged by the ill-natured earth time star. Add metal to weaken the disadvantageous water star.

South: 1M (water) 6W (metal) 7T (metal)

Metal produces water. A productive relationship bringing career advancement. No remedy is needed.

Southwest: 8M (earth) 4W (wood) 9T (fire)

Wood controls earth. A dominating relationship bringing creativity and harmony only if the conflicting situation is remedied. During Period 8 (February 4, 2004 to February 3, 2024), the ruling mountain star 8 must be supported by a mountain. The neighboring building serves as a remedy and will help bring good health and beneficial relationships to Mr. Smith and his staff. Install the fire phase to revert the cycle to a balanced one: wood-fire-earth. Fire will brighten 4 wood's creativity and lessen the possibility of inappropriate affairs. Also, fire will enhance the mountain star's ability to elicit teamwork and harmony among co-workers.

West: 3M (wood) 8W (earth) 5T (earth)

Wood controls earth. A combination bringing monetary gain only if the dominating relationship is remedied. During Period 8, the water star must be supported environmentally by a body of water or virtual water such as a roadway. In this case (and not illustrated) a parking lot is located in the back, the moving vehicles encouraging the wealth star to flow into the western entrance and windows. Inside, water is needed to activate the number 8 money star. (For the previous Period 7 [1984–2004], we would have suggested adding fire to connect the mountain and water stars.)

Northwest: 4M (wood) 9W (fire) 4T (wood)

Wood produces fire. A productive combination fostering writing and creativity. In this case, notice that the area contains two highly auspicious money numbers—9W in the northwest and 8W in the west. As you'll soon learn, we recommend that Mr. Smith move his office here. Install a table fountain to activate the money (water) stars. Disregarding the phase relationships between water (the enhancement), 9 fire and 8 earth (the water stars), remember that water activates usable water (wealth) stars (8, 9, and 1 for Period 8).

North: 9M (fire) 5W (earth) 8T (earth)

Fire produces earth. Although a productive relationship, it is not a healthy one. Although the number 9 is encouraging the innately unfavorable number 5's propensity for misfortune, the number 8 time star is warning his naughty earth brother not to misbehave. Just in case the 5 star disobeys, add moving metal to reduce the possibility of financial and health hazards.

Northeast: 2M (earth) 7W (metal) 6T (metal)

Earth produces metal. A combination bringing financial gain. During Period 7 (February 4, 1984 to February 3, 2004), we would have suggested adding water to activate the king money star 7. For Period 8, metal will strengthen the retired but still effective number 7 water star and reduce the bad-natured number 2 mountain star.

Sitting Pretty

Now that you've determined the remedy or enhancement appropriate for each area of the office, you can put the final piece in place. Look at how the desks of Mr. Smith's staff are positioned. Depending on each staff member's ming gua, you'll reposition their desk so that they face either the east or west wall (see the "after" floor plan).

Determining the staff's most favorable desk positions.

Name	Mr. Smith	Female 1	Male 2	Female 3	Female 4	Female 5	Male 6	Male 7	Female 8	Male 9
Birthdate	1948	1979	1960	1955	1982	1966	1970	1962	1958	1955
Gua	7	3	4	6	6	8	3	2	9	9
Phase	Metal	Wood	Wood	Metal	Metal	Earth	Wood	Earth	Fire	Fire
Trigram	Dui	Zhen	Xun	Qian	Qian	Gen	Zhen	Kun	Li	Li
D i r e c t i o n s										
F1	NW	S	N	W	W	SW	S	NE	E	E
F2	NE	SE	E	SW	SW	W	SE	NW	N	N
F3	SW	N	S	NE	NE	NW	N	W	SE	SE
F4	W	E	SE	NW	NW	NE	E	SW	S	S
H1	N	SW	NW	SE	SE	S	SW	E	NE	NE
H2	SE	NE	W	N	N	E	NE	S	SW	SW
H3	S	NW	SW	E	E	N	NW	SE	W	W
H4	E	W	NE	S	S	SE	W	N	NW	NW

(F1–F4 labeled "GOOD"; H1–H4 labeled "BAD")

Moving clockwise around the room, let's look at each employee, beginning with the receptionist (female 1):

1. **Gua 3 female.** The receptionist faces F4. As there is only one choice here, she's fortunate.

2. **Gua 4 male.** Currently, this salesperson faces north, his F1 qi. Although auspicious, his back is exposed. We'll move him to face the east, his F2 qi.

3. **Gua 6 female.** Facing her H2 direction (north), position the accountant's desk to face her F1 direction, west.

4. **Gua 6 female.** Currently, this secretary faces north, her H2 direction. Reposition her desk to face west, her F1 direction.

5. **Gua 8 female.** Facing north activates the secretary's H3 qi. Move her desk to face west, her F2 qi.

6. **Gua 3 male.** While facing his F1 qi (south) is auspicious, his back cannot be exposed. Reposition the sales associate's desk against the east wall, facing his F4 qi.

7. **Gua 2 male.** Currently, this sales associate faces his H2 qi (south). We'll move him so that he faces west, his F3 qi.

8. **Gua 9 female.** Although south (F4) is favorable for this salesperson, we cannot expose her back to the door. Reposition her desk toward the east wall, her F1 qi.

9. **Gua 9 male.** Now, this sales associate faces south, his F4 qi. Move his desk to the east wall, his F1 qi.

By making some simple adjustments, Mr. Smith and his staff should think and feel better.

Staff Dynamics

Let's see how Mr. Smith gets along with his staff. He's a gua 7 metal person. As you learned in Chapter 8, gua 7 people are quite stern. They're efficient, effective, and often argumentative. All in all, Mr. Smith is hard to get to know. His own kind (metal people) understand him, as do earth people (earth generates metal) and water people (metal generates water). Mr. Smith is especially hard on wood types—gua 3 and gua 4 people. He controls them. He does not like fire people, who seek to control him! All things considered, Mr. Smith gets along best with the metal accountant (female 3), the two secretaries (metal female 4 and earth female 5), and the earth sales associate (male 7). The wood receptionist (female 1) fears him. He micromanages the two wood sales associates (male 2 and male 6). In turn, the two fire sales people rub him the wrong way (female 8 and male 9). They challenge his qi. Innately, Mr. Smith is compatible with four staff members. He's incompatible with five of them. If a position becomes available among those he's incompatible with, Mr. Smith should find people with whom he's attuned. They will work with his qi and not against it.

A Means to an End

Taking into account the interior layout and the ming gua and Flying Star systems, form a conclusion. What recommendations would you suggest? Consider …

- ◆ Whether the entrance should be relocated.
- ◆ Now that you've determined a favorable sitting direction for everyone (we'll discuss Mr. Smith later on), how the cubicles can be positioned so that the design fosters harmony among the co-workers.
- ◆ How the cubicles can be positioned so qi can easily circulate.
- ◆ Given what the Flying Stars destine, whether some employees should switch desk positions.
- ◆ Whether Mr. Smith's office is best suited to him.

The following illustration shows our recommendations.

Mr. Smith's improved floor plan.

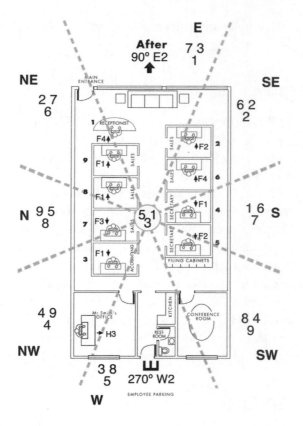

Based on this new floor plan, we suggest ...

- Relocating the main entrance—it is *the* key feng shui solution in this case study. We suggest moving it to the northeast wall. Currently, the door's location corresponds to the building's and Mr. Smith's H4 qi. By moving the entrance, it will bathe the owner, staff, and clients in an auspicious qi combination (2M-7W), inspiring financial gain. Northeast also corresponds to the building's and Mr. Smith's F3 qi.

- The cubicles should be arranged so that a middle corridor allows qi to circulate freely. The corridor will also give the staff more privacy.

- To facilitate harmony among the co-workers, entrances should be along the corridor.

- The accountant in Room 3 should switch with the salesperson in Room 6. The auspicious water stars (8 in the west and 9 in the northwest) are great for administering the company's finances.

- Mr. Smith should occupy the west-northwest office. Corresponding to his F4 and F1 qi, respectively, orient his desk so his back is against the north wall (as illustrated). Although he'll face his H3 qi (south), he'll also face the 8 water (money) star. This takes precedence.

In theory, if Mr. Smith applies our suggestions, he and his staff should coexist peacefully. He should notice an increase in motivation and production!

In Part 6, you'll learn about the Chinese Zodiac and a method of Chinese astrology called The Four Pillars of Destiny.

The Least You Need to Know

♦ Design and layout play an important role in a business's success.

♦ Study your co-workers' ming guas to determine how compatible you are with them.

♦ An employee's desk position within a particular design/layout can affect his or her job motivation and productivity.

♦ Preventing qi from circulating fosters misfortune and illness.

Part 6

Fate or Free Will: What's Your Destiny?

Part 6 is all about Chinese astrology. First, you'll learn about the Chinese Zodiac, a popular method involving 12 animals: you know, the ones featured on Chinese restaurant place mats. Based on your birth date, you'll learn which animals make your best friends and which are best avoided. Also, there's a personality profile of each animal. So, you'll know a horse is a horse, of course, of course!

Next, we'll tell you about The Four Pillars of Destiny. Unlike Western astrology, which calculates the movement of heavenly bodies to determine your destiny, The Four Pillars calculates the type of qi you inhaled at birth. That's right, the Chinese believe you inhale your destiny. Besides calculating and interpreting your fate, you'll also learn about the fates of Prince Charles and Princess Diana, and their son, Prince William; Bill and Hillary Clinton; and Ronald and Nancy Reagan—an interesting study, to be sure!

Chapter 21

Introducing the Twelve Animals of the Chinese Zodiac

In This Chapter

◆ A look at the Chinese Zodiac

◆ The 12 animals and their compatibility

◆ What's your animal sign?

◆ Personality profiles of each animal sign

You're in a Chinese restaurant waiting for your food to arrive. What else is there to do but read your horoscope, which is printed on virtually every place mat? You can learn all kinds of things from the Chinese Zodiac. Under which of the 12 animal signs were you born? Are you a sociable but crafty rat, or a proud and unpredictable tiger? Perhaps you're a nurturing and benevolent rabbit? Whatever your sign, your paper place mat will undoubtedly inform you which animals are your friends and which are your foes. You'll also learn which creature rules the current year and how its sign affects your prospects.

So, what does Chinese astrology have to do with feng shui? Not a whole lot. But, a good feng shui practitioner will incorporate elements of Chinese astrology into his or her feng shui analysis. Things like determining compatibility, your lucky colors, and careers and environments best suited to you are best described using astrology.

This chapter will take an elementary look into the popular system of Chinese astrology. Recognize, however, that although the animal zodiac can provide cursory insights into your personality, it is rarely considered in more sophisticated systems of Chinese fate calculation (you'll learn about one such method, The Four Pillars of Destiny, in Chapters 22 through 26). Nevertheless, it's fun—even if it's superficial. The character traits associated with your ming gua are more accurate. Please consult Chapter 8 for a reminder.

What Is the Chinese Zodiac?

Legend has it that just before entering Nirvana, Buddha (563– 483 B.C.E.) summoned the animal kingdom. For some reason, only 12 animals answered his call. To reward the respondents, Buddha named a year after each animal in the order of its arrival. The rat arrived first, so it was honored with the first year. Then came the ox, followed by the tiger, rabbit, dragon, snake, horse, sheep, monkey, rooster, dog, and pig. Thus, we have the 12 animals that make up the Chinese Zodiac.

But this is a legend. The truth is, no one really knows where the animal signs came from. Sima Qian (163–85 B.C.E.), considered to be one of the greatest scholars of the Han dynasty, and the Grand Astrologer to the emperor, never mentioned the animal cycle. Nor is it mentioned in the astronomical chapters of the *Jin Shu*, the history of the Jin dynasty (265–420 C.E). But, somehow, toward the end of the tenth century, the animal cycle was in full use. Interestingly, contemporary scholars agree its origins are probably not even Chinese. We'll leave it up to the scholars to discover the true origins. Let's move on.

Twelve Animals, Twelve Earthly Branches

Not one of the 12 animal signs represents a star or a constellation. Rather, the animals represent the movement of earthly qi expressed in cycles of time. Called the *Twelve Earthly Branches*, each of the 12 animal signs corresponds to a branch, or component, of 12 two-hour increments, 12 months, and 12 years.

Most Zodiac astrologers consider only the year, month, and hour of birth when determining a client's astrological chart. But, what of the day you were born? Determining the day branch requires a series of mathematical calculations that is either ignored by, or not known by, astrologers who practice this system. As you'll soon learn in Chapter 22, the Chinese believe we have eight components to our personality. If the day/animal branch is ignored, then this analysis will account for only three eighths, or less than half, of our overall makeup.

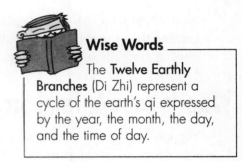

Wise Words

The **Twelve Earthly Branches** (Di Zhi) represent a cycle of the earth's qi expressed by the year, the month, the day, and the time of day.

So, what purpose do the animals serve? The animal signs attached to each branch are merely mnemonics to aid learning the different types of qi and their associated natural and human phenomena.

Take the rat, for example. A nocturnal and social creature, the rat is an ideal emblem for yin's midnight hour, for winter, and for north. The rat person is at his best at night and in a crowd. Directly opposite the rat is the horse, the emblem of noon, summer, and south. The horse symbolizes independence, passion, and masculinity—all characteristics of yang's force at its highest. This gives added meaning to the steadfast Marlboro ads, doesn't it?

Governing the earthly branches, or animal cycle, are the five phases of fire, earth, metal, water, and wood. Also, each branch corresponds to a yin and yang polarity. The following illustration shows the interplay of everything we've discussed so far.

The Chinese Zodiac and its relationship to the earth's qi.

Notice that the earth phase separates each of the other phase elements. This is because the qi represented by fire, metal, water, and wood returns to earth before transforming into another phase.

What's Your Animal Sign?

Suppose that you're a rooster. Are you a fire rooster, earth rooster, metal rooster, water rooster, or wood rooster? You could also be a fire rooster born in a water rat month, on an earth tiger day, at the time of the metal dragon. See, this stuff is a lot more complex than you thought! Even the experienced fortune-teller has much to consider. But learning to analyze each component of your destiny is beyond the scope of this chapter. We'll leave that task to Chapters 22 through 26 about The Four Pillars of Destiny, a method of Chinese astrology. For our purposes here, we'll concern ourselves with only your year sign.

The following table lists the Chinese solar years from 1924 to 2023, along with the exact time the year began. If you were born *after* the fifth of February, determining your sign is simple. However, if you were born on the third, fourth, or fifth day of February, the hour of your birth determines your Chinese birth year. Let's say you were born at 3:30 P.M. on February 4, 1925. You would use 1924 as your year of birth because 1925 didn't begin until 3:37 P.M. If you were born at 5:00 P.M. on February 4, 1925, then you would stay with 1925. Let's take another example. If you were born at 7:00 A.M. on February 5, 1940, would you use 1940, the year of the Dragon, as your Chinese birth year? No. This is because 1940 didn't actually begin until 7:08 A.M.— eight minutes after you were born. Your Chinese birth year would be 1939, the year of the Rabbit.

The question arises, why are we using the solar calendar instead of the lunar calendar to mark the beginning of the year? While traditionally, Chinese New Year (which can occur variously on a date in late January through mid-February) marks the change in animal sign, scholars and serious students of feng shui and The Four Pillars of Destiny consider the beginning of spring as the new year.

Feng Facts

The Chinese solar year begins variously on February 3, 4, or 5. It is the midpoint between the Winter Solstice (the day when daylight is at its minimum) and Spring Equinox (one of two days when day and night are of equal length). The solar calendar is based on the rotation of the earth on its axis (the solar day) and the revolution of the Earth around the sun (the solar year). The ancients also measured the interval between the successive full moons, the lunar months.

Table 1

Solar Year	Date	Time Year Began	Phase	Animal	Solar Year	Date	Time Year Began	Phase	Animal
1924	Feb 5	9:50 am	Wood	Rat	1964	Feb 5	3:05 am	Wood	Dragon
1925	Feb 4	3:37 pm	Wood	Ox	1965	Feb 4	8:46 am	Wood	Snake
1926	Feb 4	9:39 am	Fire	Tiger	1966	Feb 4	2:38 pm	Fire	Horse
1927	Feb 5	3:31 am	Fire	Rabbit	1967	Feb 4	8:31 pm	Fire	Sheep
1928	Feb 5	9:17 am	Earth	Dragon	1968	Feb 5	2:08 am	Earth	Monkey
1929	Feb 4	3:09 pm	Earth	Snake	1969	Feb 4	7:59 am	Earth	Rooster
1930	Feb 4	8:52 pm	Metal	Horse	1970	Feb 4	1:46 pm	Metal	Dog
1931	Feb 5	2:41 am	Metal	Sheep	1971	Feb 4	7:26 pm	Metal	Pig
1932	Feb 5	8:30 am	Water	Monkey	1972	Feb 5	1:20 am	Water	Rat
1933	Feb 4	2:10 pm	Water	Rooster	1973	Feb 4	7:04 am	Water	Ox
1934	Feb 4	8:04 pm	Wood	Dog	1974	Feb 4	1:00 pm	Wood	Tiger
1935	Feb 5	1:49 am	Wood	Pig	1975	Feb 4	6:59 pm	Wood	Rabbit
1936	Feb 5	7:30 am	Fire	Rat	1976	Feb 5	12:40 am	Fire	Dragon
1937	Feb 4	1:26 pm	Fire	Ox	1977	Feb 4	6:34 am	Fire	Snake
1938	Feb 4	7:15 pm	Earth	Tiger	1978	Feb 4	12:27 pm	Earth	Horse
1939	Feb 5	1:11 am	Earth	Rabbit	1979	Feb 4	6:13 pm	Earth	Sheep
1940	Feb 5	7:08 am	Metal	Dragon	1980	Feb 5	12:10 am	Metal	Monkey
1941	Feb 4	12:50 pm	Metal	Snake	1981	Feb 4	5:56 am	Metal	Rooster
1942	Feb 4	6:49 pm	Water	Horse	1982	Feb 4	11:46 am	Water	Dog
1943	Feb 5	12:41 am	Water	Sheep	1983	Feb 4	5:40 pm	Water	Pig
1944	Feb 5	6:23 am	Wood	Monkey	1984	Feb 4	11:19 pm	Wood	Rat
1945	Feb 4	12:20 pm	Wood	Rooster	1985	Feb 4	5:12 am	Wood	Ox
1946	Feb 4	6:05 pm	Fire	Dog	1986	Feb 4	11:09 am	Fire	Tiger
1947	Feb 4	11:55 pm	Fire	Pig	1987	Feb 4	4:52 pm	Fire	Rabbit
1948	Feb 5	5:43 am	Earth	Rat	1988	Feb 4	10:43 pm	Earth	Dragon
1949	Feb 4	11:23 am	Earth	Ox	1989	Feb 4	4:27 am	Earth	Snake
1950	Feb 4	5:21 pm	Metal	Tiger	1990	Feb 4	10:15 am	Metal	Horse
1951	Feb 4	11:14 pm	Metal	Rabbit	1991	Feb 4	4:08 pm	Metal	Sheep
1952	Feb 5	4:54 am	Water	Dragon	1992	Feb 4	9:48 pm	Water	Monkey
1953	Feb 4	10:46 am	Water	Snake	1993	Feb 4	3:38 am	Water	Rooster
1954	Feb 4	4:31 pm	Wood	Horse	1994	Feb 4	9:31 am	Wood	Dog
1955	Feb 4	10:18 pm	Wood	Sheep	1995	Feb 4	3:14 pm	Wood	Pig
1956	Feb 5	4:13 am	Fire	Monkey	1996	Feb 4	9:08 pm	Fire	Rat
1957	Feb 4	9:55 am	Fire	Rooster	1997	Feb 4	3:04 am	Fire	Ox
1958	Feb 4	3:50 pm	Earth	Dog	1998	Feb 4	8:53 am	Earth	Tiger
1959	Feb 4	9:43 pm	Earth	Pig	1999	Feb 4	2:42 pm	Earth	Rabbit
1960	Feb 5	3:23 am	Metal	Rat	2000	Feb 4	8:32 pm	Metal	Dragon
1961	Feb 4	9:23 am	Metal	Ox	2001	Feb 4	2:20 am	Metal	Snake
1962	Feb 4	3:18 pm	Water	Tiger	2002	Feb 4	8:08 am	Water	Horse
1963	Feb 4	9:08 pm	Water	Rabbit	2003	Feb 4	1:57 pm	Water	Sheep

continues

Table 1 (continued)

Solar Year	Date	Time Year Began	Phase	Animal	Solar Year	Date	Time Year Began	Phase	Animal
2004	Feb 4	7:46 pm	Wood	Monkey	2014	Feb 4	6:21 am	Wood	Horse
2005	Feb 4	1:34 am	Wood	Rooster	2015	Feb 4	12:09 pm	Wood	Sheep
2006	Feb 4	7:25 am	Fire	Dog	2016	Feb 4	6:00 pm	Fire	Monkey
2007	Feb 4	1:14 pm	Fire	Pig	2017	Feb 3	11:49 pm	Fire	Rooster
2008	Feb 4	7:03 pm	Earth	Rat	2018	Feb 4	5:38 am	Earth	Dog
2009	Feb 4	12:52 am	Earth	Ox	2019	Feb 4	11:28 am	Earth	Pig
2010	Feb 4	6:42 am	Metal	Tiger	2020	Feb 4	5:18 pm	Metal	Rat
2011	Feb 4	12:32 pm	Metal	Rabbit	2021	Feb 3	11:08 pm	Metal	Ox
2012	Feb 4	6:40 pm	Water	Dragon	2022	Feb 4	4:58 am	Water	Tiger
2013	Feb 4	12:24 am	Water	Snake	2023	Feb 4	10:47 am	Water	Rabbit

Considered individually, it takes 60 years for each phase's sign to reappear (5 phases × 12 branch animals = 60 years). The last complete cycle began in 1924 (the year of the wood rat), and ended in 1983 (the year of the water pig). The year 1984 ushered in a new cycle of 60 years, which will end in 2043.

Who Are Your Friends?

Many Chinese wouldn't think of proceeding with a ceremony, partnership, or anything else of importance without first seeking guidance from an astrologer. As a cursory check for compatibility, you, too, can determine the auspiciousness of a relationship.

Compatibility among the 12 animal signs.

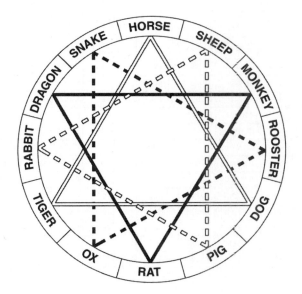

The signs that form a triangle are considered your most harmonious relationships (see the preceding figure). The rat-dragon-monkey are the best of friends, as are the ox-snake-rooster, the tiger-horse-dog, and the rabbit-sheep-pig. Upon closer examination, you'll notice each sign is four away from its compatible partner.

If you have some time on your hands, jot down the birth dates of your best friends and family members. You'll find that your affinity for your loved ones is more than a coincidence.

Who Are Your Foes?

For every two allies, you have one dangerous rival. You can determine yours by locating the animal directly opposite your sign. These are inauspicious relationships resulting in conflict, tension, and even disaster.

The animal signs that do not appear opposite each other and are not part of an affinity triad are considered compatible to varying degrees.

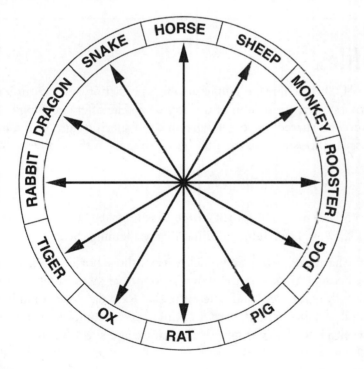

Incompatibility among the 12 animal signs.

Good Year/Bad Year

To check whether the current year is auspicious for you—or whether the upcoming year will be—simply compare your phase sign to the year in question. For example, 2005 marks the year of the wood rooster. If your element is the same as, or productive to, wood and your animal sign is compatible with a rooster, then 2005 will not feature unfavorable qi for you. But remember, this is a generality. Your year branch represents only one eighth of your personality.

Feng Alert

If you're wondering why the phase associated with your personal trigram is different than the phase assigned to your animal sign, there is a reason. The personal trigram represents the East or West *Group* to which you belong. The phase is the phase of the group, not the individual. The phase associated with your animal sign denotes the year of birth. However, the year phase also does not represent the individual. As you'll learn in the next chapter, the phase associated with the day stem characterizes a person.

Personality Profiles

Unlike other systems of Chinese fortune-telling in which prediction and precautionary measures are the cornerstones, the system of the animal zodiac offers nothing more than general characteristics shared by people born under a specific sign. In the following sections, we'll discuss the aspects of each of the 12 animals in the Chinese Zodiac.

The Industrious Rat

Famous Rats: William Shakespeare, Mozart, George Washington, Mata Hari, Jimmy Carter, Prince Charles, Doris Day, Sidney Poitier, Peggy Fleming, Sean Penn

Everyone loves a rat. Charming, social, and quick-witted, those born during a rat year are generally popular people. Always on the move, rats find safety in numbers, giving credence to the phrases "the rat race" and "the rat pack." Rats also have good business acumen. Self-motivated, detail-oriented, hard-working, and overambitious, rats are able to accumulate wealth effortlessly. Their thrifty nature and shrewdness pays off during a recession. If you have a rat boss—beware! You'll have to do a lot of negotiating to make this rat part with his reserves. Rat women make excellent wives and mothers. Budgeting, bargaining, delegating duties, and organizing hoards of stuff are her best qualities. Negatively, the rat person loves to gossip and criticize. He is often self-obsessed and greedy.

The Methodical Ox

Famous Oxen: Walt Disney, Emperor Hirohito, Richard Nixon, Vincent van Gogh, Margaret Thatcher, Robert Redford, Dustin Hoffman, Adolf Hitler, Charlie Chaplin, Saddam Hussein

The ox person succeeds by his own merits. Hard working, logical, meticulous, and tenacious, the ox can be trusted to get the job done. By nature, he is methodical, sticking to routines and tradition. It's almost impossible to get the ox to budge. His rigidity and militant style often result in an unapproachable and intimidating manner. At home, the ox man is the disciplinarian, the decision maker, and the rule setter. Disobeying an ox is cause for a rampage. Stay clear if he charges you! But, he is an excellent provider, and his family will never do without. An ox wife excels on the job and in her domestic duties. The bills are paid; the checkbook is balanced; the dinner is made; the shirts are ironed; and the kids are tucked in. Although the ox lacks a sense of humor, his affairs governed by his head rather than his heart, he is an intensely loyal creature.

The Unpredictable Tiger

Famous Tigers: Beethoven, Ho Chi Minh, Queen Elizabeth II, Dwight D. Eisenhower, Hugh Hefner, Marilyn Monroe, Rudolf Nureyev, Stevie Wonder, Jodie Foster, Tom Cruise

Tigers are romantic, charismatic, and independent. They're also fiercely adventurous, moody, impulsive, and reckless. An ardent optimist, tigers live life to the fullest and on their terms! Although he gives 110 percent to whatever catches his attention at that moment, he is notoriously unreliable. The tiger man is brash, rash, and extremely possessive. If he sees you with his lady, look out. The tiger woman is vain and indecisive. She is playful with her children, but enforces good behavior. In all, tigers are unpredictable creatures.

The Lucky Rabbit

Famous Rabbits: Albert Einstein, Orson Welles, John Dillinger, David Rockefeller, King Olav V of Norway, Jane Seymour, Nicholas Cage, Fidel Castro, Francis Ford Coppola, Sting

Rabbits are affable, even-tempered, and diplomatic. Known for their discriminating taste, rabbits are refined, cultured, and a bit snobbish! They thrive on fine wine, gourmet food, designer clothes, and stimulating conversation. In business, a rabbit is a deft negotiator. His good judgment, sound advice, and graciousness will move him up the career track—fast. Because he has few enemies, he rarely gets into trouble. Rabbits live by the Golden Rule and wouldn't think of burning a bridge. Lady rabbits are kind, considerate, and caring, but superficial.

The Dynamic Dragon

Famous Dragons: Joan of Arc, John Lennon, Jimmy Connors, Salvador Dali, Shirley Temple Black, Fred (Mr.) Rogers, Al Pacino, Pee Wee Herman, Christopher Reeves, Robin Williams

> **Master Class**
>
> In China, the dragon is the guardian of wealth and power. It is the symbol of the emperor. This is why there is an abundance of dragon artifacts throughout China and ethnic Chinese communities worldwide. If you have a keen eye, you'll notice that the dragon emblems used by the commoners have four claws on each paw. Only the emperor's emblems depict a dragon with five claws.

Among the 12 animals, dragons are the most fortunate. In fact, they're downright lucky! They're energetic, self-assured, grandiose, and egocentric. Dragons are the doers of the world. They don't sit around waiting for things to happen; they make them happen. You can always count on the no-nonsense dragon to take charge—and take risks. Their fiery enthusiasm and forceful nature rule. Dragons want things done their way. They demand perfection from themselves and from others. Even though the dragon must have the last word, he is quick to forgive. Holding grudges will slow him down. Although the dragon's magnanimous spirit draws a crowd, he has few close friends.

The Wise Snake

Famous Snakes: Picasso, Mao Tse-tung, J. Paul Getty, Brooke Shields, John F. Kennedy, Abraham Lincoln, Ryan O'Neal, Jacqueline Onassis, Oprah Winfrey

Those born under the sign of the snake are governed by their innate wisdom and intuition. Snake people think a lot. They mull things over before forming an opinion. They're intensely philosophical and make excellent listeners. Snake people are fast learners and will never make the same mistake twice. Highly skeptical and secretive creatures, snakes prefer to keep matters to themselves. They cherish their privacy, concealing their innermost wants and needs. Distrustful and somewhat unforgiving, they tend to be paranoid, even neurotic. Cross a snake, and you can be sure he'll strike at you. Most of the world's beautiful and powerful people are snakes.

The Independent Horse

Famous Horses: Rembrandt, Leonid Brezhnev, Theodore Roosevelt, Franklin Roosevelt, Billy Graham, Laura Dern, Clint Eastwood, Roger Ebert, Paul McCartney, Barbra Streisand

A horse person loves freedom. Freedom to keep his own hours. Freedom from routine. And, freedom from anyone intending to rope him in. So, if you're married to a horse, give him space, or he'll bolt. Incredibly industrious and self-reliant, horses love a challenge. Horses tend to be show-offs and self-centered, and will compliment to get a compliment. Finances are never an issue. Horses are hard-working and creative. Also, they are very headstrong, quick-minded, and don't tolerate those who are not "up to speed." Able to do 10 things at once, the horse abhors idleness. Horses are poor savers, thinking of the now and not the future.

> **CAUTION** **Feng Alert**
>
> For unknown reasons, the Chinese dread the year of the fire horse, believing that children born under this sign will bring disaster to the family. In 1966, it was reported that many Asians opted to abort, causing the birthrate to plummet. The year of the fire horse returns in 2026.

The Sensitive Sheep

Famous Sheep: Andy Warhol, Andrew Carnegie, Michelangelo, Bruce Willis, Barbara Walters, Julia Roberts, John Wayne, Malcolm Forbes, Dan Rather, Robert DeNiro

Ultra-sensitive, altruistic, compliant, sincere, gentle: This is a sheep. Although they make excellent sounding boards, don't expect the sheep to help you solve your dilemma. They're there to listen only! Prone to stress and depression, sheep prefer tranquil environments. At their worst, sheep can be pessimistic, withdrawn, and lazy. Any kind of criticism will cause them to brood for days. In the end, their self-pity will give rise to encouragement and support from friends and colleagues. Don't let a sheep manage your finances. They overspend what they have due to their generous nature. Sheep individuals follow the crowd and seldom lead.

The Mischievous Monkey

Famous Monkeys: Leonardo da Vinci, Charles Dickens, Mick Jagger, Danny De Vito, Tom Hanks, Macauley Culkin, Elizabeth Taylor, Nelson Rockefeller, Princess Caroline of Monaco, Ted Kennedy

Insatiably curious, monkeys will try anything once. Eager to learn new skills, a monkey will enthusiastically perform it over and over until he's mastered it. This gives credence to the phrase, "Monkey see, monkey do." Also, monkeys are intensely competitive. They make it their mission to do things better than anyone else. Failure is not in the monkey's vocabulary. Extremely intelligent, clever, and innovative, the monkey person will excel in any field. He truly believes he is "the top banana." On the negative side, monkeys are difficult to trust. They tend to be too self-centered to care about anyone else.

The Meticulous Rooster

Famous Roosters: Sergei Rachmaninoff, Elton John, Dolly Parton, Gene Siskel, Prince Phillip, Quincy Jones, Joan Rivers, Pope Paul VI, Emperor Akihito, Katharine Hepburn

Cocky and pretentious, the rooster loves to strut his stuff, showing off his fine feathers. Roosters are proud creatures. Their world is black and white, void of gray. Brutally honest, forthright, and candid; ask a rooster his opinion, and he'll tell you exactly what he thinks. When he wants your opinion, he'll give it to you! He is definitely not a diplomat. If the rooster could learn to sweeten his criticism, he'd be much better off. On the positive side, roosters are detail-oriented and perfectionists. Give a rooster your money, and he will account for every penny. Also, roosters are extremely focused. Their organizational skills are superlative.

The Devoted Dog

Famous Dogs: Sir Winston Churchill, Harry Houdini, Elvis Presley, Cher, Bill Moyers, Kevin Bacon, George Gershwin, Andre Agassi, Donald Sutherland, Bill Clinton

A dog is truly a person's best friend. Compatible, compromising, loyal, and unprejudiced, dogs are there when you need them. The dog person is trustworthy and dutiful, making an excellent (albeit reluctant) leader. Contrary to what you may think, dogs form friendships slowly. First, they must check you out, watch, and wait. You must win their affection. For the most part, dogs are humble animals, caring little about money. Although they can lavish you with unconditional devotion and love, when provoked, a dog can be fiercely mean-spirited, downright nasty. Of all the signs in the Chinese Zodiac, the dog is the most likeable.

The Nurturing Pig

Famous Pigs: Al Capone, Prince Rainier, Ronald Reagan, Lucille Ball, Woody Allen, Alfred Hitchcock, Kevin Kline, Billy Crystal, Arnold Schwarzenegger, Hillary Clinton

Bottom line, pigs are the nicest people on the planet. With hearts of gold, they are honest, patient, and will take every measure to ensure your safety and comfort. A pig will remain your friend for life. But, pigs are often taken for granted. Only when they're not around do you realize how dependent you are on them. Naturally naive, pigs can be gullible, falling prey to charlatans and swindlers. In all, pigs of both genders are selfless, devoted, and loving. They just can't say "no." Because of their overzealous generosity, the pig person has little money. Nevertheless, he has enough, giving credence to the phrase, "the more you give, the more you shall receive."

These are the general characteristics of the 12 animals of the Chinese Zodiac. If you're interested in a more detailed account, many books on the subject are available. One we suggest is Theodora Lau's *The Handbook of Chinese Horoscopes* (see Appendix C).

In the next chapter, you'll learn about The Four Pillars of Destiny, a method of Chinese astrology that can help you gain insight about money matters, relations with others, and the focus of your life (among other things).

The Least You Need to Know

- The 12 animals of the Chinese zodiac represent cycles of earthly qi.

- The Chinese Zodiac system of astrology is superficial, but fun.

- Once you determine your animal sign, you'll know who are your animal friends and foes.

- This system is concerned more with personality profiles than fate prediction and prevention.

Chapter 22

The Four Pillars of Destiny, Part 1

In This Chapter

- ◆ Is our destiny determined by fate or free will?
- ◆ The Ten Heavenly Stems
- ◆ The Twelve Earthly Branches
- ◆ Downloading your life chart using an online program

Let's say you're at a dinner party. You've discussed the escalating crisis in the Middle East, debated the merits of the high protein-low carbohydrate Atkins diet, argued about whether aggression is an inherent trait in specific breeds of dogs, voiced your opinion about celibacy in the Catholic Church, and chuckled over the latest celebrity foibles. Several bottles of Merlot later, there's a lull in the conversation. Here's the perfect time to pose this question to perk up the party: "Do you think your life is predictable?"

This chapter answers that question. Here, you'll learn how The Four Pillars of Destiny, a method of Chinese fate calculation, can determine a predetermined course of events—your destiny and luck. You'll learn how this method can help uncover your hidden potential so that you can enjoy a more meaningful and satisfying life.

How Free Is Free Will?

Although most Westerners believe that destiny and luck are random and unpredictable, the Chinese believe destiny and luck are measurable and knowable. Nevertheless, the Chinese believe how we think and act can help alter (positively or negatively) a predetermined course of events. So, before you discover what your four pillars say about your destiny and luck, let's take one step back and talk about free will.

We all know what free will means. It's what sets us apart from any other living, breathing thing on Earth. Free will allows us to make choices, to actively participate in building our life's path. But are we totally free? Of course not. No one has absolute free will. Not even America—the land of the free. Physical limitations and psychological conditioning restrict most of us from making choices that are harmful, or socially and morally unacceptable. For example, you have the freedom to jump off a cliff. But would you want to? Also, you have the freedom to say just about anything. It's your constitutional right. But would you want to? Do you really want to tell your best friend that you hate her new hairdo? Do you really want to tell your spouse he or she is not your soul mate? We think not.

Clearly, our decisions in some measure reflect the belief systems of our parents, society, and country. But our decisions are also influenced by our character or personality, the part of us that is largely inexplicable. Some believe our fundamental character is determined by our genetic composition. Some believe God or a Higher Power grants us our innate character, talents, and circumstances. Some also believe in reincarnation, the belief that cause and effect, or karma, determines the outcome of our lives. Basically, reincarnation holds that we are continually reborn until we achieve our full potential.

Master Class

When Song dynasty scholar Su Tong Po was asked about the criteria for passing the Imperial Examination, he answered that a person's success is based on five factors: Destiny (ming) and luck (yun) are preordained by heavenly qi. Feng shui is determined by earthly qi. And, the accumulation of virtuous deeds (ji yin de) and study (du shu) are controlled by human qi.

The Chinese believe that our character, destiny, and luck are a blend of fate and free will, a harmony of heavenly, earthly, and human qi. They believe our character is a by-product of our fate. Our fate is determined by the first breath we take. Literally, we inhale our destiny and luck, a composite of qi present at that exact moment.

Portending the Future

Anyone can predict the cycle of life: You're born; you grow up; you age; and then you die. No one can deny this most fundamental fate. On a natural level, anyone can predict that spring's rebirth leads to summer's vibrant abundance, which is followed by autumn's decay, and then winter's abyss. On a smaller scale, we can look outside and based on the season and our observation of the sky, forecast the day's weather. Also, we can use tools to help us prepare for the day ahead. For instance, we can read the thermometer posted outside the kitchen window, watch the weather vane on a neighbor's roof, or stick our finger in the air to determine the direction the wind is blowing. Yet, the five senses that we rely on to help us make judgments and decisions limit us; that is, we can't see or feel the minutia of weather patterns.

Of course, we can watch the local television news for information about the weather. Meteorologists always seem to have the answer, and they're even correct most of the time! This is because they use more sophisticated instruments to measure things like air temperature, air currents, wind speed, and humidity. In the same way, in order to predict more detailed information about a person's life, we need a sophisticated technique.

> **Feng Facts**
>
> In meteorology, there's an interesting phenomenon called the butterfly effect, so called because the flutter of a butterfly's wings (a slight change in atmospheric conditions) can cause dramatic atmospheric changes in another part of the world. On a human level, this means that the smallest act of free will can lead to an unpredictable outcome.

What Are The Four Pillars of Destiny?

In China there are two kinds of fate calculation: Ziwei Doushu (Purple Constellation Fate Computation) and Ziping Bazi (Eight Characters of Ziping). Ziping Bazi is commonly known as *The Four Pillars of Destiny*. First developed by court astrologer Li Xuzhong of the Tang dynasty (618–907 C.E.) and modified by Xu Ziping of the Song dynasty (960–1269 C.E.), the system of The Four Pillars is a method of calculating and interpreting the five phase components of the qi you inhaled at birth. Like feng shui, it is an accurate system of predicting possibilities. For example, the chart you will soon create online might indicate a potential for great wealth, thus creating an innate urge to succeed. But how you act on this urge is where your free choice comes into play. In other words, regardless of what your chart might indicate, free will helps to determine the outcome of your fate.

> **Wise Words**
>
> Called Bazi (eight characters) in Chinese, **The Four Pillars of Destiny** is a method of calculating and interpreting the five phase elements present at your birth. Each pillar represents a year, month, day, and hour. The Four Pillars of Destiny measures probabilities, not certainties, of your life's path.

So, if good fortune prevails in your chart, waiting for Publishers Clearinghouse to come knocking at your door isn't an answer. The onus is on you to act on your inborn talents and desires—to force the hand, so to speak. If you are blessed with advantageous possibility, it's up to you to bring it to fruition!

What do the "pillars" of The Four Pillars of Destiny mean? Well, each pillar is actually a time component. One pillar represents the year, one the month, one the day, and one the hour. Each time component describes the five-phase element structure present at the moment of your birth (when you took your first, qi-inspired breath). The relationship and position of each phase helps to determine your probable life path. The following chart is an example of a Four Pillars chart. It belongs to the late Princess Diana. The day-stem component is highlighted; this component is called the Day-Master. You'll learn about the Day-Master's importance in the next chapter.

Notice that each pillar is divided into a stem-branch component. Actually, stem is short for Ten Heavenly Stems, and branch is short for Twelve Earthly Branches, which we'll discuss a little later in this chapter.

Master Class

There's a fundamental difference between Western and Chinese astrology. Western astrology considers the positions of the planets, sun, and moon at your birth—a truly astral method. Chinese astrology is concerned with types of qi (heavenly, earthly, and human) and, therefore, isn't exclusively astral.

An example of a Four Pillars of Destiny life chart. This one belongs to the late Princess Diana.

Princess Diana's Four Pillars Birth Chart

	Hour	Day	Month	Year
	6:45 pm*	1	July	1961
Stem	Yi	Yi	Jia	Xin
Branch	You	Wei	Wu	Chou
Stem Phase	- Wood	- Wood	+ Wood	- Metal
Branch Phases	- Metal	- Earth	- Fire	- Earth
		- Fire	- Earth	- Water
		- Wood		- Metal

* Adjusted for Daylight Savings Time

Time, Chinese Style

Before we can get into the mechanics, let's take a moment to talk about, well, time. As we mentioned in Chapter 13, Westerners view time as linear. The year begins on January 1 and ends on December 31. The month begins on the first and generally ends on the thirtieth. The day begins and ends at midnight. Times proceed along a straight line.

The Chinese, on the other hand, think cyclically. Time is a continuous spiral. What goes around, comes around. Time does repeat itself—sort of.

The Ten Heavenly Stems

How did the Chinese develop their concept of time? As the story goes, the legendary Huang Di, known as the Yellow Emperor (2697–2597 B.C.E.), ordered a wise man named Da Nao to invent a system of recording time. To achieve this, Da Nao set about observing the intricacies of the five phases of qi, how they transformed over the course of the year. From this observation, Da Nao developed what he called the *Ten Heavenly Stems*, shown in Table 1.

Why are the stems heavenly? Harkening back to Chapter 4, the Chinese people use the word "heaven" to mean "time." Hence, the heavenly stems record how qi changes with time.

Wise Words

The **Ten Heavenly Stems** (Tian Gan) represent heavenly qi—cycles of time. The progression of stems show how the five phases alter with the passage of a year. One type of qi undergoes growth (yang) and then declines while yielding to another type (yin).

Table 1

NUMBER	PINYIN	POLARITY	POLARITY SYMBOL	PHASE
1	Jia	Yang	+	Wood
2	Yi	Yin	-	Wood
3	Bing	Yang	+	Fire
4	Ding	Yin	-	Fire
5	Wu	Yang	+	Earth
6	Ji	Yin	-	Earth
7	Geng	Yang	+	Metal
8	Xin	Yin	-	Metal
9	Ren	Yang	+	Water
10	Gui	Yin	-	Water

The Ten Heavenly Stems.

Referring to the table, each stem is associated with a yin (–) or yang (+) delineation and a phase. For example, the first stem Jia is yang (+) wood. The second stem Yi is yin (–) wood. The third stem Bing is yang (+) fire, and so forth.

The Twelve Earthly Branches

Just as the words "heaven" and "time" are interchangeable, so, too, are the words "earth" and "space." As you learned in the previous chapter, the *Twelve Earthly Branches* denote movement of qi in a given area on earth. Referring to the illustration in the previous chapter, notice that the pig, rat, and ox branches rule the north and winter. Following clockwise around the illustration, the tiger, rabbit, and dragon branches rule the east and spring; the snake, horse, and sheep (or goat) branches rule the south and summer; and the monkey, rooster, and dog branches rule the west and autumn. Why is each branch referred to by its animal name rather than a phase? This is because each branch is comprised of one or more phases. Collectively, they are called the reserved (or hidden) stems in the branches. For our purposes, we'll refer to them as the branch phases.

Wise Words

The **Twelve Earthly Branches** (Di Zhi) represent the movement of earthly qi in a given location. Each branch is assigned a zodiacal animal and contains one or more hidden stems.

The reserved stems in branches.

Table 2

NUMBER	PINYIN	ANIMAL	Hidden Stem(s) in Branches
1	Zi	Rat	- Water (Gui)
2	Chou	Ox	- Earth (Ji), - Water (Gui), - Metal (Xin)
3	Yin	Tiger	+ Wood (Jia), + Fire (Bing), + Earth (Wu)
4	Mao	Rabbit	- Wood (Yi)
5	Chen	Dragon	+ Earth (Wu), - Wood (Yi), - Water (Gui)
6	Si	Snake	+ Fire (Bing), + Earth (Wu), + Metal (Geng)
7	Wu	Horse	- Fire (Ding), - Earth (Ji)
8	Wei	Goat	- Earth (Ji), - Fire (Ding), - Wood (Yi)
9	Shen	Monkey	+ Metal (Geng), + Water (Ren), + Earth (Wu)
10	You	Rooster	- Metal (Xin)
11	Xu	Dog	+ Earth (Wu), - Metal (Xin), - Fire (Ding)
12	Hai	Pig	+ Water (Ren), + Wood (Jia)

Referring to Table 2, notice that the first rat branch Zi contains only hidden yin (-) water. The second ox branch Chou contains mainly hidden yin (-) earth, with some yin (-) water and yin (-) metal. The third tiger branch Yin contains mainly hidden yang (+) wood, with some yang (+) fire and yang (+) earth. Get the idea?

The Cycle of Sixty

The Ten Heavenly Stems and the Twelve Earthly Branches combine into a *Cycle of Sixty* stem-branch pairs, shown in Table 3. If you imagine two gears—one with 10 teeth and the other with 12 teeth—and allow them to rotate and interlock, the gear with 10 teeth would complete its rotation before the gear with 12 teeth. If you mark the first tooth of each gear and begin the rotation, you'll note that it takes six rotations of the 10 and five rotations of the 12 before the first teeth of the respective gears are aligned as they were at the start. Thus, the sixtieth interlocking will start the repeating of the cycle. Therefore, there are 60 possible pairs when the stems and branches are combined.

Wise Words

The **Cycle of Sixty** represents all possible combinations (60) of the Ten Heavenly Stems and Twelve Earthly Branches with corresponding yang and yin designations. The year 2697 B.C.E. marked the first of the 60-year, or 60-stem-branch, cycle.

Table 3

NUMBERS		STEM/BRANCH	PHASE	POLARITY	NUMBERS		STEM/BRANCH	PHASE	POLARITY
1	S1B1	Jia Zi	Wood Water	Yang	31	S1B7	Jia Wu	Wood Fire	Yang
2	S2B2	Yi Chou	Wood Earth	Yin	32	S2B8	Yi Wei	Wood Earth	Yin
3	S3B3	Bing Yin	Fire Wood	Yang	33	S3B9	Bing Shen	Fire Metal	Yang
4	S4B4	Ding Mao	Fire Wood	Yin	34	S4B10	Ding You	Fire Metal	Yin
5	S5B5	Wu Chen	Earth Earth	Yang	35	S5B11	Wu Xu	Earth Earth	Yang
6	S6B6	Ji Si	Earth Fire	Yin	36	S6B12	Ji Hai	Earth Water	Yin
7	S7B7	Geng Wu	Metal Fire	Yang	37	S7B1	Geng Zi	Metal Water	Yang
8	S8B8	Xin Wei	Metal Earth	Yin	38	S8B2	Xin Chou	Metal Earth	Yin
9	S9B9	Ren Shen	Water Metal	Yang	39	S9B3	Ren Yin	Water Wood	Yang
10	S10B10	Gui You	Water Metal	Yin	40	S10B4	Gui Mao	Water Wood	Yin
11	S1B11	Jia Xu	Wood Earth	Yang	41	S1B5	Jia Chen	Wood Earth	Yang
12	S2B12	Yi Hai	Wood Water	Yin	42	S2B6	Yi Si	Wood Fire	Yin
13	S3B1	Bing Zi	Fire Water	Yang	43	S3B7	Bing Wu	Fire Fire	Yang
14	S4B2	Ding Chou	Fire Earth	Yin	44	S4B8	Ding Wei	Fire Earth	Yin
15	S5B3	Wu Yin	Earth Wood	Yang	45	S5B9	Wu Shen	Earth Metal	Yang
16	S6B4	Ji Mao	Earth Wood	Yin	46	S6B10	Ji You	Earth Metal	Yin
17	S7B5	Geng Chen	Metal Earth	Yang	47	S7B11	Geng Xu	Metal Earth	Yang
18	S8B6	Xin Si	Metal Fire	Yin	48	S8B12	Xin Hai	Metal Water	Yin
19	S9B7	Ren Wu	Water Fire	Yang	49	S9B1	Ren Zi	Water Water	Yang
20	S10B8	Gui Wei	Water Earth	Yin	50	S10B2	Gui Chou	Water Earth	Yin
21	S1B9	Jia Shen	Wood Metal	Yang	51	S1B3	Jia Yin	Wood Wood	Yang
22	S2B10	Yi You	Wood Metal	Yin	52	S2B4	Yi Mao	Wood Wood	Yin
23	S3B11	Bing Xu	Fire Earth	Yang	53	S3B5	Bing Chen	Fire Earth	Yang
24	S4B12	Ding Hai	Fire Water	Yin	54	S4B6	Ding Si	Fire Fire	Yin
25	S5B1	Wu Zi	Earth Water	Yang	55	S5B7	Wu Wu	Earth Fire	Yang
26	S6B2	Ji Chou	Earth Earth	Yin	56	S6B8	Ji Wei	Earth Earth	Yin
27	S7B3	Geng Yin	Metal Wood	Yang	57	S7B9	Geng Shen	Metal Metal	Yang
28	S8B4	Xin Mao	Metal Wood	Yin	58	S8B10	Xin You	Metal Metal	Yin
29	S9B5	Ren Chen	Water Earth	Yang	59	S9B11	Ren Xu	Water Earth	Yang
30	S10B6	Gui Si	Water Fire	Yin	60	S10B12	Gui Hai	Water Water	Yin

The Cycle of Sixty.

Beginning with Jia Zi, the year 2697 B.C.E. marked the first of the 60-year, or 60-stem-branch, cycle. Why does the cycle begin with Jia (wood) Zi (water)? This is because the branch (Zi/water) is at the end of yin. The beginning of yang is marked by the growth of wood. It is a time of birth and renewal. What cycle are we currently in, you ask? You'll find out in a moment.

Calculating Your Four Pillars

Creating your chart takes a matter of seconds. It is error-proof—and it is absolutely free! All you need to do is to go to Joseph Yu's website: www.astro-fengshui.com. Scroll down until you find "Four Pillars Calculator." Click on "On-line calculator." You'll be taken to a page called, "Chart Your Four Pillars."

Follow these simple directions:

1. Type your name, or the name of person whose chart you will be creating, in the appropriate box.

2. Select the GMT (Greenwich Mean Time) zone for your place of birth. If you do not find the city, or a city close to where you were born, go to www.timeanddate.com. Under the Time box, click on "World Clock." Scroll down the page until you find your birth city. Click on it. For example, if you were born in Johannesburg, South Africa, GMT Standard Time is +2 or two hours ahead of Greenwich Mean Time. If you were born in Toronto, Canada, GMT Standard Time is –5 or five hours behind Greenwich Mean Time. Note: Make sure that you jot down the Standard Time and not Summer or Daylight Savings Time. Return to "Charting Your Four Pillars" page on Joseph Yu's website. Choose GMT +2:00 Athens/Helsinki for the first example and GMT –5:00 US/Eastern for the second example. Alternative references to obtain the time zone for your birth city are wwp.greenwichmeantime.com, www.astro.com (AstroDIENST), and www.hko.gov.hk/gts/time/worldtime2.htm (Hong Kong Observatory).

3. The longitude box is optional. However, you can obtain this information at the same website you might have used in Step 2: www.timeanddate.com. For example, the longitude of Johannesburg, South Africa is +27 degrees. The longitude of Toronto, Canada is –79 degrees. Anything east of Greenwich, England (Zero Longitude) gets a + and anything west of Greenwich gets a –. Longitudinal information can also be found on the alternate websites listed in Step 2.

4. Select the year and month of your birth.

5. Select the day of your birth.

6. Before you select the hour of your birth (recorded in military time; see the following conversion table), you first must adjust for Daylight Savings Time (DST), if appropriate, by subtracting an hour from the time of your birth. If you're not sure DST was in effect, go to www.astro.com. On the home page, click on "Astrology Atlas Query" located on the top left side of your screen. Select the region in which you were born and type your birth city. This will take you to another page. Next, type your birth data. If DST was in effect, it will be noted. Another good source is *The International Atlas, Fifth Edition: World Latitudes & Longitudes, Time Changes and Time Zones*, by Thomas G. Shanks (see Appendix C).

Military Time Conversion Table

00 = Midnight	01 = 1:00 A.M.	02 = 2:00 A.M.	03 = 3:00 A.M.
04 = 4:00 A.M.	05 = 5:00 A.M.	06 = 6:00 A.M.	07 = 7:00 A.M.
08 = 8:00 A.M.	09 = 9:00 A.M.	10 = 10:00 A.M.	11 = 11:00 A.M.
12 = Noon	13 = 1:00 P.M.	14 = 2:00 P.M.	15 = 3:00 P.M.
16 = 4:00 P.M.	17 = 5:00 P.M.	18 = 6:00 P.M.	19 = 7:00 P.M.
20 = 8:00 P.M.	21 = 9:00 P.M.	22 = 10:00 P.M.	23 = 11:00 P.M.

7. Click "Compute." Scroll down to find your Four Pillars chart and your Eight Luck Pillars chart (the latter will be discussed in Chapter 26). Print it out.

Remember, GMT is Greenwich Mean (or Meridian) Time. It is an imaginary longitudinal line that runs from the North Pole to the South Pole. Zero Longitude runs through Greenwich, England. Since 1884, it has been the starting point of every time zone around the world. GMT is fixed. Adjustments are not made for Daylight Savings Time.

Princess Diana's Four Pillars

As an example, let's compute Princess Diana's Four Pillars birth chart.

Princess Diana's Four Pillars Birth Chart

Hour	Day	Month	Year
- Wood [Yi]	- Wood [Yi]	+ Wood [Jia]	- Metal [Xin]
Rooster [You]	Goat [Wei]	Horse [Wu]	Ox [Chou]
-Metal [Xin]	- Earth [Ji]	- Fire [Ding]	- Earth [Ji]
	- Fire [Ding]	- Earth [Ji]	
	- Wood [Yi]		

The result of Princess Diana's Four Pillars chart obtained at www.astro-fengshui.com.

The first row represents the stems belonging to the year, month, day, and hour of Diana's birth. The second row represents the branches belonging to the year, month, day, and hour of her birth. As we mentioned earlier in this chapter, a branch contains one or more hidden components, and therefore, is referred to by its Pinyin or animal name. The third, fourth, and fifth rows represent the hidden stems within the branches (the branch phases). In Diana's chart, the ox or Chou branch in her year pillar contains only yin (-) earth. The horse or Wu branch in her month pillar contains yin (-) fire and yin (-) earth, and so forth.

To make Diana's chart easier on the eye and easier to study, we'll rearrange her chart so that the Pinyin names and phases are grouped separately. At this introductory stage, it isn't necessary to note the Pinyin names of the hidden stems in the branches. Diana's chart now looks like this:

	Hour	Day	Month	Year
	6:45 pm*	1	July	1961
Stem	Yi	Yi	Jia	Xin
Branch	You	Wei	Wu	Chou
Stem Phase	- Wood	- Wood	+ Wood	- Metal
Branch Phases	- Metal	- Earth	- Fire	- Earth
		- Fire	- Earth	- Water
		- Wood		- Metal

* Adjusted for Daylight Savings Time

Using a separate sheet of paper, take time now to arrange your pillars in the same way. With a pencil, outline your day-stem component—your Day-Master. In Diana's case, - Wood is her Day-Master. You'll learn the relevance of the Day-Master in the next chapter.

Whew! You've completed your Four Pillars of Destiny life chart. Now what? This is where the fun begins. In the next chapters, you'll learn different ways of analyzing your chart. You'll learn about your life's focus, your relations with others, and money matters (among other things).

The Least You Need to Know

- ◆ The Chinese believe the first breath we take at birth determines our destiny.

- ◆ Our free will allows us to actively participate in changing our destiny.

- ◆ The Four Pillars of Destiny is a method of determining the qi you inhaled at birth.

- ◆ Each pillar is made up of a stem-branch component(s) corresponding to a five-phase element and a yin/yang delineation.

Chapter 23

The Four Pillars of Destiny, Part 2

In This Chapter

- What is the Day-Master?
- Determining the stars that rule your chart
- Determining the timeliness of your Day-Master
- Interpreting Bill Clinton's and Princess Diana's charts
- Determining your life's purpose
- The stars that govern your chart

Now that you've obtained your chart online, how do you interpret it? Before you can obtain insight, you must know how to acquire information and where to look.

In this chapter, we'll continue with the Four Pillars method and its application with respect to the five phases. In so doing, we will zero in on the Day-Master and reveal how it offers a particularly personal assessment.

The All-Important Day-Master

Although The Four Pillars of Destiny dates to the Tang dynasty (618–907 C.E.), when astrologer Li Xuzhong developed it as a way to represent a person's birth data, the approach hasn't stayed constant. Over time, there have been many alterations. Perhaps the most significant ones involved focusing on the Day-Master as a means of illuminating a person's specific characteristics.

Focusing on the *Day-Master*, this method is also known as the *Ziping Method* after astrologer Xu Ziping and dates to the Song dynasty (960–1279 C.E.). The Day-Master helps you to identify to which of the five phases you belong. It can determine whether you have a strong or a weak chart. Knowing the relative strength of your chart can lead you to a broader understanding of your relationship to the five phases, as you'll soon see.

Wise Words

The method focusing on the **Day-Master**, or **Ziping Method**, developed by Song dynasty astrologer Xu Ziping, analyzes the five phases in your Four Pillars chart in relationship to how each phase affects the Day-Master (the day-stem component of your Four Pillars chart).

Now, referring to your life chart you just obtained online, pinpoint your Day-Master. It is equivalent to the day-stem phase component. We'll soon be analyzing the relationship between the phases and Day-Master. It might be a good idea to paperclip Appendix F, where you'll find a diagram illustrating the three cycles of qi: productive, controlling, and reductive. Understanding the phase relationships is integral to successfully analyzing your chart.

Day-Master Relations

Because this chapter is rather involved, let's review for a moment. In The Four Pillars of Destiny, there are eight components, one of which is the Day-Master. Each component is associated with a phase (fire, earth, metal, water, wood) and a yin/yang delineation. To interpret a life chart, you examine how the Day-Master is affected by the other components. How they relate to the Day-Master will lead you to understand many aspects of your life, including your purpose, finances, marriage, and relations with your family and friends, for example.

The first step is to learn about the five "stars" governing your pillars. They are …

1. **Resource Star.** If a phase produces or generates the Day-Master, it is the *resource* star. For example, if your Day-Master is fire, wood is your resource star because it generates fire. Resource corresponds to support (guidance, moral, and financial) from your parents, boss, or mentor. Resource also corresponds to

knowledge and education, rendering you a means of support. An overabundance of resource suggests that you might be spoiled. It suggests you're dependent on your parents, husband, or wife. It suggests that you might not be living up to your potential. On the other hand, a lack of resource means you are independent and self-supporting.

2. **Performance Star.** If a phase is produced or generated by the Day-Master, it is the *performance* star. For example, if your Day-Master is fire, earth is your performance star because fire generates earth. Perfor-mance corresponds to your productivity, talents, and accomplishments. A lot of performance means that you are a very talented and/or a highly accomplished person. You are recognized by others. Although your abundance of performance leads you to feel empowered and even rebellious, others are jealous of you. A lack of performance suggests that you're not a risk-taker. It also indicates you procrastinate or that you're a bit lazy.

Wise Words

The **resource** phase gives strength to, supports, and produces the Day-Master. The **performance** phase is produced by the Day-Master. The **power** phase controls, dominates, or empowers the Day-Master. The **wealth** phase challenges the Day-Master. The **parallel** phase is the same as the Day-Master.

3. **Power Star.** If a phase controls the Day-Master, it is the *power* star. For example, if your Day-Master is fire, water is your power star because it controls (or extinguishes) fire. A lot of power means that you're a natural-born leader. You're able to take on a heavy workload. Those who seek to control you also empower you to strengthen and succeed. However, since the power star challenges (or controls) the Day-Master, you might feel overwhelmed, burdened, and constrained. A lack of power could mean a lack of ambition and discipline. It suggests that your career has nothing to do with power or status.

4. **Wealth Star.** If a phase is controlled by the Day-Master, it is the *wealth* star. For example, if your Day-Master is fire, metal is your wealth star because fire controls (or melts) metal. The wealth phase represents your material possessions (money, property, jewelry, for example) and your career. An abundance of wealth suggests that you may have a lot of money-making opportunities. The key word is "may." Whether or not these opportunities will be made manifest depends on a host of factors that will become clear in successive chapters. A lack of wealth indicates that you must create opportunities yourself. It suggests you must use the strengths of the other stars to generate wealth. It does not suggest that you will not have money or a successful career.

5. **Parallel Star.** If a phase is simply the same phase as the Day-Master, it is the *parallel* star. A parallel phase assists the Day-Master to make him strong. The parallel phase also represents your friends and competitors. An abundance of parallel might mean you have to compete for everything including money and love. A lack of this phase suggests loneliness and a lack of assistance from colleagues and friends.

Are you with us so far? We know this stuff is complicated, but stick with it. In the end, it will be worth your while. Patience and perseverance prevail (say that 10 times fast).

Before you proceed, take this opportunity now to associate each phase in your chart with a star. You need correlate only each stem and the primary stems hidden in the branches (the second row of phases) with a star. For our introductory purposes, we will not analyze the lesser hidden stems in this exercise.

Star Cycles

It's important to understand how the five stars (resource, parallel, performance, power, and wealth) relate to each other. Like the producing and controlling cycles relating to the five phases, the five stars have a similar sequence as follows:

The productive and controlling cycles of the five stars.

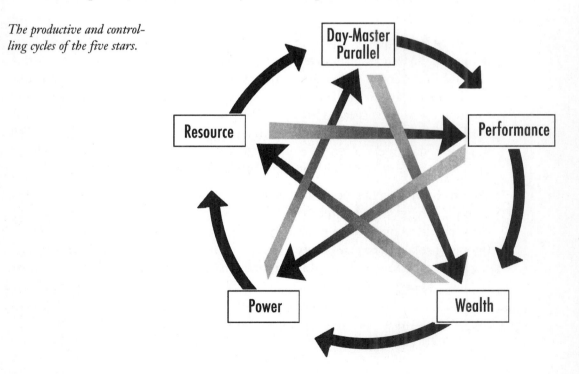

Let's analyze the productive cycle first:

◆ *Day-Master and parallel generate performance.* Your motivation and the encouragement provided by your friends and competitors drive you to perform—to hone your talent and to be more productive.

◆ *Performance generates wealth.* Your talent, productivity, and accomplishments generate an income.

◆ *Wealth generates power.* With money, you can gain power and authority.

◆ *Power generates resource.* Your authority is supported by others.

◆ *Resource generates Day-Master and parallel.* With support and knowledge, you'll gain respect from your friends and competitors.

Master Class

If a star(s) is not present in your chart, the cycle of qi is broken. However, when the star(s) in question appears on a 10-year or annual luck pillar (the subject of Chapter 26), the void is filled. When this happens, the star that's missing will come to you. For example, if the power star is absent (or untimely) in your chart, you must wait until power appears on a luck pillar to gain power, authority, and respect—a factor particularly important for a politician.

The controlling cycle works the same way:

◆ *Day-Master and parallel control wealth.* Your friends seek to take advantage of your money.

◆ *Wealth controls resource.* With money, you can influence your supporters.

◆ *Resource controls performance.* Your supporters (parents or other authority figures, for example) may prevent you from developing your talent.

◆ *Performance controls power.* Your accomplishments and talent may cause people in an authoritative position (your boss, for example) to be jealous of you.

◆ *Power controls Day-Master and parallel.* As a leader, you manage your subordinates.

In a Four Pillars analysis, it's not necessary to study the reductive cycle. Take this time now to *identify* the relationship between the stars in your chart. Before you *analyze* the relationships, you first must learn about each star's timeliness.

Too much or too little of a star will alter the forecasted prognosis. For example, let's say you have an overabundance of resource. It means you rely on others for support. If you're an adult and your parents are still supporting you, they are disabling you from being productive. On the other hand, you have no choice other than to be productive if you have very little or no resources in your chart. Get the idea?

The Timeliness of Your Day-Master and the Stars

Your month of birth determines whether a star is timely or not. Timeliness refers to the time of the year you were born—specifically, into which season you were born. For the sake of clarity, let's reiterate. Wood corresponds to and is strong in spring; fire corresponds to and is strong in summer; metal corresponds to and is strong in autumn, and water corresponds to and is strong in winter. Earth is a special case, which we will deal with in a moment. Although the ancient Chinese used the four seasons to explain the strength of a phase, we know today there are places in the world that do not have four seasons. Also, in some parts of the world, the seasons are reversed. These factors do not mean that the five-phase theory must be modified. Understand that you're studying energy coming from the universe and not just from the position of the Earth as it travels around the sun.

Add to these phase/season relationships four possible conditions: ready, vibrant, retiring, and inactive. These conditions refer to the phase's strength in the particular season into which you are born. Referring to the following chart, let's take an example. If your Day-Master is wood and you were born in spring (February, March, or April), wood is vibrant because it is predominant in the spring. In summer (May, June, and July), wood is retiring. In autumn (August, September, and October), wood is inactive. And in winter (November, December, and January), wood is ready.

Your birth month determines the timeliness of your Day-Master and the other phases in your chart.

PHASES ↓	WINTER	SPRING	SUMMER	AUTUMN
	Hai Zi Chou	Yin Mao Chen	Si Wu Wei	Shen You Xu
	Nov Dec Jan	Feb Mar Apr	May Jun Jul	Aug Sep Oct
Wood	Ready	Vibrant	Retiring	Inactive
Fire	Inactive	Ready	Vibrant	Retiring
Metal	Retiring	Inactive	Ready	Vibrant
Water	Vibrant	Retiring	Inactive	Ready
Earth	Weak Weak Strong	Weak Weak Strong	Vibrant	Weak Weak Strong

Now, what of earth? As we mentioned, earth is a special case. It's a transitional phase, as you learned in Chapter 21. We cannot apply the same terminology (ready, vibrant, retiring, and inactive) to earth. Instead, we say earth is either strong or weak. Earth is strong in October, January, and April; earth is weak in August, September, November, December, February, and March. Earth is vibrant in summer. This is because fire, the mother of earth, is strongest in summer.

Use this time now to determine the timeliness of your Day-Master and the other stars (stem phases and primary branch phases) in your birth chart.

Bill Clinton's Star Chart

Let's examine former president Bill Clinton's chart, tying together all that you've learned so far in this chapter. At this time, disregard the yin (-) and yang (+) phase delineations. You'll learn about their meaning later in this chapter and in succeeding ones. Also, for the following analysis, we only included the main phase component comprising Clinton's branches. An analysis of all the hidden phases in the branches requires advanced study.

Bill Clinton's Four Pillars Birth Chart

	Hour	Day	Month	Year
	8:51 am	19	August	1946
Stem	Geng	Yi	Bing	Bing
Branch	Chen	Chou	Shen	Xu
Stem Phase	+ Metal	- Wood	+ Fire	+ Fire
Branch Phase	+ Earth	- Earth	+ Metal	+ Earth

	Hour	Day	Month	Year
Stem	Vibrant Power	Inactive Day-Master	Retiring Performance	Retiring Performance
Branch	Weak Wealth	Weak Wealth	Vibrant Power	Weak Wealth

Born on August 19, 1946, at 8:51 A.M., Bill Clinton's Day-Master is wood. For Clinton, wood represents self and the parallel star (friends and competitors). Wood born in August is inactive. Fire is his performance (talent and accomplishments) star. Fire born in August is retiring. Earth is his wealth (money and career) star. Earth born in August is weak. Metal is his power (power and leadership) star. Metal born in August is vibrant. Water is his resource star. Water born in August is ready. Although Clinton does not have resource stars in the stems or primary branches, he does have deeply hidden resources, which is not illustrated and which we will not discuss.

Bill Clinton's main asset is vibrant power (metal). Referring to the illustration earlier in this chapter of the cycle of the five stars, vibrant power is generating support (resource) from citizens of the United States and from world leaders. Vibrant power metal is also controlling wood (self/friends/competitors). It is breathing life into and empowering his inactive self to lead the nation. The self is spurring his performance star to succeed. (Clinton's retiring performance star [fire] will burn brighter during fire years.) Performance generates wealth, which is weak, but abundant. The fact that his wealth stars are located on the branches means that wealth (money and career) is secondary to his urge to be powerful. Finally, the abundance of wealth feeds his power.

Master Class

Stars that appear on the stems represent outward expression—what is noticeable to others. Stars that appear on the branches represent inward expression—what is not noticeable to others.

Princess Diana's Star Chart

Born on July 1, 1961, at 7:45 P.M. (adjusting for DST puts her birth hour at 6:45 P.M.), Princess Diana's Day-Master is wood. For Diana, wood represents self and the parallel star (friends and competitors). Wood born in July is retiring. Fire is her performance (talent and accomplishments) star. Fire born in August is vibrant. Earth is her wealth star. Earth born in August is vibrant. Metal is her power (power and leadership) star. Metal born in August is ready. Water is her resource (support) star. Although water (resource) is not present on her stems, a trace amount of it is deeply hidden in her branches. We'll discuss how her lack of water affects her well-being in successive chapters.

Princess Diana's Four Pillars Birth Chart

	Hour	Day	Month	Year
	6:45 pm*	1	July	1961
Stem	Yi	Yi	Jia	Xin
Branch	You	Wei	Wu	Chou
Stem Phase	- Wood	- Wood	+ Wood	- Metal
Branch Phase	- Metal	- Earth	- Fire	- Earth

* Adjusted for Daylight Savings Time

	Hour	Day	Month	Year
Stem	Retiring Parallel	Retiring Day-Master	Retiring Parallel	Ready Power
Branch	Ready Power	Vibrant Wealth	Vibrant Performance	Vibrant Wealth

Diana's main assets are vibrant performance that generates vibrant wealth that generates ready power.

Your Life's Purpose

The star on the month-branch is very important because it tells you your purpose. Said another way, if a table represents your life, the centerpiece is the month-branch star. It is the focal point. Innately, it is that for which you strive. If the month-branch star is resource, you strive to be knowledgeable, usually through education. It could also mean you seek to be supported. If the month-branch star is performance, you go after fame and respect through your accomplishments and talent. If the month-branch star is parallel, you strive to be a self-confident, capable, and reliable individual. If the month-branch star is wealth, making money is your goal. If you're male, wealth in the month-branch could also mean you strive to find an ideal wife. Finally, if your month-branch star is power, you seek, well, power and authority. If you're female, it could also mean that you seek a perfect husband. Referring to Bill Clinton's four pillars chart presented earlier in this chapter, the star on the month-branch is power. Princess Diana's month-branch star is performance. Uncanny, isn't it?

Take this time now to locate your month-branch star. Does it match what you strive for?

> **Feng Facts**
>
> The star on your month-branch is always vibrant.

Star Relations

The five stars can be matched with a human relationship. With respect to how the other stars relate to the Day-Master, the star relations are as follows:

◆ Resource Star = Parents

◆ Performance Star = Children

◆ Parallel Star = Siblings, friends or competitors

◆ Wealth Star = Wife (or women) for a male only

◆ Power Star = Husband (or men) for a female only

Your parents create or generate you (Day-Master) and your siblings (parallel). You create or generate children (performance). The genesis of the wealth and power stars is controversial. In old China, a man had total control over his wife. Therefore, the star the Day-Master controls represents his wife (wealth). Conversely, for a woman, the star that controls the Day-Master represents her husband (power). There is no human correspondence for a male's wealth star. And, there is no human correspondence for a female's power star.

Let's take a look at Bill Clinton's chart:

In Bill Clinton's chart, his child and women are prominent.

	Hour	Day	Month	Year
Stem		Day-Master	Children	Children
Branch	Wife	Wife		Wife

When equating human relations with the stars present in a person's birth chart, it's best not to be literal. For example, the fact that Clinton has two children stars doesn't mean he has *two* children. It means his child (or children, if he had more than one) is prominent in his life. His love for Chelsea (his daughter) is more visible—or more important—than his love for his wife, Hillary. Regarding his wife stars, just because Clinton has three of them doesn't mean he'll marry three times. His wife stars are abundant. They're hidden in the branches. They're underground. The day-branch component represents Hillary, the star closest to Clinton's Day-Master. The other wife stars represent his lovers.

Now let's take a look at Ronald Reagan's (born on February 6, 1911, at 2:04 A.M.) chart:

Ronald Reagan's wife (and women) figure prominently in his chart. His children and parents take a secondary role.

	Hour	Day	Month	Year
Stem	Wife	Day-Master	Wife	Wife
Branch	Children	Children	Parents	

As you're learning, you read a Four Pillars chart from top to bottom—from stems to branches. You also read a chart from right to left—from year to hour. With this in mind, the wife star on the year-stem represents Reagan's first wife (Jane Wyman). The wife star on the month-stem represents Nancy Reagan. The wife star on the hour-stem represents other women who were prominent in his life. Unlike Bill Clinton, Ronald Reagan's children are underground. They're out of sight.

Finally, let's take a look at Princess Diana's chart:

	Hour	Day	Month	Year
Stem	Siblings	Day-Master	Siblings	Husband
Branch	Husband		Children	

Princess Diana's competitors and husband were prominent in her life.

The husband star on Diana's year-stem represents Prince Charles. Although he is prominent, he is far away. In fact, her siblings and friends on the month-stem stand between she and Charles. The sibling star also represents competitors (Camilla Parker-Bowles, for example). They are also prominent. Her lovers and children are underground. Her relationship with them is private.

Take this time now to study the relations in your own Four Pillars chart. You'll learn more about analyzing your mate (or prospective mate) in Chapter 25.

If you don't have the husband or wife star in your chart, it does not mean you're destined to be unmarried. When the phase the star is correlated with comes on a 10-year or yearly luck pillar, you have a chance of finding a mate. You'll learn about your luck pillars in Chapter 26. Finding a suitable mate is also discussed in Chapter 25.

In the next chapter, you'll learn how each star's yin (-) and yang (+) delineation impact your luck and destiny.

The Least You Need to Know

- Your Day-Master is the key to interpreting your life chart.

- The timeliness of your Day-Master depends on the month in which you were born.

- Each of the five phases represents a different aspect of your life: your resources, friends, talent and accomplishment, power, and wealth.

- A human relationship can also be matched with a star.

24

The Four Pillars of Destiny, Part 3

In This Chapter

- The garden of life
- Determining a strong and a weak chart
- Finding your favorable phase
- Finding your unfavorable phase

In this chapter, you'll learn that your four pillars chart resembles a garden. An ideal—or balanced—garden has a little of everything: rich soil, gentle rain, flowers and trees, and a gardener who regularly prunes them. An unbalanced garden has too much of one thing and/or a lack of something. Finding what is needed will bring balance to your life—your garden.

Also in this chapter, you'll acquire pertinent information to determine your favorable and unfavorable phases. With this knowledge, you'll learn what colors, environments, and career best suit you—the subject of the next chapter.

A Picture Is Worth a Thousand Words

Your Four Pillars chart can be expressed visually. If your life represents a painting of a landscape, each of the five phases represents an element in nature that might or might not be present in your painting. Yet understand that the picture isn't static. Depending on the phase components of the 10-year luck period you're in, as well as the phase components of the yearly pillar (subjects we'll address in Chapter 26), your landscape will change. Sometimes you can see one mountain. Sometimes more mountains will be visible. Sometimes it will rain. And sometimes a gardener will come to prune your plants and trees. But let's not put the cart before the horse. First, you must understand the components affiliated with each stem in your garden:

- Jia or yang (+) wood represents a big tree.

- Yi or yin (-) wood represents flowering shrubs.

- Bing or yang (+) fire represents the sun.

- Ding or yin (-) fire represents candlelight and artificial light.

- Wu or yang (+) earth represents a mountain.

- Ji or yin (-) earth represents garden soil.

- Geng or yang (+) metal represents an axe.

- Xin or yin (-) metal represents pruning sheers.

- Ren or yang (+) water represents a large body of water like a river, a lake, or the sea.

- Gui or yin (-) water represents rain, dew, or snow.

You can see that each stem phase has a yang side (large) and yin side (small). How they interact will help determine what you need to make your garden (your life) beautiful and harmonious.

Take this time now to match each stem and each hidden stem in the branches in your chart with a garden representation.

Princess Diana's Garden

Once again, let's look at Princess Diana's chart. Here is what her garden looks like:

	Hour	Day	Month	Year
Stem Phase	-Wood **Flowers**	- Wood **Flowers**	+ Wood **Tree**	- Metal **Sheers**
Branch Phases	- Metal **Sheers**	- Earth **Soil**	- Fire **Candle**	- Earth **Soil**
		- Fire **Candle**	- Earth **Soil**	- Water **Rain**
		- Wood **Flowers**		- Metal **Sheers**

Princess Diana needs water to nourish her garden.

Except for her month-stem phase (+ wood), Diana's entire chart is composed of yin (-) components, making her garden very delicate. There are many flowers (- wood) and ample soil (- earth). There's even a gardener that prunes (- metal) her plants. Diana's garden seems quite lovely, doesn't it? Actually, the flowers are withering, and the soil is dry. This is because there's only a scant amount of water to nourish her garden. Although there's no direct sunlight (+ fire), there is an artificial source (- fire) suggesting that Diana lives in a greenhouse. All in all, Diana desperately needs water to bring balance to her chart—to enliven her garden.

In the next chapter, you'll learn how Diana may have lived had she incorporated more water into her life.

> **Feng Facts**
>
> Diana's husband star is metal— the gardener with the pruning shears who overly trims (controls) her plants.

Prince Charles's Garden

Born on November 14, 1948, at 9:14 P.M., let's look at the Prince of Wales's garden:

	Hour	Day	Month	Year
Stem Phase	- Water **Rain**	- Water **Rain**	- Water **Rain**	+ Earth **Mountain**
Branch Phases	+ Water **River**	- Wood **Flowers**	+ Water **River**	- Water **Rain**
	+ Wood **Tree**		+Wood **Tree**	

Prince Charles is waterlogged.

The picture here is simple. It rains (- water) every day, the abundance of water joining together to form a torrential river (+ water). The river carries the plants (- wood) and trees (+ wood) downstream, and it erodes the mountain (+ earth). The soil (- earth) mixes with the river water, making it muddy. It's a downpour. Charles is waterlogged.

Unfortunately, there's no way to balance Prince Charles's chart. The only option is to follow the trend—water. In other words, if you can't beat 'em, join 'em. Therefore, Charles's garden (his innate qi) needs water. Metal and wood qi are also favorable because with water, the threesome forms a productive sequence: metal produces water and water produces wood. We'll talk more about how Prince Charles can benefit from knowing his favorable phases in the next chapter. You'll also find out whether the abundance of Charles's water qi would have sustained Diana had they remained married.

Take this time now to study your own garden. Determine the natural elements and implements that you need. They represent the phases that are favorable to you. As you'll soon find out in the next chapter, your favorable phases correlate to environments, colors, careers, and people that bring balance to your qi.

Strong or Weak Chart?

If you would like a more concrete approach to finding out what phases favor your qi, this next section will prove helpful. However, first you must learn whether your chart is one of strength or weakness. But don't think the strength or weakness of your chart reflects you, the person. Many powerful people have weak charts.

The Strong Day-Master

A chart is *strong* if the Day-Master is timely (ready, vibrant, or strong) and there is an abundance of resource and/or parallel in your chart. In other words, the person has a lot of support and knowledge (resource), and friends (parallel) who can assist him. On the other hand, he (or she) has only a little power, some opportunities to succeed and make money (wealth), but little opportunity to show his (or her) talent (performance). The resource or parallel phase is unfavorable. To bring balance to the chart, resource and/or parallel must be drained. To determine which one, follow these simple guidelines (you might want to refer to the star cycles chart in the previous chapter):

◆ If the Day-Master is timely (ready, vibrant, or strong) and there is an abundance of resource in your chart, wealth is most favorable because it controls resource. Performance is also favorable because it gives resource an outlet—something to do. Power is not favorable because it makes resource even stronger. Parallel is not favorable because the Day-Master is already strong.

♦ If the Day-Master is timely (ready, vibrant, or strong) and there is an abundance of parallel in your chart, power is most favorable because it controls parallel. Wealth is also favorable because it gives parallel an outlet—something to do. Resource is not favorable because it makes parallel even stronger. Performance is only favorable if there's no power in your chart. This is because performance attacks power—the most valuable phase.

For the most part, people with timely (ready, vibrant, or strong) Day-Masters have strong charts. If your Day-Master is untimely (retiring, inactive, or weak) and you have an abundance of parallel or resource, further investigation is required to determine your favorable and unfavorable phases. Unfortunately, these types of charts are beyond the scope of this short introduction to The Four Pillars of Destiny.

Here's an example of a strong Day-Master. Born on October 26, 1947 at 8:00 P.M., Hillary Clinton's Day-Master is strong (timely). She has an abundance of parallel (earth). Following the guidelines already given, Hillary's most favorable phase is wood (power). Water (wealth) is also favorable.

Wise Words

A **strong** Day-Master means one with more resource and parallel phases than power, wealth, and performance phases. A person with a strong chart has many friends and many competitors. He derives much support from those around him who are more experienced, while getting few chances to demonstrate his own talents.

	Hour	Day	Month	Year
Stem Phase	+ Water	+ Earth	+ Metal	- Fire
Branch Phases	+ Earth	+ Wood	+ Earth	+ Water
	- Metal	+ Fire	- Metal	+ Wood
	- Fire	+ Earth	- Fire	

Hillary Clinton has a strong Day-Master.

Those with strong Day-Masters include Al Gore, Margaret Thatcher, Monica Lewinsky, Martha Stewart, Carolyn Bessette, Brad Pitt, and Jennifer Aniston.

The Weak Day-Master

A chart is *weak* if the Day-Master is untimely (inactive, retiring, or weak) and there's an abundance of performance, power, and wealth in the chart. There is little resource and parallel phases. Although a person with a weak chart might not have enough support from friends (parallels) and those more experienced (resource), he (or she) is more likely to be independent and talented. To bring balance to the chart, performance, power, and/or wealth must be drained. To determine which one, follow these simple guidelines:

◆ If the Day-Master is untimely (retiring, inactive, or weak) and there is an abundance of power in your chart, resource is most needed to redirect the flow of qi: power generates resource, which generates and strengthens the Day-Master. The parallel phase is also favorable because it strengthens the Day-Master. Performance is not favorable because it weakens your Day-Master. Wealth is not favorable because it gives even more power to power.

◆ If the Day-Master is untimely (retiring, inactive, or weak) and there is an abundance of performance in your chart, resource is most needed because it controls performance. Parallel is also favorable because it strengthens the Day-Master. Wealth is not favorable because it attacks resource, the most needed phase. Power is favorable only if there's resource in your chart, which generates or strengthens the Day-Master. If there's no resource, power is not favorable because it attacks your Day-Master.

◆ If the Day-Master is untimely (retiring, inactive, or weak) and there's an abundance of wealth in your chart, parallel is most needed. There are many opportunities to make money, but you are too weak to grasp them. You need to strengthen yourself (Day-Master) and find partners (parallel) who can assist you. Resource is unfavorable because people with a lot of wealth usually don't bother to gain knowledge through education (resource). Performance is unfavorable because it makes wealth even stronger. Power is only favorable if there's resource in your chart. If there's no resource, power is not favorable because it attacks the Day-Master/parallel.

Wise Words

A **weak** Day-Master is one that is untimely (retiring, inactive, or weak) and that has more performance, power, and wealth than resource and parallel. A person with a weak Day-Master is usually being challenged by power and authority, yet has enough intelligence to combat such confrontations. Also, he has much potential to display his talents in favorable luck periods.

A weak chart with a timely (ready, vibrant, strong) Day-Master is very rare. In order to qualify, you must have resource or parallel in the month branch. You must not have resource or parallel anywhere else in your chart.

Those with weak Day-Masters include George W. Bush, Richard Nixon, Michael Jordan, Bill Clinton, Tom Cruise, Nicole Kidman, Arnold Schwarzenegger, and John F. Kennedy Jr.

Princess Diana has a weak chart. Referring to the illustration of Diana's garden presented earlier in the chapter, you'll see she has more performance

(2 fire phases), power (3 metal phases), and wealth (3 earth phases) than resource (1 water phase) and parallel (4 wood phases). In other words, her performance/power/wealth phases total 8, and her resource/parallel phases total 5. Diana's most favorable phase is resource (water). Parallel (wood) is not favorable for three reasons: it is untimely (retiring), it is overabundant, and it weakens her most favorable phase—water.

Master Class

If your birth month is Hai (+ water), Zi (- water), or Chou (- earth), fire will help restore balance to your chart. Said another way, if you're born in November (after the 7th), December, or January (up to February 4), your chart is too cold. Fire will warm you up. If your birth month is Si (+ fire), Wu (- fire), or Wei (- earth), water will help restore balance to your chart. Said another way, if you're born in May (after the 5th), June, or July (up to August 8), your chart is too hot and dry. Water will cool you down.

Take this time now to determine your favorable and unfavorable phases. However, as you'll learn in Chapter 26, what is favorable might change depending on the phase components comprising the 10-year and annual luck stars.

In the next chapter, you'll learn how knowing your favorable phases will benefit your well-being. You'll learn what careers, mates, environments, and colors are suited to your innate qi.

The Least You Need to Know

- A Four Pillars chart resembles a painting of a landscape. It can change over time.

- A strong Day-Master has more resource and parallel phases than power, wealth, and performance phases.

- A weak Day-Master has more power, wealth, and performance phases than resource and parallel phases.

- Favorable phases bring a chart to balance, and unfavorable phases unbalance a chart.

Chapter 25

The Four Pillars of Destiny, Part 4

In This Chapter

- How knowing your favorable and unfavorable phases can benefit you

- Determining your best environments and structures

- Using the five phases to find your best career—or to make the best of the one you've got

- Who's your ideal mate?

If we're able to change our destiny, how can we accurately forecast our future? It depends on the weapon you choose. If you're a warrior, you need the proper weaponry to successfully wield your way through the battle-field. If you choose the proper weapon—a sword, say—you'll change your destiny for the better by conquering your opponent—life's obstacles. If you choose an improper weapon—a butter knife, say—you'll lose the battle. Your destiny will take a wrong turn. Therefore, based on the weapon you choose, we can forecast a bright or a bleak future.

Your favorable and unfavorable phases are weapons that help you fulfill your potential. Use your favorable ones, and you'll succeed in this game called life!

The Phases of Our Lives

Knowing your favorable and unfavorable phases can help you in many ways. You'll know …

◆ What colors enhance your health, wealth, and relationships and what colors bring hardship and misfortune

◆ What environments are best suited to you

◆ What profession is suitable to you

◆ With whom you are compatible

◆ How to determine whether a year or 10-year period will be auspicious or inauspicious (something you'll learn more about in Chapter 26).

Let's take a simple example. Say your most favorable phase is fire, and your unfavorable phase is water. Your lucky colors then would be red, purple, dark orange, and pink. And, because wood generates fire, green is also a favorable color. Your unlucky colors are blue and black. So, following the five-phase correlations, you're best suited to hot and dry climates. Get the idea?

The following table illustrates what kind of environments and buildings correlate to each of the five phases:

Phase	Suitable Environment	Suitable Structure
Wood	Vegetated areas	High-rise buildings
Fire	Desert	Triangular structures
Earth	Mountainous	Square buildings
Metal	Dry and cool areas	Houses with domes or circular structures; houses with wrought-iron fences and security bars
Water	Living on or near any body of water; living in a rainy climate	Ranch houses

Take this time now to determine the environments and structures that resonate best with your more favorable phase—the qi type that brings balance to your being.

Professional Phases

If your career is stagnant and/or if it doesn't bring you joy and satisfaction, it might not correspond with one of your favorable phases. Essentially, you're using a weapon that's depleting your energy, getting you nowhere.

What follows are the five phases and their correlative career industries. However, please understand an industry can belong to more than one phase. For example, education is wood- and water-related. It's a wood industry because the profession uses materials made of wood—books. It's a water industry because the profession channels streams of information to its students.

Now, match the industry you're in with a phase(s). Then, study the industries that correlate with your most favorable phase.

Wood industries: Lumber, carpentry, construction work, architecture, woodcrafts, furniture making, grocery, herbs, botany, papermaking, journalism, writing, publishing, advertising, textile, fashion, ministry, education, librarianship, politics, art, music, and any field related to animals like breeding, training, and veterinary.

Fire industries: Fire fighting, electrical, lighting, laser and radiation, obstetrics, ammunition manufacturing, explosives, gas station servicing, glass and porcelain manufacturing, military, waiting tables, restaurant, food preparation, welding, and performing arts.

Earth industries: Real estate, land development, farming, ranching, natural resource mining (gas, oil, limestone, for example), gems, bricklaying, ceramic making, computer engineering, and any service-oriented career like insurance brokerage, secretarial, departmental management, accounting, law, consulting, interior and landscape design, and mortuary.

Metal industries: Metallurgy, gold and silver jewelry design, machinery, banking, automotive repair or manufacturing, mechanical engineering, bullion trading, airplane manufacturing, police, leadership, and entrepreneurial.

Water industries: Transportation, travel, fishing, sewage, housekeeping, television and radio, education, ministry, furniture moving, fortune-telling, public speaking, sales, journalism, medicine, acting, and singing.

Before you change careers, let's examine your role within your industry.

> **CAUTION**
>
> **Feng Alert**
>
> Many people are drawn to colors, environments, careers, and other people that correlate with his or her most abundant phase. This is because innately we are comfortable with it. Unfortunately, the overabundant phase in question causes imbalance and is not favorable. As the saying goes, "Too much of a good thing spoils the pudding."

The Actions of Phases

So far you've learned that each phase correlates with a color, environment, and career industry. Now, you'll learn that each phase corresponds with an action that describes what type of job you have:

◆ Earth action: *Staying* at the central part of an organization

◆ Metal action: *Decision-making*

◆ Water action: *Moving* about *communicating* with others

◆ Wood action: *Initiating* and *implementing* ideas

◆ Fire action: *Performing*, *showing off*, *presenting* to an audience.

Master Class

All industries contain jobs corresponding to one of the five phases. Finding the right job within your industry will set you on the proper path. Armed with the correct weapon, you'll win promotions and raises. Your self-esteem, happiness, and satisfaction will rise to new heights.

Although you may or may not be in an industry suitable to your most favorable phase, you can fine-tune your job so that its actions suit what's favorable to you. For example, say you're a secretary at a television station. Your job is earth action-oriented. You are stationary, your roots firmly planted in the earth. The industry you work in—television—is water-related. Upon determining your most favorable phase, you learn that wood, not earth, is good for you. Consider trying your hand at copywriting or news writing. If your favorable phase is water, consider hosting a television show. If your favorable phase is fire, sales is right for you. If your favorable phase is metal, management suits you.

The Royal Phases

In the previous chapter, we established that Princess Diana's most favorable phase is water. There's only a trace amount of it in her chart. Innately, Diana watered her wilting garden by living in London, which certainly has its share of rain. Had she known about The Four Pillars, perhaps she would have lived on or very near a large body of water. Perhaps she would have favored blue and black (water colors) clothing. Regarding her interests (dance, for example) and "career," innately she was drawn to water-based pursuits. Diana's various charities took her around the world, connecting and motivating others to contribute to her causes. She was also an effective communicator and a media darling. Had Diana survived, at age 42, water would have come into her 10-year luck pillars, nourishing her depleted spirit. (We'll discuss Diana's luck in more detail in the next chapter.)

The question arises, should Diana have stayed married to Prince Charles? As we determined in the previous chapter, his chart overflows with water. Although you may think Charles's abundance of water would have provided Diana's garden with ample nourishment, it does not. Diana needs soft misting water. Charles's gushing flow effectively overwhelms and drowns her spirit.

How would Prince Charles benefit from knowing his favorable phases are water and wood? He would understand he should stick to water- and wood-related activities. He should write, develop television programs, and continue his advocacy for organic produce, among other things. Pursuing earth-related tasks related to leadership will deplete and obstruct his qi flow. In other words, being king is not suited to him. Regarding a suitable wife, interestingly, Diana's qi favored his. Her abundance of wood provided Charles's water an outlet—something to do. For the record, Camilla Parker-Bowles's qi also favors Charles. She has a strong wood base nourished by a sufficient amount of water.

Feng Alert

An astrologer who says he or she can forecast a person's death should not be trusted. It would mean that people sharing the same birth chart must die on the same day. There is an abundance of evidence to the contrary. The date of a person's death is unknowable.

Phase Mates

As you've just learned, one qualification for a successful marriage is to find a mate whose qi contains the phase you most need. But there's another technique for determining a suitable mate. For a woman, the phase that controls her Day-Master and that is opposite in yin/yang polarity represents her ideal husband. For a man, the phase his Day-Master controls and that is opposite in yin/yang polarity represents his ideal wife. (Gay couples are also divided into husband and wife units.)

For example, let's take John F. Kennedy and his wife, Jacqueline.

John and Jackie were ideal for each other. His Day-Master was yin (-) metal. Therefore, his ideal wife was yang (+) wood. Jackie's Day-Master was yang (+) wood. Conversely, Jackie's ideal husband was yin (-) metal. John's Day-Master was yin (-) metal.

J.F.K.'s ideal wife was yang (+) wood. Jackie's ideal husband was yin (-) metal.

J.F.K.

	Hour	Day	Month	Year
	2:00pm*	29	May	1917
Stem Phase	- Wood	- Metal	- Wood	- Fire

* Adjusted for Daylight Savings Time

Jacqueline Kennedy

	Hour	Day	Month	Year
	1:30pm*	28	July	1929
Stem Phase	- Metal	+ Wood	- Metal	- Earth

* Adjusted for Daylight Savings Time

Now let's look at Ronald and Nancy Reagan's Day-Masters.

Ronald Reagan's ideal wife was yang (+) metal. Nancy's ideal husband is yin (-) fire.

Ronald Reagan

	Hour	Day	Month	Year
	2:04am	6	Feb.	1911
Stem Phase	- Metal	- Fire	+ Metal	- Metal

Nancy Reagan

	Hour	Day	Month	Year
	12:00pm*	6	July	1921
Stem Phase	+ Water	+ Metal	+ Wood	- Metal

* Adjusted for Daylight Savings Time

Ronald and Nancy Reagan were also very compatible. His Day-Master was yin (-) fire. Therefore, his ideal wife was yang (+) metal. Nancy's Day-Master is yang (+) metal. Conversely, Nancy's ideal husband is yin (-) fire. Ronald's Day-Master was yin (-) fire.

If the ideal mate phase is not the Day-Master of your spouse, it appears elsewhere in the chart. For example, if a woman's Day-Master is yang (+) earth, her ideal husband is yin (-) wood. Although her husband's Day-Master is not yin (-) wood, let's say the phase can be found elsewhere in his chart. If it correlates with his performance phase, the wife is attracted to her husband's talent. If it correlates with his resource phase, the wife seeks to be supported. If it correlates with his wealth phase, she's attracted to his money. If it correlates with his power phase, she is attracted to his power and status. If it correlates with his parallel phase, she is attracted to his kindness. If yin (-) wood is not present in his chart, then innately, she is not attracted to him.

Master Class _____

Princess Diana's ideal husband was yang (+) metal. This phase is not present in Prince Charles's chart. His ideal wife is yang (+) fire. This phase is not present in Diana's chart. They were not attracted to each other. Bill Clinton's ideal wife is yang (+) earth. Hillary's Day-Master is yang (+) earth. Hillary's ideal husband is yin (-) wood. Bill's Day-Master is yin (-) wood. They are suited to each other. George W. Bush's ideal wife is yang (+) wood. Laura Welch Bush's Day-Master is yang (+) wood. Laura's ideal husband is yin (-) metal. George's Day-Master is yin (-) metal.

Take this time now to analyze your relationship with your spouse, or a prospective one. In the next and last chapter, you'll learn about how your 10-year and yearly luck pillars affect your destiny.

The Least You Need to Know

- ◆ Favorable phases bring a chart to balance, and unfavorable phases unbalance a chart.

- ◆ Favorable phases correspond to colors, the environment, and suitable professions beneficial to your well-being; unfavorable phases are those colors, environments, and professions detrimental to your well-being.

- ◆ If your spouse's chart contains the phase you need most, the partnership is likely to be successful.

- ◆ For a woman, the phase that controls her Day-Master and that is opposite in yin/yang polarity represents her ideal husband. For a man, the phase his Day-Master controls and that is opposite in yin/yang polarity represents his ideal wife.

Chapter 26

The Four Pillars of Destiny, Part 5

In This Chapter

- What is luck?
- Determining the auspiciousness of each 10-year luck period
- Determining the auspiciousness of each year
- Looking at the charts of Ronald Reagan and Prince William

A farmer loses his horse. We say, "He's unlucky." The lost horse returns to the farm with a few wild horses. We say, "What a lucky guy!" The farmer's 18-year-old son rides one of the wild horses and is thrown, breaking his leg. We say, "He was unlucky." A war breaks out. The king summons all males from 18 to 30 years of age to join his ranks. Due to his disability, the crippled son of the farmer is exempt. We say, "Lucky boy!"

Sometimes, we are lucky. At other times, we are unlucky. Is the path written in stone? No. It's written in our Four Pillars of Destiny. How do I determine my luck, you ask? Well, you'll need to know your favorable and unfavorable phases. Also, you must have a good understanding of the five phase relationships. With this knowledge, you then can learn what components of time are destined to bring favorable or unfavorable conditions.

The Axiom of Luck

We all know luck exists. It seems some people are just plain lucky. They win drawings; they win at gambling; they win sweepstakes. Seemingly, everything they touch "turns to gold." Some say they have "the luck of the Irish." You know the type. Then there are those who can't "get a break." They are "down on their luck;" "black clouds" follow them. We consider these unfortunate people unlucky.

We all know lucky and unlucky people. In fact, each of us has experienced good luck and bad luck throughout our lives. But can luck be proven? After all, it isn't something to which we can apply our five senses. Luck can't be seen, touched, or smelled. You can't taste or feel luck. Yet, we agree it exists. Luck is a "fact" we accept without proof. In mathematics, a self-evident truth accepted on its intrinsic merit is called an *axiom*. For example, 1 + 1 = 2 is an axiom. This equation does not have to be proven because it is accepted as truth.

Wise Words

An **axiom** is a widely accepted fact based on its intrinsic merits. Because an axiom is a general truth, it does not have to be proven.

Okay, I buy this, you say. But can luck be *proven?* The Chinese believe luck is a function of time governed by the laws of nature. They believe luck is not random, but determinable. If luck were random, there would be no laws of nature. Physics would not exist. The universe would operate in a chaotic state. So, how do you determine luck? The Four Pillars of Destiny is only one method the Chinese use to measure the distribution of your luck. Let's see how.

Lucky You

Webster's New Collegiate Dictionary defines luck as "a force that brings good fortune." The Chinese believe this "force" is actually qi. Specifically, the qi you inhaled at birth determines when your luck begins. From that point on, your luck is traditionally described in periods of 10 years. So, how do you calculate your 10-year luck periods? Simply find the printout of your Four Pillars birth chart you obtained online at www.asto-fengshui.com (see Chapter 22). Your "Eight Luck Periods" (eight 10-year periods comprised of a stem and branch) were automatically calculated for you. They are located directly beneath your "Four Pillars" chart. Let's examine Princess Diana's 10-year luck pillars, which compute as follows:

31.77	21.77	11.77	1.77
+ Earth [Wu]	- Fire [Ding]	+ Fire [Bing]	- Wood [Yi]
Dog [Xu]	Rooster [You]	Monkey [Shen]	Goat [Wei]

71.77	61.77	51.77	41.77
+ Water [Ren]	- Metal [Xin]	+ Metal [Geng]	- Earth [Ji]
Tiger [Yin]	Ox [Chou]	Rat [Zi]	Pig [Hai]

Princess Diana's 10-year luck pillars computed online.

Just as you read a Four Pillars chart from right to left and top to bottom, the same applies for the luck pillars. Therefore, beginning with the first column on the right, Diana's luck began at 1.77 years of age. The stem/branch combination for that period was (-) wood [Yi]/Goat [Wei]. Ten years later at age 11.77, her second luck period began. The stem/branch combination for that period was (+) fire [Bing]/Monkey [Shen]. Let's rearrange her chart so that it's easier to analyze:

Age	2 - 11	12 - 21	22 - 31	32 - 41
Stem	Wood	Fire	Fire	Earth
Branch	Earth	Metal	Metal	Earth

Age	42 - 51	52 - 61	62 - 71	72 - 81
Stem	Earth	Metal	Metal	Water
Branch	Water	Water	Earth	Wood

An easier arrangement of Princess Diana's 10-year luck pillars.

Diana's chart now reads from left to right. We rounded up the age her luck began (1.77) to age 2. Next, we included only the phases associated with each stem and branch, omitting the yin/yang delineation. Regarding the branch, remember each animal correlates with at least one hidden stem. Use only the primary hidden stem—the first phase listed in the Twelve Earthly Branches table in Chapter 22.

Given that our life expectancy has increased over time, you might be wondering why there aren't additional 10-year luck pillars beyond what is offered in your chart. For example, even though Princess Diana died at age 36 (during her fourth luck pillar), she might have live to age 90. Adding luck pillars is easy. Referring to the printout of your Four Pillars birth chart, locate the phase occupying the year-stem. Next, depending on your gender, you'll do one of two things:

Master Class _____

If your first luck did not begin at birth, you were under your parents' luck until your first 10-year luck period began.

◆ If you're female and your year-stem is yin (-), each stem and branch in your last luck pillar moves forward.

◆ If you're female and your year-stem is yang (+), each stem and branch in your last luck pillar moves backward.

◆ If you're male and your year-stem is yin (-), each stem and branch in your last luck pillar moves backward.

◆ If you're male and your year-stem is yang (+), each stem and branch in your last luck pillar moves forward.

In Diana's case, her year-stem is (-) metal (Xin). (See her Four Pillars chart in Chapter 22.) Therefore, the stem and branch in her last luck pillar moves forward. For example, the stem in her last 10-year luck pillar is + water (Ren). Referring to the Ten Heavenly Stems table in Chapter 22, Ren is the ninth stem. Moving forward, the tenth stem is Gui or (-) water. The branch in Diana's last 10-year luck pillar is Tiger (Yin). Referring to the Twelve Earthly Branches table in Chapter 22, Tiger Yin is the third branch. Moving forward, the fourth branch is Rabbit Mao or (-) wood. Therefore, Diana's luck pillar for age 82–91 is (-) water (stem) over (-) wood (branch). To calculate her luck pillar beginning at age 92, follow the same procedure.

Take this time now to arrange your 10-year luck pillars similarly. Add luck pillars, if necessary.

Wheel of Fortune

In a nutshell, if a 10-year luck period consists of your favorable phase(s), then that decade should prove fortunate. Is it really as simple as this? Let's break it down in terms of stems and branches. The earthly branch represents the foundation, stability; the heavenly stem represents the prevailing qi for that 10-year period. It's important to note that although the stem's qi force acts quickly, the branch is more persistent. Stated another way, in the beginning of the 10-year cycle, luck is influenced mainly by the stem. The branch's influence is gradual. At the end of the cycle, the branch is more influential than the stem.

There are four possible combinations, all yielding an effect appropriate to the structure of your Four Pillars chart. They are …

1. **Favorable stem, favorable branch.** You are basically fortunate and influenced by favorable qi.

2. **Favorable stem, unfavorable branch.** You are generally unlucky, but there is favorable qi to change that from time to time.

3. **Unfavorable stem, favorable branch.** You are basically fortunate, but there is unfavorable qi to disturb you from time to time.

4. **Unfavorable stem, unfavorable branch.** You are basically unlucky; you are often subjected to the influence of unfavorable qi.

Before you set out to interpret your 10-year luck periods, let's fine-tune this general analysis. The nature of what will unfold depends on the kind of favorable/unfavorable stem-branch configuration for any given period. For example, let's take a resource/resource combination for a strong chart. This is an unfavorable/unfavorable combination, suggesting overindulgence and greed. Although things come easily to this person, he is probably spoiled rotten and would be unable to stand on his own two feet if forced to fend for himself. He's much more interested in taking than giving. Another unfavorable/unfavorable combination for a strong chart is parallel/parallel, suggesting a period of fierce competition. You'll most likely have to claw your way to the top. Unlike the first scenario, nothing will come easy in this 10-year period.

Master Class

An unfavorable stem and unfavorable branch does not mean a 10-year sentence of disaster, misfortune, and illness without possibility of peace, comfort, and happiness. Just like yin and yang can't exist without a hint of each other's opposing characteristic, misfortune can't exist without moments of fortune.

So you see, knowing the kind of qi is integral to how your free will can shape your destiny. If you knew in advance what the next 10-year luck period could bring, wouldn't you take precautions? Of course, you would. Wouldn't you carry an umbrella in anticipation of an impending storm? If you calculate a strong resource/resource period for your son, wouldn't you take care not to spoil him, enabling him to be an independent adult? If you calculate you're in a strong parallel/parallel period, wouldn't you look extra hard for any and all available angles? Wouldn't knowing your possible destiny give you an edge? We hope it will. We hope you will use the Four Pillars to your advantage.

Ronald Reagan's Chart

Born on February 6, 1911, at 2:04 A.M., Ronald Reagan's birth chart and 10-year luck chart compute as follows:

Ronald Reagan's Four Pillars chart and 10-year luck chart. Because his year stem was yin (-), luck pillars are added by counting backward from the last stem/branch combination.

	Hour	Day	Month	Year
Stem Phase	- Metal	- Fire	+ Metal	- Metal
Branch Phases	- Earth	- Earth	+ Wood	+ Water
	- Water	- Fire	+ Fire	+ Wood
	- Metal	- Wood	+ Earth	

Age	0 - 9	10 - 19	20 - 29	30 - 39	40 - 49
Stem	Earth	Earth	Fire	Fire	Wood
Branch	Earth	Water	Water	Earth	Metal

Age	50 - 59	60 - 69	70 - 79	80 - 89	90 - 99
Stem	Wood	Water	Water	Metal	Metal
Branch	Metal	Earth	Fire	Fire	Earth

Ronald Reagan's chart is uncommon because it is neither strong nor weak. Although the reasoning for this is the subject of advanced study, understand that qi flows very smoothly in his chart. This makes for a fortunate chart, and therefore, a lucky life. The wood phase in Reagan's day-branch indicates his life's purpose. For him, wood corresponds to resource. Therefore, Reagan's purpose is to gain support. Wood is also the phase that keeps his chart balanced. His power phase water that nourishes his resource wood is found only in the branches. Because water is inactive, Reagan will not reach the prime of his career until water comes on a luck pillar. When power is strong, it generates resource. Said another way, with power, Reagan will have fulfilled his purpose. At age 60, power (water) arrived on his 10-year luck stems, providing him 20 years of leadership and authority. In 1981, Ronald Reagan was elected president of the United States. He was 69 years old, halfway through his power base.

Feng Facts

Known as the Zero Year Phenomenon, each United States president elected in a year ending in zero died while in office. 1840: William Henry Harrison died of pneumonia one month after his inauguration; 1860: Abraham Lincoln was assassinated; 1880: James A. Garfield was assassinated; 1900: William McKinley was assassinated; 1920: Warren G. Harding died presumably of a heart attack; 1940: Franklin D. Roosevelt died of a cerebral hemorrhage; 1960: John F. Kennedy was assassinated; 1980: Ronald Reagan narrowly survived an assassination attempt; 2000: As of this writing, George W. Bush is alive.

In 1994, Reagan announced he was suffering from Alzheimer's disease, a neurological disorder causing memory loss. He was 83 years old. Three years prior, he entered a new luck pillar—metal (stem) over fire (branch). Unfortunately, the fire phase in the luck branch attacked Reagan's water, causing irreparable damage to his root of power.

If this happened while he was still in office, his presidency would have been in jeopardy. Because he was retired, we must find the relevancy in Reagan's health. Since power (water) is what keeps him in control, a loss of power means a loss of control. The brain controls a person's mind and actions. Therefore, fire caused his power base (his brain) to deteriorate. In 2004, at age 93, Ronald Reagan died.

Prince William's Chart

Born June 21, 1982, at 4:03 P.M., Prince William's wood Day-Master is retiring. Fire (performance) is vibrant, metal (power) is ready; water (resource) is inactive; and earth (wealth) is vibrant. His chart resembles his mother's—Princess Diana. However, William's chart contains an appropriate amount of water his mother so lacked. The phases on his month branches (his purpose) indicate that he seeks fame (fire) and fortune (earth). Because his performance phase (fire) is also located on the month-stem (stems express outward expression), we can say Prince William is born to be famous. Unlike for his father, Prince Charles, power favors William. Its location in the branches provides him with a good foundation—good training. When power arrives on a luck stem, he is ready to be crowned king. Referring to his 10-year luck pillars, power (metal) comes on his fourth luck pillar, suggesting he will mostly likely become king between the ages of 35 and 44.

	Hour	Day	Month	Year
Stem Phase	+ Wood	- Wood	+ Fire	+ Water
Branch Phases	+ Metal	+ Water	- Fire	+ Earth
	+ Water	+ Wood	- Earth	- Metal
	+ Earth			- Fire

Like his mother, Prince William seeks fame and fortune.

Age	5 - 14	15 - 24	25 - 34	35 - 44
Stem	Fire	Earth	Earth	Metal
Branch	Earth	Metal	Metal	Earth

Age	45 - 54	55 - 64	65 - 74	75 - 84
Stem	Metal	Water	Water	Wood
Branch	Water	Water	Earth	Wood

William's ideal wife is yang (+) earth. In his chart, earth is located in the branches, indicating his relationship with her will be kept private.

It Was a Very Good Year

Ten years is an awfully long time. A lot can happen. Marriage or divorce, promotion or unemployment, birth or death. It's difficult to be mindful of what a luck period brings. Can it be broken down into smaller increments? Sure! Not only can you analyze the auspiciousness of a 10-year period, you can also determine your luck on a yearly, monthly, daily, and even *hourly* basis. (We won't get into the minutia of calculating your monthly, daily, and hourly luck.)

To determine your yearly luck, simply compare your favorable and unfavorable phases to the year's stem and branch in question. Referring to the following Year Pillar table, you'll see that 2006 is a Bing Xu or fire/earth year. The year 2007 is a Ding Hai or fire/water year. The year 2008 is a Wu Zi or earth/water year.

When power comes on a yearly (or 10-year) luck pillar and power is favorable to you, you will start a business, enter the political arena, receive a promotion, or get a better-paying job. If the power phase is unfavorable, you may become entangled in litigation or be suppressed by your boss.

When wealth comes on a yearly (or 10-year) luck pillar and wealth is favorable to you, you will make a lot of money. If you have performance in your chart, you will use your talent and productivity to make money. If you do not have performance in your chart, you will inherit money, win the lottery, or enjoy the profits from a business venture. If the wealth phase is unfavorable, you will lose money through your investments. You might lose your job.

When resource comes on a yearly (or 10-year) luck pillar and resource is favorable to you, you will be supported by your boss, who will help you advance your career. If the resource phase is unfavorable, you will not find support.

When performance comes on a yearly (or 10-year) luck pillar and performance is favorable to you, your talent, accomplishments, and productivity will be recognized. If you have wealth in your chart, your talent will help you earn a living. If the performance phase is unfavorable, your power star will be hurt, which might lead to health problems.

When parallel comes on a yearly (or 10-year) luck pillar and parallel is favorable to you, you become a capable individual. You will have friends that support you. If the parallel phase is unfavorable, you will lose your competitive edge.

These are general guidelines. Although a Four Pillars analysis is based on logical deduction, variations in individual charts sometimes lead to bending the rules!

Year Pillar

YEAR	DATE	TIME	STEM / BRANCH	YEAR	DATE	TIME	STEM / BRANCH
1944	February 5	6:23a	Jia Shen	1984	February 4	11:19p	Jia Zi
1945	February 4	12:20p	Yi You	1985	February 4	5:12a	Yi Chou
1946	February 4	6:05p	Bing Xu	1986	February 4	11:09a	Bing Yin
1947	February 4	11:55p	Ding Hai	1987	February 4	4:52p	Ding Mao
1948	February 5	5:43a	Wu Zi	1988	February 4	10:43p	Wu Chen
1949	February 4	11:23a	Ji Chou	1989	February 4	4:27a	Ji Si
1950	February 4	5:21p	Geng Yin	1990	February 4	10:15a	Geng Wu
1951	February 4	11:14p	Xin Mao	1991	February 4	4:08p	Xin Wei
1952	February 5	4:54a	Ren Chen	1992	February 4	9:48p	Ren Shen
1953	February 4	10:46a	Gui Si	1993	February 4	3:38a	Gui You
1954	February 4	4:31p	Jia Wu	1994	February 4	9:31a	Jia Xu
1955	February 4	10:18p	Yi Wei	1995	February 4	3:14p	Yi Hai
1956	February 5	4:13a	Bing Shen	1996	February 4	9:08p	Bing Zi
1957	February 4	9:55a	Ding You	1997	February 4	3:04a	Ding Chou
1958	February 4	3:50p	Wu Xu	1998	February 4	8:53a	Wu Yin
1959	February 4	9:43p	Ji Hai	1999	February 4	2:42p	Ji Mao
1960	February 5	3:23a	Geng Zi	2000	February 4	8:32p	Geng Chen
1961	February 4	9:23a	Xin Chou	2001	February 4	2:20a	Xin Si
1962	February 4	3:18p	Ren Yin	2002	February 4	8:08a	Ren Wu
1963	February 4	9:08p	Gui Mao	2003	February 4	1:57p	Gui Wei
1964	February 5	3:05a	Jia Chen	2004	February 4	7:46p	Jia Shen
1965	February 4	8:46a	Yi Si	2005	February 4	1:34a	Yi You
1966	February 4	2:38p	Bing Wu	2006	February 4	7:25a	Bing Xu
1967	February 4	8:31p	Ding Wei	2007	February 4	1:14p	Ding Hai
1968	February 5	2:08a	Wu Shen	2008	February 4	7:03p	Wu Zi
1969	February 4	7:59a	Ji You	2009	February 4	12:52a	Ji Chou
1970	February 4	1:46p	Geng Xu	2010	February 4	6:42a	Geng Yin
1971	February 4	7:26p	Xin Hai	2011	February 4	12:32p	Xin Mao
1972	February 5	1:20a	Ren Zi	2012	February 4	6:40p	Ren Chen
1973	February 4	7:04a	Gui Chou	2013	February 4	12:31a	Gui Si
1974	February 4	1:00p	Jia Yin	2014	February 4	6:21a	Jia Wu
1975	February 4	6:59p	Yi Mao	2015	February 4	12:09p	Yi Wei
1976	February 5	12:40a	Bing Chen	2016	February 4	6:00p	Bing Shen
1977	February 4	6:34a	Ding Si	2017	February 4	11:49p	Ding You
1978	February 4	12:27p	Wu Wu	2018	February 4	5:38a	Wu Xu
1979	February 4	6:13p	Ji Wei	2019	February 4	11:28a	Ji Hai
1980	February 5	12:10a	Geng Shen	2020	February 4	5:18p	Geng Zi
1981	February 4	5:56a	Xin You	2021	February 4	11:08p	Xin Chou
1982	February 4	11:46a	Ren Xu	2022	February 4	4:58a	Ren Yin
1983	February 4	5:40p	Gui Hai	2023	February 4	10:47a	Gui Mao

Congratulations! You've made it through *The Complete Idiot's Guide to Feng Shui*. We sincerely hope you will apply your newfound knowledge to improve your well-being and share it with those important to you. Anyone can benefit from feng shui and The Four Pillars of Destiny. Even if your loved ones are skeptical, conduct a reading for them. Let them see how simple adjustments can improve their health, wealth, and relationships. Win them over. Allow feng shui to demonstrate to them its power. Become a booster, a feng shui fellow. You need only to be a conduit. Allow feng shui to do the rest. Allow it to tantalize your family and friends with its alluring promises of universal harmony. They'll discover what you did: Feng shui works.

The Least You Need to Know

- The Chinese believe luck is a function of time and that it is determinable.

- Your 10-year luck periods were automatically calculated for you when you computed your Four Pillars at www.astro-fengshui.com.

- If a 10-year or yearly period contains your favorable phases, the period is likely to be fortunate. If a period contains your unfavorable phases, it will probably be an unfortunate decade.

- Had Princess Diana lived, she would have entered a very lucky period beginning at age 42.

Glossary

After Heaven sequence   Called the "Hou Tian" in Chinese, this sequence of trigrams denotes motion, transformation, and the interaction of natural and human qi forces. This is the sequence used in feng shui.

annual star   A prevailing star, or number, which ushers in yearly changes in the Earth's qi field.

axiom   A widely accepted fact based on its intrinsic merits. Because an axiom is a general truth, it does not have to be proven.

azure dragon   A landform, building, trees, bushes, or fence located on the left side of your dwelling.

bagua   The eight trigrams of the *Yijing*.

Before Heaven sequence   Called the "Xian Tian" in Chinese, this is a sequence of trigrams representing an ideal reality in which natural and human qi forces are in perfect balance.

black turtle   A landform, building, grove of trees, or fence supporting the back of your residence.

Book of Burial   Written in the fourth century C.E. by Guo Pu, this is the earliest extant text on the Form School of feng shui.

celestial equator   The circular path the constellations travel perpendicular to an imaginary line joining the celestial north pole to the earth's North pole. The Chinese use the celestial equator as a baseline to observe the times when stars will appear directly overhead.

Chinese Zodiac   A popular system of astrology involving the relationships between 12 types of qi or signs expressed as animals: rat, ox, tiger, rabbit, dragon, snake, horse, sheep, monkey, rooster, dog, and pig.

Compass School   A term invented by Westerners, the Compass School holds that each of the 8 (and 24 finer distinctions) cardinal directions has a different energy. It is a very computational method, relying on intellect rather than intuitive insights. In Chinese, Compass School is known as "Liqi Pai" (Patterns of Qi School).

Confucianism   Based on the sixth century B.C.E. teachings of Confucius, it is a complex system of ethics designed to cultivate social and moral principles. The philosophy was taught in Chinese schools from the beginning of the Han dynasty to the establishment of the People's Republic of China in 1949.

conscious mind   The waking state that gives us logic, reason, and willpower. The conscious mind represents 12 percent of our total mind power.

controlling cycle   A cycle of imbalance. Each phase controls its counterpart. Fire-metal-wood-earth-water represents the controlling cycle.

crimson bird   A footstool landform or body of water that faces your dwelling.

Cycle of Sixty   Represents all possible combinations (60) of the Ten Heavenly Stems and Twelve Earthly Branches. The year 2697 B.C.E. marked the first of the 60-year, or 60-stem-branch, cycle.

Daoism   Concerned with the intuitive knowledge acquired by communing with nature and being at one with it (the Dao). The founding fathers of Daoism were a group of like-minded people who lived and taught from the fourth to the second centuries B.C.E.

Day-Master   The Day-Master is the day stem component of your chart. Also called the "Ziping Method" after astrologer Xu Ziping, The Four Pillars of Destiny analyzes how the five phases comprising your Four Pillars chart affect the Day-Master.

deductive reasoning   The method of reaching a conclusion by deducing general laws through observation.

Double Ruling Star at Facing   A dwelling that is considered Shuang Ling Xing Dou Xiang if both the ruling mountain and ruling water stars are located in the facing cell. In this case, it is easy for the occupants to make and retain money, but it is difficult for them to form stable relationships and maintain good health.

Double Ruling Star at Sitting   A dwelling that is considered Shuang Ling Xing Dou Zuo if both the ruling mountain and the ruling water stars are located in the sitting cell. In this case, it is easy for the occupants to form stable relationships and maintain good health, but it is difficult for them to make and retain money.

dragon's lair   In feng shui, all mountain ranges are called dragons. When the dragon meets the terrain, it is his lair (long xue). It is the place that attracts sheng qi and is considered the most auspicious site on which to build a home or bury the dead.

facing direction   Usually corresponds to the front side of a dwelling and is not necessarily where your front door is located.

favorable phase   A term used in a Four Pillars of Destiny analysis. It is the phase that brings balance to your chart.

feng shui   It literally means "wind water," the two natural forces that direct qi to a site. Figuratively, feng shui is the art and science of determining how your environment and your home affect you over periods of time.

Fibonacci sequence   A sequence of numbers named after a thirteenth-century mathematician, Leonardo of Pisa, also known as Fibonacci. Each number in the series is the sum of the two previous numbers.

fight or flight   A primitive and involuntary reaction triggered during moments of danger or anxiety. As man (and animals) evolved, some developed greater strength and aggressiveness (fight), and others developed agility, speed, and a sensitivity to the senses of smell, sight, and hearing (flight). Those who remained passive eventually became extinct.

five phases   Five physical elements in nature that represent the movement of qi. They are fire, earth, metal, water, and wood. The concept of the five phases is the backbone of Chinese medicine, acupuncture, and feng shui.

Flying Star   Xuankong Feixing in Chinese, it's a sophisticated and complex system of analyzing how time and space affect a building. The magnetic orientation of the dwelling, along with the year the home was built, are important factors that determine the innate character of the house.

Form School   Called "Xingfa" in Chinese, it's the first and oldest school of feng shui dating to the late Han era's publication of the *Classic of Burial* written by Qing Wuzi. Initially, its purpose was to orient tombs. The orientation of homes was later incorporated into the practice.

Fortunate Mountain Fortunate Water   A dwelling that is considered Wang Shan Wang Shui if the ruling mountain and water numbers are in their proper places. The ruling mountain star must be situated in the top, left position of the sitting cell. The ruling water star must be situated in the top, right position of the facing cell. This type of house is most favorable, bringing the highest possibility of fame, fortune, and good health.

Four Celestial Palaces   The Chinese macroconstellations called the crimson bird, azure dragon, black turtle, and white tiger represent the Four Celestial Palaces. Composed of seven constellations each, the macroconstellations comprise the 28 constellations of the Chinese zodiac.

Four Pillars of Destiny   Called Ziping Bazi in Chinese, it's a method of calculating and interpreting the five phases present at your birth. Each pillar represents a year, month, day, and hour expressed as a heavenly stem and an earthly branch. The Four Pillars of Destiny measures probabilities, not certainties, of your life's path.

Golden Ratio   Related to the Fibonacci sequence. By dividing each number in the series by the one that precedes it, the result produces a ratio that stabilizes at 1.61834. The Golden Ratio was understood by ancient builders such as the Egyptians, Greeks, and Mayans who believed everything in nature was determined by abstract universal laws that could be expressed mathematically.

Great Cycle   Called Da Yun in Chinese, it is made up of nine 20-year cycles. The nine cycles are divided into three 60-year periods called the Upper (Shang Yuan), Middle (Zhong Yuan), and Lower (Xia Yuan) cycles. The year 1864 marks the beginning of the Great Cycle we're currently in. It ends February 4, 2044.

Hetu   Also called the "River Map," it is a pattern of black (yang) and white (yin) dots purportedly found on a fantastic dragon-horse emerging from the Yellow River. The Hetu symbolizes the ideal world.

hexagram   A combination of two trigrams composes one hexagram. There are 64 total hexagrams.

house trigram   Determined by its sitting direction, which usually corresponds to the backside of a dwelling.

inductive reasoning   The method of reaching a conclusion by developing specific cases based on general laws.

kanyu   An art of divination; the precursor to feng shui. "Kan" means "way of the heaven," and "yu" means "way of the earth." Together, kanyu translates, "Raise your head and study the sky. Lower your head and study the terrain."

known   A unit of communication that has been learned earlier in life. It can be positive or negative and will be accepted into the subconscious mind.

lunar month   The interval between the successive full moons. A lunar month lasts approximately 29½ days; each lunar year lasts 354 days.

luopan   A compass containing anywhere from 4 to 40 concentric information rings. A compass, be it a luopan or Western-style, is the tool of the trade in feng shui.

Luoshu   Also known as the "Luo River Writing," it is a pattern of black (yang) and white (yin) dots said to be found inscribed on a turtle's shell. The Luoshu correlates to the After Heaven sequence of trigrams.

Magic Square of Three   Related to the Luoshu. It is considered "magical" because 3 cells add up to 15 along any diagonal, vertical, or horizontal line. The Magic Square is the numerological basis of feng shui.

ming gua   Determined by your year of birth and gender, your ming (birth) gua (trigram) is the guardian star (or number) you are born under.

mountain force   Associated with yin, it administers a person's health and relationships. Its qi enters a home through the walls; the building's mountainlike structures protecting the occupants. In classical feng shui terminology, the mountain star is synonymous with the sitting star and the stars on the top, left side of each cell.

parallel   One of five ways a phase relates to the Day-Master in a Four Pillars of Destiny analysis. The parallel phase is the same as the Day-Master.

performance   One of five ways a phase relates to the Day-Master in a Four Pillars of Destiny analysis. The performance phase is produced by the Day-Master.

personal trigram   Determined by your birth year and gender.

poison arrow qi   Qi that is directed at you in a straight line. Also known as "killing breath," this qi is extremely inauspicious, carrying misfortune, illness, and even disaster.

power   One of five ways a phase relates to the Day-Master in a Four Pillars of Destiny analysis. The power phase dominates the Day-Master.

productive cycle   A cycle of balance and creation. Each phase produces or enhances the succeeding phase. Fire-earth-metal-water-wood represents the productive cycle.

qi   The underlying and unifying substance and soul of all things. Both physical and metaphysical, qi is the nourishing force at the heart, growth, and development of the heavens, earth, and humanity. It is also called "life's breath."

reductive cycle   A cycle that reduces the power of the dominating phase and restores the sequential balance of the phases in question. Fire-wood-water-metal-earth represents the reductive cycle. In feng shui, a reductive phase is used to remedy inauspicious qi.

resource   One of five ways a phase relates to the Day-Master in a Four Pillars of Destiny analysis. A resource phase produces the Day-Master.

Reversed Mountain and Water A dwelling that is considered Shang Shan Xia Shui if the mountain and water stars are improperly placed, reversed. Here, the ruling mountain star is improperly located in the facing cell. The ruling water star is improperly located in the sitting cell. A Reversed Mountain and Water star chart brings the probability of misfortune and illness for the 20-year period to which the ruling star corresponds.

sha qi Negative qi carrying inauspicious currents that can influence your well-being.

sheng qi Positive qi carrying auspicious currents that can influence your well-being.

sitting direction Usually corresponds to the backside of a dwelling. A sitting direction is determined by a compass reading.

solar year Time based on the revolution of the earth around the sun is a solar year.

strong Day-Master A Four Pillars of Destiny chart with more resource and parallel than power, wealth, and performance phases. A person with a strong chart has many friends and many competitors. He derives support from those around him, while getting few chances to demonstrate his own talents.

subconscious mind This is the area of the mind that receives and stores information. The subconscious mind represents 88 percent of our total mind power.

swastika A universal symbol generally accepted to be a solar emblem. It is derived from the Sanskrit *svastika*, meaning lucky, fortunate, well-being. The counterclockwise swastika formed within the Magic Square expresses future time.

synchronicity A concept developed by celebrated Swiss psychologist Carl Jung (1875–1961), it expresses the connection of acausal events within a limited time frame.

taiji A symbol illustrating the eternal interaction between yin and yang. The correct orientation is with its yang "head" positioned at the top-left side.

Ten Heavenly Stems "Tian Gan" in Chinese, they represent how the five phases alter with the passage of a year. The Chinese use the word "heaven" to mean time. Hence, the Heavenly Stems record how qi changes with time.

totem An Algonquin word describing an animal or natural object with which a group feels a special attachment. Denoting group membership, the totem is worshipped by the members of the clan bearing its name.

trigram The eight trigrams are symbols representing transitional phases of all possible heavenly and human situations. Qian, Zhen, Kan, Gen, Kun, Xun, Li, and Dui represent the eight trigrams.

Twelve Earthly Branches   "Di Zhi" in Chinese, they represent cycles of earth qi expressed by the year, month, day, and hour. A zodiac animal is assigned to each branch. Each branch contains one or more hidden stems.

twenty-four mountains   Directions of a luopan compass derived from the eight fundamental trigrams: Each trigram constitutes 45 degrees of the compass (8 trigrams × 45 degrees = 360 degrees). Each trigram is subdivided into three equal parts of 15 degrees each (3 parts × 15 degrees = 45 degrees). The total number of subdivided parts (3 parts × 8 trigrams) comprise the 24 mountains, each of which has a Chinese name.

unfavorable phase   A term in a Four Pillars of Destiny analysis describing a phase that causes an imbalance in your chart.

unknown   A unit of communication that is rejected by the critical area of the mind and will not enter the subconscious.

water force   Associated with yang, it governs a person's wealth. Its qi enters a home through the windows and doors, the building's free-flowing waterlike edifices. The water star is synonymous with the facing star and the stars on the top-right side of each cell.

weak Day-Master   A Four Pillars of Destiny chart with more power, performance, and wealth than resource and parallel. A person with a weak Day-Master usually is being challenged by power and authority, yet has enough intelligence to combat such confrontations.

wealth   One of five ways a phase relates to the Day-Master in a Four Pillars of Destiny analysis. The wealth phase is dominated by the Day-Master.

white tiger   A landform, building, trees, bushes, or fence located on the right side of your dwelling.

Wuji   The beginning, the "Great Void." *Wuji* is believed to be the fountainhead of creation and is expressed as a circle.

yang   Represents the active principle in nature exhibited as light, heat, and dryness. On a human level, yang represents masculinity and the positive side of our emotions. Also, yang represents the realm of the living.

Yijing   Also known as "*The Book of Changes.*" It is the first known attempt by the Chinese to formulate a system of knowledge around the interplay of yin and yang.

yin   Represents the passive principle in nature exhibited as darkness, cold, and wetness. On a human level, yin symbolizes femininity and inertia. Also, yin represents the realm of the dead.

Zhouyi Also known as *"The Changes of Zhou,"* it is a divinatory system written by King Wen and his son the Duke of Zhou at the end of the second millennium B.C.E. In the Han dynasty (or before) commentaries were attached to the *Zhouyi* and renamed the *"Yijing."*

Ziwei Doushu Purple Constellation Fate Computation in English, it's a method of Chinese astrology that analyzes anywhere from 36 to 157 stars in accordance with your birth information. *Ziwei Doushu* uses the Chinese lunar calendar.

Common Questions and Practical Answers

Q: What exactly is feng shui?

A: Feng shui is the art and science of determining how the environment and your home affect you over periods of time. Feng shui can predict, prevent, and encourage events with great accuracy.

Q: Are there certain telltale factors that distinguish a classical-trained practitioner from one who uses modern techniques based on superstition and myth?

A: Yes. Simply, ask questions! First ask what kind of feng shui he or she practices. The answer should be classical or traditional feng shui. If the answer is Bagua School or Compass School, this could mean the consultant practices faux feng shui, in which a home is divided into sections of wealth, health, family, career, and so on. This method is too simplistic. Please see Chapter 1 for a review of authentic and faux schools of feng shui.

Q: I heard feng shui is a Daoist art. Is this true?

A: No. The philosophy of Daoism and the science of feng shui developed at the same time and share common roots. Although feng shui's origins are lost in history, the tradition actually predates Daoism, Buddhism, and Confucianism by several thousand years. As early as 6000 B.C.E., some sort of astronomical/astrological system was used to determine auspicious grave and dwelling sites.

Q: Do you need a compass to practice feng shui?

A: Yes. Just as a hair stylist needs a pair of scissors and a doctor needs a stethoscope, a feng shui practitioner needs a compass, but it doesn't have to be a Chinese luopan. A Western-style compass featuring two-degree gradations is sufficient. Without a compass, it's impossible to determine your home's trigram. Guesswork just won't do. Obtaining an accurate reading is the first step toward ensuring an accurate analysis. An incorrect assumption may cause harm to you and your family. For example, you wouldn't want your hair stylist to assume he or she has selected "Bombshell Blond"—your hair color. You would expect him or her to be certain. Furthermore, you would expect the stylist to have read and know the hair-coloring procedure thoroughly. Otherwise, your hair might fall out!

Q: Can feng shui really bring me health, wealth, and happiness?

A: Feng shui can only increase the probability of these things happening. For example, a Flying Star reading may indicate good fortune, but it's up to you to make it happen. Feng shui can create only an urge, increasing your motivation and likelihood of success. Feng shui is not a cure-all solution.

Q: Can you flush your wealth away if a toilet lid is left open?

A: Only if you empty your wallet into the bowl!

Q: Where's the best place to hang a mirror?

A: Historically, the use of mirrors to remedy qi has never been part of feng shui's tradition. The concept of mirrors as magical power devices that can stimulate, ward off, or absorb qi is a recent invention dating to the 1980s. This misconception is an excellent example of playing "telephone"—the childhood game in which one kid whispers a sentence in the next kid's ear. At the end of the line, the sentence bears no resemblance to the original.

In ancient China, mirrors were made of bronze, polished on one side, with various cosmological designs on the other. These mirrors were similar to the precursor of the luopan compass, an ancient divination tool called the shipan, which was thought to reflect, or mirror, the perfect world before the demon Gong Gong battled Zhu Rong for the Empire. During the fight, the northwest mountain (one of eight separating heaven from earth) collapsed, causing the northwest to tilt upward, and the southeast to tilt downward. As a model of the perfect world, the ancient cosmographs and bronze mirrors were thought to have magic power. Somehow, they have been mistakenly incorporated into feng shui.

Q: There are so many books and classes on feng shui. How do I know who's right?

A: It's up to you to search for the truth. Unfortunately, the ancient Chinese tradition of feng shui has been watered down and misrepresented. In large part, this is due to people not doing their homework. Our advice is to go directly to source material. Thumb through Joseph Needham's seven-volume work, *Science and Civilisation in China*. Check out scholarly material at the library or on the Internet. You do the homework. You decide fact from falsehood. Please see Appendix C for a credible list of reading material and websites about classical feng shui.

Q: When determining the construction year of a dwelling, how do you treat additions to a house?

A: The only reliable source is from Qing dynasty (1644–1911) feng shui master, Shen Zhu Reng's book, *Shen's Time and Space School (Shen Shi Xuan Kong Xue)*. He says if the new and old parts are connected so that the qi can flow freely, and the main entrance is in the new part, then the whole house is considered new. Therefore, use the construction date affiliated with the addition. On the other hand, if the main entrance is in the old part of the house, then the whole house is considered old. In this case, use the original construction date of the house. If there is a door in the new addition, but the old entrance is retained and both doors are used, then the old part is old, and the new part is new. Two Flying Star charts must be drawn.

Q: When determining the construction year of a dwelling, how do you treat a house whose roof was completely changed?

A: This is controversial. If the roof is removed and the inside of the dwelling is exposed for at least one month, the house is considered new.

Learn More About Feng Shui

Books, Magazines, and Articles

Baker, John. "Qi Through the Centuries and Around the World." *Qi: The Journal of Traditional Eastern Health and Fitness*, Vol. 1, No. 4, Winter, 1991.

Capra, Fritjof. *The Tao of Physics: Fourth Edition*. Boston: Shambhala, 2000.

Chuen, Master Lam Kam. *The Feng Shui Handbook*. Sussex, U.K.: Gaia Books, 1996.

de Bary, William Theodore, Wing-Tsit Chan, and Burton Watson. *Sources of Chinese Tradition*, Volume 1. New York: Columbia University Press, 1960.

Eisenberg, David, with Thomas Lee Wright. *Encounters with Qi: Exploring Chinese Medicine*. New York: W.W. Norton and Company, 1985.

Emoto, Masaru. *The Hidden Messages in Water*. Hillsboro, OR: Beyond Words Publishing, Inc., 2001.

Field, Stephen. *Early China: Cosmos, Cosmograph, and the Inquiring Poet: New Answers to the Heaven Questions*. The Annual Journal of the Society for the Study of Early China and the Institute of East Asian Studies, Volume 17. Berkeley, CA: University of California, Berkeley, 1992.

Garland, Trudi Hammel. *Fascinating Fibonaccis: Mystery and Magic in Numbers*. Dale Seymour Publications, 1987.

Granet, Marcel. *The Religion of the Chinese People*. Oxford: Blackwell & Mott, 1975; originally published in French in 1922.

Heisenberg, Werner. *Physics and Philosophy*. New York: HarperCollins, 1962.

Hess, Monica. *The Feng Shui of George Washington's Mount Vernon*. Morrisville, NC: Lulu, Inc., www.Lulu.com, 2004.

Kappas, John G. *Professional Hypnotism Manual*. Stouffville, Ontario, Canada: Panorama Publishing Company, 1999.

Lau, Kwan. *Feng Shui for Today*. Trumbull, CT: Weatherhill, Inc., 1996.

Lau, Theodora. *The Handbook of Chinese Horoscopes*. New York: Harper & Row, 1979.

Lippelt, Ulrich Wilhelm. *Feng Shui Demystified: A Comparative Compendium on Flying Star Feng Shui and Eight Mansion Formula*. Bloomington, IN: 1stBooks Library, 2003.

Loewe, Michael, and Edward L. Shaughnessy (eds.). *The Cambridge History of Ancient China from the Origins of Civilization to 221 B.C.E.* Cambridge, U.K.: Cambridge University Press, 1999.

Lopez, Vincent. *Numerology*. New York: The New American Library, 1961.

Major, John S. *Heaven and Earth in Early Han Thought*. Albany, NY: State University of New York Press, 1993.

Moran, Elizabeth, and Master Joseph Yu. *The Complete Idiot's Guide to the I Ching*. Indianapolis, IN: Alpha Books, 2001.

Needham, Joseph. *Science and Civilisation in China* (6 volumes). Cambridge, U.K.: Cambridge University Press, 1956.

Qi: *The Journal of Traditional Eastern Health and Fitness*, published by Insight Graphics, Inc. Call 1-800-787-2600 for more information.

Schimmel, Annemarie. *The Mystery of Numbers*. Oxford, U.K.: Oxford University Press, 1993.

Schirokauer, Conrad. *A Brief History of Chinese Civilization.* Orlando, FL: Harcourt Brace & Company, 1991.

Shanks, Thomas G. *The International Atlas, Fifth Edition: World Latitudes & Longitudes, Time Changes and Time Zones.* Columbus, OH: ACS Publications, 1999.

Skinner, Stephen. *Flying Star Feng Shui.* Boston: Charles E. Tuttle Company, 2003.

———. *K.I.S.S. Guide to Feng Shui.* New York: Dorling Kindersley, 2001.

———. *The Living Earth Manual of Feng-Shui.* London, U.K.: Arkana, 1982.

Smith, Richard J. *Fortune-tellers and Philosophers: Divination in Traditional Chinese Society.* Boulder, CO: Westview Press, Inc., 1991.

Twicken, David. *Classical Five Elements Chinese Astrology Made Easy.* Lincoln, NE: Writers Club Press, 2000.

———. *Flying Star Feng Shui Made Easy: Third Edition.* Lincoln, NE: Writers Club Press, 2000.

Tzu, Leo. *Tao the Ching.* Boston: Shambhala, 1989.

von Franze, Marie-Louise. *Number and Time.* Evanston, IL: Northwestern University Press, 1974.

Walters, Derek. *Chinese Astrology: The Most Comprehensive Study of the Subject Ever Published in the English Language.* Watkins Publishing Limited, 2004.

———. *The Chinese Astrology Workbook.* The Aquarian Press, 1988.

Wilhelm, Richard (trans.) *The I Ching or Book of Changes.* Princeton, NJ: Princeton University Press, 1950.

Wong, Eva. *A Master Course in Feng Shui.* Boston: Shambhala, 2001.

———. *Feng Shui: The Ancient Wisdom of Harmonious Living for Modern Times.* Boston: Shambhala, 1996.

Yu-Lan, Fung. *A Short History of Chinese Philosophy.* New York: The Free Press, 1948.

Websites

Val Biktashev and Elizabeth Moran

www.aafengshui.com

From the authors of *The Complete Idiot's Guide to Feng Shui* (three editions) and *The Complete Idiot's Guide to the I Ching*, the comprehensive site seeks to educate the public about classical feng shui and the *Yijing*. Master Biktashev travels worldwide providing feng shui consultations. Elizabeth Moran travels extensively offering seminars and lectures about classical feng shui.

Cate Bramble

www.qi-whiz.com

An expansive site containing many thoroughly researched essays about feng shui and related applications. Cate is known for telling it like it is with a humorous touch! We especially recommend her articles debunking Black Sect feng shui.

Feng Shui Research Center

www.fsrc.net

Launched in August 2003 by Judy Adler, this website contains everything you need to know about traditional feng shui. Sign up for her free newsletter.

Feng Shui Times

www.fengshuitimes.com

A terrific site with many informative articles written by well-known classical practitioners and masters.

Roel Hill (Heluo)

www.geocities.com/heluoarticles/index.htm

From the Netherlands, Heluo's a classical feng shui practitioner and teacher. His site is well worth visiting. If you live in the southern hemisphere, his article, "Southern Hemisphere and Universal Qi," will help you understand why feng shui methodology is not reversed.

John Mausolf

www.purefengshui.com

John is one of Australia's leading classical feng shui practitioners and teachers. His site boasts, "No gimmicks … just pure feng shui!" Check out his article debunking the southern hemisphere theory.

Danny Van den Berghe's Flying Star and Four Pillars Software

www.fourpillars.net

Here, you'll find a software package for Flying Star feng shui and for The Four Pillars of Destiny. Although the programs will create the charts, the software does not give an automated reading.

Eva Wong

www.shambhala.com/fengshui

A unique and very informative site about feng shui. Look for her interesting article about feng shui's early masters.

Joseph Yu

www.astro-fengshui.com

Master Yu offers online and worldwide in-class training courses in classical feng shui, Chinese astrology (The Four Pillars of Destiny and Zi Wei Dou Shu), and the *Yijing*. He is the co-author of all three editions of *The Complete Idiot's Guide to Feng Shui*, including this new third edition; and *The Complete Idiot's Guide to the I Ching*. Use his Four Pillars of Destiny calculator. To purchase Joseph Yu's luopan compass, please contact him at josephyu@astro-fengshui.com.

Yahoo! Discussion Groups

Astro Feng Shui

Moderated by Master Joseph Yu, this list is open to the public. Discussion centers on classical feng shui. For more information and to subscribe, go to http://groups.yahoo.com/_group/astrofengshui.

Basic Feng Shui

Moderated by Elizabeth Moran and Scott Ransom, the aim of this list is to provide a supportive atmosphere for people who are just beginning to study feng shui and who are not yet ready for elaborate technical discussions. For more information and to subscribe, go to http://groups.yahoo.com/group/basicfengshui.

Chinese Astrology

Moderated by Ray Langley, this discussion group focuses on Chinese astrology and classical feng shui. Although beginners are welcome, this list is mainly geared toward those with a solid foundation of the aforementioned traditions. Ray offers an extensive archive with many translations of Chinese texts. For more information and to subscribe, go to http://groups.yahoo.com/group/chineseastrology.

Yijing I Ching

Moderated by Master Joseph Yu, this group was established to help the reader understand *The Complete Idiot's Guide to the I Ching*, written by Elizabeth Moran and Master Joseph Yu. Although you need not own the book to participate, it would be helpful. For more information and to subscribe, go to http://groups.yahoo.com/group/yijing_iching.

Greenwich Mean Time and World Longitudes

wwp.greenwichmeantime.com (Greenwich Mean Time)

www.timeanddate.com (Time and Date)

www.astro.com (Astrodienst)

www.hko.gov.hk/gts/time/worldtime2.htm (Hong Kong Observatory)

Contact the Authors

Val Biktashev and Elizabeth Moran
American Healing Arts Institute
269 S. Beverly Drive, Suite 280
Beverly Hills, CA 90212
Phone: (323) 810-8180
Fax: (323) 852-1341
E-mail: GlobalFengShui@aol.com
Web address: www.aafengshui.com

Joseph Yu
Feng Shui Research Center
175 West Beaver Creek Road, Unit 5
Richmond Hill, Ontario L4B 3M1, Canada
Phone/Fax: (905) 881-8878
E-mail: josephyu@astro-fengshui.com
Web address: www.astro-fengshui.com

Chinese Periods and Dynasties

Chinese history is a fascinating discipline—rich, complex, and exhaustive. Remember, the Chinese have had flourishing civilizations for thousands of years. Looking at feng shui without even a rudimentary understanding of some historical basis is unwise. So much is inextricably woven into particular periods, events, and individuals. Throughout this book, we have referred to individuals, dates, and dynasties. We hope this list will compare some of feng shui's evolutions with that of Chinese history. Please note, although it appears some dynasties may overlap, in fact, they do not. Only a thorough investigation of Chinese history can adequately account for this.

The dates reflecting China's legendary and prehistoric periods, and the dynastic dates of the Shang early Zhou, are speculative and subject to dispute.

Legendary Period	
Three Emperors	2852–2597 B.C.E.
Fuxi	2852–2737 B.C.E.
Shennong	2737–2697 B.C.E.
Huang Di (Yellow Emperor)	2697–2597 B.C.E.
Shao Hao	2597–2513 B.C.E.
Zhuan Xu	2513–2435 B.C.E.

continues

continued

Legendary Period

Five Rulers	2435–2197 B.C.E.
Di Ku	2435–2365 B.C.E.
Di Zhi	2365–2356 B.C.E.
Yao	2356–2255 B.C.E.
Shun	2255–2205 B.C.E.
Yu	2205–2197 B.C.E.

Prehistoric Period

Yangshao culture	c. 5000 B.C.E.
Longshan culture	c. 2500 B.C.E.
Xia dynasty	c. 2100–c. 1600 B.C.E.

Historical Period

Shang dynasty	c. 1600–1045 B.C.E.
Zhou dynasty	1045–221 B.C.E.
Western Zhou	1045–771 B.C.E.
Eastern Zhou	770–256 B.C.E.
Spring and Autumn Period	722–481 B.C.E.
Warring States Period	403–221 B.C.E.
Qin dynasty	221–206 B.C.E.
Han dynasty	206 B.C.E.–220 C.E.
Western Han	206 B.C.E.–24 C.E.
Eastern Han	25-220 C.E.
Three Kingdoms	220–280
Wei	220–265
Shu Han	221–263
Wu	222–280
Jin dynasty	265–420
Western Jin	265–316
Eastern Jin	317–420
Southern and Northern dynasties	420–589
Southern	420–589
Northern	386–581

Historical Period	
Sui dynasty	581–618
Tang dynasty	618–907
Five dynasties and Ten Kingdoms	907–960
Song dynasty	960–1279
Northern Song	960–1127
Southern Song	1127–1279
Liao dynasty (Khitan Tartars)	916–1125
Jin dynasty (Jurchen Tartars)	1115–1234
Yuan dynasty (Mongol)	1271–1368
Ming dynasty	1368–1644
Qing dynasty (Manchu)	1644–1911
Republic of China	1912–1949
People's Republic of China	1949–present

Learn More About Taking a Proper Compass Reading Using the 24 Mountains

When you get the hang of it, taking an accurate compass reading and dividing your dwelling into eight equal sections is a snap. First, follow these steps to determine the sitting and facing directions of your house:

1. Stand in front of your house or unit, the side corresponding to the facing side. Make sure that your back is perfectly square with the house.

2. Holding your compass at waist level, rotate the compass dial until the red portion of the magnetic arrow aligns with north.

3. Read the compass grade at the index line (labeled the "bearing" line on the Silva Explorer Model 203). This is the facing direction. The grade magnetically opposite is the sitting direction.

In the following example (A) of an apartment unit, the compass grade at the index line reads 210°. The dwelling belongs to the trigram Gen and the mountain Chou (202.5° to 217.5°). The unit sits NE1 and faces SW1.

A properly divided Gen dwelling ☶ *NE1 and* ⬆ *SW1 at 210°.*

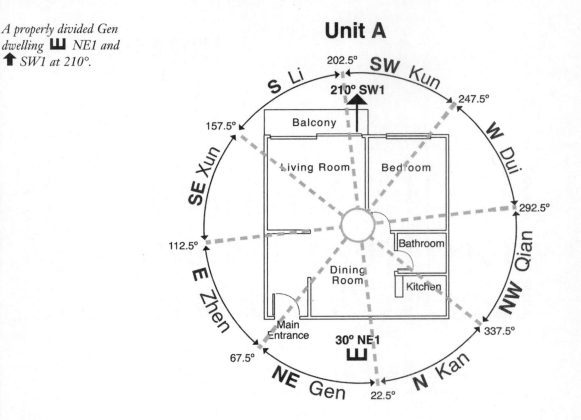

Now, follow these steps to divide your floor plan into eight equal sections corresponding to the eight fundamental directions (trigrams):

1. Note the facing degree on your floor plan (as illustrated).

2. With a pencil, mark the point where each of the eight directions begin and end (as illustrated). We suggest using a clear plastic 6-inch, 360° protractor with half-inch gradations to help with this task. Found in any office supply store, we recommend the Mars College protractor. But be careful! Read the *inside* grades that ascend around the circular instrument. Before you proceed, it might be a good idea to compare the protractor with the figure of the simplified luopan compass in Chapter 12. (If you want to purchase a luopan, please contact Joseph Yu at josephyu@astro-fengshui.com.)

3. Now, connect the dots to form eight equal sections.

Illustration B shows the same apartment sitting NE2 and facing SW2 at 225°.

Unit B

A properly divided Gen dwelling ⊔ NE2 and ↑ SW2 at 225°.

Illustration C shows the same apartment sitting NE3 and facing SW3 at 240°.

A properly divided Gen dwelling ☶ *NE3 and* ⬆ *SW3 at 240°.*

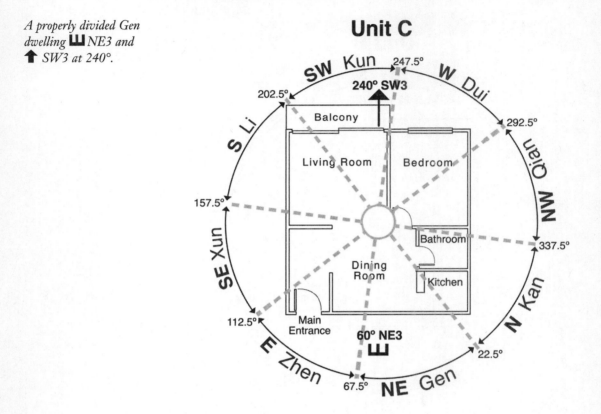

Taken together, you can see that depending on the facing degree, the sections are oriented somewhat differently for each of the three types of Gen dwellings (mountains Chou, Gen, and Yin).

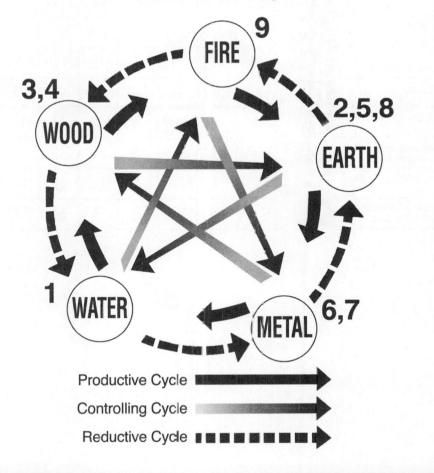

Quick Reference Charts

Five Phase Relationships

FIRE 9

3,4 WOOD

2,5,8 EARTH

1 WATER

METAL 6,7

Productive Cycle

Controlling Cycle

Reductive Cycle

Best Work / Study
F1, F2, F3, F4

➡ **F1**

Best Sleep
F4, F3. F2, F1

➡ **F4**

WANDERING
STAR AUSPICE

		1	2	3	4	6	7	8	9
		Water	Earth	Wood	Wood	Metal	Metal	Earth	Fire
		Kan	Kun	Zhen	Xun	Qian	Dui	Gen	Li
		D I R E C T I O N S							
Great Prosperity & Respectability	**F1**	SE	NE	S	N	W	NW	SW	E
Longevity & Romantic Relationships	**F2**	S	NW	SE	E	SW	NE	W	N
Good Health & Harmonious Relationships	**F3**	E	W	N	S	NE	SW	NW	SE
Peace & Stability	**F4**	N	SW	E	SE	NW	W	NE	S
Accidents, Arguments, & Injury	**H1**	W	E	SW	NW	SE	N	S	NE
Possible Malicious Encounters & Failed Relationships	**H2**	NW	S	NE	W	N	SE	E	SW
Litigation, Accidents, Injury, & Fire	**H3**	NE	SE	NW	SW	E	S	N	W
Possible Disease, Misfortune, & Unproductive Careers	**H4**	SW	N	W	NE	S	E	SE	NW

GOOD / BAD

Ming Gua Quick Reference Chart

Year	Male	Gua	Phase	Female	Gua	Phase	Year	Male	Gua	Phase	Female	Gua	Phase
1924	Xun	4	Wood	Kun	2	Earth	1964	Li	9	Fire	Qian	6	Metal
1925	Zhen	3	Wood	Zhen	3	Wood	1965	Gen	8	Earth	Dui	7	Metal
1926	Kun	2	Earth	Xun	4	Wood	1966	Dui	7	Metal	Gen	8	Earth
1927	Kan	1	Water	Gen	8	Earth	1967	Qian	6	Metal	Li	9	Fire
1928	Li	9	Fire	Qian	6	Metal	1968	Kun	2	Earth	Kan	1	Water
1929	Gen	8	Earth	Dui	7	Metal	1969	Xun	4	Wood	Kun	2	Earth
1930	Dui	7	Metal	Gen	8	Earth	1970	Zhen	3	Wood	Zhen	3	Wood
1931	Qian	6	Metal	Li	9	Fire	1971	Kun	2	Earth	Xun	4	Wood
1932	Kun	2	Earth	Kan	1	Water	1972	Kan	1	Water	Gen	8	Earth
1933	Xun	4	Wood	Kun	2	Earth	1973	Li	9	Fire	Qian	6	Metal
1934	Zhen	3	Wood	Zhen	3	Wood	1974	Gen	8	Earth	Dui	7	Metal
1935	Kun	2	Earth	Xun	4	Wood	1975	Dui	7	Metal	Gen	8	Earth
1936	Kan	1	Water	Gen	8	Earth	1976	Qian	6	Metal	Li	9	Fire
1937	Li	9	Fire	Qian	6	Metal	1977	Kun	2	Earth	Kan	1	Water
1938	Gen	8	Earth	Dui	7	Metal	1978	Xun	4	Wood	Kun	2	Earth
1939	Dui	7	Metal	Gen	8	Earth	1979	Zhen	3	Wood	Zhen	3	Wood
1940	Qian	6	Metal	Li	9	Fire	1980	Kun	2	Earth	Xun	4	Wood
1941	Kun	2	Earth	Kan	1	Water	1981	Kan	1	Water	Gen	8	Earth
1942	Xun	4	Wood	Kun	2	Earth	1982	Li	9	Fire	Qian	6	Metal
1943	Zhen	3	Wood	Zhen	3	Wood	1983	Gen	8	Earth	Dui	7	Metal
1944	Kun	2	Earth	Xun	4	Wood	1984	Dui	7	Metal	Gen	8	Earth
1945	Kan	1	Water	Gen	8	Earth	1985	Qian	6	Metal	Li	9	Fire
1946	Li	9	Fire	Qian	6	Metal	1986	Kun	2	Earth	Kan	1	Water
1947	Gen	8	Earth	Dui	7	Metal	1987	Xun	4	Wood	Kun	2	Earth
1948	Dui	7	Metal	Gen	8	Earth	1988	Zhen	3	Wood	Zhen	3	Wood
1949	Qian	6	Metal	Li	9	Fire	1989	Kun	2	Earth	Xun	4	Wood
1950	Kun	2	Earth	Kan	1	Water	1990	Kan	1	Water	Gen	8	Earth
1951	Xun	4	Wood	Kun	2	Earth	1991	Li	9	Fire	Qian	6	Metal
1952	Zhen	3	Wood	Zhen	3	Wood	1992	Gen	8	Earth	Dui	7	Metal
1953	Kun	2	Earth	Xun	4	Wood	1993	Dui	7	Metal	Gen	8	Earth
1954	Kan	1	Water	Gen	8	Earth	1994	Qian	6	Metal	Li	9	Fire
1955	Li	9	Fire	Qian	6	Metal	1995	Kun	2	Earth	Kan	1	Water
1956	Gen	8	Earth	Dui	7	Metal	1996	Xun	4	Wood	Kun	2	Earth
1957	Dui	7	Metal	Gen	8	Earth	1997	Zhen	3	Wood	Zhen	3	Wood
1958	Qian	6	Metal	Li	9	Fire	1998	Kun	2	Earth	Xun	4	Wood
1959	Kun	2	Earth	Kan	1	Water	1999	Kan	1	Water	Gen	8	Earth
1960	Xun	4	Wood	Kun	2	Earth	2000	Li	9	Fire	Qian	6	Metal
1961	Zhen	3	Wood	Zhen	3	Wood	2001	Gen	8	Earth	Dui	7	Metal
1962	Kun	2	Earth	Xun	4	Wood	2002	Dui	7	Metal	Gen	8	Earth
1963	Kan	1	Water	Gen	8	Earth	2003	Qian	6	Metal	Li	9	Fire

If you were born between January 1 and February 2, use the year prior to your actual birth year. If you were born on February 3, 4, or 5, consult Chapter 21 to determine your Chinese solar birth year. For extended dates, see Chapter 8.

Index